John Edward Stocks, W. B. Bragg

Market Harborough Parish Records

To A. D. 1530

John Edward Stocks, W. B. Bragg

Market Harborough Parish Records
To A. D. 1530

ISBN/EAN: 9783744758505

Printed in Europe, USA, Canada, Australia, Japan

Cover: Foto ©ninafisch / pixelio.de

More available books at **www.hansebooks.com**

MARKET HARBOROUGH PARISH RECORDS.

MARKET HARBOROUGH PARISH RECORDS,

TO A.D. 1530.

BY

J. E. STOCKS, M.A.,
Vicar of St. Saviour's, Leicester; formerly (1871-1884) Vicar of Market Harborough;

ASSISTED BY

W. B. BRAGG,
Of Market Harborough,

TWO OF THE TRUSTEES OF THE TOWN ESTATE.

'Our forefathers in this village were no doubt as busy and bustling, and as important, as ourselves: yet have their names and transactions been forgotten from century to century, and have sunk into oblivion; nor has this happened only to the vulgar, but even to men remarkable and famous in their generation.'—*The Antiquities of Selborne.*

LONDON:
ELLIOT STOCK, 62, PATERNOSTER ROW, E.C.
1890.

TABLE OF CONTENTS.

	PAGES
PREFACE	vii—x
INTRODUCTION	1—158
MARKET HARBOROUGH PARISH RECORDS TO 1520	159—208
EXTRACTS FROM WILLS PRESERVED AT THE DISTRICT PROBATE REGISTRY, LEICESTER	209—230
INVENTORY DISCOVERED AT LINCOLN	230—234
APPENDIX I.—PROCEEDINGS AGAINST THE RECTOR OF LITTLE BOWDEN AS TO THE PROVISION OF A CHAPLAIN FOR LITTLE OXENDON	235—242
APPENDIX II.—GRANT OF THE ADVOWSON OF LITTLE BOWDEN TO N. GRIFFYN	243
INDEX	244—267

PREFACE.

THE chief object of this volume, and of a second in course of preparation, is to place in the hands of the parishioners of Market Harborough, and of their neighbours in Great and Little Bowden, a full account of the records which have been preserved in the town, and are now in the custody of the Trustees of the Town Estate. Beyond this, it is hoped that what is brought to light in these volumes may be of some little use to the many who are at work on the remains of the past, and who have done so much in recent years to make English people understand the life and manners of their forefathers. The work of deciphering and arranging the town records was begun some years since at the request of the Trustees. For some time those who undertook it had no thought of publication, but the records proved to be more varied and of greater interest than was expected at the outset, and, ultimately, the whole body of the Trustees decided to publish them on their own personal responsibility. This volume has been prepared for the press under constant pressure of other calls and with many hindrances. No trouble, however, has been spared to attain accuracy, and while the main object in view made it necessary to give an English summary rather than the original Latin, every unusual word or phrase has been noted. I trust I may be allowed to express my lasting gratitude to my friend Mr. Bragg for his kind help. We have spent many happy hours together in mastering the records, and putting them into order, and his local knowledge and keen interest have been of the greatest service. I ought also to mention that Mr. Bragg has so arranged the records, that anyone who should wish to refer to them can do so with ease.

A few words of explanation must be given as to the Introduction, for which I alone am responsible. It was hardly possible to print the records of a town without in some way dealing with its history. Yet it was difficult to decide on the method to be followed. The history of Market Harborough, from the antiquarian point of view, has already been written at great length, and the mere repetition of this in a condensed form would have been of little use or interest. On the other hand, it was impossible altogether to ignore what has been written in the past, and an entirely new search for material, with the view of rewriting the history of the town in the full light of modern research, was beyond the scope of the work, even if it had been within the grasp of the Editor. After much thought, I decided to aim at filling up the gaps which were left by Nichols and those who have followed him, and to bring out more in detail the history of the church, and of the Scropes as Lords of the Manor. At the same time, I endeavoured, as far as possible, to gather together such facts and information as might help, not merely to the completion of an antiquarian record, but to a picture, however imperfect, of the life of the community before the Reformation. The extracts from the splendid registers and other muniments at Lincoln, which I was allowed to make through the kindness of the late and present Bishops and the Dean and Chapter, are almost entirely new material. For this reason I have transcribed them at length, and side by side with the original I have given a *précis* or translation. I have also had the privilege of using some unpublished MS. volumes belonging to Sir C. E. Isham, Bart., and I received permission from the proper authority to search and make extracts from the valuable series of wills preserved in the Registry of the District Probate Court at Leicester. All these extracts I have myself copied from the registers, muniments, or MS. volumes, but, to ensure accuracy, the Lincoln records, with few exceptions, have been compared with the originals by my friend Mr. A. Gibbons, of Lincoln.

It remains only that I should express my best thanks to those who have so kindly helped me by their suggestions and corrections, by the loan of books and MSS., and in other ways. I am specially indebted to the Lord Bishop of Oxford, whose kindness with reference to the studies of which he is a master is so well known; to the Rev. Cecil Deedes, the Rev. W. D. Macray, the Rev. Precentor Venables, the Rev. Canon Raine, the Rev. Canon Wordsworth, the Rev. A. Trollope, the Rev. G. T. Harvey, and the Rev. A. Maddison; Mr. W. H. Allnutt, of the Bodleian Library; Mr. W. W. Smith, Secretary to the Bishop of Lincoln; Sir C. E. Isham, Bart.; Mr. A. Gibbons; Messrs. W. H. Barfoot-Saunt, J. H. Douglass, E. K. Fisher, J. Flint, and P. L. Rawlins, of Market Harborough; to the Rev. T. F. Jerwood, Rector, and Mr. E. Kennard, of Little Bowden, and to the Messrs. Nevinson and Mr. W. R. Barker, of the Leicester District Probate Registry. Although unknown by name, I am also, like everyone else who has to apply to them, very much indebted to the ready courtesy of the officials at the Record Office and the British Museum.

Those who have made the subjects with which this volume deals a life-long study know well how, in the case of a first effort, each little bit of knowledge acquired seems only to reveal the extent of the learner's ignorance, and they will understand the wish which asserts itself now that the time for publication has come—that it were only possible to burn the proof-sheets and to begin again.

J. E. S.

CORRECTIONS AND ADDITIONS.

Page 19, line 29, right-hand column, *for* 'next' *read* 'last.'

Page 19, note 2, *for* 'Le Neibe' *read* 'Le Neve.'

Page 22, lines 3-5, right-hand column, *for* 'Essendon' *read* 'Bowden;' and *for* 'Bowden' *read* 'Essendon.'

Page 24, line 21, *for* '10 marks' *read* '20 marks.'

Page 24, line 24, *for* '£6 13s. 4d.' *read* '£13 6s. 8d. ;' and *for* '£30 13s. 4d.' *read* '£24.'

Page 41, lines 12 and 13, left-hand column, *for* 'conventuali' *read* 'conventualis.'

Page 57, line 37, right-hand column, *for* 'blue coverlet' *read* 'bluet coverlet.' *Bluet*, 1, a kind of woollen cloth of bluish colour.—'New English Dictionary' (Dr. Murray).

Page 99, line 37, left-hand column, *for* 'dicta' *read* 'dictæ.'

Page 99, lines 4 and 5, right-hand column, *for* 'The Court, etc.,' *read* 'Dated the day, place and year aforesaid; The Court was delivered on the 19th of November.'

Page 100, line 36, *for* '6s. 11d.' *read* '8s. 11d.'

Page 103, line 10, *for* '(50)' *read* '(51).'

Page 107, line 3, *for* 'though' *read* 'through.'

Page 137, line 1, *for* 'herbagii' *read* 'herbagio.'

Page 138, line 17, *for* 'becomes extinct' *read* 'falls into abeyance.'

Pages 145, 146. The old painting, representing the Ascension, on the north-east wall of Little Bowden Church, has recently been covered over.

Page 169, line 13, *for* 'Bondon Parva' *read* 'Boudon Parva.'

Page 215, line 12, 'bred, al and chesse.' Cf. Introduction to 'Old Mortality,' 'Funeral Charges of Robert Paterson.'

To Bread at the Founral ...	0	2	6
„ Chise at ditto	0	3	0
„ 1 pint Rume	0	4	6
„ 1 pint Whiskie	0	4	0

Page 233, line 3 and note 2, 'brandert.'—Cf. 'Guy Mannering,' ch. xxiv., 'A couple of fowls . . . soon appeared reeking from the gridiron, or brander, as Mrs. Dinmont denominated it.'

INTRODUCTION.

A STRANGER travelling to Market Harborough by the oldest line of railway which touches it, the line from Rugby, sees on the left hand, as he nears the end of his journey, what, to all appearance, is one compact little town. In the centre stands the graceful broached spire, built of that gray stone, not uncommon in the Midland counties, which is as durable as it is beautiful. From this, as a centre, the town seems to have extended itself to about the same distance at all four points of the compass, and, as the railway-station is some distance to the west of the church, the traveller has almost a complete view of it. If he is curious enough to inquire, he learns with some astonishment the main features of the local geography. The town, he finds, is really in two counties, and in four parishes. The houses which he saw as soon as the town came in sight, to the west of the church, are, for the most part, in the parish of Great Bowden; the railway-station, to the east, is in the same parish, and the houses to the south are partly in the parish of St. Nicholas, Little Bowden, partly in that of St. Mary, Little Bowden (otherwise called St. Mary's in Arden). These houses in Little Bowden are all in Northamptonshire, which is here separated from Leicestershire by the river Welland. If our traveller walks from the railway-station to the town, he remains in Great Bowden parish for the greater part of the way, and if he passes

<small>Parochial divisions of the Local Board district.</small>

through the town, either northwards towards Kibworth, or westwards towards Lubenham or Farndon, he soon comes into the same parish again. If he has had a guide, his attention will have been called to a small church and burial-ground close to the goods-station. This is the church of St. Mary in Arden, or St. Mary's, Little Bowden, standing in Leicestershire, away from its parishioners, whose houses are intermingled with those of St. Nicholas, Little Bowden, in Northamptonshire. If he should ask for the parish church of Great Bowden, the parish from which it seems so hard to escape, he will be told that it is more than a mile away, in the midst of its own good-sized village, separated from these outlying parts by considerable stretches of green field. He will also learn, rather to his further bewilderment: (1) that Market Harborough, Great Bowden, and St. Nicholas, Little Bowden, are separate ecclesiastical parishes, while St. Mary's, Little Bowden, for ecclesiastical purposes, has long been united to Market Harborough; (2) that, for civil purposes, there are only three parishes, viz., Market Harborough, Great Bowden and Little Bowden (St. Nicholas and St. Mary), and that, since the year 1880, these three parishes have formed the Local Board district of Market Harborough, Great and Little Bowden. The parish of Market Harborough is a small chapelry of the very large parish of Great Bowden. It consists of about forty acres, which are almost entirely covered with houses and gardens, and this small chapelry, a separate parish for every purpose, is bounded, north, east, and west, by Great Bowden parish, south by the Welland, and beyond that, by the two Little Bowden parishes strangely intermixed with each other.

Some such explanation of parochial divisions is necessary at the outset. Without it, many of the records now published would seem to have little to do with Market Harborough.

Thus, it will be noticed that nearly all the various portions of land, arable and pasture, which are conveyed or leased from time to time in the town documents, are either in the 'fields' of Bowden Magna alone, or in those of Bowden Magna and Harborough. Again, frequent mention is made of land called 'St. Mary's land;' and among the names of persons will be found residents in Great Bowden, and residents in Little Bowden also, as well as residents in Harborough. The explanation is to be found in the fact that Harborough never possessed separate common fields of its own. It was of old what it is now, a small section of a large parish, consisting of houses, gardens, and a few enclosures. But the 'men' of Harborough had their holdings and common-rights in the 'fields' of Bowden Magna. Hence these are frequently, though not always, called the 'fields' of Bowden and Harborough. St. Mary's land, also, consisted of holdings in the 'fields' of Great Bowden, and was under the control of the Harborough townsmen. It must not be confounded with any holdings or common-rights which the 'men' of St. Mary's, Little Bowden, may have had in the 'fields' of Little Bowden, in Northamptonshire.

The 'men' of Harborough, as such, never had any holdings or common-rights in the 'fields' of Little Bowden, but the parishes lie so close together, that some, whose interests were, in the main, in Harborough, were residents in Little Bowden, and hence the occurrence of their names in Harborough documents.

We turn, then, to the published histories, in the hope of finding some clear record of the origin and growth of the place, and some reasons for the parochial divisions which still exist. But the results are disappointing. *Evidence of the published histories, etc.*

The times before the Domesday Survey may be passed over very briefly. The histories all mention a Roman encampment on the east side of the town. Nichols gives an engraving of it, and of a few vessels and ornaments discovered at different times.[1] It is, indeed, possible that, *a. Before the Domesday Survey.*

---

[1] Nichols' Leicestershire: Gartree Hundred, pp. 478, 486. It is thought by competent students of British Roman remains that the vessels, etc., represented in the engraving are of British, not Roman,

in the course of the subjugation of the British tribes of this inland district by the Roman generals, Harborough, like the hill of Farndon, and like the low ground at Lubenham, was first a British stronghold, and afterwards a Roman station. But it cannot claim distinction as a well-known place, in the days when the Romans held Britain. It lies off the great Roman roads. The road from Dover to Chester passed within a few miles of it at Medbourne, and the Fosse Way and Watling Street were not very far distant at several points. But the road through the town, so well known afterwards, especially in coaching days, was not, apparently, a work of the Romans, and in their day Harborough was not a great thoroughfare town.[1]

Nor is there any mention of the place in such records as have come down to us from our forefathers before the Conquest. Its name does not appear in the old English chronicles, nor in the published collections of early English charters.

b. The Domesday Survey.

In the Domesday Survey we find the mother parish of Bowden Magna (Bugedone) in Leicestershire, and the adjacent parish of Bowden Parva (there also called Bugedone) in Northamptonshire, but there is no mention of Harborough, or Haverbergh, to use the earliest form of the name. An interesting question, however, arises out of what is stated about the two Bugedones, and it will be well, therefore, to give (in English) the extracts in each case.

The entries under Leicestershire are as follow. Under the heading, 'The Land of the King':

(1.) Bugedon, in Leicestershire. 'The Land of the King.'

'The King holds Bugedon (Bowden). King Edward held it. There are nine carucates and a half of land. In the demesne there are two ploughs; and thirteen sokemen, with eight villanes and sixteen bordars, have thirteen ploughs and a half, and render thirty shillings yearly.

---

workmanship. On such ancient earthworks, see paper by Mr. M. H. Bloxam, *Assoc. Soc. Papers*, vol. xiv., pp. 41 *et seq.*

[1] For the Roman roads see Dr. Guest's paper in the *Archæological Journal*, vol. xiv. Reprinted in *Origines Celticae*, ii. 218-241.

There are [   ] acres of meadow. The demesne is worth forty shillings yearly.'¹

On this it may be observed : (1) that Bugedon is one of two Leicestershire manors which had been held by Edward the Confessor, and, at the time of the Survey, were held by the Conqueror. The other was Rothley, and after both Rothley and Bowden a number of dependent manors are enumerated. Those which follow Bugedon are Medbourne, Cranoe, Carlton, Galby, Norton, Stretton, Foxton, Blaston, Shangton, Smeeton, and Ilston, but there is no mention of any second Manor of Bugedon as part of 'The Land of the King.' (2) That the Manor of Bugedon is about two-thirds the value of the Manor of Rothley, and, compared with that of other manors in Leicestershire, it is of average size; (3) that Bugedon is entered under Framland Wapentake, though really in Gartree, one amongst many proofs that 'in many cases the names have been transferred from one Hundred to another, and entries belonging to one county, either for convenience or the juxtaposition of the property of a particular landholder, or some other reason, have been confessedly placed in another.'²

In another place, under the heading, 'The Land of the Countess Judith': (2.) 'The Land of the Countess Judith.'

'[Robert de Buci holds of the Countess] three carucates of land in Bugedone. Four ploughs were there. Now in the demesne (is) one plough : and four villanes, with eight bordars, have two ploughs. There are fifteen acres of meadow. It was worth ten shillings; now, twenty shillings.'³

This is entered under Gartree Wapentake.

Under Northamptonshire there is another mention of Bugedone (i.e., Little Bowden) under Stoke Hundred : Bugedon in Northamptonshire.

'Hunfrid holds [of the Count of Mortain] two hides and

¹ Domesday for Leicestershire and Rutland, pp. 5, 6; Original Record, p. 230 b, column 1.
² Ellis, Introduction to Domesday Book, vol. i., pp. 34, 36, note.
³ Domesday for Leicestershire and Rutland, pp. 51, 52; Original Record, p. 236 a, column 2.

one virgate of land, and the third part of one virgate in Bugedone. There is land for six ploughs. In the demesne there is one (plough) with one serf: and eleven villeins with one bordar have two ploughs. There (is) a mill rendering sixteen pence, and eight acres of meadow, and three sochmen with two ploughs. It was worth sixty-four pence: now (it is worth) thirty shillings. Godwin and Ulsi held it.'[1]

The three manors in the Domesday Survey are probably the three parishes: Great Bowden, St. Mary's in Arden, and St. Nicholas, Little Bowden.

It has been supposed by Nichols,[2] and others after him, that the manor held by Robert de Buci of the Countess Judith was the Manor of Harborough. If, however, the question is carefully examined, it will be found that this supposition (for which no authority is given) is probably erroneous, and that, in these three manors enumerated in Domesday Book, we have simply three out of the four parishes which exist to-day, viz.: Great Bowden, St. Mary's in Arden, and St. Nicholas, Little Bowden, the present parish of Harborough being included in Great Bowden.

It will be noticed, in the first place, that while Bugedon, the first-named, in Leicestershire, is part of 'the Land of the King,' a royal manor, the second-named manor in Bugedone is held by a chief-tenant under the Countess Judith, and is enumerated in a different part of the record. If, next, we compare the size of the two manors, the second (the Countess Judith's) is rather more than one-third the size of the first. But the Manor of Harborough, as it existed in later times, is not in anything like the same proportion to that of Great Bowden. These two facts would suffice to throw doubt on the suggestion, if no positive proof to the contrary were at hand. If, however, we pass from the record for Leicestershire to that for Northamptonshire, and trace the first few facts in the manorial history of Little Bowden, such proof is abundant and clear.

The Count of Mortain, under whom Hunfrid held Buge-

---

[1] Domesday for Northamptonshire (S. H. Moore), p. 1; Original Record, folio 223 a, column 2.
[2] Nichols' Leicestershire: Gartree Hundred, p. 468

done in Northants, was the Conqueror's half-brother, and received, according to Domesday Book, no less than 793 manors.[1] Judith was the Conqueror's niece, and by him was given in marriage to Waltheof, an Englishman, Earl of Northampton and Huntingdon. Waltheof was condemned on the charge of complicity with rebellion, and was beheaded in 1076. The issue of their marriage was three daughters, the eldest of whom, Matilda, married (1) Simon of Senlis, the founder of Northampton Castle, to whom were granted the earldom of Huntingdon and the other possessions of Judith; (2) David of Scotland.[2] If the reader, bearing these facts in mind, will refer to the history of Bowden Parva in Bridges' 'History of Northamptonshire,' he will there find that, while part of the manor is to be traced from the Count of Mortain, part, also, is to be traced from David, King of Scotland:

'This estate, in the reign of Henry II., was in the hands of Robert Fitz-Hugh, who was certified to hold it of the Fee of Berkhamstede. At the same time, David, King of Scotland, held one hide, a third part of one virgate, and a third part of a third of a virgate in Boudon. Between the successors and descendants of these possessors, the lordship was henceforth divided. It appears by inquisition taken in the 24th Edward I., that William de Oxendon Parva held in Little Bowden twenty-seven virgates of the Earl of Cornwall, who held them of the King; and William de Latimer held fifteen virgates of the Honour of Huntingdon. These last were the lands which, in Henry II.'s time, were held of the King of Scotland.'[3]

Both manors ultimately became united in the Griffyn family, and have remained united, under different lords, up to the present time.

It is interesting to note that, at the time of the Little Bowden enclosure in 1779, it is stated in the preamble to the Act, that 'the Lands and Grounds lying and being

---

[1] Domesday Book, by W. de Gray Birch (S.P.C.K.), p. 248.
[2] Freeman's Norman Conquest (ed. 1871), vol. iv., pp. 603-605.
[3] Bridges' Northants, vol. ii., p. 4.

within the Manor, Lordship, or Liberties of Little Bowden aforesaid, are known, distinguished, or commonly called by the respective names of St. Nicholas's Land and St. Mary's Land.'[1]

Harborough probably later in date.

All, therefore, that is clear from Domesday Book with reference to the matter in hand, is the existence of Bugedon in Leicestershire as a royal manor. It would be hazardous to infer, from the silence of the record, that no such place as Harborough then existed. But, if it did exist, the relation of the two places was the same as in later days. The 'men' of Harborough had their holdings and common-rights in the 'fields' of Bowden Magna, and there was no necessity for a separate enumeration, as the manors were practically the same.

Evidence of later records. Divisions of the subject.

We come, now, to facts which are brought out by the public records of a later date. In dealing with them it will be convenient to give, or to summarize: (1) those which relate to the manorial history; (2) those which relate to the church; (3) any which bear upon the history of the parishes, though they do not fall under either of these heads.

From time to time reference will be made to the documents now published, and, as they are always dated according to the regnal years of the sovereign, it will be best to take each reign by itself, first, giving the facts drawn from different sources; next, showing the noteworthy points in the documents.

The reigns of William Rufus, Henry I., and Stephen, are a blank so far as concerns the history of Bowden and Harborough. No facts have yet come to light until the reign of Henry II. (December 19, 1154—July 6, 1189).

Grant of the manors by Henry II.

'In the twenty-sixth year of his reign,' says Nichols, 'the King granted the Manors of Bowden and Haverbergh to William de Mauduit, his Chamberlain. But Robert de Mauduit, his son, joined the rebellious barons, and his possessions were seized by the King.'[2]

---

[1] Nichols' Leicestershire: Gartree, p. 478, note 1.
[2] *Ibid.*, p. 488. The authority given is 'MS. Chetwynd.'

The reign of Richard I. (September 3, 1189—April 6, 1199) gives us also one fact, and there is one of the documents which is thought to belong to that period. In the Great Roll of the Pipe, under the heading, 'Warewichscr et Legercestrescr,' occurs the following:

Idem vice-comes reddidit computum de xs. et viii*d*. de firma de Schaftinton quæ fuit Dauid. Et de xxxii*s*. et viii*d*. de firma de Caldewella. Et de v*s*. de firma Molendini de Hauerberga. Et de ix*s*. et v . . . terra quæ est in Clauso Castelli de Kenillewurda *S*. lvii*s*. et x*d*.[1]

The Sheriff accounts for rents amounting to £2 17*s*. 10*d*., viz.: 10*s*. 8*d*. from Skeffington, which was David's, £1 12*s*. 8*d*. from Caldwell, 5*s*. from Harborough Mill, and ix*s*. v [   ] from land within the close of Kenilworth Castle.

Harborough Mill, in the Pipe Roll.

At first sight it might be thought doubtful, whether by 'Hauerberga' is meant Harborough in Leicestershire, or Harborough (Great or Little) in Warwickshire. Schaftinton (Skeffington), and Caldewella (Caldwell), a member of the Soke of Rothley, are both well-known villages in Leicestershire. Kenillewurda is, clearly, the still better-known Kenilworth in Warwickshire. What seems to decide the question is that, according to Dugdale's Warwickshire, the old form of the Warwickshire Harborough was not 'Hauerbergh,' but 'Herdeberge,' or something similar.[2] A mill, as is well known, was an important feature, and a great source of profit, in the manors of early days.

Probably Harborough in Leicestershire.

The earliest of the town documents (No. 1), though it is thought to belong to this reign, will be better considered in connexion with a later record.

In the reign of John (May 27, 1199—October 19, 1216), William de Cantilupe, the King's steward, Sheriff of Warwickshire and Leicestershire, obtained a grant of the manors. This is stated to have been in 1214, and the authority given is Collins' Peerage, iii. 182.[3] William de Cantilupe was steward of the King's household, and in constant attendance on him, taking his side in the Inter-

Grant of the manors to William de Cantilupe.

---

[1] Great Roll of the Pipe (printed), 1 Ric. I., p. 128.
[2] Dugdale's Warwickshire, pp. 65, 66.
[3] Nichols' Leicestershire : Gartree. p. 488.

dict and the Civil War. He signed the confirmation of Magna Charta. His death took place in 1239.[1]

In the sixteenth year of John, A.D. 1214, Henry de Nowres, and Juliana his wife, obtain a writ of *Novel disseisin*[2] at Westminster, against Richard Hilling, Robert de Clippeton, Ivo the son of Roger, Geoffrey the son of Bernard, and Ivo the brother of Bernard, 'de libero tenemento suo in Buchedon et Haverberg.'[3] A reference to the document already named (No. 1) will show at once the interest of this record. Richard Illing is one of the witnesses, with two Rogers. But the facts to be gleaned from the published histories and the public records are very meagre up to the end of this reign.

In the reign of Henry III. (October 28, 1216—November 16, 1272), several facts of importance come to light. We have, first, two entries in the Close Rolls, which prove the antiquity of Harborough as a market town, and show that the present custom of holding a market on Tuesdays dates back more than 660 years:

1.—Anno 4to Henr. III., A.D. 1219.

Harborough Market wont to be holden on Monday before 1219.

De mercato de Rowell.

Rex vice-comiti Northamton. salutem. Monstratum est nobis et consilio nostro quod de novo levatum est mercatum apud Rowell per diem Lunæ ad nocumentum mercati nostri de Haverberegh quod tenetur et teneri solet ibidem per diem Lune. Et idcirco tibi precipimus quod si ita est predictum mercatum de Rowell per diem Lunæ teneri prohibeas et per alium diem teneri facias.[4]

A market is being held on Mondays at Rothwell, to the detriment of Harborough Market on the same day. The Sheriff of Northamptonshire is ordered to change the day for holding the market at Rothwell.

2.—Anno 6to Henr. III., A.D. 1221.

Changed to Tuesday, 1221.

De quodam mercato habendo.

Dominus Rex concessit Rogero

The King allows Harborough

---

[1] Dictionary of National Biography (ed. Stephen).
[2] See Tomline's Law Dictionary, or, Dictionary of English History (Cassell and Co.). 'Assize of novel disseisin' was 'an action that lay with a tenant unjustly dispossessed of his lands.'
[3] Rot. de finibus in Turr. Lond. temp. Reg. Johannis (1835), p. 545.
[4] Rot. Litt. Claus. (printed), vol. i., p. 406 b.

Orget quod mercatum illud quod teneri solebat singulis septimanis per diem Lunæ apud manerium suum de Hauerberg, de cetero teneatur ibidem per diem Martis Nisi mercatum illud, etc.[1] — Market to be changed from Monday to Tuesday.

The points of importance in these extracts are: (1) that in 1219 the market is spoken of as 'held and wont to be held' on a Monday, and that, for fear of injury to it, a market on the same day at Rothwell, seven miles off, is to be stopped and changed to another day; (2) that two years later the market at Harborough was changed from Monday to Tuesday, the day on which it has always been held within living memory. Why, after all, the day for the Harborough market was altered, and not that for the Rothwell market, must remain unknown. We may notice, by the way, that Rothwell was then spelled as it is even now pronounced, 'Rowell.'

We have another entry in the same rolls, belonging to the eleventh year of Henry III., in which the name of William de Cantilupe again occurs as holding the manors granted in the previous reign:

Dominus Rex concessit Willelmo de Cantilupo quod habeat rationabile auxilium de hominibus maneriorum de Hauerberg et Bukedon quæ habet de ballivo domini Johannis Regis sicut Dominus Rex capi fecit ad opus suum de dominicis suis. Et mandatum est vicecomiti Leic' quod predictum auxilium ei habere faciat sicut predictum est. Ita quod predicti homines non sint nimis gravati. Teste Rege apud Mereton vj die Junii anno, etc., xi°.[3] — William de Cantilupe may have a reasonable 'aid'[2] from the men of the manors of Bowden and Harborough, the same as the King himself has received for his own use from the men in his demesne. The Sheriff is to see that he has this, and also that the men are not too heavily burdened by it. — William de Cantilupe is permitted to have an 'aid' from the men of Bowden and Harborough, 1227.

---

[1] Rot. Litt. Claus. (printed), vol. i., p. 485.

[2] Auxilium: 'aid,' 'a pecuniary contribution of a feudal vassal to his lord.' It might be demanded: (1) when the lord made his eldest son a knight; (2) when he gave his eldest daughter in marriage; (3) when the lord's person had to be ransomed from captivity. 'Aids' were abolished by Act of Parliament in the reign of Charles II. See New English Dictionary, ed. Dr. J. A. Murray; Encyclopædia Britannica ('Aids'); Stubbs' Select Charters ('Magna Charta'), p. 298 (ed. 1884).

[3] Rot. Litt. Claus., vol. ii., p. 188 b.

Grant to another William de Cantilupe.

According to Nichols,[1] another William de Cantilupe, son of the preceding, received a confirmation charter of the manors reviving the previous grant. The reference given is Cart. 21 Hen. III. No. 27. He also was Steward of the Household. His death took place in 1251.[2]

In the record known as 'Testa de Nevill' occurs the following, which, for the first time since the Domesday Survey, gives the value of the joint manors:

Buggedon Haverbergh sunt de dominico domini Regis Willelmus de Cantilupo eas tenet de dono Johannis Regis et valent xvij*li.* x*s.*[3]	Bowden-Harborough are of the King's demesne; William de Cantilupe holds them by grant of King John. They are worth £17 10*s.*

Sixteen years later (1251) there is the Sheriff's return as to tolls, which gives the names of two residents as jurors. The reference in Nichols is Rot. 36 Hen. III., No. 27:[4]

Tolls not paid by some who have passed through the manors.

Excellentissimo domino suo domino Henrico, Dei Gratiâ illustri regi Angliæ, domino Hiberniæ, duci Normanniæ et Aquitaniæ et comiti Andegaviæ, Vicecomes Warr' et Leic', salutem, et tam debitum quam devotum in omnibus obsequium. Noveritis me per preceptum vestrum diligenter fecisse inquisitionem qui transitum fecerunt per maneria vestra de Haverberge et Bowdon et theolonium in maneriis predictis debitum non persolverunt, sed injuste detinuerunt, per subscriptos juratores videlicet, per Ricardum Christian, Ricardum de Sadington, etc. Juratores dicunt quod Nicolaus de Bassing de Bassingburne qui mortuus est, Nicolaus capellanus de Benefend, Gosfridus Barker de eâdem et duo filii sui quorum nomina ignorantur et Hugo Justiciarius de eâdem, manentes in comitatu Northampton. transitum fecerunt per predicta maneria	The Sheriff of Warwickshire and Leicestershire, by the King's command, makes inquiry as to tolls not paid by travellers through the manors, by means of Richard Christian, Richard of Sadington, and others, as jurors. They report certain defaulters; amongst others, Nicholas Basing, of Bassingbourn; Godfrey Barker; Nicholas, Chaplain, of Benefend; and Hugh, the Justiciar, who passed through with sheep and did not pay toll.

---

[1] Nichols' Leicestershire: Gartree, p. 488.
[2] Dict. Nat. Biog. (ed. Stephen).
[3] Testa de Nevill (pub. 1807), p. 92 b.
[4] Nichols' Leicestershire: Gartree, p. 489.

cum bidentibus, et theolonium vobis debitum non persolverunt, sed injuste asportaverunt.

The name of Christian will be found many times in the town documents of later dates.

Later still, in 1270, the manors are stated to have been granted by the King to his consort, Eleanor of Provence, who held them until her death in 1291, when they reverted to the Crown.[1]

If the manorial history in this reign gives the first clear glimpse of Harborough as a place of any importance, it is in this reign that we find the earliest records as to the church. *Earliest notices as to the church.*

The 'Matriculus' of Hugh de Welles, who was Bishop of Lincoln from 1209-1235, is the first source of information. Its title is as follows :

Incipit matriculus Domini H. Episcopi Lincoln' de omnibus Ecclesiis in Archidiaconatu Leycestriæ, anno Domini M°CC^{mo}XX^{mo}. 1220.

And the entry in the original runs thus :

Ecclesiæ de Budon patronus dominus rex ut dicitur, sed contulit illud manerium domino W. de Cantilupo nescitur tamen an cum advocacione ; persona Daniel institutus, etc. Item est ibi quædam capella sive ecclesia in eadem (*sic*) feodo, quæ est ejusdem D. et habet capellanum suum residentem per matricem ecclesiam.[2]

The King is patron of Bowden. He has conferred the manor on William de Cantilupe, whether with the advowson is not known. The parson instituted is Daniel. In the same fee is a chapel or church belonging to the said Daniel. It has its own resident chaplain, provided by the mother church. *Bowden Church and St. Mary's Chapel, 1220.*

The registers of the See of Lincoln commence about the same time, but in those which belong to the episcopate of Hugh de Welles there is no mention of the Leicestershire Bowden, though there are several of its near neighbour, the Northamptonshire Bowden. It is in the records of his successor, Robert Grosseteste (1235-1254), that the Leicestershire Bowden first appears, and in one roll of the time of Henry Lexington (1254-1258), that we have the earliest mention of a church at Harborough :

[1] Nichols' Leicestershire : Gartree, p. 489.
[2] Cotton MSS. Brit. Mus., Nero, D. x., fol. 143 (140).

Market Harborough Records.

First known rector and first known vicar of Bowden, 1238.

Vicaria de Bugedon.
Willelmus de Bugedon capellanus presentatus per Danielem de Longo Campo rectorem ecclesiæ de Bugedon ad ipsius ecclesiæ vicariam, factâ prius inquisicione per J. Archid. Leirc, et interveniente assensu W. de Cantilupo patroni ejusdem ecclesiæ per quem etc. ad eandem vicariam admissus est cum onere et penâ vicariæ et mandatum, etc., eidem Archid., etc.[1]

William of Bowdon, chaplain, presented by Daniel de Longchamp, Rector of Bowden, is admitted vicar, William de Cantilupe, the patron, assenting, 1238.

From this we learn: (1) that the advowson *did* follow the manor; (2) that the full name of the rector was Daniel de Longchamp. We also have the first record of an appointment of a vicar by the rector, a fact to be carefully borne in mind when we come to later entries in the registers. The consent of the patron was given to the appointment by the rector.

But the short episcopate of Bishop Lexington, as already stated, furnishes a record of much greater importance with regard to Harborough. The document in which this is to be found is headed:

Rotulus taxacionis Arch. Leicestr. tempore Henrici Lexington Episcopi qui fuit Episcopus ab anno 1253 ad annum 1258.

Taxation Roll for the Archdeaconry of Leicester in the time of Henry Lexington, who was Bishop from 1253 to 1258.

And the entry is:

First mention of Harborough Chapel, 1253-1258.

In decanatu de Gertre cui preest Theobaldus de Picwell.
Ecclesiæ de Boudon patronus dominus Rex ut dicitur sed contulit illud manerium domino W. de Cantilupo nescitur tamen an cum advocacione; Persona Daniel Institutus, etc. Item est ibi quædam capella sive ecclesia in eodem feodo quæ est ejusdem R. [? Rectoris] et habet capellanum suum residentem. Ad eandem spectat capella de Haverberge habens capellanum suum residentem per matricem ecclesiam.
(Value of Budon. lvi marks.)

Gartree Deanery. Theobald of Pickwell, Rural Dean.
As above to the words 'resident chaplain;' then: 'To the same church belongs the chapel of Haverberg, having its own resident chaplain provided by the mother church.'

---

[1] Bishop Grosseteste's roll, third year.

It will be observed that the record follows closely upon the lines of that in the 'Matriculus'; so closely, indeed, that no notice is taken of the statement in Bishop Grosseteste's record that William de Cantilupe was the patron of the benefice. Bishop Lexington's roll gives the name of the rector as it was given thirty years before; but, in addition to the first chapel named in the 'Matriculus' as attached to the mother church, it names the chapel at Harborough as belonging to the same benefice, and as having, also, its own chaplain. Thus we have on record for the first time the three churches which, though not exactly in the same forms, exist to-day: (1) the mother church of Boudon (Great Bowden); (2) the chapel of Haverberge (Market Harborough); (3) another chapel, unnamed, which can only be that known as St. Mary in Arden. *The mother church and its two chapels.*

With regard to Harborough, the church itself, long called Harborough Chapel, proves the truth of the record, and, by the help of the record and the existing building, the date when it was built may be fixed within fair limits. An independent student of architecture, who knew nothing of what has just been stated, was asked to give approximate dates to the several parts of the church. The whole of the nave, he said, and the clerestory in the chancel, were clearly much later in date than the tower and spire, but the tower and spire, and a small part of the chancel, might be reckoned to belong to about the middle or latter part of the thirteenth century. Another indication of the rise of the chapel is to be found in its dedication—St. Dionysius the Areopagite—whose supposed works are known to have been an object of study with Bishop Grosseteste.[1] It seems reasonable to suppose that the beginning of the church is to be dated from his episcopate, when, as we have seen, the place had already some importance as a market-town, and that the building was sufficiently advanced to be consecrated before he died. Churches, it is known, were often left for a long period *Probable date of Harborough Chapel.*

---

[1] Perry's Life of Grosseteste (S.P.C.K.), p. 39.

in an unfinished state. The work of building, no doubt, was taken up at different periods, and here, as elsewhere, there is a wide interval between one part and another. The latter parts belong, in style, to a time when the manors, as we shall see, had passed to a wealthy and noble Yorkshire family, and were, perhaps, carried out by its influence and liberality.

The registers of Bishop Richard Gravesend (1258-1280) contain no reference to Bowden or Harborough.

We will now briefly consider the one document which belongs to this reign (No. 2), and with it the earliest of all, which has been already mentioned.

The oldest of the town documents, Nos. 1 and 2.

No. 1 is the only document in which the Domesday spelling of the name 'Bugedon' is to be found. It bears no date, but it is thought to belong to the closing years of the twelfth century. The name in the same form is found in the sixth year of King John, 1205.[1] The name of Bernard occurs again more than once, while that of Adam Bernard will be found more than one hundred years later, in the time of Edward I. The name of Meyners seems to account for 'Maynerdsholm' as a 'field-name' in No. 4. No. 2, also, is without date; but it is considered to have been written in the first half of the thirteenth century. The name of Adam Bernard again occurs, and for the first time we have 'field-names.'

Earliest 'Field-names.'

Two only are given, 'Tongsty' and 'Scirday Kotys,' but these two can be traced, through many varieties of spelling, for five hundred years, up to the date of the enclosure in 1776.

Edward I. began to reign November 20, 1272, and his reign lasted till July 7, 1307.

The Hundred rolls, taken under a commission at the beginning of this period, to inquire about certain abuses with regard to rights of manor, warren, chase, fishery, toll, market, etc., contain two entries which relate to Harborough.

Inquiry at Northampton, 3 Edward I.

(1) Villa Northampton.

INQUISICIO facta apud Northampton per xij juratos ejus·

Inquest held at Northampton by twelve jurors of that town in

---

[1] Rot. Litt. Claus., vol. ii., p. 32 b.

dem villæ anno regni Regis Edwardi tertio coram dominis Willelmo de Sancto Omero et Warino de Chaucombe, justiciariis domini Regis videlicet per Rogerum de Sancto Martino, Henricum ad portam, Jordanum le Chevaler, Laurentium de Bobton, Osbertum de Crouthorp, Galfridum de Oveston, Adam le Corder, Thomam de Pippewell, Radulphum de Thorp, Robertum de Keylmersh, Willelmum le Suriegien, et Johannem de Campeden qui dicunt super sacramentum. . . .

3 Edward I., before Wm. of St. Omer and Waryn of Chalcombe, the King's Justiciars, viz., by Roger of St. Martin, Henry at Gate, Jordan the Knight, Lawrence of Bobton, Osbert of Crouthorp, Geoffrey of Overston, Adam the Corder,[1] Thomas of Pipewell, Ralph of Thorpe, Robert of Kelmarsh, William the Surgeon, and John of Campden, who say, on oath. . . .

Item dicunt quod cum burgenses Northampton habeant libertatem per dominum regem et predecessores suos ut sint quieti de toloneis et omnibus consuetudinibus per totum regnum Angliæ et per portus maris, ballivi Comitis Warranniæ in Staunford, Ballivi Abbatis de Burgo Sancti Petri citra pontem Staunford, etc. . . . Ballivi dominæ Reginæ in Haverberge . . . per potestatem officii sui capiunt injuste consuetudines et tolonea de burgensibus Northampton contra libertates suas eis per Reges Angliæ concessas in contemptu regiæ dignitatis et coronæ suæ et ad grave dampnum communitatis villæ Northampton quantum æstimare nesciunt. . . .

The burgesses of Northampton, being expressly freed from toll, etc., by the King and his predecessors, have wrongfully been made to pay it by, amongst others, the Queen's bailiffs in Harborough, to their great loss, etc. . . .

Northampton burgesses wrongfully made to pay toll at Harborough.

Item dicunt quod quidam Johannes filius capellani de Haverberge attachiatus fuit tempore nundinarum Northampton iiij annis elapsis in domo Johannis le fus Juvenis pro suspicione quod furaverat ij supertunicas et ij gladios cum nichil malfecerat scilicet per Willelmum Fraunceys et Ricardum le Mustarder tunc ballivos Northampton, qui ipsum postea abire permiserunt ut fidelem sed nichil ab eo receperunt ut dicunt.[2]

John, son of a Chaplain of Harborough, was, four years before, arrested during Northampton Fair (in the house of John le fus) on suspicion of having stolen 2 overcoats and 2 swords by Wm. Francis and Richard le mustarder, the then bailiffs, who afterwards released him as having done nothing wrong, but say they did not receive anything from him.

John, son of a Harborough chaplain, arrested for theft.

---

[1] Perhaps 'the Ropemaker.' *Corder*, Fr., to twist and make ropes (Cotgrave). Corderia, the Ropery—Liber Albus (Rolls Series), vol. iii., Glossary.

[2] Rot. Hund. (Record Commission), vol. ii., pp. 4, 5.

There is also an entry in the Originalia Rolls of the Exchequer:

The manor with Gartree Hundred entrusted to Adam Bernard.

Anno Regis Edwardi filii Regis Henrici xx Rex commisit Adæ Bernard de Boudon manerium et villam de Haverbergh cum hundredo de Gertre in comitatu Leyc' custodire quamdiu Rex placuerit reddendo inde per annum executoribus, etc., Alianoræ quondam Reginæ Angliæ consortis Regis lviii*li*. xiiis. iiij*d*.[1]

20 Edward I. The King has granted to Adam Bernard, of Bowden, the manor and town of Harborough, with the hundred of Gartree, in the county of Leicester, during the King's pleasure, on payment to the executors of his late wife, Queen Eleanor, yearly, of £58 13s. 4d.

Grant as part of Queen Eleanor's dower.

The Miscellaneous Records of the Queen's Remembrancer of the Exchequer tell us that, on July 25, 1299, the manors of Bowden and Harborough were granted by the King to his second wife, Margaret of France. The King assigned his wife 'quindecim millia libratarum terræ Turōn' (£15,000, of the money of Tours in rent of land) 'nomine dotis seu dotalicii' (as dower or dowry). The account of the lands and tenements assigned for this purpose is given, and in the heading of this account it is added: 'Si quatuor denarii Turōn debeant computari pro uno denario sterling' (4d. Tours to be reckoned as equivalent to 1d. sterling). In the list we find, with 'Norh't' at the side:

Manerium de Boudon et Haverberge cum Hundredo de Gertre, lx*li*.

'The manor of Bowden and Harborough, with the Hundred of Gartree, £60.'[2]

Each of these records tells something as to the history and life of the place in the end of the thirteenth century. From the first we see that Harborough was by this time a thoroughfare town, through which the good citizens of Northampton had to pass, probably on their way to and from Leicester, and where, as at Stamford, they had to defend themselves against illegal tolls and dues. The second brings before us a Harborough man, the son of a chaplain or working priest, as we may call him, finding his

---

[1] Rot. Orig. in Cur. Scacc. Abbrev., vol. i., p. 70*b*.
[2] Documents illustrative of Eng. Hy., cent. xiii. and xiv. From Records of Dept. of Qu. Remembrancer (H. Cole, 1844), p. 348.

way to Northampton Fair, and arrested on a charge of theft by the bailiffs of the town. In the third we meet with the name of Adam Bernard, a man in a position to have the care of the manor of Bowden and Harborough with the Hundred of Gartree, and to pay a large rent to the Queen's Executors, while in the last we find the manors for the second time granted to a Queen Consort, an indication that, though the manors were not among the chief of those which belonged to the Crown, they were, nevertheless, of considerable value.

We have already seen that there is nothing relating to Bowden or Harborough in the registers of Bishop Gravesend. Bishop Oliver Sutton succeeded him, and his registers extend over a period of twenty years (1280-1300). In them are four entries, all of importance. The earliest of these is in his Memoranda, and is entitled 'Sequestrum in ecclesiâ de Boudon':[1]

Oliverus, etc., etc. Officialibus Archid., Leicr., etc. Quia magister Nicolas de Luvetoft ad parochialem ecclesiam de Boudon, in minoribus annis dudum presentatus, quibus quidem ecclesiæ et personæ certum custodem, usque ad legitimam ætatem ejusdem presentati, commisimus de gratiâ speciali, nunc major effectus et parochialem ecclesiam de Adelingflet Ebor. dioc. nuper adeptus pleno jure, institutionem in dictâ ecclesiâ de Boudon, licet ad illam sibi canonice faciendam pluries optulerimus nos paratos, a nobis recipere recusavit expresse, vobis mandamus quatenus omnes fructus et proventus dictæ ecclesiæ de Boudon post quindenam Sancti Michaelis proximo preteritam perceptos, et de cetero hujusmodi vacacione durante percipiendos, arcius sequestrantes et sub arcto se-

Nicholas of Luvetoft[2] was presented to the rectory of Bowden when under the canonical age. Since he attained the canonical age he has refused institution, though the Bishop has several times offered it. He is now presented to the benefice of Adelingfleet in the archdiocese of York. The Bishop accordingly sequestrates the benefice of Bowden, but up to a fortnight after the next Michaelmas 'of his special grace' he allows N. of Luvetoft to enjoy the profits of the benefice.

Buckden, October 15, 1290.

Nicholas of Luvetoft refuses institution. Sequestration of the benefice.

---

[1] Bp. Sutton's Register, Memoranda, fol. xi.
[2] Louvetôt in Normandy. Nicholas Lovetoft, canon of St. Paul's. Hardy's le Neibe, ii. 391 ; Newcourt, i. 156.

questro firmiter tenentes quousque aliud a nobis receperitis in mandatis, prefatum Magistrum Nicholaum de fructibus ejusdem ecclesiæ de Boudon ante quindenam predictam perceptis de nostrâ gratiâ speciali disponere libere permittatis ; et quid inde feceritis nos ante festum Omnium Sanctorum proxime futurum certiores reddatis per litteras vestras patentes harum seriem continentes. Valete. Datum apud Buckeden Id. Octobr. Pontificatus nostri anno xj.

The next in order is to be found in the list of institutions, bound up in the same volume with the Memoranda :[1]

Institution of Robert of St. Albans, 12 90/91.

Archd. de Leycestr. Magna Budon.
Robertus de Sancto Albano diaconus presentatus per dominum Edwardum dei gratiâ illustrem regem Angliæ Dominum Hiberniæ et Ducem Aquitanniæ ad ecclesiam de Magna Budon vacantem per mortem Walteri de Canciâ ultimo tenentis eandem. (Then follows a statement as to Nicholas de Luvetoft, similar to the one given in the sequestration.) Factâ prius inquisicione per Officiales R. Archidiaconi Leycestr. per quam, etc., ad dictam ecclesiam est admissus xi. Kal. ffebr. anno xi. (*i.e.*, Jan. 22, 12 90/91) apud Merlawe Monialium et rector canonice institutus in eâdem, Juratâque episcopo canonicâ obedientiâ in formâ consuetâ, Scriptum est dicto Archidiacono vel ejus officialibus quod, etc.

Robert of St. Albans, deacon, presented by King Edward to the church of Great Bowden, vacant by the death of Walter of Kent, was instituted Jan. 22, 12 90/91, at Nuns' Marlow (Little Marlow, Bucks).

This entry fills up the gap in the list of rectors which the previous registers have left. The first rector whose name is found at Lincoln is Daniel de Longchamp. He holds the benefice as early as 1220, and continues to hold it in the time of Bishop Lexington (1253-1258). Then comes Walter of Kent, of whose institution there is no

[1] Bp. Sutton's Register, Institutions, fol. lxx. (lxvii.).

record. Nicholas of Luvetoft next holds the living, before he is of the canonical age for ordination, and when he is of that age refuses institution, and in 1290-1291 Robert of St. Albans, deacon, is instituted. Already there is a clear indication that, in pre-Reformation times, the rector of the parish was rather the tenant of the church property than the pastor of the people, and this fact will become clearer as we go on.

In the following year, the Bishop's Memoranda supply an entry as to the parish and its rector which throws such light upon the time that, lengthy as it is, it must be given without abbreviation:

Dispensatio Roberti de Sancto Albano.[1]

Oliverus, permissione divina Lincoln. Episcopus, dilecto in CHRISTO filio domino Roberto de Sancto Albano Rectori Ecclesiæ de Magna Budon nostræ dioecesis presbitero salutem gratiam et benedictionem. Litteras Sanctissimi patris domini Nicholai Papæ quarti non rasas non vitiatas nec in aliquâ sui parte suspectas verâ bullâ plumbeâ et filo canapis more Curiæ Romanæ bullatas pro te nuper recepimus in hæc verba:

Nicholaus Episcopus servus servorum Dei venerabili fratri Episcopo Lincoln. salutem et Apostolicam benedictionem. Meritis dilecti filii Roberti de Sancto Albano Rectoris ecclesiæ de Magna Budon Linc. dioc. clerici carissimi in Christo filii nostri Regis Angliæ illustris inducimur ut eum speciali gratiâ prosequamur. Sane ipsius Regis petitio nobis exhibita continebat quod primo ipse ecclesiam de Esenden curam animarum habentem predictæ dioecesis ad ipsius Regis presentacionem post generale concilium Lugdunense[2] fuit canonice assecutus ipsamque

Robert of St. Albans was presented by Edward I. to the benefice of Essendon (Herts), and held it some years without offering himself to be ordained priest. He was afterwards presented by the King to the benefice of Great Bowden, and held both benefices, receiving their profits for some time without the necessary dispensation from the Holy See. But, fired by holy zeal, he has taken the Cross, and intends to go with the King to the Holy Land at his own charges. He therefore craves to be freed from the consequences of having so held the two benefices, and enjoyed their revenues. The Pope grants a Bull commanding the Bishop of Lincoln to dispense him from all such consequences, and to allow him to keep the benefices and their profits, notwithstanding any decree or other edict of a General Council to the contrary, provided only that a fit portion of the profits is reserved for the use of the benefices, that the due rites are performed, and the cure of souls not neglected.

Robert of St. Albans promises to take the Cross. Dispensation from the Pope.

---

[1] Bp. Sutton's Register, Memoranda, 12th year, fol. lvi.
[2] The Council of Lyons, A.D. 1274. Chronology of History (Sir H. Nicolas), 1838, p. 256.

pluribus annis detinens, se non fecit juxta tenorem ipsius concilii in presbiterum ordinari. Postmodum vero prefatus Robertus nominatam ecclesiam de Magna Budon ad ejusdem Regis presentacionem de novo legitime est adeptus, seque fecit statutis temporibus in presbiterum promoveri dictasque ecclesias insimul aliquamdiu tenuit et fructus percepit etiam ex eisdem, super hoc dispensacione a Sede Apostolicâ non obtentâ. Cum autem idem Robertus, qui zelo fidei et devotionis accensus signum vivificæ Crucis assumpsit, intendat cum eodem Rege suis propriis sumptibus et expensis in terræ sanctæ subsidium proficisci, nobis humiliter supplicavit ut providere sibi, tam circa detentionem dictarum ecclesiarum et perceptionem fructuum earundem quam circa statum suum, et quamlibet maculam sive notam quæ proinde sibi posset impingi, per Apostolicæ provisionis remedium misericorditer dignaremur. Nos itaque, ipsius Roberti supplicationibus inclinati et volentes sibi ob suorum exigentiam meritorum et considerationem predicti Regis, cujus idem Robertus clericus existit, gratiam facere specialem, de circumspectione tuâ plenam in Domino fiduciam obtinentes, fraternitati tuæ per Apostolica scripta mandamus quatenus, si est ita, cum eodem Roberto, ut prefatas ecclesias et fructus ex eis perceptos possit licite retinere, constitutione generalis concilii aut quâlibet aliâ super hoc in contrarium editâ non obstante, dispenses nichilominus, omnem maculam sive infamiam et quamlibet aliam inhabilitatis notam, si quam ex retentione predictarum ecclesiarum et perceptionem dictorum fructuum contraxerit, totaliter abolendo. Volumus tamen quod de fructibus prælibatis portionem congruam in evidentem utilitatem ecclesiarum ipsarum

The Bishop grants the dispensation, as commanded, and reserves 20 marks for the use of the benefice of Essendon, and 10 marks for that of Great Bowden.

Edlesborough (Bucks), May 1, 1290.

juxta tuum arbitrium idem Robertus convertere teneatur, reliquos sibi de speciali gratiâ remittendo. Proviso quod predictæ ecclesiæ debitis obsequiis non fraudentur et animarum cura in eis nullatenus negligatur. Datum Romæ apud Sanctam Mariam majorem x Kal. Marcii Pontificatus nostri anno quarto (*i.e.*, Feb. 20, 129½). Constante igitur et cognito prout res exigit de premissis, ut de Boudon et de Esenden ecclesias antedictas et fructus ex eis perceptos licite valeas retinere, constitutione generalis concilii super hoc editâ aut quâlibet aliâ contrariâ non obstante, tecum auctoritate nobis in hâc parte commissâ tenore presentium dispensamus, omnem maculam sive infamiam aut quamlibet aliam inhabilitatis notam, si quam ex retentione predictarum ecclesiarum et perceptione dictorum fructuum contraxisti, totaliter nichilominus abolentes Ita tamen quod de fructibus memoratis viginti marcas in ecclesiæ de Budon et decem marcas in ecclesiæ de Esenden evidentem utilitatem convertas, reliquis de gratiâ speciali remissis ; proviso quod dictæ ecclesiæ debitis non fraudentur obsequiis et animarum cura in eis nullatenus negligatur. In cujus rei testimonium sigillum nostrum presentibus est appensum Datum apud Edelesberg Kal. Maii anno domini M.CC. nonagesimo secundo et pontificatus nostri duodecimo.

It is worthy of note that the date of the Bull and of the dispensation is only a few weeks before the final loss of Acre (May 18, 1291[1]), which was the last scene in the Crusades. Historians tell us that, even after that event, Edward I. still dreamed of returning to Palestine, and that in his will he left £30,000 'for the equipment and maintenance of the knights who were to bear his heart to the Holy Land.' But it may be doubted whether the

[1] Gibbon, end of chapter lx.

Rector of Essendon and Great Bowden was ever called upon to fulfil his vow. The Pope himself died April 4, 1292.[1] He had refused to give money towards the crusade, and the men who had taken the cross were very different from the crusaders of former days. It is hard to avoid the suspicion that the taking of the cross may have been a ready way out of the difficulty of having acted without dispensation. Yet, on the other hand, it may be that in this King's clerk, ('cujus idem Robertus clericus existit') we have a relic of the true crusading spirit, though he never had the chance of proving it by his deeds.

Value of the benefice as given in 1291. The same Pope (Nicholas IV.) in 1288 granted an ecclesiastical tenth to the King for six years, towards defraying the cost of a crusade.[2] This taxation was made by the King's precept, and was finished in the Province of Canterbury in 1291. The whole was under the direction of John, Bishop of Winchester, and Oliver, Bishop of Lincoln. It was published by the Record Commission in the year 1802. In this volume (p. 64) we find the benefice of 'Boudon,' in the archdeaconry of Leicester, valued at £37 6s. 8d. By the terms of the dispensation, 10 marks were reserved 'in evidentem utilitatem ecclesiæ de Budon' (for the clear use of the church of Bowden). Thus £6 13s. 4d. was allowed for this purpose, and £30 13s. 4d. was to be enjoyed by the Rector absent on the crusade.

Among the muniments of the Dean and Chapter of Lincoln is preserved a fragment of a visitation record for the archdeaconry of Leicester for the year 1292, close upon the institution of Robert of St. Albans. In this fragment the name of 'Budon' fortunately occurs, and, short as it is, the record is a most useful one for this work.[3]

Budon : Rector ecclesiæ dominus Robertus de Sancto Albano.
    ,,   ,,   Rogerus de Meyner celebrans ibidem.

---

[1] Chronology of History (H. Nicolas), 1838, p. 202.
[2] Stubbs' Const. Hy. of Eng., vol. ii., p. 130.
[3] Muniments of the D. and C. of Lincoln, Press A, Shelf I, No. 14.

Budon : Dominus Nicholaus Bunney celebrans ibidem.
 „   „   Willelmus celebrans apud Harberue.
 „   „   Ricardus Illing celebrans ibidem.
Bowden : Rector, Robert of St. Albans.
 „   Roger de Meyner, saying Mass there.
 „   Nicholas Bunney,   „   „
 „   William, saying Mass at Harborough.
 „   Richard Illing, saying Mass there.

The occurrence of the two names, Roger de Meyner and Richard Illing, seems to throw some doubt upon the early date assigned to No. 1 of these documents, though names then, as now, often repeated themselves. But the chief interest of the extract lies in its bearing on the history of the church. It proves that in 1292 there were four priests in Bowden-Harborough—two at Harborough, two at Bowden; it also proves that Harborough Chapel was used for worship before the end of the thirteenth century, and so helps to confirm the inferences drawn above as to the probable date of its being built. There are more clergy in these two parishes in 1292 than, as we shall see later on, in 1492. Is this a sign that these parishes were more populous towards the end of the reign of Edward I. than just before the accession of the Tudor dynasty? It is impossible to bring out the fact without recalling the conclusions of careful writers. With the death of Edward I. (1307) began a long period of suffering, which ' may be traced in the decline of population, in the growth of crime, in the frequent returns of famine, and in the havoc caused by pestilence.'[1]

Bishop Sutton's Memoranda furnish one more entry which tells us something as to the state of the parish, and of the clergy, at this period :

Kal. April, Anno xiiij. (*i.e.*, April 1, 1294) apud Spaldwyk absolutus fuit auctoritate pontificali Magister Rogerus de Budon clericus a sententiâ majoris excommunicationis quam auctoritate Master Roger, clerk, of Bowden, is absolved from the sentence of greater excommunication which he had incurred for having laid violent hands on Master Richard of Bowden, clerk, satisfaction *Instance of clerical disorder.*

---

[1] England in the Fifteenth Century (Denton), Introd. part ii., p. 65.

canonis incurrit pro eo quod in Magistrum Ricardum de Budon clericum manus injecit temere violentas, ipsum percutiendo leviter, ut suggessit, satisfacto prius leso et impositâ sibi pro commisso penitentiâ salutari, et habuit litteram patentem testimonialem de absolucione.[1]

having been made, and salutary penance imposed.

Spaldwick (Hunts), April 1, 1294.

Comparing the names in this extract with those in the Visitation fragment, it would seem that 'Magister' Roger and 'Magister' Richard, of Bowden were two of those engaged in the performance of the due rites of the Church and the cure of souls, while the non-resident Rector enjoyed by far the larger portion of the fruits of the benefice.

Along with this instance of disorder we may take the first record as to the parish which is found in the registers of Bishop Dalderby, whose episcopate began in 1300, seven years before the death of Edward I., and lasted till 1320:

And of desecration.

Commissio ad reconciliandum cimiterium ecclesiæ de Magna Budon.[2] iij. Non. Januar. anno quinto (i.e., Jan. 3, 130⅚) apud Parcum Stowe commisit Episcopus vices suas auctoritate Apostolicâ Archidiacono Leycestr. Abbati de Osolveston (Owston) et Priori de Land (Launde) divisim ad reconciliandum cimiterium ecclesiæ de Magna Boudon sanguinis extractione violenter perpetratâ pollutum, etc., ad quod reconc. commode, etc.

Commission for the reconciliation of the burial-ground of Great Bowden Church.

The Archdeacon of Leicester, the Abbot of Osolveston [Owston] and the Prior of Launde are appointed to reconcile the burial-ground of Great Bowden Church, which had been polluted by the violent shedding of blood.

Stow Park, January 3, 130⅚.

While such records tell us of a state of social life in which violent quarrels and fierce passions had their part, they tell us also, it is fair to remember, of an authority which served to correct disorder, which strove to keep up reverence for holy things, and to bring home to men the sin of desecration.

[1] Bp. Sutton's Register, Memoranda, fol. 98.
[2] Bp. Dalderby's Register, Memoranda, fol. lxxix.

Though the reign of Edward I. gives us several facts *Town documents of the reign of Edward I.* which help us to understand the history of Bowden and Harborough, there are only two of the town documents which belong to it. Of these one (No. 3) relates to property in Stamford, and all the names, both of places and persons, are strange to Harborough; but it was found with the other documents, and is therefore published at the same time. The other (No. 4) has no date, but is thought to be about 1300. In it the name 'Buchard' of No. 1 has become 'Boccard,' and the name 'Meyners' may be traced in the field-name 'Maynersdholm.' The signatures of the witnesses in both documents tend to show how surnames gradually came about, and what were some of the early trades and occupations. On this last point there is a striking contrast between *le furbechur* (furbisher [1]), *le parmenter* (tailor), *le orfevure* (goldsmith), of a town like Stamford, and *le sweyn* (herdsman) and *folur* (fowler) of the country village, with its low-lying lands, often flooded by the sluggish Welland, with its swamps and stretches of wild moorland, with its cattle and hogs feeding on the common-land and eating acorns in the thick woods.

Edward II.—'Edward the son of Edward,' as he was styled (see No. 5)—reigned from July 8, 1307, to January 20, 1327. The episcopate of Bishop Dalderby covers the first thirteen of these years, and the remaining seven form part of the episcopate of Henry Burwash, or Burghersh (1320-1342).

In this reign the manors of Bowden and Harborough *The manors held by Queen Isabella.* were held by Queen Isabella, as they had been by Queen Margaret. An interesting MS. volume belonging to Sir C. E. Isham, Bart., of Lamport, gives an extract from the Great Roll of 15 Edward II. to this effect:

In magno Rotulo de anno decimo quinto RR.E secundi in Warr. Leic.	Queen Isabella has the manors of Bowden and Harborough in dower from Feb. 14, in the eleventh

---

[1] *Armorum politor*, one who brightens arms (Bailey's Dictionary).

[   ] Maneria de Bowdon et Haverbergh a xiiij die ffebruarii anno xj° quo die M. (Margaret) Regina obiit sicut continetur in rotulo xi° regni regis hujus, sed Isabella Regina habet eadem maneria in dotem per duo brevia inter communia de anno xi° videlicet a predicta xiiij die.[1]

year of the King, on which day Queen Margaret died.

Queen Margaret died in 1317, ten years after her husband, while Edward II. married Isabella of France in 1308. The manors were thus held by the Queen Dowager for ten years, and then became part of the dower of the Queen Consort. Isabella, as is well known, did not die till long after the accession of her son, Edward III., so that this one grant will account for the manorial history for the whole reign.

Robert of St. Albans an infirm old man. Appointment of assistant.

The Bishop's registers bring the crusading rector again before us. He is now an old man, afflicted with the loss of sight and other bodily and mental infirmities, unable to take due care of himself, and in need of help. Both the Bishops of this reign grant him such help. First, Bishop Dalderby:

Deputacio coadjutoris Rectori Ecclesiæ de Magna Boudon.[2] X°. Kal. Febr. (*i.e.*, Jan. 23, 1316) apud Parcum Stowe deputatus fuit Johannes de Ardern Rector ecclesiæ de Wakele coadjutor Roberto de Sancto Albano Rectori ecclesiæ de Magna Boudon et Rectori ecclesiæ de Esenden, ad petitionem suam expressam prout ....decanus de Hertford Episcopo litteris suis patentibus intimavit, qui quidem Robertus senio confractus tantâ cecitate et adversâ valetudine erat detentus quod ad ipsius regimen non sufficiebat nec suorum.

John of Ardern, Rector of Wakely, is appointed assistant to Robert of St. Albans, Rector of Great Bowden, who is so afflicted with old age, blindness, etc., that he cannot take care of himself or his possessions.

Stow Park, January 23, 1316.

Bishop Burghersh, or Burwash, succeeded Bishop Dalderby, and in his registers we find a longer record on the same subject:

---

[1] Isham MSS., TT., fol. 199.
[2] Bp. Dalderby's Register, Memoranda, fol. cccxl.

Ienricus, divinâ providentiâ coln. Episcopus, dilecto nostro Christo filio Roberto de Culle-th clerico salutem gratiam et edictionem. Cum Robertus Sancto Albano Rector ecclesiæ Magna Boudon adeo corporis ilitate et infirmitate laboret, io ut dicitur jam confractus et ersâ valetudine sic detentus, o quod ad sui ipsius regimen non icit nec suorum, Nos ex officii tri debito, tam ecclesiæ pre- tæ quam personæ Roberti rec- s predicti providere volentes, tuâque fidelitate fiduciam ob- entes, te eidem rectori ad ipsius suorum regimen et ad curam tæ ecclesiæ suæ tam in tem- alibus quam in spiritualibus liter peragendam, dum tamen sensus predicti rectoris ad accedat, coadjutorem tenore fato deputamus, Mandantes , in virtute prestiti a te ad sancta evangelia juramenti, quatenus bonis prefati rectoris et ecclesiæ predictæ nunc extantibus et iris inventario per te fideliter to, eundem rectorem secundum ultates suas manuteneri curam- parochiæ dictæ ecclesiæ et ra eidem incumbentia peragi iatis et agnoscatis, te in hac parte ter habiturus quod de facto tuo liter possis reddere rationem, n ex parte nostrâ congrue fueris uisitus, et de facto tuo debeas rito commendari, potestatem o cuicunque alteri in hujus-modi dministracionis officio alias nmissam, ceteris de causis nos ventibus, tenore presentium re- amus. Datum apud Rykhale or. dioc. xij Kal. Jul. Anno nini 1322 (*i.e.*, June 20, 1322).[1]

Robert of Culworth, clerk, is appointed to be Robert of St. Albans' assistant. He is to exhibit careful inventories, and to see that the parochial duties and obligations are duly discharged.

Dated at Riccall, York diocese, June 20, 1322.

But, after all, the old man lived on, and did not die until the beginning of the next reign. He held the benefice irty-eight years.

[1] Bp. Burghersh, Reg., Memoranda, fol. lviii.

30   *Market Harborough Records.*

<small>Document of the reign of Edward II.</small>

The town possesses only one document of this reign (No. 5). The only point of local interest in it is the mention of Foxton Moor. This proves that the rood and a half of land therein mentioned must have been in what was afterwards known as the North, or Gallow, Field. There is, however, a change in the terms used, which shows how local legal documents bear witness to the changes made by authority. For the first time in these papers we read the words, which will be found commonly in later documents, 'to hold the same of the chief lord of the fee at the due and accustomed services' ('Habendum ... de capitali domino feodi illius per servicia inde debita et de jure consueta'). This is due to the statute called 'Quia Emptores,' which was enacted in 1290, and required that in the transfer of land the new tenant should hold the land, not of the alienor, but of the chief lord, and should pay him feudal duty.[1]

The long reign of Edward III. lasted from January 25, 1327, to June 21, 1377. The Bishops of Lincoln during these fifty years were (1) Henry Burghersh, whose episcopate ended in 1342; (2) Thomas Bek (1342-1347); (3) John Gynewell (1347-1363); (4) John Bokingham, who held the see till nearly the end of the century. The records supply a good deal of material of interest as to Bowden and Harborough, and there are ten of the town documents which belong to this reign.

<small>Grant of the manors to John of Eltham, the King's brother, 1330.</small>

Nichols states that on December 1, 1330, the King granted the manors to his brother, John of Eltham, Earl of Cornwall. The reference given is 'Cart., 4 Edw. III., No. 12.'[2] In the former reign, as we have seen, the manors had been granted to the King's mother, Queen Isabel, on the death of Margaret, the relict of Edward I. For the first few years of this reign 'all real power lay in the hands of the Queen-mother and of Mortimer.'[3] The

---

[1] See Stubbs' Const. Hy., vol. ii., pp. 115, 132; Green's Short History (1888), p. 173.
[2] Nichols' Leicestershire: Gartree, p. 489.
[3] Hist. of Eng. to 1509 (York-Powell), p. 218.

Queen-mother 'contented herself with an enormous settlement, which left to her son only a third of the Crown lands to maintain his royal dignity.'[1] But on October 19, 1330, Mortimer was arrested at Nottingham. He was afterwards tried and condemned, and was put to death as a traitor on November 29, while Isabel was sent to Castle Rising, and kept in retirement on an allowance of £3,000 a year.[2] 'From this time,' says the historian, 'Edward ruled as well as reigned.'[3] The grant of these manors to his brother two days after the death of Mortimer is, perhaps, one out of many signs of his rule.

But the King's brother died in 1336,[4] and the manors reverted to the Crown. In the same year the King made a fresh grant of them to Geoffrey le Scrope, Chief Justice of the King's Bench. The following copy of the grant is taken from the Isham MSS.:[5]

Grant of the manors to Geoffrey le Scrope, 1336.

'In original' de anno decimo E tertii Rot. xxxiiij ex parte rem' Thesaur.

Rex Archiep., etc., salutem. Sciatis quod cum dilectus et fidelis noster Galfridus le Scrop, qui manerium de Whytegifta cum pertinenciis una cum membris de Redenesse, Usseflet, Houk et Ayreminne in Com. Ebor. tenuit in feodo, idem manerium cum membris et aliis pertinenciis suis nobis ad requisicionem nostram concesserit et reddiderit, habendum et tenendum nobis et heredibus nostris, simul cum feodis militum, advocacionibus ecclesiarum, ac omnibus aliis ad manerium et membra illa qualitercumque spectantibus, imperpetuum, Ita quod nos vel heredes nostri prefato Galfrido aut heredibus suis alibi infra regnum nostrum in loco

Geoffrey le Scrope, at the King's request, has granted to the King his manor of Whitgift, with its members, Reedness, Ousefleet, Hook and Airmyn, in Yorkshire, on condition that the King will make provision for him to the same amount in lands and tenements within the kingdom. The King, accordingly, has granted to Geoffrey le Scrope the manor and town of Nayland, with its members, etc., Stoke, Great Horkesley, Little Horkesley, Wiston and Leavenheath, in the counties of Suffolk and Essex, which Queen Philippa had held and had restored to the King. A return made in the King's Chancery shows that the manor of

---

[1] Stubbs' Const. Hy. of Eng., vol. ii., p. 402.
[2] Stubbs, vol. ii., p. 406, York-Powell, pp. 220, 221.
[3] Stubbs, vol. ii., p. 406.
[4] Longman's Edw. III., i. 73. Nicolas, Historic Peerage (Courthope), 126.
[5] TT., fol. 199. See also Rot. Orig. in Cur. Scacc. Abbrev., ii., p. 111a.

competenti de terris et tenementis ad valorem manerii predicti cum membris et aliis pertinenciis suis supradictis provideri faceremus, ac nos nuper juxta condicionem illam dederimus et concesserimus pro nobis et heredibus nostris prefato Galfrido manerium et villam de Neylond una cum membris et omnibus terris et tenementis nostris in Stoke, Magna Horksley parva Horksley, Wyston et Leuensheth, Quæ quidem maneria et villam simul cum membris et terris predictis Philippa Regina Angliæ consors nostra carissima tenuit ad terminum vitæ suæ ex concessione nostrâ et quæ eadem consors nostra nuper reddidit in manum nostram, Habendum et tenendum eidem Galfrido et heredibus suis una cum feodis militum et advocacionibus ecclesiarum ac omnibus aliis ad ea spectantibus, tam in Com. Suffolk. quam in Com. Essex, volentes et concedentes pro nobis et heredibus nostris quod, factis extentis tam predictorum manerii de Whytegeft et membrorum ejusdem quam dictorum manerii et villæ de Neylond et membrorum suorum ac terrarum et tenementorum predictorum, et in Cancellariâ nostra retornatis, prefato Galfrido et heredibus suis de aliis terris et tenementis in loco competenti infra regnum nostrum ad valorem illius, quod sicubi sic defecerit de valore dicti manerii de Whytegeft et membrorum suorum ultra valorem dictorum manerii et villæ de Neylond ac membrorum terrarum et tenementorum predictorum, juxta extentas, per nos vel per heredes nostros provideatur imperpetuo possidendum, prout in cartâ nostrâ eidem Galfrido inde confectâ plenius continetur. Ac jam dictum manerium de Whytegift cum membris et aliis per-

Whitgift, etc., is worth £133 15s. 9½d. per annum, while the manor, etc., of Nayland and its members was worth £97 9s. 0¼d. The King, therefore, grants to Geoffrey le Scrope the manors of Bowden and Harborough, lately held by his brother John, Earl of Cornwall, deceased, with knights' fee, advowsons of churches and chapels, fairs, markets, liberties, etc., etc., which are worth £42 13s. 4d. per annum; but Geoffrey le Scrope is to pay into the Exchequer, by half-yearly payments, at Easter and Michaelmas, the sum of £6 6s. 7d. yearly, the amount in which the value of the manors of Nayland, etc., and Bowden with Harborough, exceeds that of the manor of Whitgift, etc.

Given by the King's own hand at Nottingham, October 3, 1336.

Witnesses: J. Archbishop of Canterbury, Primate of All England, Chancellor (John Stratford), H. Bishop of Lincoln, Treasurer of the Household (Henry Burghersh); W. Bishop of Winchester (W. must be a mistake; the Bishop of Winchester at that date was Adam de Orlton[1]), John de Warrenne, Earl of Surrey, Richard, Earl of Arundell, William de Clynton, Robert de Ufford, Steward of the Household, and others.

---

[1] Historic Winchester (Bramston and Leroy), p. 146.

tinenciis suis predictis, ad centum et triginta et tres libras, quindecim solidos, novem denarios et unum quadrantem, et predictum manerium de Neylond, cum dictis membris et aliis pertinenciis suis ad quatuor viginti et decem et septem libras, et novem solidos, et unum quadrantem extenditur per annum, sicut per extentas inde per quosdam fideles nostros de mandato nostro captas et in Cancellariâ nostrâ retornatas est computum, Nos, volentes eandem concessionem nostram juxta dictam condicionem prout decet effectualiter adimplere, dedimus et concessimus pro nobis et heredibus nostris et hac cartâ nostrâ confirmavimus prefato Galfrido maneria de Bowdon et Harebergh cum pertinenciis in Com. Leic. quæ Johannes nuper Comes Cornubiæ frater noster jam defunctus tenuit sibi et heredibus de corpore suo legitime procreatis ex concessione nostrâ, et quæ, pro eo quod idem Comes obiit sine hujusmodi heredibus, ad manus nostras jam devenerunt, quæ etiam valent per annum quadraginta et duas libras, tresdecim solidos, et quatuor denarios, sicut per quasdam extentas et alias evidentias in Cancellariâ nostrâ residentes plene liquet, Habendum et tenendum eidem Galfrido et heredibus suis, una cum feodis militum, advocacionibus ecclesiarum et capellarum, feriis, mercatis, libertatibus et omnibus aliis ad maneria illa qualitercumque et ubicumque spectantibus sive pertinentibus, adeo plene et integre sicut prefatus Comes ea tenuit de nobis et heredibus nostris ac aliis capitalibus dominis feodi illius, per eadem servicia per quæ tenebantur, antequam ad manus nostras sic devenerunt, imperpetuum, Reddendo inde nobis et heredibus nostris per annum ad Scaccarium nostrum sex libras, sex solidos, et septem denarios, quæ excedunt valorem dicti manerii de Whytegyft juxta extentas predictas, sicut superius est expressum, unam videlicet medietatem ad Scaccarium nostrum Paschæ et alteram medietatem ad Scaccarium nostrum Sancti Michaelis. Quare volumus et firmiter precipimus, pro nobis et heredibus nostris, quod idem Galfridus habeat et teneat sibi et heredibus suis predicta maneria de Boudon et Harebergh, cum pertinenciis, una cum feodis militum, advocacionibus ecclesiæ et capellarum, feriis, mercatis, et libertatibus ac omnibus aliis ad maneria illa qualitercumque et ubicumque spectantibus sive pertinentibus, adeo plene et integre sicut prefatus Comes ea tenuit, de nobis et heredibus nostris ac aliis capitalibus dominis feodi illius, per eadem servicia per quæ tenebantur antequam ad manus nostras sic devenerunt, imperpetuum, reddendo inde nobis et heredibus per annum ad Scaccarium nostrum dictas sex libras, sex solidos, et septem denarios, quæ excedunt valorem dicti manerii de Whytegift juxta extentas predictas, sicut superius est expressum, unam videlicet medietatem ad Scaccarium nostrum Paschæ et alteram medietatem ad Scaccarium nostrum Sancti Michaelis sicut predictum est. Hiis testibus venerabilibus patribus J. Cantuar. Archiepisc. totius Angliæ primate, Cancellario nostro, H. Lincoln. Episcopo, Thesaurario hospicii nostri, W. Wynton Episcopo, Johanne de Warrenna, Comite Surr., Ricardo, Comite Arundell, Willelmo de Clynton, Roberto de Ufford, Senescallo hospicii nostri, et aliis, Datum per manum nostram apud Nottingham tertio die Octobris.

Thus began the connection between Bowden and Harborough and the Scrope family, which lasted, with but one break, for 200 years. Geoffrey le Scrope was the second son of Sir William le Scrope, of Bolton, Yorkshire. He was appointed Chief Justice of the Common Pleas in 1323, and of the King's Bench in 1324. He purchased the manor of Masham, in Yorkshire, early in this reign, and his branch of the family is known as Scrope of Masham. He died at Ghent in 1340, and was buried in Coverham Abbey Church, Yorkshire. By his marriage with Ivetta, daughter of William Roos, of Ingmanthorp, he had five sons and three daughters. Henry, the eldest son, was created Lord Scrope of Masham, and held the manors for the remainder of this reign. Geoffrey, the fifth son, as we shall see presently, was Rector of Great Bowden from 1366-1378.[1] It will be observed that the value of the manors had risen from £17 in the reign of Henry III. (see p. 12) to £42 13s. 4d.; also that in 1336, as in 1235, the manors are valued together, and not separately. *Comparison of the values of the manors, 1235 and 1336.*

An extract from the Originalia, in the tenth year of this reign, gives the first instance of a grant of the rent which the holders of the manors had to pay yearly to the Crown:[2]

Et mandatum est Johanni de Melbourn, firmario villarum de Haverbergh et Boudon, quod firmam quam pro villis predictis prefato Comiti (*i.e.,* John of Eltham, Earl of Cornwall) pro instanti termino Sancti Michaelis solvere tenebatur, prefato Willelmo (*i.e.,* William de Cusanciâ) solvat, etc.

John of Melbourn, 'farmer' of the towns of Bowden and Harborough, is ordered to pay to William de Cusanciâ the Michaelmas rent due. *Grant of the reserved rent, 1336-37.*

Notices of similar grants are to be traced in later reigns.

The Isham MSS., to which we are indebted for the grant to Geoffrey le Scrope, also contain a copy of a document, by which John of Gunwardeby gives, grants, and confirms several manors, and among them 'Boudon and Herbergh,' to 'the lord Henry le Scrope, knight, son and heir of the lord Geoffrey le Scrope, knight, and his lawful *Settlement of the manors with the other estates, 1352-53.*

---

[1] Scrope and Grosvenor Roll, vol. ii., pp. 96 *et seq.*
[2] Rot. Orig. in Cur. Scacc. Abbrev., vol. ii., p. 106.

heirs.' The witnesses of this deed are 'Richard le Scrope and William le Scrope, knights; Thomas de Synyngthwait, clerk; William de Synyngthwait, rector of the church of Anderby with Stepil; John Fawdon, rector of the church of Sturneton; William de Rowth (?), bailiff of the liberty of Richmond, John de Fletcham, and others.' Dated, Coverham, February 22, 25 Edward III., 1352-53.[1] It is stated in this deed that John of Gunwardeby holds all the property which he grants 'ex dono et feoffamento dicti domini Henrici.' The said John of Gunwardeby was an executor under the will of Richard le Scrope, Lord of Bolton, in 1400.[2] This suggests the idea that he was a friend, retainer, or adviser of the family, who was available for business purposes. In this case he appears to have been the channel by which the family estates were entailed, and, a hundred years later, the claim to all these estates by John le Scrope is based on this or similar deeds. The Statute of Westminster II., passed in 1285, had 'enabled estates to be settled in a family from parent to child for ever.'[3]

The entries in the episcopal registers are numerous and varied. First, we have the institution of a successor to Robert of St. Albans:

John of Melbourn instituted Rector of Great Bowden, 1328.

Johannes de Melbourn accolitus presentatus per Dominam Isabellam, Dei gratiâ Reginam Angliæ illustrem, Dominam Hiberniæ et Comitissam Pontivi, ad ecclesiam de Magna Boudon Linc. Dioc. vacantem per mortem Roberti de Sancto Albano ultimi Rectoris ejusdem, factâ prius inquisicione per... officialem Archid. Leyc^r per quam, etc., ad dictam ecclesiam est admissus nona Kal. Octobr. Anno Domini 1328 (*i.e.*, September 23, 1328) apud Norwycum et Rector canonice institutus in eâdem, Juratâ

John of Melbourn, acolyte. presented by Queen Isabella to the Rectory of Bowden, vacant by the death of Robert of St. Albans. Instituted at Norwich, September 23, 1328.

---

[1] Isham MSS., TT., fol. 204.
[2] Testamenta Eboracensia, ii. 278.
[3] York-Powell's Hist. of Eng. to 1509, p. 185.

episcopo canonicâ obedientiâ in formâ consuetâ, Scriptum est dicto officiali quod, etc.[1]

This John of Melbourn, as we have seen, was held responsible for the rent reserved to the King after the grant of the manors to Geoffrey le Scrope. When instituted he had only taken one of the lowest of the minor orders, and there are two entries in the same Bishop's registers which make his position still clearer:

Quarto non. April. A.D. MCCCXXXI. (*i.e.*, April 2, 1331) apud Waltham Sanctæ Crucis licentiatus fuit Johannes de Melbourn, Rector ecclesiæ de Boudon Magna Linc. Dioc. quod posset studere intra Regnum Angliæ per unum annum et fructus, etc., percipere, etc., Ita tamen, etc.[2]

April 2, 1331, at Waltham Holy Cross, John of Melbourn receives licence to study for a year within the realm of England, and to receive the fruits of his benefice.

Licences to John of Melbourn.

Eisdem die et loco (17 Kal. Nov., 1331—*i.e.*, October 16, 1331 —apud vetus Templum Lond.) licentiatus fuit Johannes de Melbourn, Rector ecclesiæ de Boudon Magna, quod possit se absentare ab ecclesiâ suâ pro suis et ecclesiæ suæ negotiis per biennium et fructus, etc., in termino dimittere ad firmam, Ita tamen, etc.[3]

October 16, 1331, at the Old Temple, London, John of Melbourn, Rector of Great Bowden, receives licence to be absent from his benefice for two years, and to give a lease of its fruits for that period.

In another part of the same volume occurs an entry of a different kind:

H. permissione divinâ Linc. Episcopus dilectis in CHRISTO filiis, magistris Hugoni de Walmessford et Willelmo Bacheler, Ecclesiæ nostræ Linc. canonicis, et Roberto de Welton consistorii nostri Linc. advocato, salutem gratiam et benedictionem Ad cognoscendum excessus quoscumque Galfridi de Yonge de Haverbergh nostræ dioecesis reformandumque puniendum necnon cognoscendum procedendum et diffiniendum in

Hugh of Walmesford and William Bacheler, Canons of Lincoln, with Robert of Welton, Advocate in the Consistorial Court, appointed Commissioners to take cognizance of the offences of Geoffrey Yonge, of Harborough, and to determine the suit brought against him by Richard of Whitewell. Waltham Holy Cross, March 31, 1331.

---

[1] Bp. Burghersh, Reg., Institutions, fol. cxxv.
[2] *Ibid.*, Reg., Memoranda, latter part, fol. 10.
[3] *Ibid.*, Reg., Memoranda, earlier part, fol. 41.

causâ seu negotio quocumque inter dominum Ricardum de Whitewell, actorem ex parte unâ, et eundem Galfridum ex alterâ, moto seu movendo, vobis, communiter et divisim, et cuilibet vestrum in solido, vices nostras committimus, cum, cohibitionis canonicâ potestate, Datum apud Waltham Sanctæ Crucis II. Kal. April. MDCCCXXXI.[1] (*i.e.*, March 31, 1331).

Geoffrey le Scrope, fifth son of the Chief-Justice, Canon of Lincoln, etc.

In a part of the same book, separately paged and headed 'licenc. celeb. in orator,' fol. 16, we have the first mention of Geoffrey le Scrope, fifth son of the Chief Justice, who was afterwards Rector of Great Bowden.

xvij. Kal. Januar. A.D. MDCCCXXXIX. (*i.e.*, December 16, 1339) licenciatus fuit Magister Galfridus le Scrop canonicus Linc. quod posset facere celebrari divina in oratorio infra mansum suum in parochiâ beatæ Mariæ Oxon per unum annum Ita tamen, etc., in formâ consuetâ.

December 16, 1339, Geoffrey le Scrope, Canon of Lincoln, receives licence to have the Divine Offices celebrated in his own oratory, within his house in St. Mary's parish, Oxford, for one year.

At the very end of Bishop Gynewell's Memoranda, Geoffrey le Scrope is stated to be thirty-six years of age.[2] As Bishop Gynewell's episcopate lasted till 1363, Geoffrey le Scrope must have been a Canon of Lincoln long before he was twenty. There are many other stray notices of him in the different registers which bring out his position socially and ecclesiastically. Bishop Burghersh, in 1340, gives him licence to choose his own confessor—'etiam in casibus reservatis.'[3] Bishop Gynewell, in 1355, appoints him a commissioner, with Anthony of Goldesburgh, precentor, and Hamon Belers, subdean, to hear and determine certain actions brought by the master and choristers of the church of Lincoln against the Rectors of Lafford (Sleaford) and Kirklyngton ('ad audiendum et terminan-

---

[1] Bp. Burghersh, Reg., Memoranda, fol. ccxxxi.
[2] Bp. Gynewell's Reg., Memoranda, fol. clxxiii.
[3] Bp. Burghersh, Reg., Memoranda, fol. lxxii.

dum de causis Magistri et Choristarum Ecclesiæ Lincoln contra Rectores ecclesiarum de Lafford et Kirklyngton."[1]

In the registers of Bishop Bokingham, who succeeded Bishop Gynewell in 1363, we have still further entries, which complete the picture of a noble and wealthy church dignitary of the fourteenth century. First, there is the record of the institution of John of Bolton to the Rectory of Bowden, vacant by the death of John of Melbourn, and almost at the same time a commendatory letter in favour of Geoffrey le Scrope, who is about to leave England. One year after the institution of John of Bolton, we have the institution of Geoffrey le Scrope himself to the same rectory—a lengthy document, differing in many respects from previous institutions. Apparently John of Bolton only held the benefice until Geoffrey le Scrope could return for institution and induction.

Johannes de Bolton, clericus, presentatus per Willelmum de Ailyngton, Rectorem ecclesiæ de Fifhede, attornatum nobilis viri domini Henrici le Scrop militis ad presentandum personas ydoneas ad quæcunque beneficia ecclesiastica ad presentacionem dicti domini Henrici qualitercumque spectantia, ipso in remotis agente, specialiter deputatum, ad ecclesiam de Boudon Magna Linc. Dioc. per mortem domini Johannis de Melburn ultimi Rectoris ejusdem vacantem,[2] etc., etc.

Date. Id. April. A.D. 1364 (April 13, 1364), at Lydington.

Litteræ commendaticiæ pro magistro Galfrido le Scropp.

Universis sanctæ matris ecclesiæ filiis presentes litteras inspecturis, Johannes permissione divinâ Linc. Episcopus salutem in omnium Salvatore, Cum dilectus filius Magister Galfridus Scrop, Canoni-

John of Bolton, clerk, presented by William of Allington, Rector of Fifehead, attorney for Henry le Scrope, knight, instituted to the Rectory of Great Bowden, vacant by the death of John of Melbourn. Instituted through his proctor, Geoffrey, vicar of the north portion of the Prebendal Church of Graffham (?) April 13, 1364.

John of Bolton instituted Rector of Great Bowden, 1364.

Geoffrey le Scrope, Canon of Lincoln, has duly received all the Holy Orders, is of good and honest life, and is under no criminal charge or sentence of excommunication, etc. Lest he should be

Commendatory letter on behalf of Geoffrey le Scrope, 1364.

---

[1] Bp. Gynewell's Reg., Memoranda, fol. lix.
[2] Bp. Bokingham's Reg., Institutions, part i., fol. 232.

cus ecclesiæ nostræ Linc. presentium exhibitor, ad omnes sacros ordines temporibus debitis a sacris canonibus constitutis rite et canonice ordinatus, ac bonæ honestæque conversacionis et vitæ ac nonnullis aliis virtutum donis multipliciter decoratus, nullo quoque crimine irretitus, nec aliquâ excommunicationis suspencionis aut interdicti sententiâ innodatus, a nobis cum nostrâ gratiâ et benedictione licentiatus, ad partes longinquas et ignotas habeat proficisci, ne idem Galfridus, tanquam ignotus clericus, ab execucione suorum ordinum in dictis officiis alicubi arceatur, Universitatem vestram in Domino requirimus et rogamus quatinus prefatum Magistrum Galfridum, cum per partes vestras transitum fecerit, ex causis rationabilibus et honestis per nos approbatis, sub mutuæ vicissitudinis obtentu ac caritatis intuitu ad execucionem dictorum ordinum et alias benigniter admittatis et favorabiliter pertractetis, scientes quod, pro vobis et vestris, si oportuerit, vices consimiles rependemus, In quorum omnium testimonium has litteras nostras sibi fieri fecimus et nostri sigilli munimine roborari, Datum apud Lydington, iij Kal. Maij A.D. MCCCLXIIIJ. et consecrationis nostræ primo.[1]

debarred from the due exercise of his office whilst travelling abroad, the Bishop certifies this to all whom it may concern, and prays that, wherever he may be, he may be allowed to perform the duties of his sacred office. Lydington, April 29, 1364.

Geoffrey le Scrope, Canon of Lincoln, instituted Rector of Great Bowden, 1365.

Galfridus le Scrop presentatus per Willelmum de Ailyngton (then, as before, in the institution of John of Bolton, as far as the word 'deputatum') ad ecclesiam de Boudon Magna Linc. dioc. vacantem vij Idus Aprilis, A.D. MCCCLXV. (April 7, 1365) in monasterio de Parco Lude est admissus et Rector institutus, in personâ Lamberti de Irnham capellani procuratoris sui sufficientem potestatem habentis,

Geoffrey le Scrope, presented by William of Allington (as above, p. 39), instituted Rector of Great Bowden, at Louth Park, in the person of Lambert of Irnham, Chaplain, his proctor, April 7, 1365. The record recites the terms of a commission issued by the Bishop to the Abbots of St. Mary of the Meadows, Leicester, and Owston, and the Prior of Launde, authorizing them to

---

[1] Bp. Bokingham's Reg., Memoranda, fol. xxv.

canonice in eâdem et inductus in possessionem corporalem ejusdem ecclesiæ, in personâ ejusdem procuratoris, per Abbatem Monasterii de Osolveston, auctoritate commissionis sibi in hac parte factæ cujus tenor talis est :—Johannes permissione divinâ Linc. Episcopus dilectis filiis beatæ Mariæ de Pratis Leycestr. et de Osolveston monasteriorum Abbatibus, necnon Priori Ecclesiæ Conventuali de Landa, Ordinis Sancti Augustini, nostræ diocesis, salutem gratiam et benedictionem. Presentavit nobis Willelmus de Alyngton, etc. (described as before) dilectum filium Magistrum Galfridum le Scrop, canonicum ecclesiæ nostræ Lincoln. ad ecclesiam de Boudon Magna, nostræ diocesis ut dicitur jam vacantem, Super cujus vacacione et aliis articulis consuetis ac jure presentantis ad eandem, per Officiales Archidiaconi nostri Leycestr. inquisicionem fieri fecimus diligentem, Ad recipiendum igitur certificatorium inquisicionis predictæ illudque examinandum, et in eventu quo, per inquisicionem hujusmodi, dictam ecclesiam inveneritis jam vacare, ipsaque inquisicio pro presentante et presentato faciat memoratis, et nichil in hac parte obviaverit de canonicis institutis, ad admittendum prefatum Magistrum Galfridum le Scrop ad ecclesiam de Boudon predictam, ipsumque Rectorem instituendum canonice in eâdem, necnon ad inducendum inducive mandandum seu faciendum ipsum Magistrum Galfridum vel procuratorem suum ejus nomine in corporalem possessionem dictæ ecclesiæ de Boudon Magna jurium et pertinentium ejusdem, ac cetera omnia et singula facienda et expedienda, quæ circa premissa fuerint oportuna, vobis communiter et divisim tenore presentium committimus vices nostras cujuslibet cohibicionis make inquiry as to the vacancy, etc. Dated, March 10, 1364/5. The return made by the commissioners is dated, March 14, 1364/5, and the confirmation of the proceedings by the Bishop, April 7, 1365.

canonicæ potestate, mandantes, quacumque de toto processu super hiis coram vobis habendo, nos, expedito dicto negocio, certificet ille vestrum qui presentem nostram commissionem fuerit executus, litteris suis patentibus habentibus hunc tenorem ; Datum in Monasterio de Parco Lude vj Idus Marcij A.D. MCCCLXIIIJ. (*i.e.*, March 10, 136¼) et consecrationis nostræ secundo. Cujus auctoritate mandati reverendi noveritis me certificatorium inquisicionis predictæ a dicto Officiali Archidiaconi Leycestr. recepisse, illudque examinasse, per quod inventum est, prefatam ecclesiam de Boudon tempore presentacionis predictæ vacasse, inquisicionemque pro presentante et presentato sufficienter fecisse, nichilque in hac parte de canonicis institutis obviasse, Quocirca prefatum Magistrum Galfridum ad ecclesiam de Boudon predictam admisi, ipsumque Rectorem, in personâ domini Lamberti de Irnham, capellani, procuratoris sui sufficientem potestatem in hac parte habentis, institui canonice in eâdem, Salvis in omnibus juribus episcopalibus et ecclesiæ cathedralis Lincoln. dignitate, necnon prefatum Magistrum Galfridum, in personâ dicti procuratoris sui, in corporalem possessionem dictæ ecclesiæ de Boudon Magna jurium et pertinentium ejusdem induxi, et ipsum sic inductum in pacificâ possessione dimisi in eâdem, quæ omnia et singula vestræ paternitati reverendæ significo per presentes, sigillo meo consignatas, Datum apud Boudon Idibus Marcij anno domini supradicto (March 14, 136¼) Postmodum confirmatus fuit totus processus per dominum sub hiis verbis, Nos igitur considerantes dictum commissarium nostrum in premissis rite et legitime processisse, omnia et singula per eum in hâc parte acta et gesta ratificamus, approbamus, et nostrâ auctoritate pontificali tenore presentium confirmamus, In cujus rei testimonium sigillum nostrum fecimus hiis apponi, Datum in Monasterio de Parco Lude vij Idus Aprilis, A.D. supradicto et consecrationis nostræ.¹

In the same Bishop's Memoranda, among the records of the taxation of benefices held by members of the cathedral body, occurs the following :² *Benefices held by Geoffrey le Scrope.*

Nomina beneficiorum Magistri Galfridi le Scroop, nat' quondam nobilis viri domini Galfridi le Scroop militis, Magist' in artibus et Baccalar' in legibus.	Benefices of Geoffrey le Scrope, son of Geoffrey le Scrope, knight, Master of Arts and Bachelor of Laws.
Prebenda de Haydor cum Walton in ecclesiâ Cathedrali Linc. quæ quondam taxabatur lx marc'	Haydour cum Walton, Prebend in the Church and Archdeaconry of Lincoln, formerly taxed at £40
Sed modo quia una vicaria est ordinata de porcione ejusdem quæ taxatur ad xii marc' dicta prebenda taxatur ad xlviij marc'	Now, because one vicarage has been constituted from a part of the same, taxed at £8, the said prebend is taxed at £32
Item Ecclesia de Boudon Magna Linc. Dioc. taxatur ad lvj marc'	The Church of Great Bowden, Linc. Dioc. is taxed at £37 6s. 8d.
Item in Archiepiscopatu Ebor. Prebenda de Apesthorpe in ecclesiâ Cathedrali Ebor. taxatur ad ... xv marc'	In the Archiepiscopate of York, Apesthorpe, Prebend in the Cathedral Church, is taxed at £10
Item in eodem Episcopatu Capella seu ecclesia cur' de West Vittu' quæ taxabatur quondam ... xij marc'	The Chapel or Church of West Witton in the same, formerly taxed at £8
Sed modo taxatur ad v marc'	Now at ... ... £3 6s. 8d.

Judging from this, Bowden was the richest, though not the most dignified, preferment he held. The whole amount at which his benefices are taxed is over £80, equivalent to between twelve and twenty times as much of our money.³

A document which is of great importance, as helping

¹ Bp. Bokingham's Reg., Institutions, part i., p. 234.
² *Ibid.*, Reg., Memoranda, fol. xliii.
³ The estimate varies considerably. See Hallam, Middle Ages (edit. 1837), iii. 448; Longman's Edward III., i. 126, note; Longman's Lectures on the History of England, i. 416, note.

Exchequer Lay Subsidy Roll, 1 Edward III., names in Bowden and Harborough.

towards an estimate of the comparative wealth of Leicestershire townships, and as a record of their chief inhabitants, has recently been published. It is the earliest of the Exchequer Lay Subsidy Rolls which have been preserved, the record of the 'twentieth' granted by the first Parliament of Edward III., held at Lincoln from September 15 to September 23, to defray the expenses of a campaign against the Scots.[1] 'Boudon' and 'Hauerbergh' are given separately under 'Gertre' Hundred.[2]

BOUDON.			HAUERBERGH.	
De Magistro Johanne de budon	x*s*.		De Ricardo de Stonton	iij*s*.
			Willelmo de Godesalve	vj*s*.
Ricardo le Dekene	viij*s*.		Roberto Waryn	xij*d*.
Thomas Aucrey	vj*s*.		Hugone Luff	ij*s*.
Ricardo ad ecclesiam	iiij*s*.		Willelmo de Corby	xij*d*.
Adam de Sutton	iiij*s*.		Johanne Gladman	iij*s*.
Thoma atte Mor	iiij*s*.		Waltero Bate	iij*s*.
Isabell Mayners	iij*s*.		Thoma Reigner	v*s*.
Ricardo Boner	v*s*.		Thoma Bate	ij*s*.
Thoma Gerard	ij*s*. vi*d*.		Thoma de Ranesby	iiij*s*.
Willelmo Walkere	xviij*d*.		Rogero de Thedyngworth	ix*s*.
Willelmo Mawdit	vj*s*.		Oliua Kyng	v*s*.
Agnete Herberd	iij*s*.		Johanne berth	v*s*.
Ricardo Harpere	iij*s*.		Galfrido de Cotes	iiij*s*.
Willelmo Pachet	iiij*s*.		Johanne Andrew	iij*s*. vj*d*.
Adam Ingold	iij*s*.		Willelmo Mayners	xij*d*.
Rogero filio Reginaldi	v*s*.		Rogero Cristien	v*s*.
Roberto Sparewe	iij*s*.		Rogero Robyn	iij*s*.
Adam Mayners	iiij*s*.		Hesteln' Andrewe	iiij*s*.
Thoma Pere	iiij*s*.		Rogero Andrew	ij*s*.
			Johanne Iue	ij*s*.
Summa	iiij*li*. x*s*.		Rogero Mayner	ij*s*.
			Ricardo de Oxendon	xij*d*.
			Thoma Kyng	vj*d*.
			Galfrido Yonge	xij*d*.
			Thoma filio Hugonis	xij*d*.
			Thoma filio Thomæ	xij*d*.
			Summa	iiij*li*.

Comparison with other places in the Hundreds of Framland and Gartree.

From this roll it is clear that, for the purposes of taxation, Bowden and Harborough were nearly equal in value, the former being rather the more valuable of the two, but it is equally clear that even then Harborough had the

---

[1] Stubbs' Const. Hy., vol. ii., p. 402.
[2] Assoc. Soc. Reports, etc., vol. xix., part i., pp. 235-257.

larger population. Comparing the two places with others in the Hundreds of Framland and Gartree, it will be found that only the Borough of Leicester produces a larger sum than Bowden and Harborough together—the amount produced there being £16 0s. 4d., while only seven places produced more than £4, viz., Wymondham (with Edmondthorpe), £8 13s. 4d.; Melton Mowbray, £8 1s. 0d.; Bottesford, £6 15s. 4d.; Hallaton, £5 13s. 6d.; Medbourne, £4 17s. 0d.; Evington, £5 0s. 1d.; Great Easton, £4 15s. 9d.

A comparison of the names, both in Bowden and Harborough, with those quoted in extracts from public records, and also with those in the town documents, will show many points of correspondence, while some found in this roll are new. The name 'Mayners,' which has been already traced in the field-name 'Maynerdsholm,' is found both at Bowden and Harborough. Geoffrey Yonge of Harborough is evidently the same with whose 'offences' Hugh of Walmesford and William Bacheler, Canons of Lincoln, with Robert of Welton, advocate in the Consistory Court, were commissioned to deal. Master John of Boudon is, perhaps, John of Ardern, the then Rector's deputy, or possibly John of Melbourn, not yet instituted as Rector. The date is close upon the death of Robert of St. Albans, and just before John of Melbourn's institution in September, 1328.

Comparison of names in the roll with those in the town papers, etc.

Atte Mor, Andrewe, Reyner or Reigner, Waryn, with Mayner, are names which have occurred in the documents of previous reigns. Robert Warin, who grants land in the only document of Edward II. (No. 5), must be the very same who pays xij*d.* to the subsidy; and Thomas Rayner, who is witness to the grant, must be the same who pays vs. The same Thomas Rayner grants the twenty acres of land in No. 6. Richard Harper of Bowden, who pays iijs., Richard Boner, who pays vs., Richard le Dekene, who pays viijs., and William Pachet, who pays iiijs., are all witnesses to No. 7 in this reign. John Andrewe is a witness to No. 6 and No. 8, and the following names occur in the long list of property in No. 6: Adam de Sutton (B.), Hugh Luffe (H.), Geoffrey Yonge (H.), William Pachet (B.), William de Godesalve (H.), John Andrew, chaplain (H.), Thomas Auerey (B.), Thomas Piere (B.).

Examination of Document No. 6.

There are, as said before, ten of the town documents which belong to this reign. One of these, however (No. 6), was not among the number which were preserved in the town chests. It was purchased from a catalogue of deeds, etc., for sale in 1882, by the Ven. Assheton Pownall, F.S.A., the late Archdeacon of Leicester, and afterwards presented to the town. It is by far the most important of them all. In it we have, for the first time, a long list of field-names, most of which were kept in use, though with some changes, up to the date of the Enclosure Act in 1776. The following table will show which of the names were to be found in 1655, and also in what forms the survivors were afterwards known. From 1655 to the enclosure in 1776 the changes were very slight.

Field-names in 1343 and 1655.

1343.	1655.[1]	1343.	1655.
Stanyhull,	Stonehill.	Kyngestirne,	Kingsterne.
Sevenewell,	? Laconwell.	Broddole.	
Holbergh.		Shirdaycotes,	Shirtycotes.
Ouerrademylde,	Over Redmyles.	Portgates,	Portgate.
Netherrrade-mylde,	Nether Redmyles.	Galhou,	Gallowe.
		Westwell.	
Shorthilrene,	Short Elderne.	Le Brest,	Brest.
Hethirne,	Elderne.	Toucroft,	Toecroft.
Gasewell,	Gaswell Sicke.	Nethirportgate.	
Longehilrene,	Long Elderne.	Godwynes Oxe,	Goodwyn's Ox.

'Godwynes oxe.'

But the most interesting fact in the document is the explanation given by it of the last-mentioned field-name. Here, instead of the name only, we have ' ubi Godwynes oxe morieabatur ' (*sic*)—a clear proof that one amongst the many sources of field-names is to be found in simple local facts, the memory of which soon passed away, though the name remained. It will be noticed that in this deed the land of 'Master Geoffrey' is twice named. This

---

[1] Rouse's Harborough Charities, pp. 29-49.

would seem to refer to Geoffrey le Scrope. We again meet with Geoffrey Yonge.

Taking the other documents of this reign in order of date, in No. 7 (17 Edward III., 1343-44) we have another instance of how a field-name took its rise. William Fidel gives his name to 'Fiddeliswonge.' In this, too, we have once again the name Bernard, 150 years after its first occurrence. In No. 8 (18 Edward III., 1344) is to be found the first mention of a property which will recur many times, and which was only sold by the trustees in 1805 to obtain funds for the redemption of the Land Tax. The stall is one of what were afterwards called the 'Four Stalls'—butchers' stalls—on a place in the main street now covered by offices. *Review of the remaining documents, temp. Edward III.*

In Nos. 10 and 11 (38 Edward III. and 39 Edward III., 1364 and 1365) we have again descriptions of residents, each of which helps to fill up the picture of the time— 'Magister Ricardus le leche,' 'Hugh le Milner,' 'John le bailif,' 'Thomas Skynare, chaplain.' We have also the first mention of another property which was long held in trust for the town, and was only sold in 1869. The description given in No. 11 is as follows: 'That is to say, in length from the King's highway in the town as far as the field of Magna Boudon' ('scilicet in longitudine a viâ regiâ in villâ usque in campum de Magna Boudon'). Of all the various properties held in trust, there are only two which tally with this description, viz., the two which for many years were known as the George and the Hind. In No. 12 we have the name of John of Bolton, *chaplain*, in 41 Edward III., 1367, two years after the institution of Geoffrey le Scrope to the rectory, and three years after the institution of John of Bolton, given above (p. 39). This supports the conjecture that the institution of John of Bolton was only a matter of convenience, because, for some reason or other, on the death of John of Melbourn, Geoffrey le Scrope could not then be instituted. *Descriptive names of persons.* *John of Bolton.*

From No. 13 (42 Edward III., 1368) we learn that in

The Fraternity of the Holy Cross.

Harborough, as in other towns before the Reformation, there was at least one Guild with its chaplain. Unfortunately, we have this one fact, and only this, that there was a Guild, or Fraternity, of the Holy Cross. It is not mentioned in any later document, nor is there any hint of any other Guild.

The reign of Richard II. almost finishes the century. It began June 22, 1377, and ended September 29, 1399. Bishop Bokingham's episcopate lasted till 1398, and he was succeeded by Henry Beaufort, afterwards Bishop of Winchester, and a Cardinal.

The Isham MSS. contain a copy of a charter granted by the King to Henry le Scrope, confirming the right of his tenants in Bowden and Harborough to be free from contributing to the wages of the representatives of the county returned to Parliament.

Bowden and Harborough freed from payment to Members of Parliament.

Ricardus dei gratiâ rex Angliæ et Franciæ et dominus Hiberniæ vicecomiti Leycestr. qui nunc est vel qui pro tempore fuerit salutem, etc. Cum dilectus fidelis noster Henricus le Scrop, dominus maneriorum de Boudon et Haverbergh, nobis veraciter dedit intelligi, quod homines et tenentes sui de maneriis predictis, quæ sunt de antiquo dominico coronæ Angliæ, ut dicitur, ac eorum antecessores tenentes de eisdem maneriis, a tempore quo non extat memoria, semper hactenus quieti consueverunt de expensis militum ad parliamenta nostra vel progenitorum nostrorum quondam Regum Angliæ, pro communitate dicti comitatus venientium, et nobis supplicaverit ut novæ et insolitæ exactiones hujusmodi expensarum militum eisdem hominibus et tenentibus factæ supersederi jubere velimus NOS, NOLENTES nostros homines et tenentes in hac parte indebite pregravari, vobis precipimus, quod ab inquietacionibus et districtionibus prefatis hominibus et tenentibus

Richard, by the grace of God, etc., etc., to the Sheriff of Leicestershire.

Henry le Scrope, lord of the manors of Bowden and Harborough, has informed the King that, whereas from time immemorial the tenants of manors of B. and H., being of ancient demesne of the Crown, have been free from all payments towards the expenses of knights sent by the county to Parliament, such payments are being wrongfully, and contrary to custom, demanded of them. The King, therefore, orders the Sheriff to abstain from all disturbance or distraint on this ground.

Northampton, December 4, 4 Richard II., A.D. 1380.

occasione premissa faciendis desistentes, ipsos ad contribuendum expensas militum ad parliamenta nostra pro communitate dicti comitatus venientium nullatenus compellatis aliter quam fieri consuevit temporibus retroactis Teste me ipso apud Northampton quarto die Decembr. Anno regni nostri quarto.[1]

The payment of Members of Parliament was the custom of the period, and is stated to have been fixed at four shillings a day for knights of the shire, and two shillings a day for citizens and burgesses, in the seventh year of Edward II. The sheriffs collected the money from the 'communities of the counties and towns represented.' But the power of election was not at that time highly valued, and, therefore, many petitions for exemption from the charge were made to the King. Among the pleas for exemption was the fact that lands were part of the ancient demesne of the Crown—or, in other words, had been held by the Crown since the reign of Edward the Confessor.[2] In the case of Bowden and Harborough this plea was allowed, and an exemption was granted. To the tenants of these manors 'the exemption from payment was far more valuable than the privilege of voting.'

In the 15th year of King Richard, Henry le Scrope died, July 31, 1391, aged 78, and the manors passed to his second son, Stephen, the eldest, Geoffrey, having been killed at the siege of Piskre, in Lithuania, in 1362.[3] In the Inquisitions *post mortem*, 16 Richard II., 'Henricus le Scrop Chivaler' is stated to have died seised of the manor of 'Boudon,' with the advowson of the church, and of the manor of 'Harebergh,' in the county of Leicester.[4] *Death of Henry, first Lord le Scrope of Masham, 1391.*

Stephen le Scrope was about forty years old when his father died. He was Justice of Munster, Leinster, and *Stephen, second Lord le Scrope.*

[1] Isham MSS., TT., fol. 206.
[2] Stubbs' Const. Hy., i. 454; ii. 251, 252; iii. 523, 524.
[3] Scrope and Grosvenor Roll, ii. 119, 120.
[4] Inquis. post mortem, vol. iii., p. 156, num. 28.

Uriell in Ireland, and as such his conduct is said to have been iniquitous. He was made captive with King Richard at Flint, and bore the sword of state when Richard surrendered. Early in the following reign (August 4, 1400) he was tried in the Moothalle, Newcastle-upon-Tyne, on the charge of being privy to an insurrection, but acquitted. He was afterwards taken into Henry IV.'s service, and went again to Ireland, as deputy of the King's son, Thomas of Lancaster. This time, owing, it is said, to the influence of his wife, he ruled excellently. He died in 1406.[1] William of Husè, Rector of Bowden, was one of the executors to his will, but the will makes no other mention either of Bowden or Harborough.[2]

Resignation of Geoffrey le Scrope, Rector of Great Bowden, 1378.

Turning from the manor to the church, we find from Bishop Bokingham's Institutions that Geoffrey le Scrope resigned the benefice of Bowden in 1378. His death did not occur till 1382. He was buried in Lincoln Cathedral, and his will, which is preserved among the muniments of the Dean and Chapter,[3] is as follows:

	Translation.
In Dei nomine Amen. Ego Galfridus le Scropp Canonicus Ecclesiæ beatæ Mariæ Lincoln compos mentis meæ viij Kal. Febr. viz: die Conversionis Sancti Pauli Apostoli in hospicio meo intra clausum ecclesiæ Lincoln. anno domini Millesimo CCC^{mo} octagesimo secundo condo testamentum meum in hunc modum.	In the name of God, Amen. I, Geoffrey le Scrope, Canon of the Church of the Blessed Mary, at Lincoln, being of sound mind, on January 25, the Feast of the Conversion of St. Paul, in my house within the close of the said Church, in the year of our Lord 1382, do make my will as follows:
Imprimis lego animam meam deo et beatæ Mariæ et omnibus sanctis ejus et corpus meum ad sepeliendum in ecclesiâ Lincoln juxta sororem meam sub campanili Ita tamen quod corpus meum ultra triduum super terram	First, I leave my soul to God, to the Blessed Mary, and to all His saints, and my body to be buried in the Church of Lincoln, next to my sister, beneath the belfry,[4] provided that my body be in no case kept above ground

---

[1] Archæologia, xvii. 334, 335; xx. 89, note e; 249.
[2] Testamenta Eboracensia, iii. 37.
[3] D. ii. 60, 3.
[4] See Peck's Desiderata Curiosa, lib. viii., p. 17 (Monumental Inscriptions, as in 1661, by Dr. R. Sanderson, etc.): 'Near the choir door, under the Lanthorn, on a Marble, this circumscribed on brass.' Then follows an imperfect Latin inscription, which is variously given by Peck and by Nichols (Gartree, p. 475).

minime præservetur : quoad pastum relinquo arbitrio executorum meorum nolo tamen quod modum excedant.

Item volo quod ij cerei ponderis xx lb. cere tunc circa corpus meum accendantur et missâ finitâ ponantur in dexterâ et levâ magni altaris accendendi juxta disposicionem custodis dicti altaris Item xx torches longitudinis xij pedum per ulnam de quibus ij remaneant ad magnum altare et ij remaneant ad altare ubi celebratur missa de beatâ Mariâ in honorem Corporis Christi et j ad quodlibet altare in ecclesiâ Item in distribucione pauperum in domibus jacentium et aliorum mediocrium ac debilium quinque marcas, et aliis pauperibus prout executoribus videbitur Item cuilibet canonico residenti et presenti in exequiis meis vjs. viij$d$. et celebranti missam preter hoc ijs. Item custodi altaris beati Petri vjs. viij$d$. Item cuilibet vicario iijs. iiij$d$. Item cuilibet capellano gerenti habitum ijs. Item cuilibet pauperi clerico ijs. Item cuilibet choristæ xij$d$. Item cuilibet deferenti virgam presenti xij$d$. Item pulsantibus cum eisdem ministrantibus vjs. viij$d$. Item volo quod una ymago argentea et deaurata summæ Trinitatis de meo fabricetur et in medio summi altaris ponatur in summo tabernaculo Item fabricæ ecclesiæ Cathedralis Lincoln quinque marcas Item eidem ecclesiæ albam capam meam de serico cum orfray de bluete velveto cum ymaginibus Apostolorum de auro intextis

beyond the space of three days : as to the entertainment [during that time] I leave it to the discretion of my executors, but I will that they do not go beyond what is fitting.

Item, I will that two wax tapers, each weighing 20 lb. in wax, be lighted at that time round my body, and that, when Mass is ended, they be set to burn on the right and left of the high altar, according to the direction of the custodian of the same. Item, I leave 20 torches, 12 feet in length by the ell, of which two shall remain at the high altar and two at the altar where is celebrated the Mass of the Blessed Mary, in honour of the Body of Christ, and one at each altar in the church. Item (I leave) to be distributed to the poor who lie in their own homes, and to other lowly and infirm persons, 5 marks, and to other poor people, as shall seem fit to my executors.[1] Item, to each canon in residence. present at my funeral 6s. 8d., and to the one who celebrates the funeral Mass 2s. in addition. Item, to the custodian of the altar of St. Peter 6s. 8d., to each vicar 3s. 4d., to each chaplain wearing the habit[2] 2s., to each poor clerk 2s., to each chorister 12d., to each verger who is present 12d., to the ringers with their attendants 6s. 8d. Item, I will that a silver-gilt figure of the Most High Trinity[3] be made at the cost of my estate, and placed in the midst of the high altar on the top of the tabernacle. Item, to the fabric of the Cathedral Church, Lincoln, 5 marks. Item, to the

---

[1] On doles to the poor at funerals. See *Rock*, Church of our Fathers (C. Dolman, 1849), vol. iii., 36 *et seq*.

[2] *I.e.*, wearing the choral habit. There were at Lincoln other priests having chantries—'sacerdotes cantarias habentes'—or 'altaristæ,' who did not form part of the choir—'non sequentes chorum'—and therefore did not wear the habit.

[3] See Bury Wills (Camden Soc.), pp. 35, 36, 138, for similar bequests.

Item lego altari ubi celebratur missa de beatâ Mariâ unam casulam rubiam cum magno orfray de auro cum ij tuniculis et dalmaticâ eidem casulæ pertinentibus Item volo quod reponantur in custodiâ subcancellarii et succentoris L marcæ et fiat inde obitus meus quamdiu duraverit, prout fit in obitu quondam Magistri Johannis Stretlay decani ejusdem ecclesiæ Item lego vicariis commorantibus in Boungarth xx marcas ad reponendum cum pecuniâ eisdem datâ per dominum Henricum de Edenstowe et Magistrum Willelmum de Burton et eodem modo expendendum et conservandum Item lego vicariis de secundâ formâ in unum commorantibus x marcas ut inde fiat per omnia sicut de pecuniâ eis datâ per dominum Henricum de Edenstowe et Magistrum Willelmum de Burton superius est ordinatum superioribus vicariis, et annuatim reportentur subcancellario et succentori et ab eisdem pro providentiâ faciendâ de novo annuatim recipiatur Item lego duobus capellanis meis, viz., dominis Hugoni Bussy et Johanni Vaux de Quadryng celebraturis per v annos pro animâ meâ et omnium benefactorum meorum et precipue Magistri Johannis de Fandon et domini Lamberti de Irnham quolibet anno cuilibet eorum C[s] Item lego ecclesiæ de Boudon ad usum magni altaris same church my white silk cope, with orphreys of blue velvet, embroidered with figures of the Apostles in gold. Item, I leave to the altar where the Mass of the Blessed Mary is said a red chasuble with a great gold orphrey, with 2 tunicles and a dalmatic belonging to the same. Item, I will that there be laid by, in the charge of the Vice-Chancellor and the Succentor, 50 marks, and that my *obit* be kept from that sum so long as it shall last, as is done with regard to the *obit* of Master John Streatley, late Dean of the same church.[1] Item, I leave to the vicars dwelling in Boungarth[2] 20 marks, to be laid by with the money given to them by Sir Henry of Edenstowe[4] and Master William of Burton, and to be expended and kept in the same way. Item, I leave to the Vicars of the second form,[3] dwelling in common, 10 marks, that it may be dealt with in every respect as it has been ordained for the Vicars of the higher grade with regard to the money given to them by Sir Henry of Edenstowe and Master William of Burton, and be yearly reported to the Vice-Chancellor and the Succentor, and that such report be annually received anew by them with a view to making provision. Item, I leave to my two chaplains, viz., Sirs Hugh Bussy and John Vaux of Quadring, to say Mass for 5 years for

---

[1] See below, p. 61. 'The year's mind, anniversary, or obit.' *Rock*, Church of Our Fathers, vol. iii., 97 *et seq*.

[2] See Maddison's Vicars-Choral of Lincoln, pp. 34, 43. Bishop Sutton granted a building on a site called Boungarth, on the west side of Vicars' Court, next the Palace, to the senior or Priest-Vicars. Provision was made for junior Vicars also to live in the Court in 1328. *Ibid.*, p. 8.

[3] Junior Vicars, Acolytes, Subdeacons or Deacons. They were advanced to the higher grade in choir, and ordained priest as vacancies occurred. *Ibid.*, p. 5.

[4] Preb. of Thorngate 1328, Karlton Kyme about 1331. He was also Prebendary of Llandaff and Southwell.

calicem meum majorem cum foliis in pede ejusdem   Item optimum corporale meum   Item lego ecclesiæ beatæ Mariæ in parva Boudon in campis album vestimentum meum cum toto apparatu   Item lego capellæ Herbergh unum orfray de Coloniâ pro unâ capâ quod [possit?] se habere pannum de serico   Item lego ecclesiæ beatæ Mariæ Oxon optimum et integrum vestimentum meum de auro cum orfrays de rubio velveto broudatum cum floribus liliorum de auro cum toto apparatu   Item unam amitam (*sic*) de rubio velveto broudatam cum tribus M literis integris ad induendam cum capâ vestimenti supradicti   Item lego aulæ de Balliolo xx*li.* bonæ monetæ ut exinde libri domui predictæ necessarii emantur et perpetuis usibus sociorum in eâ commorancium pro perpetuo applicentur   Item lego Abbati et Conventui de Choverham x marcas   Item lego domui de Bellivalle optimum calicem meum cum fiolis majoribus de argento et xl*s*. pro pietanciâ die illo quo commemoracionem pro animâ meâ inter ipsos fecerint celebrari   Item lego domui de Haynton ejusdem ordinis xl*s*.

my soul, and for the souls of all my benefactors, especially Master John of Fandon and Sir Lambert of Irnham, each year to each of them 100*s*. Item, I leave to the Church of Bowden, for the use of the high altar, my greater chalice with leaves at its foot. Item, my best corporal.[1] Item, I leave to the Church of the Blessed Mary in Little Bowden in the fields my white vestment with all its belongings. Item, I leave to the chapel of Harborough one orphrey of Cologne,[2] for a cope,[3] that it may have cloth of silk. Item, I leave to the Church of the Blessed Mary, Oxford, my best complete vestment of gold, with orphreys of red velvet broidered with lilies of gold, together with all its belongings. Item, an amice[4] of red velvet, broidered with three letters, MMM,[5] complete, to be worn with the cope of the suit aforesaid. Item, I leave to Balliol Hall[6] £20 of good money, that therefrom books needful to the said house may be bought and applied to the use in perpetuity of the fellows dwelling in it. Item, I leave to the Abbot and Monastery of Coverham[7] 10 marks.

---

[1] The white cloth spread by the priest in the midst of the altar.

[2] In the fifteenth century Cologne became famous for the manufacture of orphrey-web, inferior to those of Florence or Venice, and frequently using blue for faces of the figures introduced. Textile Fabrics, *Rock-Maskell*, p. 59. The orphreys of a vestment (chasuble or cope), or a frontal, are the bands, ornamented or otherwise, which divide it into parts. In a chasuble they run up behind and before in the form of a Y. See *Rock*, Church of our Fathers, i. 363.

[3] Cope. *Rock*, vol. ii., chap. vi., sect. 3.

[4] Amice. *Rock*, i., chap. v., sect. 11, p. 463. On the vestments generally, as in use in England before the Reformation. See *Rock*, vol. iii., sect. 18 *et seq*. *Bloxam*, Companion to Gothic Architecture Eccl. Vestments, chap. i.

[5] Perhaps simply meaning 'Mary' repeated; or it might be interpreted 'Maria Mater Misericordiæ.'

[6] Probably Balliol College. For Balliol Halls see Wood's City of Oxford, Oxf. Hist. Soc., vol. xv.

[7] Coverham, Premonstratensian Abbey, in Wensleydale. Dugdale's Monasticon (edit., 1846), vol. vi. 920.

Item domui de Witham ejusdem ordinis xl*s.* Item domui London ejusdem ordinis xl*s.* Item domui de Hull ejusdem ordinis xl*s.* Item lego cuilibet ordinum fratrum mendicantium in civitate Lincoln commorancium xx*s.* Item lego quatuor domibus monialium, viz., Irford, Gaukewell, Heynenges et Fosse cuilibet domui v marcas Item lego fratri Willelmo de Hebden xl*s.* Item lego domino Willelmo capellano parochiali de Boudon xl*s.* Item lego in distribucionem pauperum illius parochiæ parvæ Boudon et Herbergh juxta ordinacionem predicti Willelmi xl*s.* Item lego ecclesiæ meæ de Frampton crucem meam argenteam et dauratam (*sic*) et lapidibus incertam ad reponendam prout capellanis ecclesiam regentibus melius videbitur Item lego ecclesiæ de Haydor calicem meum cotidianum Item lego ecclesiæ Sanctæ Margaretæ infra clausum Lincoln vestimentum meum stragulatum de auro et velveto cum toto apparatu Item ecclesiæ de Apulthorp albam et amitam (*sic*) cum paruris stolâ et fanone consutas de serico cum diversis armis et quod ematur una casula prout disposui pro capellâ

Item, I leave to the house of Beauvale[1] my best chalice, with the silver cruets of larger size, and 40*s.* for a pittance[2] on the day on which they cause commemoration to be made for my soul amongst themselves. Item, I leave to the house at Haynton,[3] belonging to the same order, 40*s.*; to the house at Witham,[4] of the same order, 20*s.*; to the London[5] house 40*s.*; to the house at Hull,[6] of the same order, 40*s.* Item, I leave to each of the orders of mendicant friars dwelling in the City of Lincoln 20*s.* Item, I leave to the four houses of nuns, viz., Irford,[7] Gaukewell,[8] Heynenges,[9] and Fosse,[10] to each house 5 marks. Item, I leave to brother William of Hebden 40*s.* Item, I leave to Sir William, parish chaplain of Bowden. 40*s.* Item, I leave for distribution to the poor of that parish, of Little Bowden and Harborough, according to the orders of the aforesaid William, 40*s.* Item, I leave to my Church of Frampton my silver cross, gilt, and inlaid with stones, to be placed as shall seem best to the chaplains who rule that church. Item, I leave to the Church of Haydor my everyday chalice. Item, I leave

---

[1] A Carthusian house in Gresley Park, Notts, founded by Nicholas de Cantilupe in 1338. Dugdale, Monasticon, vi. 11.

[2] An allowance over and above the stated commons on particular occasions. Bury Wills (Camden Soc.), p. 242.

[3] Henton: Carthusian Priory in Somerset, founded 1222. Dugdale, vi. 3.

[4] Witham. Carthusian Priory in Somerset, founded 1181. Dugdale, vi. 1622.

[5] Charterhouse. Dugdale, vi. 6.

[6] Carthusian Priory, founded *temp.* Edward III. Dugdale, vi. 19.

[7] Irford. Small house of Premonstratensian nuns in Lincolnshire, founded *temp.* Henry II. Dugdale, vi. 936.

[8] Gokwell or Gowkeswell. Cistercian nunnery in Lincolnshire, founded before 1185. Dugdale, v. 721.

[9] Or Hevenynge. Cistercian nunnery in Lincolnshire, founded about 1180. Dugdale, v. 723.

[10] Near or without Torkesey, Lincolnshire. Small Benedictine nunnery, founded *temp.* Henry III. Dugdale, iv. 292.

meâ propriâ et eidem ecclesiæ de Apulthorp tradatur Item lego domino Henrico fratri meo meliorem cupam meam cum aquario ejusdem sectæ deaurato Item dominæ Johannæ consorti suæ secundam cupam meam meliorem Item lego domino Stephano le Scropp tertiam cupam meam cum rosis incertam et deauratam Item lego eidem et dominæ Matildæ consorti suæ duodecim discos argenteos quos emi de executoribus domini de Huntyngfeld Item lego domino Johanni le Scropp vj goddetis (sic) infra septimam cum coopertorio inclusis Item lego domino Ricardo le Scropp portiforium meum de usu Ebor. quem habet penes se Item lego gildæ de Corpore Christi cercum (?) meum de velveto cum perles et xxs. Item lego Johannæ Perte unum ciphum vocat' 'Nuts' cum coopertorio et pede deaurato Item lego domino Roberto de Plumpton et dominæ Isabellæ consorti suæ duas pecias cum coopertoriis inclusas in corio bulliet' Item domino Henrico Fitzhugh unum par tabellarum annelit' quas habui de Archidiacono Item lego Magistro Ricardo le Scropp Ostiensem in lectura quem habet penes se et librum meum Beringarium Item lego Magistro Henrico Gategang magnum anulum meum cum magno peridod. et ciphum meum vocat' 'Boll' de argento cum armis domini fratris mei in summitate coopertorii Item lego domino Petro de Halton Rectori ecclesiæ de Claypole rotundam peciam cum

to the Church of St. Margaret, below the close at Lincoln, my vestment, diversely striped with gold and velvet, with all that belongs to it. Item, to the Church of Apulthorpe[1] an alb and amice, with apparels,[2] stole, and maniple,[3] wrought in silk, with divers coats of arms; and that a chasuble[4] be bought, as I have arranged for my private chapel, and given to the same Church of Apulthorp. Item, I leave to the Lord Henry, my brother, my best cup, with the gilt laver belonging to the same set. Item, I leave to the Lady Johanna, his wife, my second best cup. Item, I leave to Sir Stephen le Scrope my third cup inlaid and gilt, with roses. Item, I leave to the same, and to the Lady Matilda, his wife, the twelve dishes of silver which I bought of the executors of Lord Huntingfield.[5] Item, I leave to Sir John le Scrope six cups, enclosed within a seventh, with the cover. Item, I leave to Sir Richard le Scrope my breviary, of the York use, which he has in his possession. Item, I leave to the Guild of Corpus Christi my velvet circlet (?) with pearls, and 20s. Item, I leave to Johanna Perte a cup, called 'Nuts,' with its cover and gilt foot. Item, I leave to Sir Robert of Plumpton and the Lady Isabella, his wife, two pieces with covers enclosed in stamped leather. Item, to Henry Lord Fitzhugh[6] a pair of chessmen enamelled, which I had of the Archdeacon. Item, I leave to Master Richard le Scrope (my copy of)

---

[1] Apesthorpe, Notts, the testator's prebend in the cathedral church of York.

[2] *Paroures*, rich embroidered ornaments. See Promptorium Parvulorum (Camden Soc.), vol. ii. 384, note 2. For full description, with illustrations, see *Rock*, vol. i., chap. v., sect. ix.

[3] *Fanon*, maniple. See Prompt. Parv., i. 149. note 2.

[4] Worn by the celebrant at Mass. See *Rock*, vol. i., chap. v., sect. I.

[5] William de H., 1st Baron by writ, 1351. Nicolas, Historic Peerage (ed. Courthope), p. 264.

[6] 2nd Baron by writ. Nicolas, Historic Peerage, p. 194.

co-opertorio quæ fuit Magistri Johannis de Kellesey Item lego Johanni de Apulthorp x marcas et optimum equum meum quem duxerit eligendum Item Willelmo fratri suo solidum michi debitum remitto Item lego Willelmo de Plumpton unum par plates velveto rubio co-opert' et cassem optimam cum euentali meliori Item Johanni de Bautre parvum librum qui incipit cum rubro 'Cum Cubas dicas' et v marcas Item Waltero Warner xx*s*. Item domino Johanni Burgh capellano portiforium de usu Sarum notatum sic quod post mortem ejusdem remaneat Priori et Conventui domus de Kirkeby pro animabus sororum mearum de Luterell et Hathern et meæ imperpetuum Item domino Roberto de Donyngton ciphum murreum nigrum de quo solebam potare Item eidem unam peciam cum co-opertorio cum tribus glandinibus Item domino Roberto de Preston duos libros quos habet penes se, viz., Sextum et Clementinum cum singulis glosis Item domino Johanni de Feliskirk unum goddetum de argento cum co-opertorio habens scriptum verbum 'Y' Item eidem parvum librum vocat' 'forma fratris Monardi de casibus' Item Johanni Harpham zonam meam de viridi Ostiensis' lecture,[1] which he has in his possession, and my Beringarius.[2] Item, I leave to Master Henry Gategang my large ring with the large chrysolith, and my cup, called 'Boll,' of silver, with the arms of my lord brother on the top of the cover. Item, I leave to Sir Peter of Halton, Rector of Claypole, the round piece with a cover which belonged to Master John of Kellesey. Item, I leave to John of Apulthorp 10 marks and my best horse, which he may think fit to choose. Item, to William, his brother, I forgive the shilling he owes me. Item, I leave to William of Plumpton a pair of plates covered with red velvet, and my best helmet with the best ventaille.[3] Item, to John of Bawtry the little book which begins thus: 'Cum Cubas dicas,' in red ink, and 5 marks. Item, to Walter Warner 20*s*. Item, to Sir John Burgh, chaplain, my breviary noted, of the use of Sarum, so that after his death it shall be in remainder to the Prior and Monastery of Kirkeby,[4] for the souls of my sisters de Lutterell[5] and Hathern, and for my soul in perpetuity. Item, to Sir Robert of Donnington the black mazer cup from which I used to drink. Item, to the same a piece with a cover with three

---

[1] *I.e.*, Cardinal Henry de Segusio on the Decretals. H. de Segusio, d. 1271. 'Lectura Super Prologo Bibliorum.'

[2] In the Brit. Mus. are two MSS. under this name: (1) Berengarii Tusculanensis Episc. Casus in quibus sententia excommunicationis major fertur ex jure. Royal MSS., 8 a, ix. (6). (2) Berengarii Recantatio. Royal MSS., 9 b, xii., p. 306.

[3] The breathing part of the helmet. See Du Cange, s.v. *ventaculum*.

[4] Kirby Belers, Leicestershire. Augustinian Priory. (Dugdale, vi. 511.)

[5] Foss, Judges of England (iii. 495), says that two daughters of the Chief Justice married into the family of Lutterell. Beatrix m. Sir O. Lutterell; Constance m. Sir Geoffrey Lutterell. Gervase Holles (Linc. Church Notes), states that in one of the north windows of the nave in Haydor church there was an inscription: 'Orate pro animâ Galfridi le Scrope, Prebendarii hujus Ecclesiæ et pro animâ Beatricis Le Outrell sororis ejus.' Pray for the soul of Geoffrey le Scrope, Prebendary of this Church, and for the soul of Beatrice Le Outrell his sister.

serico unum quart' ferri duo quart' brasii medietatem j bovis salsi et unum porcum recentem vel duas parvas salsas eligat ipse Item lego pauperibus clericis prout supra Johanni Harpham legatum est preter zonam Item chorustis lego per eundem modum et eisdem unam ollam bonam cum aliquâ patellâ sufficienti prout executoribus meis videbitur Item lego Aliciæ de Spridlyngton unum firmaculum aureum cum j par' Avez de corall cum gaudez de albo Item remitto Thomæ marito suo et sibi v marcas de debito eorundem dum tamen residuum debiti executoribus meis persolvant fideliter Item lego domino Johanni Vaux capellano xx*s*. Item lego Thomæ camerario meo lectum meum de Northfolchia cum avibus cum tapetis et banquers et coopertorium de blueto cum avibus sive tapeto cum cillor curtinis et j par linthiaminum blanketez canvaz ac alia cotidiana in camerâ extenta et v marcas argenti et unum equum prout executoribus videbitur cum ix cussynez Item lego Willelmo Coco magnam ollam quam dedit michi Harpham et unam patellam juxta disposicionem executorum et v marcas argenti Item Willelmo Pistori xl*s*. Item lego Mauricio de Coquinâ et Roberto Balme de Pistrino cuilibet xx*s*. si sint mecum in officio tempore mortis meæ Item lego Thomæ de Stabulo xiii*s*. iiij*d*. Item Thomæ Lillyng xiii*s*. iiij*d*. Item lego Johanni garcioni acorns. Item, to Sir Robert of Preston two books which he has in his possession, viz., the Sixth Book of the Decretals[1] and the Clementines,[2] each with its gloss. Item, to Sir John of Feliskirk a silver mug with a cover, having inscribed on it the letter 'Y.' Item, to the same the little book called 'Forma fratris Monardi de casibus.'[3] Item, to John Harpham my girdle of green silk, a quarter of iron, two quarters of brass, half a salted ox, and one fresh pig, or two little salt pigs, whichever he may choose. Item, I leave to the poor clerks as was left above to John Harpham, except the girdle. Item, to the choristers I leave after the same manner, and also to the same one good pot with a suitable platter as shall seem good to my executors. Item, I leave to Alice of Spridlington a gold clasp[4] with a pair of Ave Marys (beads) of coral, with white gaudes (Pater Nosters). Item, I forgive Thomas, her husband, and herself 5 marks of the debt due from them, provided that they faithfully pay to my executors the residue of the debt. Item, I leave to Sir John Vaux, chaplain, 20*s*. Item, I leave to Thomas, my chamberlain, my Norfolk bed with birds with tapestry and bankers,[5] and a blue coverlet, with birds or tapestry with canopy,[6] curtains and one pair of sheets, blankets, canvas, and other things in daily use in the chamber, and 5 silver

---

[1] Liber Sextus Decretalium cum glosis, added to previous Decretals by Boniface VIII. in 1298 (Stephen's Blackstone, i. 42). This was one of the earliest printed books, fol. 1465, reprinted 1473.

[2] Clementinæ seu Liber Constitutionum; decrees of Clement V. added in 1317. (Stephen's Blackstone, i. 42.)

[3] ? *Monaldus*, Minorite. Summa de Casibus. He died about 1330.

[4] *Firmaculum*, a buckle. Liber Albus (Rolls Series), Glossary (Latin).

[5] *Bankers*, 'hanging tapestry work.' See Prompt. Parv., i. 23, note 1.

[6] *Celure* (obs. forms, silour, cylour, etc.), a canopy covering a bed, daïs, altar, etc. New Eng. Dict. (Murray).

de Coquinâ vjs. viijd. Item parvo Willelmo de Coquinâ vjs. viijd. Item parvo Johanni Brounc et Johanni filio Roberti carectarii cuilibet iijs. iiijd. et volo quod omnes servientes mei tam majores quam minores ad proximum terminum stipendii proxime futuri post mortem meam solvendi integrum feodum recipiant quantumcunque diu ante me mori contigerit Item lego Anachoritæ de Hampole xxs. Item lego Anachoritæ ad ecclesiam Sanctæ Trinitatis Lincoln xxs. cum tunicâ de russeto furrat' cum calabr' cum capicio duplicato et cum armilausâ ejusdem sectæ furrat' cum grice Item lego Anachoritæ de Kirkeby Wysk xiijs. iiijd. Item lego Anachoritæ ad ecclesiam Sancti Pauli Staumford xijs. iiijd. Item Anachoritæ apud Doncastre vjs. viijd. Item Beatrici de Estlyngton xls. Item lego Ceciliæ Whatlous xijs. iiijd. Item lego Roberto carectario et Waltero Mathewe cuilibet vjs. viijd. Item lego sorori Henrici Warde moniali de Irford xijs. iiijd. Item lego Willelmo filio Thomæ Barbour xiijs. iiijd. Hujus autem testamenti executores ordino facio et constituo Magistrum Henricum Gategang Rectorem ecclesiæ de Welton ultra Humbriam dominum Johannem Sacristam in ecclesiâ Cathedrali Lincoln. dominum Johannem de Fiskerton vicarium in choro ejusdem ecclesiæ dominum Johannem Ingham capellanum ac socium in cantariâ Burghersch et Johannem de Apulthorp armigerum meum quibus lego residuum bonorum marks and a horse, as shall seem good to my executors, with 9 cushions. Item, I leave to William the cook the pot which Harpham gave me, and a platter at the discretion of my executors, and 5 marks in silver. Item, to William the baker 40s. Item, I leave to Maurice of the kitchen and to Robert Balme of the bakehouse, each xxs. if they be in my service at the time of my death. Item, I leave to Thomas of the stable 13s. 4d. Item, to Thomas Lillyng 13s. 4d. Item, I leave to John the kitchen-boy 6s. 8d. Item, to little William of the kitchen 6s. 8d. Item, to little John Browne and John, son of Robert the coachman, each 3s. 4d.; and I will that all my servants, as well upper as under, at the next term when their wages are due after my death, shall receive the whole sum then due, however long before that date death may have befallen me. Item, I leave to the anchorite of Hampole 20s. Item, I leave to the anchorite at the Church of the Holy Trinity, Lincoln, 20s., with a russet tunic furred with calaber,[1] with a double hood, and with a cloak[2] of the same suit furred with gris.[3] Item, I leave to the anchorite of Kirkby Wiske 13s. 4d. Item, I leave to the anchorite at St. Paul's Church, Stamford, 13s. 4d. Item, to the anchorite at Doncaster 6s. 8d. Item, to Beatrice of Estlyngton 40s. Item, I leave to Cecilia Whatlows 13s. 4d. Item, I leave to Robert the coachman and Walter Mathew each 6s. 8d. Item,

---

[1] A kind of fur. See Cowel's Interpreter, 'furre.' New English Dictionary (J. A. H. Murray), 'calaber.'
[2] Liber Albus, Riley (Rolls Series), Glossary.
[3] *Grice*, gris. 'Precyowse furrure.' See Prompt. Parv., i. 211, note 2, reference to Chaucer.

'I saw his sleeves purfiléd at the hond
With gris, and that the finest of the lond.'
      Prologue to Canterbury Tales—The Monk.

meorum ut de eisdem disponant prout eis coram deo melius videbitur expedire Et lego predictis executoribus meis, viz., Magistro Henrico Gategang dominis Johanni Sacristæ Johanni de Fiskerton et Johanni de Ingham capellanis et Johanni de Apulthorp cuilibet eorum pro labore suo v marcas et volo ac rogo dominos meos reverendos de Capitulo quatenus, compoto istius testamenti reddito, omnes et singuli executores prenominati administracionem recipientes bene et laudabiliter si quid residuum superfuerit per eosdem ultra legatum eisdem per prius remunerentur.

I leave to Henry Ward's sister—a nun of Irford—13s. 4d. Item, I leave to William, son of Thomas Barber, 13s. 4d. Of this my will, I ordain, make, and constitute executors Master Henry Gategang, Rector of Welton beyond the Humber, Sir John, Sacrist in the Cathedral Church of Lincoln, Sir John of Fiskerton, Vicar choral of the same church, Sir John Ingham, chaplain and fellow of the Burghersh Chantry, and John of Apulthorp, my Esquire, to whom I leave the residue of my goods not bequeathed, that they may dispose of the same as shall seem best to them before God. And I leave to the aforesaid, my executors, viz., Master Henry Gategang, Sirs John, Sacrist, John of Fiskerton, and John of Ingham, chaplains, and John of Apulthorp, each of them, for their trouble 5 marks. And I will and pray my reverend brethren of the Chapter that, account being rendered of this will, all and each of my forenamed executors receiving administration, may be by them well and laudably remunerated if there be any overplus beyond what has been bequeathed to them by the foregoing.

Presens testamentum coram nobis Subdecano et Capitulo Ecclesiæ beatæ Mariæ Lincoln in domo capitulari ibidem die Sabbati proxime post festum Conversionis Sancti Pauli, viz., ultimo die mensis Januarii Anno Domini MCCC. octogesimo secundo fuit exhibitum probatum approbatum et insinuatum administracioque bonorum defuncti suprascripti commissa erat per nos tunc ibidem executoribus suprascriptis omnibus et singulis in forma juris juratis In cujus rei testimonium sigillum nostrum commune fecimus hiis apponi.

This present will before us, the Subdean and Chapter of the Church of the Blessed Mary, Lincoln, in the Chapter-house there, on the Saturday next after the Feast of the Conversion of St. Paul, viz., the last day of the month of January, in the year of our Lord One Thousand Three Hundred and Eighty-two, was exhibited, proved, approved, and enrolled, and administration of the goods of the deceased was by us then and there granted to the above-written executors, each and all being sworn in due legal form. In witness whereof we have caused our common seal to be affixed to these presents.

A similar record of probate before the official of the Archdeacon of Lincoln, at Frampton, February 15 in the same year.

A similar record of probate before the Chapter of St. Peter's, York (the Dean 'in remotis agente'), Friday, April 10, 1383.

A similar record of probate before the Vicar-General of the Archdeacon of Richmond, York, April 11, 1383.

A careful examination of the records preserved in the Chapter muniment room would, doubtless, reveal many interesting particulars of the time when Geoffrey le Scrope was a Canon. Here it must suffice to give two or three extracts from the accounts of the Clericus Communæ. From these we gather that Geoffrey le Scrope was one of the Canons who kept what is called the great term of residence, and he appears to have done so every year. Thus, in the accounts of the year 1368, under the heading 'Facientes Magnam Residenciam,'[1] we have John of Welborn, for the Prebend of *Asgarby*; Hamon Belers, Subdean, for *Welton*; Geoffrey le Scrope, for *Haydor*, William Hugate, for *Carlton Kyme*. In those of the year 1382 his name appears, for the last time, under the same heading, together with John of Belvoir, Subdean, for *Welton*, Thomas of Sutton, for *Decem Librarum*, John of Rouceby, for *Carlton-cum-Thurlby*, Richard of Beverley, for *Liddington*, John of Carlton, for *St. Botolph's*, Richard of Winwick, for *North Kelsey*, John of Warsopp, for *Welton Rivall*, and William Welburne, for *Sexaginta Solidorum*. The amount of income seems to have been variable, coming, as it did, from different sources, and being sometimes in arrears. The following is a specimen record for one year:

In communis Magistri Galfridi Scroppe canonici ecclesiæ Lincoln ... ... xx*li.* viij*s.*
Item eidem pro vinis ... cx*s.* vj*d.*

For the Commons of Master Geoffrey Scrope, Canon of Lincoln. £20 8*s.* 0*d.*
Likewise to the same for wine £5 10*s.* 6*d.*

---

[1] *I.e.*, in Le Scrope's case, a residence for thirty-four weeks and four days in the year, he not electing to reside on his prebend of Haydor-cum-Walton. He must have put a Vicar in that parish, instead of paying a Priest-vicar to follow the choir at Lincoln.

Item eidem pro obitu de communâ ... ... xxxixs. ijd. ob.	Likewise to the same for obits from the common allowance £1 19s. 2½d.
Item eidem pro obitu ex parte W. Lexington ... xliiijs. vjd.	Likewise to the same for W. Lexington's obit £2 4s. 6d.
Item eidem de residuo compoti lli. xjs. ijd.	Likewise to the same from the surplus of the (audit) account £50 11s. 2d.
Item eidem de arreragiis anni preteriti ... xxxili. xvjs. ob. qa.	Likewise to the same for arrears of the past year £31 16s. 0¾d.
Item eidem de arreragiis diversorum annorum xxxjs. jd. ob. qa.	Likewise to the same for arrears of divers years ... £1 11s. 1¾d.
Item eidem pro missâ regis ijs. ijd. ob.	Likewise to the same for the King's Mass[1] ... ... 2s. 2½d.
Item eidem pro redditu debito ecclesiæ Sanctæ Margeretæ iiijs.	Likewise to the same for rent due to the Church of St. Margaret ... ... 4s. 0d.
Summa ... cxiiijli. vijs. ijd. qa.	Total ... ...£114 7s. 2¼d.

In the year 1383 there is an entry stating that his *obit* was kept 'a die Sabbati proximâ post festum Conversionis Sancti Pauli' (January 25), 'quo die obiit, usque in diem dominicam proximam post festum Exaltationis Sanctæ Crucis proxime sequentem per triginta tres septimanas et unum diem'—from the Saturday after the Conversion of St. Paul, the day on which he died, to the Sunday after the Feast of the Exaltation of the Holy Cross (September 14), *i.e.*, for thirty-three weeks and one day.[2] The date of death is about six years earlier than that which is given in the Scrope and Grosvenor Roll.

Geoffrey le Scrope was succeeded by Richard le Scrope, apparently the third son of Henry le Scrope, and brother of Stephen.

Magister Ricardus le Scrop presbiter presentatus per nobilem virum dominum Henricum le Scrop militem ad ecclesiam de Magna Boudon Linc. dioc. per resignationem Magistri Galfridi le Scrop ultimi rectoris ejusdem in manibus reverendi patris domini Johannis Dei gratiâ Linc. Episcopi factam et per ipsum acceptatam vacantem, factâ nullâ inquisicione in hâc parte	Richard le Scrope, priest, presented by Henry le Scrope, knight, to the Rectory of Great Bowden, vacant by the resignation of Geoffrey le Scrope. Instituted December 20, 1378.	Richard le Scrope (afterwards Archbishop of York), Rector of Great Bowden, 1378.

---

[1] Mass on the anniversary either of death or accession.
[2] Muniments of the D. and C. of Lincoln, B. j. 3, numbers 6 and 7.

quia eidem patri constabat de jure patronatus ad quam, etc.[1]

Date xiij Kal. Jan. A.D. 1378 (*i.e.*, December 20, 1378).

Instituted in the person of William Fisshwyk, clerk, of the diocese of York.

His after-career.

According to the genealogy of the family given by Sir H. Nicolas in his account of the Scrope and Grosvenor suit, this Richard le Scrope was the same who, as Archbishop of York, is well known to history.[2] In other genealogies—*e.g.*, the one in Blore's 'Rutland'—the Archbishop is given as a son of the Lord of Bolton, but reasons are given in the authority here quoted why this is incorrect.

Richard le Scrope was appointed Dean of Chichester and Chancellor of the University of Cambridge in 1383,[3] Prebendary of Lincoln and afterwards Bishop of Coventry and Lichfield, in 1386,[4] and Archbishop of York in 1398.[5]

He was one of King Richard's proctors appointed to present his resignation to the Parliament of 1399, and after Richard's deposition, with Archbishop Arundel of Canterbury, he led Henry IV. to the throne.[6] But in 1405 he joined the Earl of Northumberland and others in drawing up and circulating articles of indictment against Henry, and in a rising to arms. The proposals in these articles, we are told, were such as 'touched all the weak points in Henry's administration,' and, on the part of the Archbishop, were dictated by a hope of reform. But the result to the lords who drew it up was disastrous. The Archbishop was arrested, and brought to trial as a traitor. Though Archbishop Arundel pleaded for him, and Sir William Gascoigne, the Chief Justice, refused to sentence him, he was beheaded on June 8, 1405.[7] The effect is thus summed up:

'It was no wonder that the body of the murdered

---

[1] Bp. Bokingham's Reg., Inst., vol. i., fol. 270.
[2] Scrope and Grosvenor Roll, ii. 121.
[3] Le Neve's Fasti, i. 256; iii. 599.
[4] Le Neve, ii. 187; Browne Willis, Cathedrals, iii. 220.
[5] Browne Willis, ii. 39. [6] Stubbs' Const. Hy., ii. 553.
[7] *Ibid.*, iii. 52-55, 61, 82.

Archbishop began at once to work miracles; he was a most popular prelate, a member of a great Yorkshire house, and he had died in the act of defending his people against oppression. Nor is it wonderful that in popular belief the illness which clouded Henry's later years was regarded as a judgment for his impiety in laying hands on the Archbishop. English history recorded no parallel event; the death of Becket, the work of four unauthorized, excited assassins, is thrown into the shade by the judicial murder of Scrope."[1]

In the same Bishop's Institutions we have Richard le Scrope's resignation and the appointment of his successor. The date of the institution, it will be observed, is a few months after Richard le Scrope's appointment to the Deanery of Chichester.

| Johannes de Clone clericus presentatus per dominum Henricum le Scroope militem et dominum de Masham ad ecclesiam parochialem de Boudon Magna Lincoln. Dioc. per resignationem Magistri Ricardi le Scroope ultimi Rectoris ejusdem in manibus Reverendi in Christo patris domini Johannis dei gratia Linc. Episcopi factam et per eundem reverendum patrem acceptatam vacantem, nullâ inquisicione captâ quia eidem Reverendo patri constabat, etc., ad quam quinto die mensis Octobr. A.D. 1384 (October 5, 1384) apud Lydington fuit admissus et Rector in personâ Willelmi de Ludelowe vicarii ecclesiæ parochialis de Ricall Ebor. dioc. procuratoris sui sufficienter et legitime in hâc parte constituti institutus canonice in eâdem Juravitque idem procurator canonicam obedientiam, etc., etc.[2] | John of Clone, clerk, presented by Henry le Scrope, knight, Lord of Masham, to the parish church of Great Bowden, vacant by the resignation of Richard le Scrope. Instituted at Lydington October 5, 1384, in the person of William de Ludlow, Vicar of Riccall, York Diocese, his lawful proctor. | John of Clone, clerk, Rector of Great Bowden, 1384. |

John of Clone, as will be seen from the next extract from the Bishop's Institutions, held the benefice only seven years, and we gather from three entries in the

---

[1] Stubbs' Const. Hy., iii. 55.
[2] Bp. Bokingham's Reg., Instit., vol. ii., fol. 198.

Bishop's Memoranda, that he had little to do with anything but the revenues.

Licences of non-residence, etc., granted to him.

Item septimo die ejusdem mensis (*i.e.*, October, 1384) ibidem concessa fuit litera non residenciæ pro domino Johanne de Cloñ Rectore ecclesiæ parochialis de Magna Boudon Linc. dioc. quod posset se absentare, etc., per triennium et dimittere fructus ejusdem ad firmam per idem tempus contemplacione domini Archiepiscopi Ebor. quia suus familiaris et commensalis, etc.[1]

October 7, 1384, licence of non-residence is granted on behalf of John of Clone, Rector of Great Bowden, for three years, with power to lease the profits of the benefice, out of regard for the Lord Archbishop of York, because he is his Grace's private chaplain, and sits at his table.

Item eisdem die et loco (July 2, 1388, apud Parcum Lude) concessa fuit litera non-residenciæ domino Johanni de Clone Rectori ecclesiæ parochialis de Boudon Magna quod possit se absentare per biennium locis honestis commorando fructus interim percipiendo ac si. etc., contemplacione domini Ricardi Chesterfeld Canonici Ecclesiæ Lincoln.[2]

July 2, 1388, at Louth Park, licence of non-residence is granted to John of Clone, Rector of Great Bowden for two years, with power to receive the profits, etc., out of regard for Sir Richard Chesterfield, Canon of Lincoln.

Item primo die mensis Julii A.D. supradicto (1391) ibidem (apud Sleford) concessa fuit litera non. res. domino Johanni Clone Rectori rec. de B. M. per biennium fructus percipere contemplacione Ricardi Chesterfeld.[3]

July 1, 1391, at Sleaford, licence of non-residence is granted to John Clone, Rector of Great Bowden (as in the last).

From these we learn that John of Clone was in some capacity attached to the household (1) of the Archbishop of York, (2) of one of the Canons of Lincoln, and that by their favour he was allowed to live away from his benefice while receiving its profits, or letting them out at a rent.

Returning to the Bishop's Institutions, we find the following:

Magister Willelmus Wolstanton presbiter presentatus per dominum Henricum le Scrope militem

William of Wolstanton, priest, presented by Henry le Scrope, knight, to the parish church of

---

[1] Bp. Bokingham's Reg., Memoranda, fol. 287 (cciiii××vij.).
[2] Bp. Bokingham's Reg., Memoranda, fol. cccxlix.
[3] Bp. Bokingham's Reg., Memoranda, fol. ccclxxviii.

ad ecclesiam parochialem de Boudon Linc. dioc. vacantem per mortem domini Johannis Clune ultimi rectoris ejusdem, captâ inde inquisicione, etc. xxij Nov.. A.D. 1391, apud Parcum Stowe.[1]	Bowden, vacant by the death of John Clune, the last rector. November 22, 1391, at Stow Park.

One more reference must be made to Bishop Bokingham's Memoranda, which brings out a feature in the history of the time, and shows that the religious movements of the day made themselves felt in these parishes. In a Parliament which sat from May 7 to May 22, 1382, a statute was passed against heretic preachers.[2] The Bishop's Memoranda give an instance of the way in which this statute was carried out. William of Swinderby, a hermit-priest, had preached heresy within the diocese of Lincoln. He was examined and convicted of the same, but, on submission, he was restored to the bosom of the Church. He was then commanded to read his recantation in eight churches of the diocese, on eight successive Sundays, at Mass. The eight churches were, the Cathedral at Lincoln, the Prebendal Church of St. Margaret, Leicester, St. Mary's Church in the Newarke, Leicester, and the parish Churches of St. Martin, Leicester, Meltone Moubray (Melton Mowbray), Halughton (Hallaton), Hareburgh (Harborough), and Loucheborough (Loughborough). The date is June 6, 1382.[3]

William of Swinderby ordered to read his recantation in Harborough Church.

In the Bishop's Memoranda the whole process is to be found, very beautifully and distinctly written. It is headed, 'Processus domini Johannis Lincoln Episcopi contra Willelmum Swynderby Wycclevistam et impietates ejus hereticas.' The form of the recantation to be read is given at length.

The documents which belong to the reign of Richard II. are Nos. 16-24. There is not much in them which calls for remark. No. 17 gives the name to the place where

Town documents of the reign of Richard II.

---

[1] Bp. Bokingham's Reg., Institutions, vol. ii., fol. 220.
[2] Stubbs, Const. Hy., ii. 506, note 2.
[3] Bp. Bokingham's Reg., Memoranda, fol. ccxl. *et seq.*; Fasciculi Zizaniorum (Rolls Series), pp. 334-336.

the stalls already mentioned were situated—'le fleyschschamelis,' or, to use a later word, the 'shambles.' In No. 19 we have an example of the growth of surnames—'John le bailif' and 'Hugh le Milner' have become John Baly and Hugh Milner. In No. 20 the list of field-names receives two additions, 'Smethmewe' and 'Watyrlakes,' and in the last (No. 24) we have a designation of property as being in 'le west ende' of Great Bowden. This enables us to identify it as a property still held by the trustees, and shows that it has formed part of the Harborough Town Estate for 500 years.

As there is only one document preserved to the town which belongs to the reign of Henry IV., and not one which belongs to that of Henry V., it will be convenient to take these two reigns together. Henry IV. reigned from September 30, 1399, to March 20, 1413, and Henry V. from March 21, 1413, to August 31, 1422. The Bishops of Lincoln during this period were, Henry Beaufort, whose episcopate lasted till 1405, Philip Repingdon (1405-1420), and Richard Fleming, 1420.

Death of Stephen, Lord le Scrope, of Masham, 1406.

The death of Stephen le Scrope, in 1406, and the 'judicial murder' of Richard le Scrope, Archbishop of York, in the previous year, have been already noted. The Inquisitions *post mortem* record that Stephen le Scrope, of Masham, died seised of the manor of Bowden with the advowson of the Church, and of the manor of Harborough in the county of Leicester.[1] His eldest son, Henry le Scrope, was a Knight of the Garter, and high in the service of Henry IV. He became Treasurer of England at the very end of Henry's reign, but when Henry V. came to the throne, the Earl of Arundel was appointed in his place. In 1415 he was arrested and tried, on charge of complicity with what is known as the 'Southampton' plot. The charge was, that, bribed by the French, against whom the King had declared war, he, with the Earl of Cambridge and others, had 'concocted a design of carrying off the Earl of March, the legitimate heir of

---

[1] Inquis. post mortem (1828), vol. iii., p. 308, No. 52.

Edward III., to Wales, as soon as Henry had sailed for France, and there proclaiming him heir of Richard II.' In the end Lord le Scrope was condemned and executed on the August 5, 1415.[1]

This is but the barest outline of an event which has left its mark in many long records. The outline may be filled up at pleasure. Thus, if we turn to the documents printed in Rymer's 'Fœdera,' we find lengthy accounts of the preparations for the King's journey. Among these is the will of Henry le Scrope, which fills nine pages, and gives a clear idea of his wealth and consequence.[2] The date of this will is June 23, 1415. He leaves a cope to each of several churches, ' Boudon, Aynderby, Kilvyngton,' etc.[3] A little later comes the commission to Thomas, Duke of Clarence, to hear and determine, etc., the charge against the conspirators, including Henry le Scrope, of Masham, knight.[4] Then follows the confession of the Earl of Cambridge, in English.[5] As Scrope's position was rather different to that of the other conspirators, the main part of this must be given :

My most Dredfulle and Sovereyne Lege Lord, Lyke to zoure Hynesse, to wete, touching the Purpose cast agens zowir hye Estate, havyng the Erle of Marche by his awne assent, and by the assent of my self (wherof y most me repent of all worldly thyng) and by the Accorde of the Lord Scrop and Sir Thomas Grey, to have hadde the forseyd Erle in to the Lond of Walys wythoutyn zoure Lycence, takyng up on hym the Sovereynte of zys Lond, zyf yonder manis Persone, wych they callen Kyng Richard hadde nauth bene alyve, as y wot wel that he wys not alyve ;

For the wych poynt I putte me holy in zoure Grace : And as for the forme of a Proclamacyoun, wych schudde hadde bene cryde in the Erle name, as he Heyre to the Coroune of Ynglond, ageyns zow, my Lege

---

[1] Stubbs' Const. Hy., iii. 67, note 5, 81, 91.
[2] Rymer's Fœdera (ed. 1709), vol. ix., pp. 272 *et seq.* On page 230 of the same volume there is an indenture (in Norman-French) by which Henry le Scrope binds himself to go with the King, and serve him for a year in his Duchy of Guienne and Kingdom of France. He is to take with him 30 men-at-arms, of whom 3 are to be knights, 26 esquires, and 90 archers on horseback.
[3] Rymer's Fœdera, ix. 275 : Item lego cuilibet ecclesiarum parochialium de Boudon, Aynderby, Kilvyngton, etc., post decessum meum unam capam secundum disposicionem executorum meorum.
[4] Rymer's Fœdera, ix. 300.   [5] *Ibid.*, ix. 300, 301.

Lord, calde, by an untreu Name, Harry of Lancastre Usurpur of Ynglond, to the entent to hadde made the more People to hade draune to hym, and fro zow,

of the wych Crye Scroope knew not of by me but Grey dyd .... And as for the purpose, takyn by Unfrevyle and Wederyngtonn, for the bryngyng yn of that Persone, wych they name Kyng Rychard, and Henry Percy oute of Scotland, with a power of Scottys, and theyre Power togedyrs semyng to theyme able to geve zow a Bataylle, of the wych entent Sir Thomas Grey wyst of, and I also, but nauth Scrop as by me ....

Still further particulars of the proceedings which ended in Scrope's execution may be gleaned from the Rolls of Parliament.[1] The conspirators were first tried on August 2, the names of the jurors being John Chonde, John Lok, John Steer, John Veel, Robert Upham, Laurence Hamelyn, John Welere Fysh, John Colyn, John Penyton, Walter Hore, John Halle, and John Snelle. The details of the plot are given, and the charges are laid. The charge against Scrope is, that he had communications with the Earl of Cambridge and Thomas Grey with regard to the design for the destruction of the King, the King's brothers, and others, and that he treacherously concealed the same from the King. The conspirators are brought up from the Tower of Southampton by Sir John Popham, the Constable. They are separately invited to answer the charges against them. Cambridge and Gray confess all, and throw themselves upon the King's mercy. Scrope acknowledges that he had communications with the others as to all the designs, except that of bringing about the King's death and that of the King's brothers, but declares that he had these communications with the intention of frustrating the evil designed. As to the concealment of the fact, he places himself at the King's mercy. He denies that he is any way guilty of having planned or consented to the King's death. Moreover, he pleads that he is 'dominus,' and one of the Peers of England, and demands that, according to custom, he may be tried and judged by his Peers.

[1] Rolls of Parliament (printed), vol. iv., pp. 65 *et seq*. See some interesting papers in the 43rd Report of the Deputy-Keeper, pp. 579, *et seq*.

The prisoners are sent back to the Tower in custody. The court pronounces Sir Thomas Grey guilty, and sentences him to be led out on foot from the Watergate to the Northgate of Southampton, and there to be beheaded. His head is to be set up, in sight of the people passing by, at Newcastle-on-Tyne, and all his lands and tenements, goods and chattels, are to be forfeited to the King. Cambridge and Scrope are to be tried by their Peers.

Accordingly, the two are again brought up for trial on the following Monday. Thomas, Duke of Clarence, is the President of the court, and with him are Edmund, Earl of March, John, Earl of Huntingdon, Thomas, Earl of Arundell, John, Earl Marshal, Thomas, Earl of Dorset, Thomas, Earl of Salisbury, Richard, Earl of Oxford, Michael, Earl of Suffolk, John, Lord de Clifford, Gilbert, Lord de Talbot, William, Lord de Zousche, John, Lord de Haryndon, Robert, Lord de Wylughby, William, Lord de Clinton, John, Lord de Mautravers, Hugh, Lord de Boucer, and the Lord de Botreaux. By these, their Peers, both are adjudged traitors, Cambridge as the chief designer of the treason, Scrope as consenting to it, frequently holding communications with the traitors, and concealing the fact. They are sentenced to be hanged, beheaded, and dismembered. But the sentence is partially remitted in each case; Cambridge, because he is of the blood royal, is only to be beheaded; Scrope, because he is a Knight of the Garter, is to have the same punishment as Grey. His head is to be set up on one of the gates of York, in sight of the passers-by.[1] Everything is to be forfeited to the King, with the saving clause that the forfeiture is to be within the limits of the common law of the kingdom, and that all lawful rights in respect of it are reserved.[2] For the time being the forfeiture

---

[1] 'Mickellyth (*i.e.*, Micklegate) Bar.' Drake's Eboracum, p. 108.
[2] 'Ita quod forisfactura hujusmodi se extendat dumtaxat prout Lex communis Regni Angliæ in hac parte exigit et requirit. Jure tamen omnium et singulorum qui forisfacturas in hoc casu virtute Libertatum et Franchesiarum suarum habere clamant semper salvo.'

seems to have been very complete in the case of Henry le Scrope. In the inventory of the effects of Henry V. a good many articles are enumerated which were formerly his property—*e.g.* :[1]

I Lite d'Arras d'or de Chessis, q̄ jadis estoit a Sr̄ d'Escrop, q̄ forfist a Roy, le Celour cont' iiii verg' de longur', et iiii verges de large, en tout cont' xvi verges quarr', le Testour cont' iiii verges di de longur', et III verges III quarter de large, en tout xvii verges quarres ; le Conterpoynt cont' vi verges de longur', et v verges di de large, en tout xxxiii verges quarres. La Somme en tout cont' lxvi verges quarres, pris le verge vjs.
xix*li*. xvi*s*.
Item III Curtyns de vert Tarterin raies ... pris xxvj*s*. viij*d*.
I Tapite de bloy Tapicerie, ovec arm' d'Escrop ... pris iis.
II Tentes de bloy carde, linez de toill linge queux furent au Sr̄ Herry d'Escrop ovec i Porche, et i Alcy, pris de tout vi*li*. xiij*s*. iiii*d*.

In the volume of the Isham MSS., quoted above, we find an extract from the records, which shows that out of the vast possessions of the family, the manors of Bowden and Harborough were at once granted to Sir William Porter, knight.

Grant to Sir William Porter.

Rex etc. escaetori suo Com'. Leic' salutem Cum de gratiâ speciali concesserimus dilecto armigero nostro Willelmo Porter manerium de Harburgh et Bowedon cum pertinenciis in Com. predicto quod fuit Henrici le Scrop de Masham Chivaler defuncti qui erga nos nuper forisfecit, et quod ad nos pertinet occasione forisfacturæ predictæ, habendum eidem Willelmo manerium predictum cum pertinenciis a die forisfacturæ ejusdem Henrici quamdiu in manibus nostris occasione illâ contigerit remanere, adeo plene et integre sicut idem Henricus manerium illud habuit et tenuit dum vivebat, reddendo inde nobis et heredibus nostris per annum extentam inde factam vel faciendam, vel prout inter Thesaurarium Angliæ qui pro tempore fuerit et prefatum Willelmum poterit con-

The King to the Escheator for Leicestershire, health, etc.

The King has granted to his esquire, William Porter, the manor of Harborough and Bowden, which was formerly the property of Henry le Scrope, knight, and was forfeited by him to the King. The said William Porter is to have and to hold the same from the day of the forfeiture so long as it shall remain in the King's hands by reason of the forfeiture, paying each year to the King or his heirs the valuation already made or to be made or as shall be agreed upon between the Treasurer of England for the time being, and the said William Porter. The Escheator is to hand over the manor to him to be held on these terms. Southampton, August 8, 3 Henry V., 1415.

---

[1] Rolls of Parliament (printed), iv., pp. 235, 240.

cordari, prout in litteris nostris patentibus inde confectis plenius continetur; tibi precipimus quod eidem Willelmo manerium predictum cum pertinenciis liberes habendum juxta tenorem litterarum nostrarum predictarum; volumus enim te exonerari Teste me ipso apud Southampton octavo die Augusti anno regni nostri tertio.[1]

Rex omnibus ad quos, etc., salutem; sciatis quod nuper de gratiâ nostrâ speciali per litteras nostras patentes concesserimus dilecto et fideli nostro Willelmo Porter chivaler manerium de Harburgh Bowdon cum pertinenciis in Com. Leic^r, quod nuper fuit Henrici le Scrope de Masham chivaler defuncti, qui erga nos forisfecit et quod ratione forisfacturæ predictæ ad nos pertinet, habendum prefato Willelmo manerium predictum cum pertinenciis a die forisfacturæ predictæ Henrici quamdiu in manibus nostris occasione predictâ existeret, adeo plene et integre sicut idem Henricus manerium predictum habuit et tenuit dum vivebat; reddendo inde nobis et heredibus nostris extentam inde factam vel faciendam vel prout inter thesaurarium Angliæ qui pro tempore foret et prefatum Willelmum posset concordari, prout in litteris nostris patentibus inde confectis plenius continetur. Nos pro eo quod idem Willelmus litteras nostras predictas nobis in Cancellariâ nostrâ restituit cancellandas, de gratiâ nostrâ speciali concesserimus prefato Willelmo manerium predictum cum pertinenciis quocunque nomine idem manerium censeatur seu nuncupatur aut censeri vel nuncupari poterit, cum feodis militum et advocacionibus ecclesiarum, wardis, maritagiis, releviis, eschaetis, parcis, feriis, mer-

The King to all, etc., etc.

The previous grant of the manor of Harborough and Bowden to William Porter, chivaler, has been returned by him to the King's Chancery to be cancelled. The King now grants the same manor to the same, with knights' fees, advowsons of churches, wards, reliefs, etc., etc., for the term of his life, without payment of rent; and further wills that, in regard to this manor, he shall be wholly free from all 'aids' and 'sheriff's courts.' Westminster, January 15, 14$\frac{15}{16}$.

---

[1] Isham MSS., TT., fol. 200.

catis, reversionibus, libertatibus, regalitatibus, franchesiis et omnimodis aliis membris et commoditatibus ad manerium illud qualitercunque pertinentibus sive spectantibus, una cum omnibus arreragiis firmarum reddituum serviciorum consuetudinum finium et amerciamentorum ac omnium aliorum proficuorum inde provenientium, ac prefato Henrico die forisfacturæ suæ predictæ debitis ; habendum et tenendum prefato Willelmo manerium cum feodis militum et advocacionibus ecclesiarum, wardis, maritagiis, releviis, eschaetis, parcis, warreniis, feriis, mercatis, reversionibus, libertatibus, regalitatibus, franchesiis et omnibus aliis membris et commoditatibus ad idem manerium quovismodo pertinentibus sive spectantibus una cum arreragiis predictis a die forisfacturæ predictæ pro termino vitæ ipsius Willelmi absque aliquo nobis seu heredibus nostris inde reddendo, et ulterius uberiori gratiâ nostrâ concessimus eidem Willelmo quod ipse durante vitâ suâ de auxiliis et curiis vicecomitis quoad manerium et pertinencia predicta totaliter quietus et exoneratus existet, eo quod expressa mencio de aliis donis et concessionibus prefato Willelmo ante hæc tempora factis seu de vero valore eorundem aut de vero valore manerii predicti cum pertinenciis et aliis supra dictis iuxta formam statuti inde editi in presentibus facta non existit non obstante ; IN CUJUS, etc., teste Rege apud Westm. xvº die Januarii,

In rotulo patenti regis Henrici quinti Anno tertio secunda pars.[1]

It will be noticed that in the first grant, three days after the execution of Henry le Scrope, the manors are granted 'so long as they shall remain in the King's hands by

[1] Isham MSS., TT., fol. 200.

reason of the forfeiture,' and the sum to be paid is left to be settled between Sir William Porter and the Treasurer of England. In the second grant it is stated that the first has been returned into the King's Chancery to be cancelled, and a second is made for Sir William Porter's life, without any payment, and with entire freedom from 'aids' and 'sheriff's courts' in respect of the manor and its appurtenances. The date of the second is five months after that of the first—January 15, 1415-16. In the next reign, as we shall see, the manors were restored to the Scrope family.

William of Wolstanton, who had been presented to the benefice in 1391, died on August 31, 1403. He was buried, according to his own directions, in the chancel of Great Bowden Church, and a small brass long remained there to his memory, with the following inscription : *[Death of William of Wolstanton.]*

hic jacet Magister Willelmus Wolstonton quondam Rector istius ecclesiæ qui obiit ultimo die mensis Augusti anno domini MCCCCIII. cujus animæ propicietur Deus.

Here lies Master William Wolstanton, formerly Rector of this church, who died the last day of the month of August in the year of our Lord 1403. On whose soul, God have mercy ! *[Brass in Great Bowden Church to his memory.]*

A copy of his will is preserved at Lincoln :[1]

In nomine, Amen A.D. MCCCC^{mo} tertio mensis Augusti die xxiii^{to} Ego Willelmus de Wolstanton Rector ecclesiæ parochialis de Boudon Magna Linc. dioc., compos mentis et sanæ existens memoriæ, condo testamentum meum in hunc modum In primis lego et commendo animam meam individuæ Trinitati Sanctæ beatissimæque Virgini Mariæ genitrici Jesu Xti Petro et Paulo Sanctissimæ Virgini Margaretæ cum omnibus sanctis ac civibus ecclesiæ triumphantis corpusque meum sepeliendum in cancello ecclesiæ predictorum Apostolorum Petri et Pauli de Boudon predictâ Item volo quod constituantur circa corpus meum tempore exequiarum ac sepulturæ meæ quinque torci

In the name, etc., Amen. A.D. 1403, August 23. I, William of Wolstanton, Rector of the parish church of Bowden Magna, in the diocese of Lincoln, being of sound mind and good memory, do make my will as follows : First, I leave and commend my soul to the Holy and Undivided Trinity, to the Most Blessed Virgin Mary, the mother of Jesus Christ, to Peter and Paul, and to the most holy Virgin Margaret, with all the saints and citizens of the Church Triumphant, and my body to be buried in the chancel of the Church of the aforesaid Apostles Peter and Paul, of Bowden aforesaid. Item, I will that there be set up round my body at the time of my funeral *[His will.]*

---

[1] Bp. Beaufort's Reg., Memoranda, fol. 57.

quorum quilibet contineat in pondere quinque libras   Item volo quod unus lapis marmoreus ematur pretii centum solidorum ad ponendum super sepulcrum meum et ut ordinetur et disponatur modo et formâ quibus mei executores me noverint constituisse   Item volo quod omnia debita mea ubilibet persolvantur   Item lego Johannæ de la Mount quinque marcas et unam vaccam ac unum cotagium juxta molendinum ad terminum vitæ suæ quod quidem cotagium post terminum vitæ ejusdem Johannæ meis executoribus totaliter revertatur   Item lego Johannæ de Halle sex solidos et octo denarios   Item lego cuilibet sacerdoti in ecclesiâ de Boudon predictâ tempore exequiarum mearum vjs. et viijd.   Item lego domino Johanni le Scrope portiforium meum de usu Ebor.   Item Willelmo de Ocle viij porcos et iiijor quarteria fabarum   Item lego ecclesiæ Sancti Wilfridi de Kylvyngton xxxs. ad emendum vestimentum quod ad laudem et honorem Dei in dictâ ecclesiâ poterit usitari   Item lego Ricardo Barnard meum optimum equum carectarium   Item lego Johanni le Scrop equum meum vocatum 'prank'   Item volo quod successor meus habeat de bonis meis de libero dono meo unam pelvim cum lavacro ac manutergio et unam mappam unam ollam eneam unum plumbum et unum massefactum, si se habeat erga executores meos benevolum et modestum   Hujus ergo meæ ultimæ voluntatis ac testamenti expletores et executores constituo dominos Johannem Fynche ac Johannem de Alton capellanos ac Ricardum Bernard et Willelmum de Ocle de Boudon predictâ supervisorem vero omnium predictorum constituo

and interment five torches, each containing five pounds in weight. Item, I will that a marble stone be bought at a cost of 100 shillings, to be set over my grave, and that it be ordered and arranged in such form and manner as my executors know that I have appointed. Item, I will that all my debts, wheresoever they may be, shall be discharged. Item, I leave to Joan de la Mounte five marks, a cow, and a cottage next the mill, for the term of her life, which said cottage, after her death, shall wholly revert to my executors. Item, I leave to Joan de Halle 6s. 8d. Item, I leave to each priest in Bowden Church aforesaid at the time of my funeral 6s. 8d. Item, I leave to Sir John le Scrope my breviary[1] of the York use. Item, I leave to William of Oakley 8 pigs and 4 quarters of beans. Item, I leave to the Church of St. Wilfrid of Kilvyngton 30s., to buy a vestment, which shall be used in the said church to the praise and glory of God. Item, I leave to Richard Barnard my best cart-horse. Item, I leave to Sir John le Scrope my horse called 'Prank.' Item, I will that my successor shall have from my goods, of my free gift, a basin, with a bath and hand-napkin,[2] and a table-cloth,[2] a brazen-pot, a weight, and a mash-vat, if he shall bear himself with goodwill and modesty towards my executors. Of this my last will and testament, I appoint as completors and executors, Sir John Fynche and Sir John of Alton, chaplains, Richard Bernard and William of Oakley, of Bowden aforesaid. As overseer of all the above, I appoint Sir John Holt, of Brampton, knight, and to their disposal I entrust and bequeath the

---

[1] Office-book, '*Portos*.' Bury Wills (Camden Soc.), p. 229.
[2] Bury Wills (Camden Soc.), p. 230.

dominum Johannem Holt de Brampton militem, quorum quidem disposicioni commendo et lego residuum bonorum meorum ut ipsi exinde pro salute animæ ac animabus omnium quibus potissime teneor ordinent et disponant qualiter eis videbitur michi commodius expedire In quorum vero omnium et singulorum fidem et testimonium ego Willelmus de Wolstanton Rector antedictus huic testamento ac meæ ultimæ voluntati sigillum meum apposui Datum et actum apud Boudon predictam die et anno domini supradictis.

Memorandum quod quinto die mensis Novembr. A.D. MCCCC. tertio apud Lidyngton probatum fuit dictum testamentum et approbatum et insinuatum et commissa est administracio omnium bonorum dictum defunctum et ejus testamentum concernentium infra dioc. Linc. existentium executoribus in dicto testamento nominatis in formâ juris pro eo quod idem defunctus quamplura bona et diversa in diversis diocesibus tempore mortis suæ obtinuit cujus pretextu ipsius testamenti probacio et insinuacio ac administracio bonorum commissio calculi, etc., ad reverendum patrem Linc. episcopum et nullum alium jure et nomine Ecclesiæ Lincoln. ac consuetudine laudabili, etc., dinoscuntur pertinere, probacione et approbacione administracioneque bonorum commissione et aliis inde secutis, per officialem Archidiaconi Leycestr. contra jura ecclesiæ attemptatis per eundem Episcopum Lincoln. primitus cassatis irritatis ac pro nullis cassis et irritis judicialiter pronunciatis.

rest of my goods, that they may therefrom order and arrange as they shall deem most fitting for me, with the view to the welfare of my soul and of the souls of all to whom I am specially beholden. In witness whereof, all and singular, I, William of Wolstanton, Rector aforesaid, have affixed my seal to this my last will and testament. Given, etc., at Bowden as aforesaid.

In William of Wolstanton we have the first example of a resident rector in priest's orders. The others before him have been either dignified pluralists, or, practically, laymen, having just sufficient of an ecclesiastical character to enable them to hold ecclesiastical revenues. William

William of Wolstanton.

of Wolstanton is a priest, residing and having property at Great Bowden. He cares for his church, for the priests who serve at its altars, and for the rector who shall step into his place. He is on friendly terms with his patron's family. Apparently he is a Staffordshire man by birth, but he has north-country associations and interests. He leaves a vestment to a church in Yorkshire, and his office-book is of the York use. He is a man of substance, with houses and horses, farm-stock and produce, and he does not forget his friends in the disposition of his goods. If we may guess from the name of one of his horses, he is a man of kindly humour, and we can almost fancy we see him enjoying the young colt's vigorous play, as he gives it a name. He is a man who likes a little state, and this taste goes even so far as to influence the ordering of his own funeral; but he is a generous man, and he takes care to reward those who will have the trouble of the funeral arrangements. Altogether the picture is of a wealthy man, whose possessions are in different parts of the country, and, for this last reason, there is a struggle about the probate of the will between the Bishop of Lincoln and the Archdeacon of Leicester, in which the Bishop, as was fitting, was the conqueror.

Discovery on the reverse of the brass in 1886.

At the restoration of Great Bowden Church, in 1886, the brass plate was taken up, and it was found that on the under side was 'engraven, in deeply-incised lines, the figure of a layman under a canopy of tabernacle work of a decorated character.' The following description is given in the *Transactions of the Leicestershire Architectural and Archæological Society*, together with a drawing of both sides of the brass :

'The work appears to be of foreign, perhaps Flemish design, and is incomplete; possibly the wife was also represented on one side. The work appears never to have been finished, the incisions never having been filled up with colour. It was thought by some members that it was probably a subordinate figure of a large brass, never finished, and cut up for use in smaller designs. The figure represented on the under side was that of a man in a civilian's dress of the fourteenth century, bareheaded, with curly flowing hair, beard, and moustache. He was habited in a close-fitting tunic, slightly open at the throat, and buttoned down to the front, with cape covering the shoulders, vandyked at the lower edge. The sleeves of the tunic reached to the middle of the arm between the shoulder and elbow, and then hung down nearly to the knees, showing the sleeve of a very close-fitting undergarment, with buttons, or studs, close together on the outside, reaching to the middle of the back of the hands. The tunic was fastened round the waist by a girdle, buckled on the left side. Nether stocks and shoes, tied in front, covered the lower limbs. The figure of a lion was placed at the feet.'[1]

On the death of William of Wolstanton, William of Husè, or Hosè, became Rector. He has been already mentioned as one of the executors of the will of Stephen le Scrope.

William of Husè, or Hosè, Rector of Great Bowden, 1403.

Willelmus Hosè Rector ecclesiæ de Carleton in Kesteven presentatus per honestum virum Stephanum le Scropp dominum de Masham ad ecclesiam parochialem de Boudon Linc. dioc. per mortem Magistri Willelmi de Wolstanton ultimi rectoris ejusdem vacantem ad quam tertio die mensis Septembris A.D. 1403 apud Lidyngton fuit admissus et Rector institutus canonice in eâdem, nullâ inquisicione previâ, etc.[2]

William Hosè (= Hussey), Rector of Carlton in Kesteven, presented by Stephen le Scrope, Lord of Masham, to the parish church of Bowden, vacant by the death of William of Wolstanton. Instituted at Lydington, September 3, 1403.

Again the rector is non-resident, and possibly not in more than minor orders. There are three entries in Bishop Repingdon's Memoranda which show that William Hose was allowed the same license in regard to residence and the use of church revenues which had been granted to so many of his predecessors.

[1] *Transactions of the Leicestershire Architectural and Archæological Society*, vol. vi., part iv., pp. 222-224.
[2] Bp. Beaufort's Reg., Institutions, fol. 82.

Licenses granted to him.

Magna Bouden dimissio ad firmam.
 Item ultimo die Julii A.D. supradicto (1407) apud Wroxton concessa fuit consimilis licencia domino Willelmo Hosy rectori de Magna Bouden Linc. dioc. quod possit dimittere fructus dictæ ecclesiæ ad firmam per triennium.[1]

Boudon Magna licencia absentare.
 Item eisdem die et loco et anno domini (*i.e.*, August 1, A.D. 1407, apud Wroxton) licenciatum fuit domino Willelmo Hosy, Rectori de Magna Bouden Linc. dioc. quod possit absentare se a dictâ ecclesiâ suâ scolis insistendo per triennium percipiendo interim fructus ejusdem ac si, etc.[2]

Husè dimissio ad firmam.
 Item xxvj^{mo} die mensis Aprilis loco et anno domini supradictis (apud Sleford, A.D. 1408) concessa fuit licencia domino Willelmo Husè Rectori de Magna Bouden Linc. dioc. quod possit dimittere omnes fructus illius ecclesiæ ad firmam domino Johanni Fynche capellano per triennium.[3]

July 31, 1407, at Wroxton, William Hosy, Rector of Great Bowden, receives license to lease the profits of this benefice for three years.

August 1, 1407, at Wroxton, William Hosy, Rector of Great Bowden, receives license to be absent from his church and attend the schools for three years, receiving the profits, etc.

April 27, 1408, at Sleaford, William Husè, Rector of Great Bowden, receives license to lease the profits of his church to John Fynche, chaplain, for three years.

Litigation as to the right of presentation on the death of William de Hose.

William of Hosè, or Husè, held the living till nearly the end of Henry V.'s reign, and on his death the right of presentation to the advowson was a matter of litigation between the widow of Henry le Scrope and Sir William Porter, and it would appear from the following extract from Bishop Repingdon's Institutions that the Lady Marjory won the day. The date of the avoidance of the benefice by William Hosè's death is not known, but that of the final institution of Robert Felton is November 25, 1416. If the reader will refer to the two grants from the King to Sir William Porter, given immediately after the execution of Henry le Scrope, he will see that the first is dated August 8, in the third year, and the second January 15, in the third year. Now, the third year

---

[1] Bp. Repingdon's Reg., Memoranda, fol. xxiii.
[2] *Ibid.*, Memoranda, fol. xxiv.
[3] *Ibid.*, Memoranda, fol. xxvii.

of Henry V., according to the table of regnal years in Sir H. Nicolas's 'Chronology of History,' began March 21, 1415. The second grant was, therefore, six months later than the first. As in the first grant there is no mention of the advowsons of the churches connected with the manors, while in the second they are twice mentioned, it seems probable that the death of William Hose took place either before the forfeiture of the manors or between the two grants, and, if the latter, that the establishing of her right by the Lady Marjory was the reason why the first grant was returned to be cancelled, and a new one made out.

The record of the Institution is as follows:

Institution of Robert Felton presented by the Lady Marjory Scrope, 1416.

Vacante ecclesiâ parochiali de Magna Bowdon Linc. dioc. per mortem Magistri Willelmi Husè ultimi Rectoris ejusdem, prepotens vir dominus Willelmus Porter miles Robertum ffelton clericum ad dictam ecclesiam reverendo in Christo patri et domino domino Philippo Dei gratiâ Linc. episcopo per suas litteras patentes presentavit, super cujus quidem ecclesiæ vacacione ac jure presentantis nunc ad dictam ecclesiam et ultimo ad eandem ac aliis articulis in hâc parte necessariis et consuetis per Archidiaconum suum Leycestr. et ipsius officialem conjunctim et divisim mandavit inquiri, quibus dedit potestatem et commisit vices suas quod, si inquisicio sufficienter faceret pro presentante et presentato, quod ipsum presentatum admitterent instituerent et facerent induci ac cetera peragerent in hâc parte necessaria et oportuna Cujus quidem commissionis vigore prefatus Robertus se ad dictam ecclesiam per dictos commissarios admitti et institui in eâdem ac in corporalem possessionem ejusdem per Archidiaconum loci induci procuravit et obtinuit et sic diucius dictam ecclesiam de facto occupavit Tandem altercato ut

The parish church of Great Bowden, being vacant by the death of William Husè, William Porter, knight, presented Robert Felton, clerk, to the same. After due inquiry, the said Rober Felton was duly instituted and inducted, and held the benefice for some time. A suit, however, arose in the King's Court, as to the right of patronage between the Lady Marjory le Scrope and [Sir William Porter]. The said Robert Felton then renounced his title to the benefice, on the ground of its insufficiency, and procured a fresh presentation, under the hand and seal of the Lady Marjory, under which he was instituted at the Old Temple, London, November 25, A.D. 1416.

dicebatur aliquamdiu in curiâ domini Regis inter nobilem dominam dominam Marjoriam dominam le Scrop pro jure patronatus dictæ ecclesiæ tandem idem Robertus renuncians titulo suo quem prius obtinuit in dictâ ecclesiâ propter ejus insufficientiam, obtinuit se presentari ad eandem ecclesiam per prefatam dominam le Scrop et litteras presentacionis suæ sub sigillo ejusdem dominæ confectas Reverendo patri domino Philippo dei gratiâ Linc. episcopo in camerâ suâ infra hospicium suum apud vetus templum London situatâ exhibuit et realiter demonstravit xxv^{to} die mensis Nov. A.D. 1416 quibus literis per dictum reverendum patrem receptis, admissâ etiam per eundem resignacione dicti Roberti de ecclesiâ predictâ quam ad tunc in sacras manus dicti reverendi patris resignavit, habitâ etiam sufficienti informacione de jure dictæ presentantis, idem reverendus pater eundem Robertum ad dictam ecclesiam de Bowdon Magna, ad quam per prefatam nobilem dominam dominam Marjoriam dominam le Scrop predictam extitit presentatus, admisit et Rectorem instituit canonice in eâdem Nullâ inquisicione previâ quia, etc. Juratâ canonicâ obedientiâ, vero, ut in formâ consuetâ, scriptum fuit Archidiacono Leyestr seu ipsius officiali ad inducendum eundem, etc.[1]

One Town Document, temp. Hen. IV. The one document above mentioned as belonging to the reign of Henry IV. (No. 25, 7 Henry IV., 1406) presents few special points for remark. A steward of the manor, Richard de Leycester, is mentioned for the first time, and two chaplains' names are given—Roger Petlyng and Thomas Bate. Roger Petlyng's name occurs afterwards in No. 50. The property mentioned is another stall in ' le Fleschameles.'

The long reign of Henry VI. lasted from September 1,

[1] Bp. Repingdon's Reg., Institutions, fol. 188.

1422, to March 4, 1461. During this period there were five Bishops of Lincoln—Richard Fleming, who continued till 1431; William Grey, 1431-1436, William Alnwick, 1436-1450, Marmaduke Lumley, 1450-1452, and John Chedworth, 1452.

Here we reach a point in the manorial history at which the records are even more voluminous than at the date of the execution of Henry le Scrope. In Nichols' History there is a distinct gap. He only states that 'William Caleys, or Cales, parson of Aynderby, and William Vincent had a joint grant of the manors, and conveyed and assigned them to John le Scrope, and Elizabeth, his wife, in 1451.'[1] The grants to Sir William Porter by Henry V. are not noticed, and thus there is an unexplained interval of about thirty-six years. If, however, we refer again to the Rolls of Parliament, we find that the family estates were restored to John le Scrope, the brother of Henry le Scrope, in the reign of Henry VI. The process of restoration took some time before it was accomplished, and incidentally it brings out the wealth and dignity of the family, and traces very accurately the line of the entail. John le Scrope was the fourth son of Stephen le Scrope. He is described in history as a friend of the Duke of Gloucester, and as having been made Treasurer of England through the Duke's influence over Henry VI., on February 26, 143½. On the return of Cardinal Beaufort to England changes in the administration were brought about, and on August 11, 1433, Lord Cromwell was made Treasurer.[2] John le Scrope died on November 15, 1455. His will is preserved at York, and has been printed by the Surtees Society.[3] In it mention is made of 'Sir William Caleys, of Ainderby' (*i.e.*, Ainderby, Yorkshire, *not* Enderby, Leicestershire), 'my Confessour.' From this it seems probable that the estates, after they were restored, were again entailed,

Restoration of the estates to John le Scrope, brother of Henry le Scrope.

---

[1] Nichols' Leicestershire: Gartree, p. 490.
[2] Stubbs' Const. Hy., iii. 122, 126.
[3] Testamenta Eboracensia, ii. 193.

and that William Caleys and William Vincent filled the same useful office in 1451 which John of Gunwardeby had filled in the previous century.

Turning, then, to the Rolls of Parliament we find that, as early as A.D. 1421, in the 9th year of Henry V., John le Scrope petitions for the restitution of the forfeited lands, etc.[1] The greater part of them, he declares, were entailed by deed—'par force de certeins donnes ent faitz en la taille a ses auncestres.' He prays that he may be allowed to enter upon them without being compelled to prosecute any suit in Chancery, or in any other court. He is ready to produce evidences of the grant in tail, etc. He pleads his necessities, and his inability to meet the expense of his service to the Crown.[2] This petition seems to have been in part successful, and yet not at once to have won the day, for, in 1423, we find that the Archbishop of Canterbury and the Bishop of Durham bring before Parliament a paper, with reference to a certain matter in dispute between John le Scrope and Henry, Lord FitzHugh. In this there is fuller information as to the claim. Going back to the time of the forfeiture, it is stated that the Duke of Exeter, returning to England after the death of Henry V., recounted how Henry had confessed to the said FitzHugh certain troubles of conscience which weighed upon him, because he had learned that some of Henry le Scrope's lands were entailed, and ought to have passed by force of the entail to his brothers, Geoffrey, Stephen and John. These lands he had granted to FitzHugh and others. FitzHugh declared his willingness to relieve the King's mind by surrendering the lands granted to himself, and Sir William Porter made a similar declaration. The King wished them to restore only those lands to which John le Scrope should prove his right

---

[1] Rolls of Parliament (printed), vol. iv., pp. 160, 161.

[2] 'Que le dit suppliant, pour le temps q'il a este en la service nostre dit Sr le Roy en ses Gueres es parties par dela, a este a ses graundes costages et expenses, quel service il desire de tout son cœur a continuere, et quel desire il sera impotent a perfourmer en caas q'il soit mis a pursuere son dit Droiture par la Commune Leye.'

before the Archbishop of Canterbury, the Duke of Exeter, the Bishop of Durham, and one William Kynwolmersh, clerk. After the King's death John le Scrope produced his evidences, before persons indifferent, in Westminster Abbey. FitzHugh denied that they proved his right. Arbitration was impossible; the parties must be left to the Common Law.[1]

But in spite of this rebuff John le Scrope was not daunted. A little later, in 1425, there is another and a stronger petition from him.[2] In this he partly goes over the same ground as before, and partly brings out new points in the proceedings. He recounts Henry V.'s conscientious scruples, the fact of letters patent having been issued ordering entailed estates to be restored,[3] the production of evidences before the Archbishop, the Duke, the Bishop, and William Kynwolmersh, the stopping of further proceedings by the deaths of the Duke and William Kynwolmersh. Then he states that he has preferred 'divers petitions,' and that 'divers commissions' have been issued and returned into the King's Chancery, by which it was found that the greater part of the estates were entailed. Yet John le Scrope, because of great and wilful delays on the part of certain persons, has not been able to recover, to his great impoverishment, and even to the destruction of his inheritance. He prays that, by authority of the present Parliament, he may have livery of his lands, etc., of which he has been the lawful inheritor now for six years. The answer to this is, that the King, with the assent of the Lords, and at the request of the Commons, grants the entire petition. To this answer, however, a long proviso is added, to the effect that, if at any time it should be found by any escheator, etc., that any of the lands of Henry le Scrope, now restored, were

---

[1] Rolls of Parliament (printed), iv. 213.   [2] *Ibid.*, iv. 287, 288.
[3] The Patent Rolls (2 Henry VI., part iv., M. 5) contain a grant from the King of all the forfeited estates. etc., of Henry le Scrope to John le Scrope, for four years, John le Scrope to prove, within that period, that they were entailed, or to restore to the Crown. Dated at Westminster, February 15.

held at the time of the forfeiture in fee-simple, the King or his heirs may enter upon them. A memorandum is appended that this proviso was added by the advice of the Lords Spiritual and Temporal, and of the King's Serjeants-at-Law.[1]

This caused John le Scrope further trouble before he was quite secure in possession. In 1442, seventeen years afterwards, there is yet another petition,[2] which recites the old one, together with the King's answer and proviso, and then proceeds, in English, to complain that the proviso had been added 'withouten Knowlech or assent of your seide Communez, and ayenst the statuit in suche cas made in tyme of the seide Kyng your noble Fader; of the whiche Estatuit a copy ys annexed to this Bille.' John le Scrope had come before the Bishop of Winchester, the Chancellor 'in the chauncellarie' in Trinity term, and had 'showed his good and sufficiantz taillez,' 'entre' had been granted him, and he had 'enterid and peasibly enjoyed . . . unto now late that Cristofre Conyers, late the Escheitour of Yorks, seised certeins of the seid lordships, etc., unto your noble honds be vertue of certein Inquisitions taken before hym . . . coloured be matier conteyned in the seide clause of Purveu.' . . . . 'In whiche Inquisition hit was founden, be men unenfourmed in eny wise of the right of the seide Besecher.' . . . . that the lands had been held in fee-simple. The petitioner represents that the King can have no avail by the clause of Purveu because all the lands were granted to different persons by Letters Patent. Prayer therefore is urged that 'the King will ordeyne the Besecher's entre may be good, juste, effectuall and availlable in lawe, be auctorite of this same Parliament; the seide Clause of Purveu, or anythyng conteyned thereyn, and all thyng folowed, de-

---

[1] Responsio. Le Roi, de l'assent des Seigneurs esteantz en cest Parlement, et a la request des ditz Communes, ad graunte toute la contenue en la dite Petition. (At the close of the Proviso): Mem. quod ista clausula de Purveu, facta fuit de avisiamento Dominorum Spiritualium et Temporalium et Servientum Domini Regis ad legem.

[2] Rolls of Parliament (printed), v. 41, 42.

pendyng and executed there oppon, notwithstondyng'; that the King will remove his 'hondes' from the lands, and that the Chancellor may be directed to issue the needful writs, etc. The King assents to this petition in every point, and this time without a proviso.[1]

In the foregoing extracts from the Rolls of Parliament mention is made of 'divers commissions' issued to inquire as to the manors which had been forfeited, and of returns from these commissions made to the Chancery. Although these commissions do not add to the story of the restoration of the lands as a whole, yet, incidentally, they bring out the great wealth of the family, and show in what it consisted. On July 5, in the second year of Henry VI., a commission is issued to Henry Percy, Earl of Northumberland, Ralph Nevill, Earl of Westmoreland, and Sir Richard Nevyll, John, Lord Graystock, Robert Tirwhit, and John Preston, with Sir Robert Hilton, Sheriff of Yorkshire, to inquire as to the manor of Masham. The terms of the commission refer to John le Scrope's petition, and to a deed of entail therein stated to have been executed by one John Alburgh, September 22, 13 Edward III. The descent of the estates by this deed (secundum formam donacionis predictæ) is traced down to John le Scrope. The fact of the forfeiture is then recited, and the grant of this forfeited estate to Henry Fitzhugh. The commissioners are to inquire by jury as to the truth of all the matters contained in the petition, and send the result without delay to the Chancery. Then follow other commissions relating to other manors, and in most cases details are given as to the extent of the possessions. Thus the manor of Coverham, Yorks, consisted of 10 messuages, 12 cottages, 3 bovates of land, 12 acres of meadow, and 2s. rent in certain other villages; the manors of Burton

---

[1] Quâ quidem Petitione, in Parliamento predicto lectâ, auditâ et plenius intellectâ, eidem Petitioni de avisiamento et assensu predictis, taliter fuit responsum :

Le Roy, de l'advys et assent de lez Seignrs Espirituels et Temporelx, et lez Communes, esteantz en cest Parlement, ad graunte tout le continue en icell Petition en toutz pointz.

Constable, Clifton, 'Aynderby wyth the Stepill,' Hunton, Garston and Bellerby, contained 14 messuages, 13 cottages, 27 bovates of land, 127 acres of land, and 24 acres of meadow and 12d. rent in two other villages. Later on, a number of Yorkshire manors are all grouped together, and there are said to be, in all, 102 messuages, 24 cottages, 12 tofts, 50 acres of land, 133 acres of meadow, 1,000 acres of pasture, 140 acres of wood, and £33 rent, in 'Masham, Helagh, Ellyngton, Ellyngstryng, Sutton Freerby, Burton Constable,' and other places, to the number of thirty. The manors of Silton and Upsal contain 100 messuages, 24 cottages, 18 tofts, 3 carucates, and 1,000 acres of land, 200 acres of meadow, 1,200 acres of pasture, 330 acres of wood, and £40 rent in those villages and eleven others in various parts of the county.[1] The claim to most of these is based on deeds executed by John of Gunwardeby, similar to the one given above (pp. 35, 36) in connection Bowden and Harborough in 1352.

In the Roll of the next year another group of commissions is recorded. These are concerned in the main with the estates in Essex, but almost at the end of them is one to inquire as to Bowden and Harborough.[2] It is addressed to Sir William de Ferrars of Groby, Sir Richard Hastynges, John Cokayn, James Strangways, Bartholomew Brokesby, and the Sheriff, and follows the lines of the earlier commissions. Unfortunately it gives no details similar to those given with regard to the Yorkshire or the Essex properties. The return made by the commissioners is preserved in part in the Isham MSS., and is now given, because it traces accurately the line of the family descent. But it is imperfect, several folios being missing from the volume in which it is contained. In all probability the missing parts would have given just the detailed information which the record of the commission does not give.

[1] Patent Rolls, 2 Henry VI., Part iii., *a tergo*. See Fisher's History of Masham, where several extracts from Rolls are given.
[2] *Ibid.*, 3 Henry VI., Part i.

Inquisicio capta apud Leycestr. xxvj^{to} die mensis Februarii in Com. Leycestr. anno regni regis Henrici sexti post conquestum Angliæ tertio (*i.e.*, February 26, 142$\frac{5}{6}$) coram Willelmo de Ferariis de Groby milite Johanne Cokayn Jacobo Strangways et Bartholomeo Brokesby Commissionariis dicti domini Regis virtute cujusdam commissionis dicti domini Regis eisdem Willelmo Johanni Jacobo et Bartholomeo ac Ricardo Hastynges militi et Johanni Malory vicecomiti comitatus predicti directæ ad inquirendum per sacramentum, etc. Qui dicunt super sacramentum suum quod Johannes de Gunewardeby per factum suum cujus datum est apud Coverham xxij^{do} die mensis Februarii anno regni domini Edwardi nuper Regis Angliæ tertii post conquestum progenitoris prefati domini Regis nunc defuncti xxx^{to} inter alia dedit Henrico le Scrop militi per nomen domini Henrici le Scrop militis filii et heredis domini Galfridi le Scrop militis et heredibus de corpore suo procreatis maneria de Bowdon et Harburgh cum pertinenciis in comitatu predicto per nomen maneriorum suorum de Boudon et Harburgh in Com. Leycestr. simul cum feodis militum advocacionibus ecclesiarum et capellarum feriis mercatis et libertatibus et omnibus aliis ad eadem maneria pertinentibus absque aliquo retenemento, quæ quidem maneria cum pertinenciis inter alia ipse nuper habuit ex dono et feoffamento predicti domini Henrici, virtute cujus dicti doni prefato Henrico facti ipse fuit seisitus de maneriis predictis cum pertinenciis in dominico suo ut de feodo et de jure per formam donacionis predictæ tempore pacis tempore dicti nuper Regis Edwardi : et expletias inde percepit ut in locacione mesuagiorum bladis herbagio falcacione prati succisione bosci et subbosci red-

Inquest held at Leicester February 26 (3 Henry VI.), 142$\frac{5}{6}$, before William de Ferrars, of Groby, knight, John Cokayn, James Strangeways, and Bartholomew Brokesby, the King's Commissioners, under a commission addressed to them, and to Richard Hastings, knight, and John Mallory, Sheriff of the County, to enquire, etc.

The Commissioners say on oath that on February 22 (30 Edward III.), 135$\frac{3}{5}$, John of Gunewardeby by his deed gave to Henry le Scrope, knight, son and heir of Geoffrey le Scrope, knight (inter alia), the manors of Bowden and Harborough, etc., etc., of which he was seised by the gift and feoffment of the said Henry, and of which he received the profits from the letting of houses, from corn, right of pasture, meadow-mowing, wood and underwood cutting, rents, arrears, etc., to the amount of £20 and upwards according to the terms of the gift.

The title to the manor is then traced, according to the terms of the same gift—

1. To Stephen, son and heir of Henry le Scrope.
2. To Henry, son and heir of Stephen le Scrope, who died without issue.
3. To Geoffrey, brother of Henry le Scrope, who died without issue.
4. To Stephen, brother of Geoffrey le Scrope, who died without issue.
5. To John, brother of Geoffrey le Scrope.

The Commissioners then say that King Henry V. was seised of the manors through a sentence of forfeiture for high treason passed on Henry le Scrope, at Southampton, on Monday, August 5 (3 Henry V.), 1415, before Thomas, Duke of Clarence, and others, which sentence was afterwards

ditibus arreragiis reddituum aliisque modis exituum maneriorum ad viginti libras et plus attingentium ut de feodo et de jure, per formam donacionis predictæ ¶ Et de predicto Henrico descendebat jus maneriorum predictorum cum pertinenciis et descendere debuit Stephano, ut filio et heredi predicti Henrici, per formam donacionis predictæ ¶ Et de eodem Stephano descendebat jus maneriorum predictorum cum pertinenciis et descendere debuit Henrico, ut filio et heredi ipsius Stephani, per formam donacionis predictæ ¶ Et de eodem Henrico filio Stephani, eo quod ipse obiit sine herede de corpore suo, descendebat jus eorundem maneriorum cum pertinenciis et descendere debuit Galfrido, ut fratri et heredi predicti Henrici filii Stephani per formam donacionis predictæ ¶ Et de eodem Galfrido fratre Henrici, eo quod idem Galfridus obiit sine herede de corpore suo, descendebat jus maneriorum predictorum cum pertinenciis et descendere debuit Stephano, ut fratri et heredi predicti Galfridi fratris Henrici per formam donacionis predictæ ¶ Et de eodem Stephano fratre Galfridi, eo quod idem Stephanus obiit sine herede de corpore suo, descendebat jus eorundem maneriorum cum pertinenciis et descendere debuit Johanni le Scrop, ut fratri et heredi predicti Stephani fratris Galfridi, per formam donacionis predictæ ¶ Et quæ post mortem predictorum Henrici patris Stephani et Stephani filii et heredis ejusdem Henrici et Henrici filii et heredis ejusdem Stephani filii Henrici et Galfridi fratris ejusdem Henrici filii Stephani et Stephani fratris ejusdem Galfridi fratris Henrici prefato Johanni Lescrope, ut fratri predicti Stephani fratris Galfridi ac etiam fratri et heredi prefati Henrici filii Stephani, descendere debent per formam donacionis predictæ, eo quod quilibet confirmed by Parliament, that afterwards, the said King Henry, by letters patent, granted the manors to William Porter, knight, for the term of his life.

predictorum Henrici Galfridi et Stephani fratrum predicti Johannis Lescrope obiit sine herede de corpore suo. Et quæquidem maneria cum pertinenciis dominus Henricus nuper Rex Angliæ pater domini Regis nunc defunctus seisivit in manus suas, pretextu cujusdam judicii forisfacturæ de altâ prodicione apud Suthampton versus predictum Henricum filium Stephani per nomen Henrici domini Lescrope de Masham de Flaxflete in Com. Ebor. militis, die Lunæ quinto die Augusti anno regni dicti domini Henrici patris domini regis nunc defuncti tertio, coram Thoma nuper Duce Clarencie et aliis diversis paribus predicti Henrici filii Stephani per ipsum nuper ducem sibi vocatis, virtute cujusdam commissionis ejusdem Henrici patris domini Regis nunc defuncti prefato nuper duci inde directæ redditi. Et quod quidem judicium in Parliamento prefati Henrici patris domini Regis nunc defuncti apud Westm. eodem anno tertio cito postea fuit affirmatum Postmodumque idem Henricus pater domini Regis nunc defunctus eadem maneria cum pertinenciis per litteras suas patentes concessit Willelmo Porter militi pro termino vitæ suæ. ¶ Et sic prefati jurati dicunt—[1]

Thus, in the end, John le Scrope was successful; the forfeited estates were restored to the family in the third year of Henry VI., and he held them till his death in 1455. An Inquisition *post mortem* soon after, (36 Henry VI.), states that 'Johannes Lescrop de Masham, miles' died seised of 'Bowdon Magna maner' and Haverburgh maner', in the county of Leicester.'[2] If the supposition is correct that in 1451 he made a fresh settlement of the estates, it would seem that his widow held them after him, and in 1460 we shall find that she had the right of presentation to the living.

[1] Isham MSS., TT., fol. 245.
[2] Inquis. post mortem, vol. iv., p. 269 (36 Henry VI.), No. 14.

Returning to the history of the benefice, we find that, if Sir William Porter failed to establish his right as patron in 1416, he certainly exercised it in 1425.

John Forster, clerk, Rector of Great Bowden, 1425.

Bowedon Magna Eccl.
5 die. Julii 1425 dominus apud Lambeth admisit Magistrum Johannem Forster clericum ad ecclesiam parochialem de Bowedon Magna Lincoln dioc. sede episcopali ibidem vacante, per resignationem domini Roberti Felton ultimi rectoris ejusdem vacantem ad presentacionem Willelmi Porter Militis ecclesiæ patroni.¹

On July 5, 1425, at Lambeth, John Forster, clerk, was instituted to the Rectory of Bowden, on the resignation of Robert Felton, by Archbishop Chicheley, the See of Lincoln being then vacant, on the presentation of William Porter, Knight, the patron.

In Bishop Alnwick's Institutions is to be found the record of an exchange between this John Forster and John Wraby, priest, Rector of Biddenden, in Kent.

John Wraby, Rector of Biddenden, Kent; Rector of Great Bowden by exchange, 1438.

Permutacio de ecclesiâ de Bowdon et de ecclesiâ de Bydyngdon.
Johannes Wraby, presbiter, presentatus per dominum Johannem dominum le Scrope ad ecclesiam parochialem de Bowdon Linc. dioc. per resignacionem domini Johannis Forster ultimi Rectoris ejusdem ex causâ permutacionis de ipsâ cum ecclesiâ parochiali de Bydynden Cantuar. dioc. quam dictus Johannes ultimus obtinuit in manibus Episcopi factam et per ipsum, tam Reverendi in Christo patris Cantuar. Episcopi totius Angliæ primatûs et Apostolicæ sedis legati sibi commissâ, quam suâ auctoritate ordinariâ, discussis primitus et approbatis causis permutacionis hujus, admissam, vacantem, ad eandem fuit admissus apud Vetus Templum London xvij die mensis Maii A.D. 1438 et Rector ex causâ permutacionis hujusmodi institutus canonice in eâdem, nullâ inquisicione, etc., etc.²

Exchange between Bowden and Biddenden.
John Wraby, priest, presented by John, Lord le Scrope, to the parish church of Bowden, vacant by the resignation of John Forster, on his obtaining the parish church of Biddenden, in the diocese of Canterbury (which resignation was accepted by the Bishop on his own authority, and that entrusted to him by the Archbishop of Canterbury, Primate of all England and Legate of the Apostolic See). Instituted at the Old Temple, London, May 17, 1438.

---

¹ Reg. Chichele, fol. 260, a; Add. MSS., Brit. Mus., 6,078, p. 552.
² Bp. Alnwick's Reg., Institutions, fol. 149; see also Add. MSS. (as before), p. 475.

John Wraby held the living till 1460, and was succeeded by John Lilleford, LL.D., whose institution is recorded in the register of Bishop Chedworth.[1]

Magister Johannes Lilleford legum doctor presentatus per discretam mulierem Elizabeth Scroopp nuper uxorem domini Johannis Scroopp de Upsall ad ecclesiam parochialem de Bowdon Magnâ Linc. dioc. per resignacionem domini Johannis [Wraby] ultimi Rectoris ejusdem in manus domini Episcopi factam et per eum admissam, vacantem, ad eandem xxv die Octobr. Anno Domini 1460 apud London fuit admissus et Rector in personâ Magistri Johannis Woulhouse procuratoris sui sufficienter et legitime in hac parte constituti institutus canonice in eâdem, nullâ inquisicione previâ quia, etc. Juratâ canonicâ obedientiâ, etc. Scriptum fuit Archidiacono Leycestr. seu ejus officiali ad inducendum eundem.

John Lilford, LL.D., presented by Elizabeth Scrope, late wife of John Scrope, of Upsall, to the parish church of Great Bowden, vacant by the resignation of John [Wraby.] Instituted in London, October 25, 1460, in the person of John Woulhouse, his lawful proctor.

John Lilford, LL.D., Rector of Great Bowden, 1460.

In Bishop Alnwick's Memoranda is recorded the will, or an extract from the will, of a parishioner of Harborough, which is of interest as showing that then, as until within recent years, St. Mary's, otherwise St. Mary's in Arden, or St. Mary's in the Fields, was the burial-place for the town. It may be compared with the will of William Neell (No. 33), which belongs to the same reign, and is of very nearly the same date.

Testamentum Katerinæ Caumbrygge.[2]

In Dei nomine Amen die Martis proximo ante festum S. Mathei Apostoli A.D. MCCCCXLIII. ego Katerina Caumbrygge de Haverbrugh compos mentis et sanæ memoriæ condo testamentum meum in hunc modum Inprimis lego animam meam Deo Beatæ Mariæ matri suæ et omnibus

Will of Katharine Caumbrygge, of Harborough.

Dated Tuesday next before the Feast of St. Matthew, 1443. My soul to God, to the Blessed Mary, his Mother, and to all the saints. My body to be buried in the burial-ground of the church of the Blessed Mary in the Fields in Great Bowden. The residue of all my goods not bequeathed I

Will of Katherine Caumbrygge 1443.

---

[1] Bp. Chedworth's Reg., Inst., fol. 99. The name of the last Rector is given as John Kelyng. Probably the entry was made long after date, and this is an error made by the scribe.

[2] Bp. Alnwick's Reg., Memoranda, fol. 49.

sanctis ejus corpusque meum ad sepeliendum in cimiterio ecclesiæ Beatæ Mariæ in campis in Magna Boudon residuum vero omnium bonorum meorum non legatorum do et lego Willelmo Welden Thomæ Baverey de Haverbergh et Willelmo Toft de eâdem Capellano quos facio meos executores pro salute animæ meæ hiis testibus Henrico Smyth de Haverbrugh Thoma Mathon et aliis.

Approbacio dicti testamenti: dato die et loco et anno domini supradictis xvi die Januar. A.D. 1443 apud Lidyngton fuit probatum presens testamentum per dominum Willelmum Toft capellanum executorem ejusdem testamenti exhibitum et probatum, etc., approbatum fuit et commissa fuit administracio dicto domino Willelmo Toft in formâ, etc.

give and bequeath to William Welden, Thomas Baverey, of Harborough, and William Toft, of the same, chaplain (whom I make my executors), for the health of my soul. Witnesses: Henry Smyth, of Harborough, Thomas Mathon, and others. Proved at Lidyngton, January 16, 144¾, by William Toft, chaplain, and administration granted to him.

Town Documents *temp.* Henry VI.

Repair of bridges. 'The great bridge.'

Nineteen of the town documents belong to this reign (Nos. 26-44). In these there are many points of interest. Beginning with names of persons: in No. 26 William Neell, mercer, of Harborough, is first mentioned. No. 33 is his will, and in this we have the mention of St. Mary's as the burial-ground, and a bequest to 'the church of S. Mary and the chapel of Haverbergh.' But this will is especially worthy of note, because in it money is left for the repair of 'the great bridge.' Thus, one of the objects to which the town estate has always been devoted, and one still recognised in the scheme under which it has been administered since 1868, can be traced back to the year 1439. In No. 38 another William Neell is mentioned, and is said to be 'of Keylmersh,' about four miles from Harborough. Probably this was the son of the former, and the one referred to in Nichols' History.[1] It is there stated that in an Act of resumption or adnullation passed in 1455, it was provided that the Act should not extend nor be prejudicial to 'William Neel ... one of our groomes of our chambre, in or for a grant made by us unto him of the £6 6s. 8d. which Geoffrey le Scrope and his heirs to us

[1] Nichols' Leicestershire: Gartree, p. 490.

yerely owe for to be gelde, of the residue of the maner of Boweden and Haverbergh . . . for eight years.'[1]

In No. 27 occurs the name of Everard Digby. This can only be the head of the family of Digby, at that time Lord of Tilton and Stoke Dry, and the ancestor of Sir Kenelm Digby. He was killed at the battle of Towton, in 1461. Along with his name occurs that of Thomas Palmer. He was lord of the manor of Holt, near Medbourne, and died 15 Edward IV. (1475). By marriage with Katharine, his daughter, William Nevill, of Rolleston and Holt, acquired his possessions.[2] This is the first of the documents which suggests the idea of a number of feoffees holding property for the benefit of the town.

<small>Everard Digby.</small>

<small>Thomas Palmer, of Holt.</small>

No. 40 is the first deed which mentions the saint to whom the chapel of Harborough is dedicated—St. Dionysius the martyr. The feast of St. Dionysius is on October 9, and before the change of style, Harborough Fair always began on this day. It seems reasonable to infer from the fixing of the date in this document, that the fair was in existence in that year, viz., 1453. Here also we have the first hint that any sort of cloth manufacture was carried on in the town.

<small>First mention of St. Denis.</small>

There are several names connected with the open fields, or with tenements or other features in the two parishes. Thus, to the list of field-names must now be added 'Branglondis,' afterwards 'Brandlands,' 'le Hayeleyis,' and 'Cranesworth.' 'Le Gallowfield' is now found as the designation of one of the open fields. We have, also, the expression 'against the sun,' which is found in the latest terrars before the enclosure. In No. 29 we have three Bowden names—'Gunnesbrok,' the brook which still runs there, 'Chapelensthing,' as the name of a tenement, and 'le Kylnzerde.' In No. 30 'Haverbergmore' tells us of another piece of waste ground, probably on the hill between Harborough and Bowden, then not brought into cultivation, now neatly enclosed as arable or grazing ground. In No. 35 we learn, for the first time, that Har-

---
[1] See Rolls of Parliament (printed), v. 313.
[2] Visitation of Leicestershire (Harleian Soc.), p. 21.

borough had a market cross, while in Nos. 39 and 41 we have the first inn sign—' le bere super le hoope.'

The reign of Edward IV. began March 4, 1461, and lasted till April 9, 1483. None of the documents now published fall within the brief period (October 9, 1470 to about April, 1471) during which Henry VI. was restored to the throne.

Death of Elizabeth le Scrope, 1466.

Elizabeth le Scrope died in the sixth year of the reign (1466). The Inquisitions *post mortem* record that 'Elizabetha quæ fuit uxor Johannis le Scrop de Massham' was seised of 'Bowdon magna maner' et advoc' ecclesiæ' and 'Haverbargh maner.'[1] The manors then passed to Thomas le Scrope, the third son of John le Scrope, and the fifth Baron. He held them nine years, and died in 1475. In the Inquisitions *post mortem* he is described as 'Thomas Scrope de Masham, miles,' and as having been seised of the two manors.[2] His eldest son, Thomas, held them after him, and lived till 1493. According to Sir Harris Nicolas's note on the Scrope and Grosvenor Roll, the first-named Thomas le Scrope received a pension of 20 marks for services against the House of York.[3] This is the only fact which connects the locality with the Wars of the Roses. Though the Scropes were Lancastrians, the regular succession to their property does not seem to have been affected by the struggle.

Thomas, 5th Lord le Scrope, died 1475.

Thomas, 6th Lord le Scrope, died 1493.

John Kelyng, priest, Rector of Great Bowden, 1463.

In 1463 John Kelyng, priest, became Rector of Great Bowden on the resignation of Dr. John Lilleford.

Dominus Johannes Kelyng presbiter presentatus per Elizabetham le Scrop nuper uxorem domini Johannis le Scrop de Upsall ad ecclesiam parochialem de Magna Boudon per liberam resignacionem Magistri Johannis Lyliford ultimi Rectoris ibidem in manus Episcopi factam et per eum ad-	John Kelyng, priest, presented by Elizabeth le Scrope, late wife of John le Scrope, of Upsall, to the parish church of Great Bowden, vacant by the resignation of John Lilford. Instituted at Stevenhythe (Stepney), October 23, 1463, in the person of John Rudyng, his lawful proctor.

---

[1] Inquis. post mortem (1828), vol. iv., p. 336, No. 41.
[2] *Ibid.*, vol. iv., p. 372, No. 41.
[3] Scrope and Grosvenor Roll, ii. 136. Cf. Rymer's Fœdera (edit. 1741), v. ii., 90.

missam, vacantem, ad eandem xxxiii die Octobris A.D. 1463 apud Stevenhith fuit admissus et Rector in personam Magistri Johannis Rudyng procuratoris sui, etc., institutus canonice in eâdem Nullâ inquisicione previâ quia, etc. Juratâ canonicâ obedientiâ, etc.[1]

John Kelyng held the benefice till 1474, and near the end of his time, in the 12th year of Edward IV., he founded a chantry in the parish church. A copy of the record as to this chantry and its endowment was procured in 1827, and is as follows: *John Kelyng founds a chantry at Great Bowden, 1472.*

Inter Recorda Curiæ Cancellariæ in Turri London' asservata; Scilicet, Inquis: ad quod damnum de anno regni regis Edwardi quarti duodecimo n. 54, sic continetur.

Edwardus Dei gratiâ Rex Angliæ et Franciæ et Dominus Hiberniæ Escaetori suo in Com. Leyc. salutem Precipimus tibi quod per sacramentum proborum et legalium hominum de ballivâ tuâ, per quos rei veritas melius sciri poterit, diligenter inquiras si sit ad dampnum vel prejudicium nostrum aut aliorum, si concedamus Johanni Kelyng clerico, quod ipse novem mesuagia unum molendinum ventriticum centum acras terræ octo acras prati et duodecim acras pasturæ cum pertinenciis in Magna Boudon et Haverbergh dare possit et assignare cuidam capellano perpetuo, divina singulis diebus in ecclesiâ de Magna Boudon in Com. Leyc. pro bono statu nostro ac perdilectissimæ consortis nostræ Elizabeth reginæ Angliæ et ipsius Johannis dum vixerimus et pro animabus nostris cum ab hac luce migraverimus ac pro animâ Excellentissimi principis Ricardi nuper Ducis Ebor

Records of the Court of Chancery. Inquisitions *ad quod damnum* 12 Edward IV., No. 54. 'Edward, by the grace of God, King of England, etc., etc., to his Escheator for the County of Leicester, health, etc.'

The said Escheator (Thomas Ward) is to inquire, on the oaths of trusty and lawful men of his bailiwick, whether it would be to the loss of the King, or of others, for John Kelyng, clerk, to assign to a certain chaplain, 9 messuages, 1 windmill, 100 acres of land, 8 acres of meadow, and 12 acres of pasture, in Great Bowden and Harborough, who shall celebrate the divine offices daily in Great Bowden Church, for the good estate of the King himself, and Elizabeth, Queen of England, his consort, and the said John Kelyng, during life, and after their death for their souls, for the soul of Richard, Duke of York, the King's father, for the souls of the said John Kelyng's parents, friends, and benefactors, and for all the faithful departed, to have and to hold to the said chaplain and his successors celebrating the divine offices, etc., for ever. If to the loss of the King, etc., to what, whose,

---

[1] Bp. Chedworth's Reg., Institutions, fol. 101.

patris nostri et animabus parentum amicorum et benefactorum predicti Johannis ac omnium fidelium defunctorum, juxta ordinacionem in hac parte faciendam celebraturo, Habendum et tenendum eidem capellano et successoribus suis capellanis, divina in ecclesiâ predictâ pro animabus predictis singulis diebus sicut predictum est celebraturis imperpetuum, necne, Et si sit ad dampnum vel prejudicium nostrum aut aliorum, tunc ad quod dampnum et quod prejudicium nostrum et ad quod dampnum et quod prejudicium aliorum et quorum, et qualiter et quo modo et de quo vel de quibus predicta mesuagia molendinum terræ prata et pasturæ teneantur et per quod servicium, et qualiter et quomodo et quantum valeant per annum in omnibus exitibus juxta verum valorem eorundem, et qui et quot sunt medii inter nos et prefatum Johannem de mesuagiis molendino terris pratis et pasturis predictis, et quæ terræ et quæ tenementa eidem Johanni ultra donacionem et assignacionem predictas remaneant et ubi et de quo vel de quibus teneantur et per quod servicium, et qualiter et quomodo et quantum valeant per annum in omnibus exitibus, et si terræ et tenementa eidem Johanni remanentia ultra donacionem et assignacionem predictas sufficiant ad consuetudines et servicia, tam de predictis mesuagiis molendino terris pratis et pasturis sic datis, quam de aliis terris et tenementis sibi retentis debita facienda et ad omnia et singula onera quæ sustinuit et sustinere consuevit, ut in sectis, visibus franci plegii, auxiliis, tallagiis, vigiliis, finibus, redempcionibus, amerciamentis, contribucionibus, et aliis quibuscunque oneribus emergentibus sustinendis Et quod heredes ipsius Johannis in assisis, juratis, et aliis recognici-

and in what way, etc. Of whom the said messuages are held, and by what service, etc. What is the true yearly value, and who are the mesne tenants between the King and the said John Kelyng? What lands and tenements remain to the said John Kelyng, over and above these, of whom and by what service they are held, what is their yearly value, and whether they will suffice for the payment of all dues and services, as well as for the property given as for that remaining? And that the said John Kelyng's heirs in assizes, juries, and other recognisances, may be put in the same position as their predecessors, so that the patrimony may not be unduly burdened by the gift to the detriment of his heirs.

The inquest when truly made to be sent, without delay, under the seals of the Sheriff and Jurors to the Chancery. Westminster, October 26 (12 Edward IV.), 1472.

onibus quibuscumque poni possint prout antecessores sui ante donacionem et assignacionem predictas poni consueverunt Ita quod patrimonia per donacionem et assignacionem predictas in heredum ipsius Johannis defectum magis solito non oneretur seu gravetur Et inquisicionem inde distincte et aperte factam nobis in cancellariam nostram sub sigillo tuo et sigillis eorum per quos facta fuerit sine dilatione mittas et hoc breve. Teste me ipso apud Westm. xxvj die Octobris anno regni nostri duodecimo

DAVYSON

In dorso
Thomas Ward Escaetori infranominato.
Execucio istius brevis patet in quadam inquisicione huic brevi consuta.

Inquisicio capta apud Magnam Boudon in com. Leycr. secundo die Novembris anno regni regis Edwardi quarti post conquestum duodecimo coram Thoma Warde escaetore domini regis in comitatu predicto virtute cujusdam brevis domini regis eidem escaetori directi et huic inquisicioni consuti per sacramentum Thomæ Gilberd de Haverbergh Roberti Janyn de eâdem Willelmi Harper de Boudon magna sen Willelmi Grange de eâdem Ricardi Knight de eâdem Johannis Annes de eâdem Johannis Shepper de eâdem Ricardi Merston de eâdem Willelmi Clerk de eâdem Thomæ Harper de eâdem Ricardi Petnale de eâdem et Rogeri Cristyan de eâdem juratorum proborum et legalium hominum de comitatu predicto. Qui dicunt super sacramentum suum quod non est ad dampnum nec prejudicium domini regis nunc neque aliorum, si idem Dominus rex concedat Johanni Kelyng clerico, in dicto brevi infranominato, quod ipse novem

Inquest held at Great Bowden, November 2 (12 Edward IV.), 1472, before Thomas Ward, Escheator for the County of Leicester, under a writ from the King addressed to him, on the oath of Thomas Gilbert and Robert Janyn, of Harborough, William Harper, William Grange, Richard Knight, John Annes, John Shepper, Richard Merston, William Clerk, Thomas Harper, Richard Petnale, and Roger Cristyan, all of Great Bowden, sworn trusty and lawful men of the county.

The jury say on oath :

That the grant by John Kelyng of the property before enumerated, for the purpose before stated, is not to the King's loss or that of others.

That all the before-mentioned property, except five acres of land, are held of Thomas, Lord le Scrope, of Masham and Upshale, paying yearly to the said Lord le Scrope and his heirs, by way of service, 8s. 11d. yearly, together with a suit of court at Bowden for

mesuagia unum molendinum ventriticum centum acras terræ octo acras prati duodecim acras pasturæ cum pertinenciis in Magna Boudon predicta et Haverbergh dare possit et assignare cuidam capellano perpetuo, divina singulis diebus in ecclesiâ de Magna Boudon in comitatu predicto pro bono statu domini regis nunc ac perdilectissimæ consortis suæ Elizabeth Reginæ Angliæ et ipsius Johannis, dum vixerint, et pro animabus suis cum ab hâc luce migraverint, ac pro animâ excellentissimi Principis Ricardi nuper ducis Ebor patris predicti domini regis nunc et animabus parentum amicorum et benefactorum predicti Johannis ac omnium fidelium defunctorum juxta ordinacionem in hâc parte faciendam, celebraturo, Habendum et tenendum eidem capellano et successoribus suis capellanis divina in ecclesiâ predictâ pro animabus predictis singulis diebus sicut predictum est celebraturis imperpetuum Et ulterius jurati predicti dicunt super sacramentum suum quod mesuagia molendinum terræ prata et pasturæ predicta cum suis pertinenciis, exceptis quinque acris terræ cum pertinenciis de terra predicta, tenentur de Thoma domino Le Scrop de Masham et Upshale, per servicium reddendi inde annuatim eidem domino Le Scrop et heredibus suis octo solidos et undecim denarios et faciendam sectam curiæ suæ de Boudon predicta pro omnimodis serviciis secularibus et cunctis demandis Et quod nulli sunt alii medii inter dictum dominum regem et prefatum Johannem Kelyng de mesuagiis molendino terrâ prato et pasturis predictis cum pertinenciis, exceptis preexceptis, nisi dictus Thomas dominus Le Scrop qui est medius Et dicunt quod mesuagia molendinum terræ prata et pasturæ

all manner of secular services and demands.

That there are no other mesne tenants between the King and the said John Kelyng in regard to the said property.

That the property is of the yearly value of £6 0s. 3d., after all deductions.

That the said five acres are held of William Derby and William Mannyng, by what services the jury know not.

That there are no other mesne tenants of the said five acres between the King and the said John Kelyng.

That the said five acres are of the yearly value of 12d., after all deductions.

That one messuage in Bowden and one messuage in Harborough, with three acres of land, remain to the said John Kelyng, after the said gift; that the messuages are of the yearly value of 40s., after all deductions, and are held of Thomas, Lord le Scrope, by what services the jury know not; and that the three acres of land are held by William Derby and William Mannyng, and are of the yearly value, after all deductions, of 9d.

That the said two messuages in Bowden and Harborough, with the said three acres of land, suffice for all customs and dues in respect as well of the said 9 messuages, 1 windmill, 100 acres of land, 8 acres of meadow, and 12 acres of pasture in Great Bowden and Harborough, as of the other messuages and lands retained, as in suits, view of frankpledge, aids, tallages, etc., etc.

That the heirs of the said John Kelyng, in assizes, juries, and other recognisances, can be placed in the same position as their predecessors before the gift, so that the patrimony will not be unduly burdened to the detriment of his

predicta cum pertinenciis valent per annum ultra reprisas juxta verum valorem eorundem in omnibus exitibus singulis annis exceptis preexceptis, sex libras et tres denarios Et ulterius iidem jurati dicunt quod predictæ quinque acræ terræ cum pertinenciis preexceptæ tenentur de Willelmo Derby et Willelmo Mannyng per quæ servicia jurati predicti penitus ignorant Et quod non sunt alii medii de predictis quinque acris terræ preexceptis inter dictum dominum Regem et prefatum Johannem Kelyng preter Willelmum Derby et Willelmum Mannyng qui sunt medii Et quod illæ quinque acræ terræ cum pertinenciis valent per annum juxta verum valorem eorundem in omnibus exitibus ultra reprisas duodecim denarios Et etiam jurati predicti dicunt quod unum mesuagium cum pertinenciis in Boudon predictâ et aliud mesuagium in Haverbergh predictâ cum tribus acris terræ et suis pertinenciis ibidem ultra donacionem et assignacionem predictas remanent prefato Johanni Kelyng, et valent per annum in omnibus exitibus ultra reprisas quadraginta solidos, et eadem mesuagia tenentur de predicto Domino le Scrop per quæ servicia jurati predicti penitus ignorant, et dicta tres acræ terræ cum pertinenciis in Haverbergh predicta tenentur de dictis Willelmo Derby et Willelmo Mannyng et valent per annum in omnibus exitibus juxta verum valorem eorundem ultra reprisas novem denarios Et dicunt quod predictum messuagium in Boudon et aliud messuagium in Haverbergh cum tribus acris terræ ibidem sufficiunt ad consuetudines et servicia, tam de predictis novem mesuagiis uno molendino ventritico centum acris terræ octo acris prati et duodecim acris pasturæ cum pertinenciis in

heirs. In witness, etc., the Escheator and the jurors have affixed their seals.

The Court was delivered day, year, and place aforesaid, November 19.

Magna Boudon et Haverbergh sic datis, quam de aliis mesuagiis et terris sibi retentis debita facienda, ut in sectis visibus franciplegii auxiliis tallagiis vigiliis finibus redempcionibus amerciamentis contribucionibus et aliis quibuscumque oneribus emergentibus sustinendis Et quod heredes ipsius Johannis Kelyng in assisis, juratis, et aliis recognicionibus quibuscumque poni possint prout antecessores sui ante donacionem et assignacionem predictas poni consueverunt Ita quod patrimonia per donacionem et assignacionem predictas in heredum ipsius Johannis defectum magis solito non oneretur seu gravetur. In cujus rei testimonium huic Inquisicioni tam predictus Escaetor quam predicti jurati sigilla sua apposuerunt Datum die loco et anno supradictis.

Deliberata fuit curia xix die Novembris.

From these extracts it appears that the whole property held by John Kelyng in Bowdon and Haverbergh was: 9 houses, 1 windmill, 100 acres of land, 8 acres of meadow and 12 of pasture, together with 2 other houses (one in Bowdon, and another in Harborough), and 3 acres of land, also in Harborough. The whole of the first-named property he gives for the maintenance of a chaplain to celebrate the Divine offices in Great Bowden parish church. This property (except 5 acres of land) is held of Thomas le Scrope, at a yearly rent of 6s. 11d. The 5 acres of land are held of William Derby and William Mannyng. The yearly value of the whole property is £6 1s. 3d. The value of the property which will remain in John Kelying's possession, after this grant, is £2 0s. 9d., but this is sufficient to pay all dues and customs for all the property. There is no record at Lincoln of the foundation of the chantry, nor of the institution of any chantry priest, but the wills given in this volume prove that the chantry was there, and was duly served.[1] Tradition says that it was on the south side of the church, and that the eastern part of it was afterwards used as the vestry.

The records of a visitation are preserved at Lincoln which, from the mention of John Kelying's name, belongs to this period. Under the head of 'Bowdon' four church-wardens' names are given, viz.: Richard Merston, William Clerk, William Grainge and John Annys. These complain that one, John Typler, had 'kept back' from the church vjd. due for repairs in the same. On the 3rd of June he appears and denies the charge. Also that Johanna Langton, of 'Herburgh,' has 'kept back' iijd., and has done this for ten years. At the foot of this entry there is a short note to the effect that, like so many of his predecessors, John Kelyng was non-resident.[2]

From Bishop Rotherham's Institutions, we learn that John Kelyng resigned the benefice in 1474, and was succeeded by Robert Booth, LL.D.

Magister Robertus Booth Legum doctor presentatus per venerabilem virum Thomam Dominum le Scrop de Massham ad ecclesiam parochialem de Bowdon Linc. dioc. per resignacionem domini Johannis Kelyng ultimi Rectoris ejusdem in manus Reverendi patris Linc. Episcopi factam et per ipsum admissam vacantem Ad eandem x die Jan. A.D. 1474 apud Lincoln fuit admissus et Rector, in personâ Thomæ Howdenby literati procuratoris sui sufficienter et legitime in hâc parte constituti, nunc (?) institutus canonice in eâdem, nullâ inquisicione previâ quia, etc.	Robert Booth, LL.D., presented by Thomas, Lord le Scrope of Masham, to the parish church of Bowden, vacant by the resignation of John Kelyng. Instituted, in the person of Thomas Howdenby, literate, his lawful proctor, at Lincoln, January 10, 1474.	Robert Booth, LL.D., Rector of Great Bowden, 1474.

---

[1] See, especially, the will of William Sotherey, Chantry Priest.

[2] Bowdon: Ric' Merston, Willm Clerk, Willm Grainge, Johes Anys } dic' q^{d.} Johes Typler subtrahit ab ecc' ibm vj*d.* concess' ad reparacionem ejusdem. iij die Junii compt. et negat. Itm Joh'na Langton de herburgh subtrahit ab eadem iij*d.* et subtraxit per x annos.

Dns Joh'es Kelyng non residet.

Juratâ canonicâ obedientiâ, etc. Scriptum fuit Archid. Leyc. seu ejus officiali ad inducendum eundem.[1]

Town documents, temp. Edward IV.

Field-names.

Of the documents now published, thirty-seven belong to this reign, viz.: Nos. 45 to 79. In these we have the following additions to the list of field-names: Bukwelmore (49), Lyttylhill (*ib.*), le Estlonge (*ib.*), le Threnge (*ib.*), Warpart (*ib.*), Lyttylbergh (*ib.*), Snakesyke (*ib.*), Sandefurlong (*ib.*), Musfurlong (*ib.*), Lakefurlong (*ib.*), Yngbarowefelde (No. 54), Fargatys (No. 58), Midillfurlonge (58), Banlonds (58), Comyn marle pytts (58), Efilde (66), Stockefurlong (66), Stretefurlong (66), Shorte Rockhill (66), Netherwylardisgatys (66), Penytherne (67).

Names of streets.

In No. 46 we read of 'Dag Lane' in Harborough. This is the lane leading from the south-east corner of the church to the Sheep Market. In the map published with Harrod's History in 1776, it is called New Street. In No. 71 we have the first instance of a name still in common use—Lubenham Lane—though, since the beginning of the present century, 'Coventry Street,' or 'Coventry Road' has also been used. For the first part of the road 'Lubenham Lane' is the usual name, and this document shows that the name was in use in 1479. In No. 66 it is stated that the arable land and meadows, etc., lie dispersed or scattered (divisim) in the fields of Bowdon. This is put still more distinctly in 49, 'in diversis locis separatim jacentes,' lying separately in different places. No. 59 contains a very full description of the property conveyed, proving it to have been on the west side of the High Street. It also mentions 'the common rope-walk,' and 'the common bakehouse. In Nos. 50 and 51 we find the name of Robert Smyth, who is described as 'bailiff of Haverbergh.' In 56 we meet with Robert Janyn's name. He is there described as 'yoman,' but in 62 he is called 'bailiff of Harborowe and Bowdon,' and in 79 'bailiff of Sybertoft,' six miles off, in Northants. In No. 59 John Kelyng,

---

[1] Bp. Rotherham's Reg., Institutions, fol. 68.

clerk, is mentioned, and his house in Harborough. This also was on the west side of the High Street. In Nos. 62 and 72 the Fishmongers' and Grocers' Companies of London are incidentally mentioned. Henry Pentyng, citizen and fishmonger, was the heir of William Neell before mentioned (see No. 47). The following chaplains' names occur: Thomas Fyssher (50), Roger Petelyng (50), John Belyngham and William Blake (74), and also the following descriptions or designations: 'bucher,' or 'bocher' (50); 'gentelman' (51, 62 and 65); 'husbondman' (54), 'yoman' (56 and 61), 'webster' (65). No. 49 is, perhaps, the most important of all. The situation of the house is clearly defined, and there is no mistake as to where it was. The land, as in all cases before the Enclosure, lies dispersed in the common fields; but the house can be traced through succeeding deeds and leases to the Enclosure Act.

Chaplains' names.

Edward V., the son of Edward IV., and the elder of the two boys, whose supposed murder in the Tower has marked for ever the name of King Richard III., had a short reign, from April 8, 1483, to June 25, 1483. The Camden Society has published the grants made in this short period, and one of these grants relates to the manors of Bowdon and Harborough.

Grant by Edward V., 1483.

Rex omnibus ad quos te salutem. Sciatis quod nos de gratiâ nostrâ speciali ac ex certâ scientiâ et mero motu nostris perdonavimus remisimus et relaxavimus Thomæ Trigot et Willelmo Johnson omnimodas donationes alienationes et perquisitiones de maneriis de Bouden et Haverbergh cum pertinentiis in Com. Leycestriæ, ac de quodam redditu centum solidorum per annum in Heltwelle et Abbeketelby cum suis pertinentiis in eodem comitatu, quæ nuper fuerunt Thomæ Scrop de Massham militis defuncti, et quæ de nobis tenentur in capite per servitium militare, ante hæc tempora factas absque licentiâ regiâ, una cum

The King to all, etc., etc., health, etc.

The King has released and remitted to Thomas Trigot and William Johnson all gifts, alienations, and acquisitions, from the manors of Bowden and Harborough, and from a yearly rent of 100 shillings in Heltwelle and Ab. Kettelby, which were late the property of Thomas Scrope, of Masham, knight, deceased, and which are held of the King in chief by knights' service, which gifts, etc., were heretofore made without the King's licence, together with all issues and profits thence heretofore accruing.

The King has, moreover, granted

exitibus et proficuis inde ante hæc tempora perceptis. Et ulterius de uberiori gratiâ nostrâ concessimus eisdem Thomæ Trigot et Willelmo Johnson omnia et omnimoda exitus proficua et reventiones maneriorum et reddituum predictorum cum pertinentiis ante hæc tempora provenientia et nobis ex causis supradictis seu earum aliqua debita aut aliquo modo nobis ante hæc tempora pertinentia. Habendum et percipiendum, tam per manus suas proprias, quam per manus vicecomitum escaetorum ac nuper vicecomitis et nuper escactoris comitatus predicti seu aliorum occupatorum maneriorum et reddituum predictorum cum pertinentiis pro tempore existentium, adeo plene et integre sicut nos ea haberemus si præsens concessio nostra eis inde facta non fuisset. Eo quod expressa mentio de vero valore annuo maneriorum et reddituum predictorum vel certitudine premissorum aut de aliis donis sive concessionibus per nos eisdem Thomæ Trigot et Willelmo Johnson seu eorum alteri ante hæc tempora factis in presentibus minime facta existit, aut aliquo statuto acto ordinatione seu restrictione in contrarium facto edito sive ordinato, vel aliquâ re causâ vel materiâ quâcunque non obstantibus In cujus rei, etc.[1]

to the same, all manner of issues, profits, and revenues of the aforesaid manors and rents heretofore forthcoming, due or belonging. To have and to hold, etc., etc.

Whoever Thomas Trigot and William Johnson may have been, and whatever was the force or meaning of this grant to them, it seems clear that there had been no forfeiture of the estates. Gifts had been made to them without licence of alienation from the Crown, and are now assured to them notwithstanding such defect of title.

The reign of Richard III. (June 26, 1483, to August 22, 1485) falls within the time when Thomas le Scrope, the 6th Baron, was living. There are no new facts either as to the manors or the church. Dr. Robert Booth continued to hold the benefice until 1487.

[1] Grants by Edward V. (Camden Soc.), p. 51.

Five documents belong to this reign (Nos. 82-86). Of these No. 86 gives four additional field-names: 'Fulforth,' 'Paddokispyltche,' 'Overgyfhoke,' and 'Le Halough.' No. 81 contains the first piece of English. Though the bond itself is in Latin, the condition on the back is in English. It speaks of 'Mekell' Boudon, and, for a long period, the parish was as often called 'Much' Bowden as 'Great' Bowden. Town documents, *temp.* Edward IV.

We now come to the reign of Henry VII., which is reckoned from August 21 or 22, 1485, and which lasted till April 21, 1509. The Bishops of Lincoln were John Russell, who had been consecrated in the reign of Edward IV., and William Smith, consecrated in 1496.

According to the genealogy of the Scropes, given in the notes on the Scrope and Grosvenor Roll, Thomas le Scrope, 6th Baron, died April 25, 1493, and was succeeded by his brother Henry, who died sometime before the 6th Henry VIII., A.D. 1514. He was succeeded by another brother, Ralph, who died September 17, 1515, and he by yet another, Geoffrey, who died in 1517. The barony then went into abeyance among his three sisters.[1] It would appear, however, from the record of the institution given below, that, early in the sixteenth century, the advowson of the church, and therefore, probably, the manors, were in the possession of Elizabeth le Scrope, the widow of the last-named Thomas le Scrope. This genealogy is in contradiction to the one given by Nichols. He states that Thomas le Scrope left an only child, Alice, who married her kinsman Henry, Lord le Scrope, of Bolton, and that in this way the manors passed to that, the older, branch of the family.[2] But Ralph le Scrope's will, dated August 6, 1515, has been printed since Nichols wrote, and in it he leaves the manors of Harborough and Bowden to his brother Geoffrey, for his life.[3] Differences in the Scrope genealogies.

On the death of Dr. Robert Booth, Thomas Bowde was presented to the benefice. Thomas Bowde, Rector of Great Bowden, 1487.

[1] Scrope and Grosvenor Roll, ii. 137.
[2] Nichols' Leicestershire: Gartree, p. 490.
[3] Testamenta Eboracensia, iv. 64.

Magister Thomas Bowde presentatus per Thomam dominum de Scrope de Upsale militem ad ecclesiam parochialem de Bowdon Linc. dioc. per mortem Magistri Roberti Bouth ultimi Rectoris ejusdem vacantem ad eandem vii die Febr. A.D. 1487 apud Oxon' personaliter fuit admissus et Rector institutus canonice in eâdem, nullâ inquisicione previâ, scriptum fuit Archid. Leycr. seu ejus officiali ad inducendum eundem.[1]

Thomas Bowde, presented by Thomas, Lord le Scrope, of Upsale, knight, to the parish church of Bowden, vacant by the death of Robert Bouth, instituted in person at Oxford, February 7, 1487.

The next institution to the benefice to be found at Lincoln does not give the name of the Rector vacating it, but only speaks of his death. If Thomas Bowde was the last Rector, he held the living twenty-one years.

John Chambre, M.D., Rector of Great Bowden, 1508.

Magister Johannes Chambre in medicinis Doctor presentatus per probam mulierem Elizabetham Scrope nuper uxorem domini Scrope de Upsale ad ecclesiam parochialem de Bowden Linc. dioc. per mortem ultimi Rectoris ejusdem vacantem ad eandem ix die Aprilis A.D. 1508 apud Lidyngton fuit admissus et Rector institutus canonice in eâdem, nullâ captâ inquisicione quia etc. Juratâ canonicâ obedientiâ scriptum fuit Archid. Leycr. seu ejus officiali ad inducendum eundem.[2]

John Chambre, M.D., presented by Elizabeth Scrope, late wife of Thomas Scrope, of Upsale, to the parish church of Bowden, vacant by the death of the last Rector. Instituted at Lidyngton, April 9, 1508.

Town documents, temp. Henry VII.

'The dede frō yᵉ friste feffies.'

The documents belonging to the reign of Henry VII. are thirty-two in number, viz., from 87 to 117. Of these No. 115, dated September 24, 1508, is the most noteworthy. It is thus endorsed: 'The dede frō yᵉ friste feffies In truste too oother feffies,' and by it the town estate is traced back, as being under the control and management of a body of feoffees, to the very beginning of the sixteenth century. A comparison of the names in this deed with those in No. 112, dated five years earlier, shows that a considerable part of the property came to the first feoffees from John Janen or Jenyn, and thus, in

---

[1] Bp. Russell's Reg., Institutions, fol. 91.
[2] Bp. Smith's Reg., Institutions, fol. 290.

part, the town estate can be traced to a still earlier date through his father, Robert Jenyn, who was Bailiff of Bowden and Harborough, and though the names of Joye, Smyth, Harper, Swane, and others, in earlier deeds. Various properties seem to have accumulated in the hands of Robert and John Jenyn, and, by the last-named, to have been finally settled for charitable purposes in the town. In the time of Edward VI., an inquiry was held, in which this deed and others were matters of deposition, though they do not seem to have been produced. To the field-names already given, must now be added: 'Shulfebrode' (96), 'More-furlong' (*ib.*), 'Wasshford' (*ib.*), 'Overtoftys' (*ib.*), 'Russhygore' (*ib.*), 'Shortebanham' (*ib.*), 'Pylwelfur-long' (98); while Nos. 103 and 117 give a description with the name, 105 speaks of 'Smeton leys,' and it is endorsed 'for ye leis w'in ye willows in ye horse faire at hau'browge.' This identifies the ground with part of that which, since the Enclosure, has been known as the Horsefair Close. No. 117 speaks of 'a holme called Pyllokesholme;' 'holme' meaning in old records 'a hill, or fenny ground, encompassed with little brooks.'[1] The house to which the lands are attached is one of those already referred to, as situated on the west side of Harborough High Street; probably, therefore, the 'holme' would be part of the rising ground behind, the property there held for so long a period by the feoffees. No. 87 speaks of 'the bridge of Haverbergh.' This must mean what was afterwards called the Chain Bridge, a way for foot-passengers across the Welland on the road to the south. No. 89 tells of a place in Bowden called Hyrn Lane. With this we may connect the name given before, 'Thomas in le Hyrne.' In after-times the three little words coalesced and formed the surname 'Incleherne.' No. 90 speaks of 'le mylne house cum uno molendino equino in dicto messuagio edificato'—'the mill-house with one horse-mill built in

---

[1] Kersey's General English Dictionary, 1721.

the said house.' No. 110 describes another part of Bowden as 'Ferrōs Lane.' A notion of the kind of 'messuage' so frequently mentioned in one place or the other, is given by No. 117, where the tenant is required 'to repeyr as in thacke and modd.' No. 94 gives four names outside Harborough: 'Ralph Shirley, knight; Margaret Staunton, widow; Thomas Kewell, Serjeant-at-Law, and Thomas Entwysall, esquire.' Nos. 99, and 115, give the name of Miles Roos, 'baylly of Myche Bowden and Haverbergh.' No. 95 gives the name of another Everard Dygby, of Stoke Dry, the son of the one who was killed at Towton.

The end of the reign of Henry VII. has been called 'a line of real division in English history, the line at which the Middle Ages, with their forms of life and thought, and their systems of Church and State, land and labour, close: and the age of the New Learning and the New Faith, which are known as the Renaissance and the Reformation, came in to reshape and recast the life and thoughts of men.'[1]

For some reasons it would be convenient at this point to review the facts which have been brought out, and to realize, if possible, the picture which they set before us of Bowden and Harborough before the Reformation. But, in the town documents, there is a very marked break between the twelfth and twenty-fourth years of the reign of Henry VIII., and for this and other reasons, the main facts will be continued up to the year 1530. Before reviewing what has been told, a brief statement will be made as to the other Bowden—Bowden Parva, Little Bowden, or Bowden St. Nicolas—which, as before stated, is so closely connected, geographically and in other ways, with St. Mary-in-Arden and with Harborough.

Henry VIII. began his reign April 22, 1509, and reigned till January 28, 1547. The Bishops of Lincoln during his reign were William Smith, Thomas Wolsey, 1514; William Atwater, 1514-1521, and John Longlands, 1521-

[1] York-Powell's History of England to 1509, p. 369.

1547. The registers are complete only up to 1547, after which date they are imperfect, there being two distinct gaps, viz., from 1547-1560, and from 1608-1660.

Ralph le Scrope, as we have seen, succeeded his brother Henry, and died without issue, September 17, 1515. Geoffrey le Scrope, the last remaining brother, and the 9th Baron, died in 1537, aged thirty-two. The barony then fell into abeyance, and its possessions passed to those of another name.[1] The manors of Bowden and Harborough had been held by the direct line of the Scropes, with one short forfeiture, for just two hundred years. Although there is no documentary evidence to prove the fact, it seems reasonable to suppose that the completion of Harborough Church, and the rebuilding of parts of Great Bowden Church were the work of the Scrope family. The nave of Harborough, and the clerestory of the chancel belong to the fifteenth century, as clearly as the spire belongs to the latter part of the thirteenth, and the work at Great Bowden bears a strong likeness to that at Harborough.

There is no entry of any institution to the Rectory of Bowden in the registers of Bishops Smith, Wolsey, Atwater, or Longlands, and other records do not help to show clearly whether there was a change of Rector or not.

Three different visitation notes give three different Rectors. Happily, while they perplex us on this point, each of them is interesting on others. At a visitation of the Archdeaconry of Leicester, held in St. Mary's, Scraptoft, April 17, 1509, it is recorded that 'Master Chamber' was the Rector of Bowden, and Sir John Freyby's name is given as the only other priest. Miles Rose and Richard Dekyn are wardens. Sir Thomas Kesten is chaplain of Harborough; Thomas Smyth and John Harlande are wardens; they say that all is as it should be.[2] At a visitation held

---

[1] Scrope and Grosvenor Roll, ii. 137.
[2] In visitacione Archidiaconali Leicestriæ tentâ in ecclesiâ parochiali beatæ Mariæ de Scraptoft xvij die mensis Aprilis A.D. M. quinquagesimo nono.
Bowdon Mᵃ M. Chamber, r. ibm. dñs Johes Freyby. Milo Rose

in the parish church of 'Boresworth,' on September 18, in
the same year, by Dr. William Mason, the Bishop's Vicar-
General, no names are given. The Rector of Bowden
failed either to appear, or to pay his dues. The parochial
chaplain of Harborough was present, and said that all
was well.[1] In the next year, also, we have both an
Archdeacon's and a Bishop's visitation, contrary to the
modern custom according to which the Archdeacon omits
his visitation in the years when the Bishop holds one.
The Archdeacon's was held in the parish church of
St. Margaret, Gumley, on April 16. The entry as to
Bowdon Magna gives 'Master Polydore'[2] as Rector, Sir
John Fraby as chaplain, Richard Dekyn and Miles Rose
as wardens. The entry as to Harborough gives Sir
Richard Watkyn as chaplain, William Browne and John
Asplande as wardens. These last acknowledge the ruinous
condition of the chancel of St. Mary's. The entry is badly
written, and is in parts difficult to read, but it is sufficiently distinct to show that the roof, the windows, and the
stone work were very defective. An order is given for
repairs to be done under a penalty of 10s.[3] The Bishop's
visitation was held in the parish church of St. Mary,

Ricus Dekyn. yco. dicunt. Harborough. Dns. Thomas Kesten
Cap^s. Thoms Smyth Johes harlande yco, dicunt omnia bene.

[1] In visitatione ven. viri M'g'ri Willi Mason utriusque juris doctoris
Rev. in Xto. patris et dni dni Willi. d.g. linc. Epis. in Arch. Leyc^r
sequestratoris et communis generalis dicti rev. patris tentâ et celebratâ
in ecclesiâ parochiali de Borresworth xviij die mensis Septr. A.D. 1509.

Bowdon. rec. non p^t neque solvit aliquid. Haverbrugh. cap^s paroch.
p^t omnia bene.

[2] Polydore Vergil was Rector of the adjoining parish of Church
Langton from 1503-1535. Nichols : Gartree, p. 666.

[3] In visitatione domini Archidiaconi Leyc^r tentâ in ecclesiâ parochiali Sanctæ Margaretæ de Gomondeley xvi° die mensis Aprilis anno
MCCCCC decimo.

Bowdon M. Mag'r Polidorus rector

Dns. Johes Fraby Capellanus. Ricardus Dekyn, Milo Rose yconomi
inquisiti dicunt bene.

Harburgh. Dns Ricardus Watkyn capellanus. Willelmus Browne,
Johannes Asplande, yconomi, inquisiti dicunt quod cancellus ecclesiæ
beatæ Mariæ est ruinosus in tector' et latomia [   ] muracione et
In vitriacone fenestrarum et ord' habet ad reparand' eum ante festum
S. Mich. prox. futur. sub pena xs.

Carlton (Carlton Curlieu), on September 19. On this occasion we read, under Bowden, that 'Sir Geoffrey Pyfford,' the Rector, did not appear. John Frayby's name is given as chaplain, William Wayver and Robert Browne as wardens. They report that Robert Dekan, 'farmer' there, has cut down a certain gate on the north side of the churchyard. This gate, commonly called the Parsonage Gate, he had been ordered to repair before the Feast of All Saints. Under Harborough the name of Sir Thomas Kestin is given as parish chaplain, and Sir John Watkyn as chaplain. The wardens, William Weyver and Richard Browne, declare that the will of Thomas Francys was not proved, and had been without probate for half a year.[1]

In addition to these visitations, Nichols states that Wolsey, before he left the See of Lincoln for that of Winchester, held a visitation, and reported as to the churches of the diocese. He gives extracts from this report in one of the notes to the history of Lutterworth, and in this it is stated that Bowden is vacant, and has been so for some time. It has neither Rector, nor Vicar, and the Rectory is held by Mistress Stirlay (Strelley), who acquired it from her husband lately deceased.[2] To reconcile these statements is hopeless, but it would seem that these visitation records are only lists prepared for use beforehand, in which, at the time of the visitations, notes were somewhat hurriedly entered. It is easy to

[1] In visitatione Rev^{di} in X^{to} Patris et dni dni Willelmi d.g. Linc. Epi. tentâ et celebratâ in ecclesiâ parochiali beatæ Mariæ de Carleton nonodecimo die mensis Septr. A.D. M. quingentesimo decimo.

Bowdon. dns Galfridus Pyfford. Rect. non p^{r}. Dñs Johannes ffrayby Cap^{ns} Wills Wayver Rob^{ts} Browne yco. dicunt qd. Robtus dekan desecavit quandam portam cimiterii ex pte boriali quæ porta communiter appellatur 'the parsonage gate,' ord' habet ad rep^{d} citra festum Omn' Sctorum sub penâ incumben.

Haverbrugh. dominus Thomas Kesten cap^{nus} paroch. dominus Johannes Watkyn cap^{nus}. Willmus Weyver, Ricus Browne yco inquis dicunt qd test^{m} Thomæ Francys ibm non est probatum et per medium anni sic remansit.

[2] Nichols' Leicestershire, Guthlaxton, p. 261, note.

Bowden. Vacat, et diu vacat : non habet rectorem nec vicarium. Magistra Stirley (Strelley) habet rectoriam in suos usus ; perquisitam per virum suum, modo defunctum ; sed non antea appropriatam. Fiat melior inquisitio.

understand that errors and slips might be made by clerks or notaries in a diocese of the size of Lincoln, and in days of difficult intercommunication. One other fact remains to be told, which throws doubt on the names of the Rectors in all the later visitation notes. The Valor Ecclesiasticus, or Liber Regis, made in 1534 (26 Henry VIII.), gives the name of Mr. Chambers, as Rector. The value of the benefice is £37, the same as in 1291, when Robert of St. Albans received his dispensation and allowance as a Crusader.

The local interest of these visitation notes is considerable. The names of Miles Rose, or Roos, Richard Dekyn, and William Browne are all found in the town documents. In John Jenen's deed (No. 112) there is a William Browne, baker, and in No. 115, the deed from the first feoffees, he is named as one of the body, together with another William Browne, weaver. The old Rectory of Great Bowden, now the property of Christ Church, Oxford, and long inhabited by their lessee, is at the north-west corner of the churchyard, and there is a gate into the churchyard from the Rectory premises. The reference to the 'chancel' of St. Mary's as being ruinous in certain points, proves that, in the earliest years of the sixteenth century the whole church was standing, while the fact that there is no mention of a separate chaplain, or even separate wardens, leads to the conclusion that, even before the Reformation, St. Mary's was only, or chiefly, the place of burial.

We turn now to the parish of Bowden Parva. The manorial history can only be very roughly summarized. The extract from the Domesday Survey, which describes the Manor of Bugedun, in Northamptonshire, held by Humfrey, Count of Mortain, has already been given (pp. 5,6), and reasons have been stated which lead to the conclusion that the second manor of Bugedun, held by Robert de Buci under the Countess Judith, and reckoned under Leicestershire, was the present parish of Bowden St. Mary, or St. Mary-in-Arden. A reference has also been made to Bridges' 'History of Northamptonshire,' from which it appears that William le Latymer held a certain part of the manor in the 24th Edward I., of the honour of Huntingdon. The descent of this latter manor, or part of a manor, is given with tolerable clearness. It remained, almost entirely, in the hands of the Latimers (who have left their name behind them in Burton Latimer, and after whom Corby was at one time called Corby Latimer) down to the 9th Henry V. (1422), when it passed to the Griffyns; John Gryffyn, the first to hold it, being the grandson of Elizabeth le Latimer. Part of the Latimer property passed into the family of the Burtons by the marriage of Alianore de Latimer with Sir William de Burton in 30 Edward III. (1357), and this gave rise to the names Burton's Fee and Latimer's Fee, as used for different parts of the lordship. But this part came back to the Latimers in 2 Henry IV. (1401), and ultimately the whole of the Latimer property passed to the Griffyns. The descent of that manor, or part of a manor, which did not belong to the Latimers, and was not of the honour of Huntingdon, is not clear. In Edward I.'s reign it was held by William de Oxendon Parva, of the King; in the time of Henry VI. it seems to have been in the possession of the Beaumonts, one of whom was taken prisoner at Towton and attainted. It was granted to Richard Hastyngs by Edward IV., and, in the reign of Henry VII., it was restored to the Beaumonts, and was then stated to be held of Arthur, Prince of Wales, as of the honour of Berkhamsted. The Knights Hospitallers, also, had manorial rights in Bowden Parva, and in the 3rd Edward III. were summoned to show by what authority they held them.[1] The subsequent history of the manor does not belong to the period with which this introduction deals, but it is clear that there was latterly only one lord of the manor, and that the manor included both St. Mary and St. Nicolas. The fact of there being a division within the period now under consideration, and the fact that part was held of the King, and part was of

[1] Bridges' Northamptonshire, ii., pp. 4-6.

the honour of Huntingdon, is a confirmation of what has been suggested in speaking of the manors of Bowden and Harborough, that in the Northamptonshire 'Bugedun' of Domesday, and in the manor held by Robert de Buci of the Countess Judith, who married the Earl of Huntingdon, we have the originals of Bowden St. Nicholas and Bowden St. Mary's, otherwise St. Mary-in-Arden.

The benefice of Bowden St. Nicholas, so far back as it can be traced, was in the gift of the Prior and monks of Launde. It is not mentioned in the earliest documents which enumerate the benefices belonging to that abbey, but it is thus described in a charter of confirmation granted by Hugh, Bishop of Lincoln, about the end of the twelfth century, 'Ecclesiam S. Nicolai de Buggeden de dono Roberti filii Hugonis'—the Church of St. Nicholas, Bowden, the gift of Robert, the son of Hugh.[1]

As in the case of Great Bowden, we shall trace some points in the history of the benefice, and the succession of those who held it, by the help of the Lincoln Registers and other public records.

In the Rolls of Hugh de Welles there are two entries:

John of Rowell, acolyte, Rector of Little Bowden, 1220.

Johannes de Rowell acolitus presentatus per Priorem et conventum de Landa ad ecclesiam de Bugedon factâ prius inquisicione per R. Archid. Northampton. per quam, etc., admissus est et in eâ canonice persona institutus Salvâ Henrico cappellano vicariâ suâ quam habet in eâdem, qui totam ipsam ecclesiam nomine vicariæ suæ quoad vixerit tenebit, reddendo inde dicto Johanni viginti solidos annuos nomine pensionis Injunctum est eidem Johanni ut scolas sub periculo beneficii sui frequentet et addiscat et quod ad proximos ordinaciones domini Episcopi veniat ordinandus Et mandatum est dicto Archidiacono ut, etc., xviii Kal. Octobr. anno undecimo (September 14, 1220).[2]

John of Rowell, acolyte, presented by the Prior and Monastery of Launde to the church of Little Bowden. Instituted September 14, 1220. Reserving to Henry the chaplain the Vicarage he has, who (the said Henry) holds the whole church in the name of his Vicarage for his life, paying therefrom to the said John a yearly pension of xxs.

The said John is ordered, on pain of losing his benefice, to frequent the schools and to learn, and to present himself to be ordained at the next ordination held by the Bishop.

---

[1] Nichols' Leicestershire: East Goscote, p. 302.
[2] Bp. Hugh de Welles' Rolls, Inst. Northampton, 15th year.

Anno 19º Bugedun.

Omnibus, etc. Noverit universitas vestra nos ad presentacionem dilectorum filiorum Prioris et Conventus de Landa patronorum ecclesiæ de Buggedon dilectum in Christo filium Johannem de Rouweil clericum ad eandem ecclesiam admisisse ipsumque in eâ canonice personam instituisse Salvâ Henrico cappellano vicariâ suâ quam habet in eâdem Qui quidem totam ipsam ecclesiam nomine vicariæ suæ tenebit quoad vixerit, reddendo inde predicto Johanni et successoribus suis ejusdem ecclesiæ personis xx solidos annuos nomine pensionis Salvis etiam in omnibus, etc. Quod ut perpetuum, etc. Testibus Magistris W. de Beningworth cappellano. A. de Buggedun et W. de Winchcumb canonicis Lincoln. Magistris R. Beuon (?). Clement. Pigiun et A. de Arundell. Ricardo de Oxon. G. de Moris et Th. de Askerby clericis Datum per manum R. de Waravill canonico Linc. apud Buggeden iii Non. Octobr. pontificatus nostri anno xixº (October 5, 1228.[1]

(The second—four years later—is almost the same as the first. The names of the witnesses are added, viz., W. of Benniworth, chaplain; A. of Bowden, and W. of Winchcombe, Canons of Lincoln; R. Beuon, Clement Pigiun, and A. of Arundel, Richard of Oxford, G. de Moris, and Thomas of Askerby.)

Little Bowden, under the hand of R. de Waravill, Canon of Lincoln, October 5, 1228.

Again instituted 1228.

In the Roll of Bishop Grosteste (1235-1254) there are two entries, both, apparently, referring to the same institution.

Herbertus de Burton subdiaconus presentatus per Priorem et Conventum de Landa ad personatum ecclesiæ de parva Buwedon factâ prius inquisicione per E. Archidiaconum Northampton, per quam, etc., ad eundem admissus est et in eâdem ecclesiâ canonice Rector institutus Salvâ Magistro Henrico vicariâ suâ quam optinet in eâdem ecclesiâ, qui dictam ecclesiam possidet solvendo inde annuatim dicto Herberto xx solidos sterlingorum nomine pensionis et mandatum est dicto Archidiacono ut Herbertum,[2] etc.

Herbert of Burton, subdeacon, presented by the Prior and Monastery of Launde to the 'parsonate' of the church of Little Bowden. Instituted in the 13th year (1248), reserving to Master Henry his Vicarage, etc., etc. (as before).

Herbert of Burton, subdeacon, 'Parson' of Little Bowden, 1248.

---

[1] Bp. Hugh de Welles, 'Rotulus Cartarum,' Northampton, 19th year.
[2] Bp. Grosteste's Roll, Inst. Northampton, 13th year.

Omnibus, etc. Noverit universitas vestra nos ad presentacionem dilectorum in Christo filiorum Prioris et Conventus de Landa patronorum ecclesiæ de parva Buwedon dilectum in Christo Herbertum de Burthon subdiaconum ad eandem ecclesiam admisisse ipsumque in eâdem canonice rectorem instituisse, salvâ dilecto filio Henrico vicario ipsius ecclesiæ vicariâ suâ quam optinet in eâdem quamdiu vixerit honeste in habitu seculari, salvisque in omnibus Episcopalibus consuetudinibus, etc. Quod ut imperpetuum. etc. Hiis testibus, etc.[1]

(The second entry records the institution in the form of a certificate. 'To all, etc. Be it known, etc.' And after the mention of 'Henry,' the Vicar, and his 'Vicarage,' is added, 'so long as he shall live with good report in the secular habit.')

In the Roll of Bishop Gravesend (1258-1280) there are again two entries:

Geoffrey of Cave, Rector of Little Bowden, 1266.

Magister Galfridus de Cava presentatus per Priorem et Conventum de Landa ad ecclesiam de Budon, vacantem per mortem Herberti ultimi rectoris illius, factâ prius inquisicione per E. Archid. Northampton per quam, etc., ad ipsam ecclesiam est admissus apud Aston Sabbato quatuor temporum in septimana Pentecostes anno viii° et in eâ canonice rector institutus et demandatum est dicto Archid. ut ipsum, etc.[2]

Geoffrey of Cave, presented by the Prior and Monastery of Launde to the church of Bowden, vacant by the death of Herbert, the last Rector. Instituted at Aston, the Saturday in Whitsun Week, 1266.

Ralph, son of Ralph de Arnhale, clerk, Rector of Little Bowden, 1274.

x Kal. Octobr. anno XVI. apud Stamford Radulphus filius Radulphi de Arnhale clericus presentatus per Priorem et Conventum de Landa ad ecclesiam de parva Boudon, vacantem per mortem Magistri Galfridi de Cave ultimi rectoris ejusdem, factâ prius inquisicione per E. Archid. Northampton per quam acceptum est, etc., in subdiaconum est ordinatus ibidem et ad dictam ecclesiam admissus et rector canonice institutus in eâdem Quia tamen nondum legitimæ ætatis existit juravit tactis evangeliis sacrosanctis

September 22, 1274, at Stamford, Ralph, son of Ralph de Arnhale, clerk, presented by the Prior and Monastery of Launde to the church of Little Bowden, vacant by the death of Geoffrey of Cave, ordained subdeacon and instituted. Being under the lawful age, he takes oath that until he is of lawful age he will abide by the directions of the Bishop in all things concerning his benefice.

---

[1] Bp. Grosteste's Inst. Roll, Northampton, 15th year (*in dorso*).
[2] Bp. Gravesend's Inst. Roll, Northampton, 8th year.

quod super rata temporis quod restat de ætate suâ stabit ordinacioni domini Episcopi de plano in omnibus quæ ad ecclesiam spectant supra dictam.[1]

No entry occurs as to the benefice of Little Bowden either in the registers of Bishop Oliver Sutton (1280-1300), or of Bishop Dalderby (1300-1320). Ralph de Arnhale, appointed while not of age, and when only in minor orders, held the living for fifty years. In the registers of Bishop Burghersh (1320-1342), is recorded at length the fact of his deposition and deprivation for contumacy, and the institution of his successor.

Ricardus de Whitewell accolitus presentatus per Priorem et Conventum de Landa ad ecclesiam de Boudon parva Linc. dioc. vacantem per diffinitivam sententiam privacionis et amocionis a curâ et regimine ecclesiæ supradictæ contra Radulphum de Arnale, pro Rectore ejusdem ecclesiæ nuper se gerentem et possessioni ipsius ut dicebatur de facto incumbentem, in auditorio episcopi latam prout inferius continetur, factâ prius inquisicione super ætate vitâ moribus et conversacione dicti presentati et aliis articulis consuetis, per quam acceptum fuit quod prefato presentato nichil de canonicis institutis obviare quominus ad dictam ecclesiam admitti deberet, et Rector institui in eâdem, ad dictam ecclesiam est admissus Non. Januarii A.D. 1324 apud Lydyngton et Rector institutus in eâdem Juratâque episcopo canonicâ obedientiâ in formâ consuetâ. Et scriptum est Officiali Archid. Northampton quod, etc. Presentibus Magistris Waltero de Maydenston dicti patris cruciferario Willelmo de Stauren et Johanne de Farendon notario publico.[2]	Richard of Whitwell, acolyte, presented by the Prior and Monastery of Launde to the church of Little Bowden, vacant by reason of the final sentence of deprivation and removal from the cure of souls promulgated in the Bishop's Court, against Ralph de Arnhale, etc., etc. Instituted at Lydington, January 5, 1324. Present: Walter of Maidstone, crucifer to the Lord Bishop, William of Stauren, and John of Farendon, notary.	Richard of Whitwell, acolyte, Rector of Little Bowden, 1324.

---

[1] Bp. Gravesend's Inst. Roll, Northampton, 16th year.
[2] Bp. Burghersh, Reg., Inst., fol. clxiii.

Then follows the account of Ralph de Arnhale's trial, non-appearance, and sentence of deprivation.

According to this lengthy and involved document, Ralph de Arnhale had been instituted and inducted when just about twenty-one years of age, and had persistently refused to be ordained priest as the needs of his benefice required. When called to account for this, before Master Gilbert of Buckingham, the Bishop's Chancellor, he had at first acknowledged his error, but afterwards he had appealed to Canterbury and to the Holy See. In these appeals, though they consumed a good deal of time, he was ultimately unsuccessful, and the Bishop then appoints a commission, consisting of the Abbot of Bourne, and John Harington, Canon of Lincoln, to proceed further with the matter. Before this commission Ralph de Arnhale presents a schedule of exceptions to his own acknowledgment of error. This is discussed, and a day appointed for decision on it. A further commission is then issued to Gilbert of Buckingham, who, after all due formalities have been observed, including that of waiting in Liddington Church for six hours for Ralph de Arnhale to appear, there pronounces him contumacious, and propounds the sentence of deprivation and removal from the cure of souls. The date of the first commission to Gilbert of Buckingham is July 11, 1323, of the commission to the Abbot of Bourne, and John Harington, December 15, 1324, and of the deprivation January 3, 132$\frac{4}{5}$, 'about the ninth hour.' Two certificates are appended: (1) from the Dean of Bow Church (St. Mary de Arcubus), official and commissary of the court of Canterbury, in reference to the appeal; (2) from the Archdeacon of Northampton, dated May 25, 1325, stating that Richard was inducted on January 6, previous.

In the same volume, five years later, is recorded the fact of an exchange between Richard of Whitwell, and Simon Laurence of Preston Capes, Rector of Oadby.

Simon Lawrence,

Simon Laurencius de Presten Capes clericus presentatus per

Simon Laurence, of Preston Capes, clerk, presented by the

Priorem et Conventum de Landa ad ecclesiam de Bouden parva Linc. dioc. vacantem per resignacionem domini Ricardi de Whitewell ultimi rectoris ejusdem, sub nomine permutacionis quam idem Ricardus cum ecclesiâ de Oudeby quam prefatus Simon ut rector prius tenuerat auctorisante Episcopo rite factam, factâ prius inquisicione super articulis inquirendis per quam, etc., ad dictam ecclesiam est admissus iiij Id. Aprl. A.D. 1329 apud Dorkecestr. et Rector in personâ Willelmi de Kyldesby procuratoris sui canonice institutus in eâdem Juratâque episcopo canonicâ obedientiâ informâ consuetâ scriptum est Officiali Archid. Northampton quod ipsum Simonem vel procuratorem, suum, etc.[1]

Prior and Monastery of Launde to the church of Little Bowden, vacant by the resignation of Richard of Whitwell, who exchanged the church with the said Simon Laurence for the church of Oadby, under the authority of the Bishop. Instituted at Dorchester, April 10, 1329, in the person of William of Kilsby, his lawful proctor.

<small>of Preston Capes, Rector of Little Bowden, 1329.</small>

It will be convenient here to insert two extracts from the public records. The first gives the value of the benefice in 1288, the second the assessment on the benefice for a subsidy in 1341.

<small>Taxation of the benefice, 1291.</small>

Taxatio Ecclesiastica P. Nicholai. Dioc. Linc. Decanatus de Rowelle.[2]

Ecclesia de Parva Boudon
£6 13s. 4d.

Beneficia ecclesiastica Ad x marcos et infra taxata quorum possessores aliunde non sunt beneficiati.[3]
Ecclesia de parva Boudon
£6 13s. 4d.

Inquisitiones Nonarum.

Hæc indentura testatur quod Rogerus le Yonge Willelmus Chace Thomas Mayner Ricardus de Foxton Rogerus Abonetoun Alexandrus Wybern Thomas atte Persones Robertus le Merchere Hugo Smyth Thomas Human Alexandrus Bould et Rogerus de

Taxation of Pope Nicholas IV. Lincoln Diocese. Rothwell Deanery.
Little Bowden ... £6 13s. 4d.

Ecclesiastical benefices taxed at 10 marks and under, the holders of which are not beneficed elsewhere.
Little Bowden ... £6 13s. 4d.

This indenture witnesseth that Roger le Yonge, William Chace, Thomas Mayner, Richard of Foxton, Roger Abonetoun, Alexander Wybern, Thomas at Parson's, Robert the Mercer, Hugh Smyth, Thomas Human, Alexander Bould, and Roger of Kel-

<small>Assessment for the subsidy, 1342.</small>

---

[1] Bp. Burghersh, Reg., Inst., fol. clxxi.
[2] Taxation of Pope Nicholas (Record Comm., 1802), p. 39.
[3] *Ibid.*, p. 42b.

Keilmersh jurati coram Abbate Sancti Jacobi extra Northampton et sociis suis assessoribus et collectoribus nonæ garbarum vellerum et agnorum domino Regi in Com. Northampton et Roteland concessorum die Lunæ proximo post festum Sancti Petri in Cathedra anno regni Regis Edwardi tertii post conquestum quinto decimo dicunt per sacramentum suum quod ecclesia de parva Boudon extenditur ad decem marcas.

Item dicunt quod nonæ garbarum vellerum et agnorum ecclesiæ predictæ decima feni oblaciones obvenciones mortuaria vituli porcelli et alia minuta valent hoc anno ij marcas.

Item dicunt quod nulli sunt mercatores seu catallarii ibidem prater illos qui vivunt de agricultura In cujus rei testimonium tam predictus abbas quam predicti jurati predictis indenturis sigilla sua alternatim apposuerunt.[1]

marsh, jurors, before the Abbot of St. James without Northampton and his fellows, assessors and collectors of the ninth sheaf, fleece, and lamb, granted to the King in the counties of Northampton and Rutland, on the Monday next before the Feast of St. Peter in Cathedra, 15 Edward III., 134½, say, on oath, that the church of Little Bowden is valued at 10 marks.

Item, they say that the ninth sheaf, fleece, and lamb, from the said church, the tenth of hay, the gifts, offerings, mortuaries, calves, sucking-pigs, and other small tithes are, this year, worth 2 marks.

Item, they say that there are no traders or dealers there except those who live by agriculture. Sealed by the said Abbot and the jurors.

The date of the proceedings here mentioned appears to be the Monday after February 22, 134½. In the Parliament of January, 1340, 'a ninth sheaf, fleece and lamb were granted by the prelates, barons and knights of the shire for two years.'[2] In the Parliament of 1341, the question of taking means 'for collecting the second year's produce of the last grant' was debated. This was the same Parliament in which Archbishop Stratford defended himself successfully against charges made by the King, and in which the King made important concessions, which he repudiated in the following October.[3] It brings Northamptonshire before us as a sheep-farming district, and Little Bowden, especially, as having no inhabitants, but those who lived by agriculture. The statement of the jurors may possibly be a local illustration of the fact that, owing

---

[1] Inquisitiones Nonarum (Record Comm., 1807), p. 29*b*.
[2] Stubbs' Const. Hy., ii. 415.
[3] *Ibid.*, ii. 421-425.

to the importance at this time of the imports on wool, the King 'began to deal with the merchants collectively apart from Parliament and representative merchants were summoned to wait upon the Council.'[1]

Simon Laurence died in 1346, and his will is entered in the Lincoln Registers, in Bishop Bek's Memoranda:

Testamentum quondam Simonis Rectoris ecclesiæ de Boudon parva.

In Dei nomine Amen die Sancti Jacobi Apostoli anno domini Millesimo CCC^{mo} quadragesimo sexto Ego Simon Rector ecclesiæ de Boudon parva condo testamentum meum in hunc modum In primis lego animam meam Deo et corpus meum ad sepeliendum in ecclesiâ Sancti Nicholai de Boudon parva Item lego ad expensas circa funus meum x marcas Item lego fabricæ matricis ecclesiæ Lincoln. xij denarios Item lego ad capellam Sanctæ Mariæ in ecclesiâ de Boudon parva v marcas et meam cistam meliorem Item lego Thomæ Baddeby vj marcas quas Rogerus cognatus meus habet in manibus Item lego Thomæ Fallisle xx solidos et Johanni fratri ejus xx solidos et Simoni filio Hugonis de Catesby xx solidos et Johanni fratri ejus xx solidos. Item lego cuilibet ex filiolis meis xij denarios Item lego Domino Alexandro le Grene capellano unam dimidiam marcam et domino Johanni Page xl denarios et domino Willelmo in ye crofte x denarios et domino Willelmo in ye feld iij solidos Item lego Hugoni famulo meo equum meum meliorem Item quicquid residuum fuerit de bonis meis non legatum lego executoribus meis Executores meos ordino facio et constituo Hugonem de Catesby Rogerum de Preston cognatos meos et Aliciam sororem meam

Will of Simon, Rector of Little Bowden. St. James's Day, 1346.

My soul to God. My body to be buried in the Church of St. Nicholas. For funeral expenses 10 marks. To the fabric of the Mother Church, Lincoln, 12*d.* To the Chapel of St. Mary in Little Bowden Church 5 marks and my best chest. To Thomas Baddeby 6 marks, which Roger, my kinsman has. To Thomas Fallisle 20*s.* To John, his brother, 20*s.* To Simon, son of Hugh of Catesby, 20*s.* To John, his brother, 20*s.* To each of my godchildren 12*d.* To Sir Alexander le Grene, chaplain, half a mark. To Sir John Page 40*d.* To Sir William in ye Crofte 10*d.* To Sir William in ye Field 3*s.* To Hugh, my servant, my best horse. The rest, etc., to my executors, viz., Hugh of Catesby, Roger of Preston, my kinsmen, and Alice, my sister. May they have God before their eyes, and dispose of it, as shall seem best, for my soul's weal.

Simon Laurence's Will, 1346.

---

[1] Stubbs' Const. Hy., ii. 412, 413.

ut deum pro oculis habeant faciant et disponant pro salute animæ meæ prout melius viderint expedire.¹

William Sumpter of Somerby, Rector of Little Bowden, 1346.

On the death of Simon Laurence of Preston Capes, William Sumpter of Somerby was instituted.² He is described in the record of institution as 'a poor priest (pauper presbiter) of the Diocese of Lincoln,' and as having been instituted in obedience to letters from Rome. But in Bishop Bek's will he is said to be 'chaplain and custodian of the palace at Lincoln.' He receives several bequests, and is named as present when the will was executed.³ It seems probable that the Bishop provided for his chaplain and servant by means of the Papal power, and, if so, it is easy to understand the statement that forty-five years later, in 1390, when the second Statute of Provisors was passed, 'the Bishops protested against the infringement of the Papal right by the Statute.'⁴ In this case the record of institution states that the Bishop had received letters from Pope Clement VI. requesting him to provide for William Sumpter by collating him to some benefice, out of any that may be vacant in the patronage of the Prior and Monastery of Launde. Under the authority of these letters the Bishop had at first issued a commission to Gilbert Weston, Canon of Lincoln. Now, revoking this and any other like commission, and learning that William Sumpter has in due form signified his acceptance of the Rectory of Bowden Parva, vacant by the death of Simon Laurence of Preston Capes, within the time allowed by the Pope, he confers the same upon him, provides for him by that benefice, and invests him personally with the same by the imposition of the biretta.'⁵ William Sumpter reserves his claim under the Papal

---

[1] Bp. Bek's Reg., Memoranda, fol. cvi.
[2] *Ibid.*, inst., fol. lxxviii.
[3] Testamenta Eboracensia, i. 25, 28.
[4] Stubbs' Const. Hy., ii. 528, note 3.
[5] 'Predictam ecclesiam . . . tibi conferimus et de eâ tibi providemus ac te per birretum nostrum investimus presentialiter de eâdem.'

letters, if the benefice should prove to be due to another than himself, and the Bishop declares that what is done shall not derogate from such claim. Letters are appended directing the Dean of Gartree to induct, and the whole record is certified by William de Askeby as notary. It is dated at Lydington on August 10, 1346, 'about the hour of Prime,' and the witnesses are: Master Richard of Retford, D.D. (sacræ paginæ professor); Walter of Greenwich, and Augustin of Stockton, learned in the law (juris periti); Sir Nicholas of Denton, Rector of Wrawby; the Dean of Gartree, and others.[1] The first Statute of Provisors, which checked the Pope's encroachments on patrons' rights, was passed in 1351, and the disputes on the subject, which were carried on for many years, are regarded as one of the precursors of the final break with Rome.[2]

Bishop Gynewell's Registers contain the record of William Somerby's resignation and the institution of his successor.

William Sewale, of Southwell, Rector of Little Bowden, 1349.

Willelmus Sewale de Suthwell presbiter presentatus per Priorem et Conventum de Landa ad ecclesiam de parva Boudon Linc. dioc. vacantem per resignacionem Willelmi de Somerby ultimi rectoris ejusdem, factâ prius inquisicione per officialem Northt. per quam, etc., ad dictam ecclesiam est admissus ij Kal. Dec. anno domini 1349 apud Lydyngton et Rector institutus canonice in eadem Juratâ, etc. Scriptum est, etc.[3]

William Sewale, of Southwell, priest, presented by the Prior and Monastery of Launde to the church of Little Bowden, vacant by the resignation of William of Somerby. Instituted at Lydington, November 30, 1349.

Exchange between William Sewale and William Freeman, Rector of Colwick, 1366.

From Bishop Bokingham's Institutions we learn that on August 16, 1366, William Sewale exchanged with William Freeman, Rector of Colwick, in the Diocese of York. The record is purely formal, and tells nothing of

---

[1] For most of these names see Bp. Bek's will, Test. Ebor., i. 24-28.
[2] Stubbs' Const. Hy., ii. 446. York-Powell, p. 233. Warburton's Edward III. (Epochs of History), pp. 94, 140.
[3] Bp. Gynewell's Reg., Inst., fol. cxxxiiii.

local interest. Both parties appeared in person before the Bishop of Lincoln, at Yardley; the Bishop instituted William Sewale to the Rectory of Colwick, by authority of a commission which is recited, from John, Archbishop of York (John Thoresby), dated at Thorpe by York (Bishopthorpe), November 6, 1365.[1] How long William Freeman held the benefice is not clear. The next institution recorded at Lincoln is in the registers of Bishop Beaufort (1398-1405), but in Bishop Bokingham's Memoranda (fol. ccccxxv.), there occurs the record of a commission of sequestration in the Archdeaconry of Bedford which is addressed to 'our beloved son, Master Thomas Tyberay, Rector of the church of Boudon Parva in our diocese.' The date of this is Aug. 1, 1395. Sometime towards the close of the fourteenth century, the patronage changed hands. From 1228 up to 1365 it was the property of Launde Abbey. But the presentation in 1401 is by Robert Michel, of Harborough, and John Bale. From this date the advowson has remained in what is now called private patronage.

Thomas Tyberay, Rector of Little Bowden.

Change of patronage.

The next Rector, whose institution is recorded at Lincoln is John Cryspe:

John Cryspe, chaplain, Rector of Little Bowden, 1401.

Johannes Cryspe capellanus presentatus per Robertum Michell de Haverbergia domicellum et Johannem Bale vicarium ecclesiæ parochialis de Tokby ad ecclesiam parochialem de Bowdon parva Linc. dioc. per resignacionem Magistri Thomæ Tyberay ultimi Rectoris ejusdem in manibus reverendi in Christo patris et domini domini Henrici dei gratiâ Linc. Episcopi factam et per eundem admissam vacantem, ad quam sexto die Decembr. A.D. MCCCC primo (December 6, 1401) apud Oxon. fuit admissus et Rector institutus canonice in eâdem, Nullâ inquisicione previâ quia,

John Cryspe, chaplain, presented by Robert Michell, of Harborough, gentleman, and John Bale, Vicar of the parish church of Tokby (? Tugby), to the parish cnurch of Little Bowden, vacant by the resignation of Thomas Tyberay, the last Rector. Instituted at Oxford, December 6, 1401.

---

[1] Bp. Buckingham's Reg., Inst., vol. i., fol. 162 *et seq.*

etc. Juratâ canonicâ obedientiâ ut in formâ consuetâ scriptum fuit Archidiacono Northampton seu ejus officiali ad inducendum eundem vel procuratorem suum ejus nomine in corporalem,[1] etc.

In the Memoranda of the same episcopate is an entry which nearly fixes the date of the building of a chapel at Little Oxendon, and shows that even at that time Little Oxendon 'parished' to Little Bowden.

Oxenden oratorium.

Item eisdem die et loco (January 31, 1398) concessa fuit litera incolis et inhabitatoribus hamelettæ de Oxenden parva in parochiâ de Boudon parva Lincoln dioc. quod possent facere celebrari divina in capellâ dictæ hamelettæ nondum dedicatâ.[2]

January 31, 1398, letters granted to the inhabitants of the hamlet of Little Oxendon, in Little Bowden parish, permitting them to have the Divine Offices celebrated in the chapel there, not yet consecrated, at the pleasure of the Lord Bishop.

The chapel of Little Oxendon in Little Bowden parish.

Bishop Repingdon's Institutions record another exchange of livings by which John Cryspe became Master of St. John's Hospital, Lutterworth, and Stephen Brackele, Rector of Little Bowden. The patron is now stated to be John Leyot, Dean of Chester. A later record shows that the presentation of John Cryspe was also made by him.

Exchange between John Cryspe and Stephen Brackele, or Brake, Master of St. John's Hospital, Lutterworth, 1414.

Boudon parva Lutterworth } permutacio.

Stephanus Brackele presbiter presentatus per honestum virum Magistrum Johannem leyot decanum Cestr. ad ecclesiam parochialem de parva Bouden Linc. dioc. per resignacionem domini Johannis Crysp ultimi Rectoris ejusdem ex causâ permutacionis de ipsâ cum hospitali S. Johannis de Lutterworth dictæ dioc. quod ut magister ejusdem ultimo tenuit

Exchange between Little Bowden and Lutterworth.

Stephen Brackele, priest, presented by Master John Leyot, Dean of St. John's, Chester,[3] to the parish church of Little Bowden, vacant by the resignation of John Cryspe, who exchanges the benefice for the Hospital of St. John, at Lutterworth. Instituted at Louth Park, October 1, 1414, in the person of William Mondeyn, his lawful proctor.

---

[1] Bp. Beaufort's Reg., Inst., fol. cxi. (111).
[2] *Ibid.*, Mem., fol. vii.; Bridges' Northamptonshire, ii. 9.
[3] John Leyot, 1395. List of Deans of the Collegiate Church of St. John the Baptist, Chester, quoted in Dugdale's Monasticon, vi., 1448.

faciendæ in manibus domini Episcopi factam et per ipsum, discussis primitus et approbatis causis permutacionis hujusmodi, admissam vacantem, ad eandem fuit admissus apud Parcum Lude primo die mensis Octobris A.D. 1413 et Rector in personâ W. Mondeyn procuratoris sui sufficienter et legitime in hac parte constituti per modum et ex causâ permutacionis predictæ institutus canonice in eâdem, nullâ inquisicione previâ quia, etc., Juratâ canonicâ obedientiâ ut in formâ consuetâ scriptum fuit Archid. Northampton seu ejus officiali ad inducendum eundem vel procuratorem suum ejus nomine, etc.[1]

In Bishop Fleming's Registers a third case of exchange is recorded, and a third name is given as presenting to the benefice. This entry is specially interesting as showing that the advowson of the church was attached to a particular part of the manor.

Exchange between Stephen Brake, or Brakele, and Richard Rychevyl, Rector of Drayton, 1429.

parva Bodon } permutacio.
Dreyton }

Ricardus Rychevyl presbiter presentatus per magistrum Willelmum Mundeyn armigerum ad ecclesiam parochialem de parva Bodon Linc. dioc. per resignacionem domini Stephani Brake ultimi Rectoris ejusdem, ex causâ permutacionis de ipsâ cum ecclesiâ parochiali de Dreyton ejusdem Linc. dioc. quam ut Rector ejusdem ultimo tenuit faciendæ in manibus domini Episcopi factam et per ipsum, discussis primitus et approbatis causis permutacionis hujusmodi, admissam vacantem, ad eandem fuit admissus xx^{mo} die mensis Maii A.D. 1429 apud Lidyngton et Rector in personâ Johannis Storer procuratoris sui sufficienter et legitime in hâc

Exchange between Little Bowden and Drayton.

Richard Rychevyl, priest, presented by William Mundeyn, esquire, to the parish church of Little Bowden, vacant by the resignation of Stephen Brake, who has exchanged the benefice with the parish church of Drayton in the same diocese. Instituted at Lidyngton, May 20, 1429, in the person of John Storer, his lawful proctor.

The said William Mundeyn is the true patron . . . and has full right of presentation . . . by reason of a certain rood of arable land, part of the manor obtained by the said William from John Layet, the true lord of the said rood, to which rood the advowson of the said church is affixed.

---

[1] Bp. Repingdon's Reg., Inst., fol. 256.

parte constituti institutus canonice in eâdem, captâ prius inquisicione per quam compertum est quod dictus Willelmus est ejusdem ecclesiæ verus patronus et habet plenum jus presentandi nunc ad dictam ecclesiam racione cujusdam rodæ terræ arrabilis de manerio Johannis layet dictæ rodæ veri domini per ipsum Willelmum nunc presentantem adepto, ad quam appendens est dictæ ecclesiæ advocacio Juratâ canonicâ obedientiâ ut in formâ consuetâ scriptum fuit Archid. Northampton ad inducendum eundem.[1]

From a later institution it will be seen that William Mundeyn, who was proctor for Stephen Brackele in 1414, received the advowson from the Dean of Chester, and that the presentation of John Cryspe was made by the Dean of Chester, though the names which appear in the institution given above are Robert Michel and John Bale.

Bishop Alnwick's Registers record two more exchanges made by Rectors of Little Bowden, and by these we can trace the passing of the advowson from one patron to another.

Permutacio de ecclesiâ de Bowdon parva et vicariâ de Oxon.

Magister Radulphus Prestbury decretorum doctor presbiter presentatus per Rogerum Clerke ad ecclesiam parochialem de Bowdon parva Linc. dioc. per resignacionem domini Ricardi Rychevyll ultimi Rectoris ibidem ex causâ permutacionis de ipsâ cum ecclesiæ parochialis perpetuâ vicariâ beatæ Mariæ Magdalenæ Oxon' dictæ Linc. dioc. quam ut vicarius perpetuus ibidem ultimo obtinuit faciendæ in manibus Episcopi factam et per ipsum, discussis

Exchange between Little Bowden and a Vicarage at Oxford.

Ralph Prestbury, Doctor of Canon Law, priest, presented by Roger Clerke to the parish church of Little Bowden, vacant by the resignation of Richard Rychevyll, the last Rector, who has exchanged his benefice for the Perpetual Vicarage of St. Mary Magdalene, Oxford. Instituted at Lidyngton, June 12, 1438.

Richard Richevyll exchanges with Ralph Prestbury, Vicar of St. Mary Magdalene's, Oxford, 1438.

---

[1] Bp. Fleming's Reg., Inst., fol. 78.

primitus et approbatis causis permutacionis hujus, admissam vacantem, ad eandem fuit admissus apud Lydyngton xiij die mensis Junii A.D. MCCCCXXXVIII. et Rector per modum et ex causâ permutacionis predictæ institutus canonice in eâdem nullâ inquisicione previâ quia, etc. Juravit canonicam obedientiam; scriptum fuit Archid. Northampton vel ejus officiali ad inducendum eundem.[1]

Ralph Sandon, priest, Rector of Little Bowden, 1442.

Radulphus Sandon presbiter presentatus per honestum virum Rogerum Clerke ad ecclesiam parochialem de Bowdon parva Linc. dioc. per mortem Radulphi Prestbury ultimi Rectoris ibidem vacantem, ad eandem fuit admissus apud Tychemarsche xxviij die Junii A.D. 1442 et Rector institutus canonice in eâdem, factâ prius inquisicione prout per in fine hujus folii Juratâ canonicâ obedientiâ scriptum fuit Archid. Northampton seu ejus officiali ad inducendum eundem.

Ralph Sandon, priest, presented by Roger Clerke to the parish church of Little Bowden, vacant by the death of Ralph Prestbury, the last Rector. Instituted at Titchmarsh, June 28, 1442.

(*At the end of the folio.*)

per quam (inquisicionem) compertum est quod Magister Johannes Layed nuper habuit justum titulum presentandi ad dictam ecclesiam de Boudon parva et fuit in possessione juris advocacionis ejusdem hac vice ut verus patronus suo tempore presentavit dominos Johannem Cryspe et Stephanum Braklay presbiteros successive ad eandem, qui quidem Magister Johannes Layed per cartam suam dedit et concessit Willelmo Munden dum vixit de Boudon parva predicta heredibus et assignatis suis jus et titulum advocacionis ecclesiæ de Boudon predictâ Idem Willelmusque premissarum pretextu in possessione juris advocacionis hujus-

by which inquiry it was found that Master John Layed lately held the right of presentation to the said church ... and was in possession of the advowson, and in his time presented to it, successively, John Cryspe and Stephen Braklay, priests, who, the said John Layed, by his charter, while he lived, gave and granted to William Munden, of Little Bowden, his heirs and assigns, the right and title to the advowson of the said church; that the said William Munden, being in possession of such right, presented one Richard Rechvile to the same, from whom the said William Munden, the beforenamed Roger Clerke, now presenting, and in possession of the

---

[1] Bp. Alnwick's Reg., Inst., fol. 117.

modi existens quondam Ricardum Rechvile presentavit ad eandem ecclesiam de quo quidem Willelmo Munden prenominatus Rogerus Clerke jam presentans ac in possessione juris presentandi existens jus advocacionis patronatus ejusdem ecclesiæ cum suis pertinenciis justo titulo perquesivit ac ultimo presentavit Radulphum presbiterum ad eandem.[1]

right of presentation, acquired the right to the advowson, etc., by lawful title, and has presented Ralph, a priest, to the same.

In Bishop Chedworth's Institutions is a long record of yet one more exchange. In this case Ralph Sandon exchanged with Ralph Spyer, Rector of Lapworth. The date is August 15, 1452. Both parties, Ralph Spyer, in person, and Ralph Sandon, by his proctor, Thomas Colston, notary public, appeared before the Bishop of Lincoln at Grantchester, and gave in their respective resignations. The Bishop then instituted Ralph Spyer to the Rectory of Bowden Parva on the presentation of Roger Clerke, gentleman, of Haloughton, in the county of Stafford, and Ralph Sandon to Lapworth, by virtue of a commission from John, Bishop of Worcester (John Carpenter), dated at his manor of Hillingdon, August 12, 1452. In this commission the presentation to Lapworth is stated to have been made by the Warden and Scholars of Merton College, Oxford (per discretos viros custodem et scolares domus scolarium de Merton in Oxon).[2]

Ralph Sandon exchanges with Ralph Spyer, Rector of Lapworth, 1452.

Ralph Spyer held the benefice eleven years, but the record of his successor's Institution does not state whether it was vacated by his death, or by his resignation. Another change in the patronage took place some time during his incumbency. The advowson became the property of the Griffins, with whom it remained until 1545.[3]

Magister Petrus Rykeman presbiter presentatus per honestum virum Nicholaum Gryffyn Armigerum ad ecclesiam parochialem

Peter Rykeman, priest, presented by Nicholas Gryffyn, Esquire, to the parish church of Little Bowden, vacant. Instituted

Peter Rykeman, priest, Rector of Little Bowden, 1463.

---

[1] Bp. Alnwick's Reg., Inst., fol. 128.
[2] Bp. Chedworth's Reg., Inst., fol. 49.
[3] Bridges' Northamptonshire, ii. 7. See Appendix II., p. 243.

de parva Bowdon Linc. dioc. vacantem ad eandem primo die Novembris A.D. 1463 apud Stevenhithe fuit admissus et Rector institutus canonice in eâdem Nullâ inquisicione previâ quia, etc. Juratâ canonicâ obedienciâ, etc. Scriptum fuit Archid., etc., in personâ Ricardi Karlyll, literati, procuratoris sui sufficienter et legitime in hac parte constituti fuit admissus, etc.[1]

at Stevenhith (Stepney), November 1, 1463, in the person of Richard Karlyll, his lawful proctor.

Three years later Peter Rykeman resigns, and William Sherman is instituted:

William Sherman, priest, Rector of Little Bowden, 1466.

Dominus Willelmus Sherman presbiter presentatus per honestum virum Nicholaum Gryffyn Armigerum ad ecclesiam parochialem de Boudon parva Linc. dioc. per resignacionem Magistri Petri Rykman ultimi Rectoris ibidem in manus Episcopi factam et per eum admissam vacantem ad eandem iiij^{to} die Aprilis A.D. 1466 apud Bukden fuit admissus et Rector in personâ Magistri L. Bertlot procuratoris sui, etc., institutus canonice in eâdem Nullâ inquisicione previâ, etc. Jurata, etc.[2]

William Sherman, priest, presented by Nicholas Gryffyn, Esquire, to the parish church of Little Bowden, vacant by the resignation of Peter Rykman, the last Rector. Instituted at Buckden, April 4, 1466, in the person of Master L. Bertlot, his lawful proctor.

From the same Bishop's Institutions (fol. 95), we learn that Ralph Sandon, on February 28, 1456, exchanged the Rectory of Lapworth for that of Gumley, with J. Hill.

Unlike many of his predecessors, William Sherman held the benefice for a long period. There is no record in the Lincoln Registers until 1503, when, on his death, John Slake was instituted by Bishop Smyth.

John Slake, priest, Rector of Little Bowden, 1503.

Dominus Johannes Slake presbiter presentatus per providum virum Nicholaum Gryffyn militem ad ecclesiam parochialem Sancti Nicholai de Boudon parva Linc. dioc. per mortem domini Willelmi Sherman ultimi Rectoris ejusdem

John Slake, priest, presented by Nicholas Gryffyn, Esquire, to the parish church of Little Bowden, vacant by the death of William Sherman, the last Rector. Instituted at Banbury August 22, 1503.

---

[1] Bp. Chedworth's Reg., Inst., fol. 66.
[2] *Ibid.*, fol. 69.

vacantem ad eandem vicesimo secundo die mensis Augusti A.D. 1503 apud Banbury personaliter fuit admissus et Rector institutus canonice in eâdem Nullâ inquisicione previâ quia, etc. Juratâ canonicâ obedienciâ ut in formâ, scriptum fuit Archid. Northampton seu ejus officiali ad inducendum eundem.[1]

There is but one more record at Lincoln which belongs entirely to the old state of things. John Slake died in 1526, and George Malory was instituted in his place. Six years afterwards there is the record of another institution, but this shows some trace of the great changes made in the reign of Henry VIII., and does not belong to the period included in this volume.

Dominus Georgius Malory clericus presentatus per Thomam Gryffyn armigerum ad ecclesiam parochialem de Bowden parva Linc. dioc. vacantem per mortem naturalem domini Johannis Slake ultimi Rectoris ejusdem ad eandem fuit admissus apud Bowdon predictam ix die mensis Marcii A.D. 1526 et Rector personaliter institutus canonice in eâdem Captâ prius inquisicione per quam compertum fuit etc., juratâ obedientiâ canonicâ Scriptum fuit, etc.[2]	George Malory, clerk, presented by Thomas Gryffyn, Esquire, to the parish church of Little Bowden, vacant by the death of John Slake, the last Rector. Instituted at Bowden, March 9, 1526.

Georgo Malory, clerk, Rector of Little Bowden, 1526.

Comparing the records as to the benefice of Little Bowden with those already given as to Great Bowden, there are points of likeness, and points of difference. The first record is remarkable as showing that sometimes the 'Parson' or Rector of a parish was not only practically a layman, living a lay life, and taking minor orders as a qualification for holding the benefice, but that he received only a sort of pension, or, as we should say, rent-charge, from the profits of the benefice, the rest being reserved for the 'Vicar,' who was resident, and

Comparison between the records as to the two Rectories, Great and Little Bowden.

[1] Bp. Smyth's Reg., Inst., fol. 214.
[2] Bp. Longland's Reg., Inst., fol. 98.

who was engaged in the offices and duties of the church and parish.

Up to the time when the benefice was held by Simon Laurence of Preston Capes, whose tenure lasted from 1329 to 1346, the Rectors were, as in the case of Great Bowden, only in minor orders. But after that time the Rectors of Little Bowden were nearly all in priest's orders. Simon Laurence himself was a man of substance, but his successor is described as a 'poor priest' of the diocese, and was attached to the Bishop's household. Non-residence in each case seems to have been the rule. Only William of Wolstanton is known to have been buried at Great Bowden, only Simon Laurence at Little Bowden. The average tenure of the benefices is short, and exchanges, especially in the case of Little Bowden, are frequent.

Extracts from the lists of ordinations at Lincoln.

At this point a few extracts may usefully be given from the entries in the lists of ordinations preserved at Lincoln. These are not so perfect as the Institutions. Yet they are too numerous to be given entire. In some episcopates they are altogether missing. Those which are now printed will help to fill up what is wanting in the picture of the Church before the Reformation in these parishes. The names, etc., will be given in English.

Bishop Bek.

BISHOP BEK (1342—1347).

In the Parish Church of All Saints', Northampton, by Thomas, Bishop of Annadown (Enachdunensis), 'die Sabbati iiii^{or} temporum xv Kal. Jan. A.D. 1345,' *i.e.*, Saturday in Ember Week, December 18, 1345.

Deacons unbeneficed: John Browne, of Harborough, on a title from Pipewell Abbey.

In the same Bishop's Memoranda, Richard Gryffyn, of Great Oxendon, subdeacon, is granted leave to be advanced to the order of deacon; and on March 27, 1346, at Buckeden, Robert, son of William atte Thorn, of 'Parva Bowdon,' deacon, is granted leave to be ordained priest, and Roger, son of Robert Waryn, of 'Harberge,' acolyte, to be ordained subdeacon.[1]

Bishop Beaufort.

BISHOP BEAUFORT (1398—1405).

General ordination by the Bishop himself in the Conventual Church of Peterborough, Ember Saturday (Feast of St. Matthew), 1398.

Acolytes unbeneficed: John Merston, of Great Bowden.

---

[1] Bp. Bek's Reg., Mem., fol. xxxiv., xliii.

General ordination in the Church of the Austin Friars, at Stamford, Ember Saturday (the Vigil of Trinity), 1399, by 'Willelmus episcopus Prissinensis.' 'Vice et auctoritate Reverendi in Christo patris et domini Henrici d.g. Linc. Episcopi de mandato Ven. viri Magistri J. Burbache legum doctoris canonici Ecclesiæ Linc. dicti Reverendi patris in remotis agentis in spiritualibus vicarii generalis.'

Subdeacons unbeneficed: John Merston, of Great Bowden, on a title from St. Mary's Abbey, Leicester, to all the holy orders.

Priests unbeneficed: John Bell, of Harborough, on a title from Sulby Abbey.

Ordination by Bishop Beaufort, in the Prebendal Church of Lidyngton, Ember Saturday, in the first week of Lent, A.D. 1399.

Deacons unbeneficed: John Merston, of Great Bowden, on a title from St. Mary's Abbey, Leicester.

10 Kal. Januar. 1402 (December 23, 1402), by 'Willelmus episcopus Prissinensis,' in the Prebendal Church of Lidyngton.

Acolytes unbeneficed: John Couper, of Harborough.

March 6, 1402, by the same, in the same church.

Acolytes unbeneficed: Thomas Prentys, of Harborough.

BISHOP REPINGDON (1405—1420).

Bishop Repingdon.

In the Parish Church of Holbech, Lent ordination, 1425, by the Bishop.

Deacons unbeneficed: Richard Coft, of Harborough, on a title from Pipewell Abbey.

Priests unbeneficed: Thomas Smyth, of Bowden, on a title from Sulby Abbey.

BISHOP FLEMING (1420—1431).

Bishop Fleming.

Ember Saturday, next after the Feast of St. Lucy, by John Bishop of Soltania, at Lidyngton.

Deacons unbeneficed: John, son of Richard Baxster, of Great Bowden, on a title from Sulby Abbey.

xv. Kal. Marcii 1423 (February 15, 1423), by the same, at Lidyngton.

Subdeacons unbeneficed: John, son of John Sadyler, of Harborough, on a title from Sulby Abbey, to all the holy orders.

Priests unbeneficed: John Baxster (as before).

vi. Id. Aprilis 1424 (April 8, 1424), at Lidyngton, by John, 'episcopus Ancoradensis.'

Deacons unbeneficed: John Sadyler (as above).

Trinity, 1424, at Lidyngton, by the same.

Priests unbeneficed: John Sadyler (as above).

BISHOP ROTHERHAM (1472—1480).

Bishop Rotherham.

Id. Marcii A.D. 1474 (March 15, 1474), by Thomas, 'episcopus Rathlurensis,' in the Prebendal Church of Sleaford.

Acolytes unbeneficed: William Burton, of Harborough.

On the Vigil of Trinity, 1477, by the same, in the Parish Church of All Saints', Northampton.

Acolytes unbeneficed: John Wakelyn, of Great Bowden.

Subdeacons unbeneficed: William Cristian, of Great Bowden, on a title from Pipewell Abbey.

On the Vigil of St. Matthew (September 20, 1477), in the Prebendal Church of Banbury, by Thomas, Bishop in the Catholic Church.
Deacons unbeneficed: William Cristian (as above).

xiii. Kal. Jan. 1477 (December 20, 1477), in the Prebendal Church of Buckden, by Thomas, 'episcopus Rathlurensis.'
Acolytes unbeneficed: Robert Annes, of Great Bowden.

v. Kal. April 1479 (March 28, 1479), in the Parish Church of St. Mary at the Bridge, Stamford, by the same.
Subdeacons unbeneficed: John Wakelyn, of Bowden, on a title from Pipewell Abbey.

xiv. Kal. Octobr. 1479 (September 18, 1479), in the Prebendal Church of Lidyngton, by the same.
Acolytes unbeneficed: John Annes, of Bowden.
Subdeacons unbeneficed: Robert Annes, of Bowden, on a title from Sulby Abbey.
Deacons unbeneficed: John Wakelyn (as above).

xiv. Kal. Jan. 1479 (December 19, 1479), in the Parish Church of Luton, by the same.
Deacons unbeneficed: Robert Annes (as above).
Priests unbeneficed: John Wakelyn (as above).

iv. Kal. Marcii 1479 (February 26, 14$\frac{79}{80}$), in the Prebendal Church of Buckden, by the same.
Priests unbeneficed: Robert Annes (as above).

On the Vigil of Trinity, 1480, by the same, in All Saints', Northampton.
Deacons unbeneficed: John Annes, of Bowden, on a title from Hengham Castle.

Bishop Russell.

BISHOP RUSSELL (1480—1496).

On the Vigil of Trinity, 1481, in the Prebendal Church of Lidyngton, by Thomas, 'episcopus Rathlurensis.'
Acolytes unbeneficed: John Marshall, of Harborough.

On the Vigil of St. Matthew (September 20, 1488), in the Prebendal Church of Buckden, by John, Bishop of Lincoln.
Acolytes unbeneficed: Thomas Parson, of Bowden.

1st Sunday in Lent, 1490, in the same, by Augustine, Bishop of Lydda.
Acolytes unbeneficed: John Christian, of Bowden.
Subdeacons unbeneficed: John Bridgeman, of Harborough, on a title from Sulby Abbey.

March 19, 1490, in the Prebendal Church of Lidyngton, by the same.
Acolytes unbeneficed: Thomas Wellingore, of Harborough.
Deacons unbeneficed: John Bridgeman, of Harborough.

1st Sunday in Lent, 1491, in the Prebendal Church of Buckden, by the same.
Subdeacons unbeneficed: John Christian, of Bowden, on a title from the Carthusian Priory near Coventry.
Priests unbeneficed: John Bridgeman (as above).

April 7, 1492, in St. Mary's, Stamford, by the same.
Deacons unbeneficed: John Christian (as above).

September 22, 1492, in the Prebendal Church of Bikyllswade (Biggleswade), by the same.

Subdeacons unbeneficed: John Marshall, of Harborough, on a title from Sulby Abbey.

December 22, 1492, in the Parish Church of St. Paul, Bedford, by the same.

Deacons unbeneficed: John Marshall (as above).

Priests unbeneficed: John Marshall (as above); John Christian (as above).

BISHOP THOMAS WOLSEY (1514).

[Bishop Thomas Wolsey.]

1st Sunday in Lent, 1513, in the Prebendal Church of Buckden, by John, Bishop of Mayo.

Acolytes unbeneficed: Thomas Westby, of Harborough.

Such are the main facts as to the history of these parishes gathered from the Bishops' Registers, and the most accessible of the Public Records; and such are the chief points of local interest to be traced in those documents, which, at Harborough, have escaped decay and destruction, and are in the possession of the town at the present time. Do they help us, in any way, to form a picture of life here in pre-Reformation times? Can we, by the aid of these fragments, see anything that is clear and accurate as to the conditions and development of that life, or learn how the local institutions of to-day have their roots in the deep soil of the past?

In attempting to find an answer to these questions the first point which suggests itself is the manor. Without doubt the manors of Bowden and Harborough exist to-day, and the right to hold them, and the succession of holders, can be traced with tolerable certainty from the days of Edward the Confessor until now. But the picture of the manor suggested by the pre-Reformation records is something very different from that singularly quiet and little-known institution under which men now live, and the relations of the lord of the manor to the dwellers in the manor are of a very different character in the two periods. The manor of old times, even as it is made known by the scattered and fragmentary notices which have been given, must have been one great dominant fact in the life of all who lived and worked here. In the earliest record of all, the manors include 23 'villanes,' 25 'bordars,' 13 sokeman, and 1 serf. The 'sokeman' held his land in the *soc*, or franchise of a lord, and had to pay suit to a lord's court, or soken. The 'villein,' with his family, was in a state of subjection to his lord, could be disposed of with the land, yet had cattle of his own, and some comforts and rights. The 'bordar,' or cottager, a little lower in the social scale then the 'villein,' was, nevertheless, like him, in a semi-servile state, but his services were 'more continuous, more trivial, and more servile.'[1] The serf was his lord's bondsman, a little lower still than the 'bordar.' All were in varying degrees dependent on the lord, to an extent which most of us in modern days find it hard to understand. Historians tell us that the tendency of 'both law and social habit' under the Norman Kings was to bring all those thus described in the Domesday Survey into one class, that of born villeins,[2] and for a time, at any rate, to depress the condition of that one class, while, on the other hand, the beginnings of education through the monasteries, the Black Death, the rise of guilds, the wars of the great families, and other causes, ultimately righted the balance and raised the general condition of the people. Some of these influences, *e.g.*, the existence of guilds, and the attraction of the monasteries, are to be traced in these records and documents. But the means by which the feudal system in its day was maintained can also be traced. The mills of the lord of the manor, let out at a rent, at which the tenants were bound to grind their corn; the 'aids,' 'suits of court,' market tolls, the 'expletiæ,' or

---

[1] Pioneers and Progress of English Farming (R. E. Prothero), p. 10. For the discussion and explanation of some or all of these denominations, see Stubbs' Const. Hy., vol. i., chap. xi.; Seebohm's Eng. Village Community, chap. ii.; Sir H. Ellis, Introd. to Domesday. A popular summary is given in Domesday Book by W. de Gray Birch, F.S.A. (S.P.C.K.).

[2] Stubbs' Const. Hy., i. 428. On the manor generally, see the same work (i. 451 *et seq.*); Seebohm's English Village Community, chap. iii.; Denton's England in the Fifteenth Century, Introd. (part i.), and chap. ii.

profits, 'in locacione mesuagiorum bladis herbagii falcacione prati succicione bosci et subbosci,'[1] and all forms of rent and service. The question naturally occurs how far the services of the men of the Bowdens and Harborough were required in war? When Henry III. called up a force to besiege Rockingham, only twelve miles off,[2] when Edward I. marched into Scotland, when Henry le Scrope followed the king to Crecy, in the days of the terrible struggle between Lancaster and York, at Towton or at Wakefield, at Barnet or at Northampton, may we think that some from these quiet inland towns and villages followed and fought, because they had no choice but to do so?[3] There is no indication in these records or documents to give an answer; but, at least, there is proof that the land never lacked cultivators, and that the quiet stream of local life went on almost unruffled by the storms of national conflict. The lords of the manor, the kings, or the heads of the great Yorkshire house, formed their plans, and chose their sides, and no doubt called on some of their 'men' on these manors to do them service; but all the while the land is tilled and the crops are gathered, both land and houses change hands in due form, charitable gifts are made, and there is no sign of desolation or ruin in a district where at that time no fierce battle took place.

[1] See above, p. 87.   [2] Stubbs' Const. Hy., ii. 35.

[3] In Rymer's Fœdera are abundant details as to the raising of a force at a particular time from the different counties. Thus, *e.g.*, in 1339 Henry, Earl of Lancaster, Thomas of Astley, and William Trussel are to supply from the county of Leicester xxx. men-at-arms (homines ad arma), cxx. armed men (homines armati), and cxx. archers (sagittarii), out of a total force of 1,247 men-at-arms, 6,230 armed men, and 5,600 archers (edit. 1821, ii. 1070-72). In 1346 the Mayors, Bailiffs, etc., etc., of different cities and towns are commanded to see that certain armed men, etc., are chosen, arrayed, tried, and furnished with horses and armour, and brought to the King at Portsmouth within a certain time. The Bailiffs of Harborough are to supply 3 armed men, those of Leicester 12, of Melton 4, of Loughborough 3 (*ibid.*, iii. 71). In 1350 there is a similar demand. The place of gathering is Sandwich. Harborough is to send 1, Leicester 6, Melton 2, Lutterworth 1 (*ibid.*, iii. 193, 194). In 1360, men arrayed from the counties of Nottingham, Derby, Leicester, Rutland, and Northampton are to go to the defence of the sea-coast of Lincolnshire (*ibid.*, iii. 471).

If we pass from the manor to the lords of the manor, the facts which have been stated tell of the rise and fall of a great family. The younger son of a Yorkshire house rises high in the service of his king, and is rewarded with gifts. His son settles the property in due form, is a soldier fighting with the king abroad, or a courtier, filling high office and mingling in the strife between persons or parties at home. Another descendant is in office in Ireland, and a witness of one of the tragedies of our history; another, after gaining the confidence of his sovereign, is accused, condemned, and executed for high treason. A little later, and his forfeited estates are restored to his brother. For nearly a hundred years they remain with the descendants of him to whom they were restored, until, at last, on the very 'edge of the storm,' in the early part of the sixteenth century, the last of four brothers dies young, the peerage becomes extinct, and these manors, only a small part of very large possessions, pass to those who are near of kin, but who bear another name.

The name of Geoffrey le Scrope, the founder of this branch of the great Yorkshire house, and the first holder of the manors, is not prominent in the pages of the histories of England, and some of the biographers of the judges make no mention of it.[1] But in the records it is a name of frequent occurrence, and a reference to those only which have been printed shows that he had a busy and varied career. A Chief Justice seems, in his day, to have played many parts. To treat with 'them of Scotland,' or the representatives of the King of France, on terms of peace;[2] to inquire as to the price paid by the men of Ripon to save their city from being harried and burnt;[3] to see to the safe-guarding of the city of York;[4]

---

[1] Lord Campbell, Lives of the Chief Justices (i. 85, 86), omits Geoffrey le Scrope, though he notices his brother Henry; Foss, Judges of England (iii. 493-502), gives an account of both the brothers.
[2] Rymer's Fœdera (edit. 1821), ii. 434, 437, 524, 577, 578, 704, 1065, etc.
[3] *Ibid.*, ii. 437.
[4] *Ibid.*, ii. 711.

to negotiate as to the espousals of David of Scotland, or the son of the King of France and the King's sister;[1] to cross over with the king to France;[2] to make inquiry as to those who spread false and dangerous rumours;[3] to open the Parliament at York;[4] to see to the condition of Pontieu;[5] to negotiate with any of the nobility of France, etc., with a view to procuring a wife for John of Cornwall, the King's nephew, and to inquire, not only as to the future wife's dower, but as to her birth, manners, and personal beauty[6]—these are only a few out of the many duties which Geoffrey le Scrope discharged in company with archbishops, bishops, nobles and knights, in the course of his long life, while other records bear witness to his more regular legal work as itinerant justice, or as sitting in his own court. He seems to have been one of those useful and trusted servants of kings, whose work is unceasing, though, from a historical point of view, it is always in the background. And the king recognised his services by other gifts than those of the manors of Bowden and Harborough. In the year 1340 Edward III. grants him and his heirs a yearly pension of 200 marks, in consideration of his faithful, unwearied and continuous services to the king himself, to his father, and of the expense he has been put to in rendering them, and that he may be able to prepare for a voyage across the sea in attendance on the king. The year is the same in which he died.[7]

[1] Rymer's Fœdera (edit. 1821), ii. 730, 766. [2] *Ibid.*, ii. 764.
[3] *Ibid.*, ii. 775. [4] *Ibid.*, ii. 848.
[5] *Ibid.*, ii. 870, 884. [6] *Ibid.*, ii. 883.
[7] Rymer's Fœdera (edit. 1821), ii. 1123: 'Attendentes grata et utilia obsequia quæ dilectum et fidelem Galfridum Lescrop, domino Edwardo, nuper Regi Angliæ, genitori nostro, et nobis, tam in Angliâ, presertim in officio Justiciarii et consiliarii ipsius genitoris nostri, nostrique, et totius regni nostri Angliæ, communia negotia laboriosè et providè dirigendo, quam in partibus Scociæ, et etiam in partibus transmarinis, se variis periculis exponendo, novimus multipliciter impendisse; necnon labores continuos et indefessos, ac sumptus et expensas intolerabiles, quos ipse . . . sustinuit temporibus antedictis. Nos, premissorum contemplatione, ac pro eo quod prefato Galfrido jam districtius diximus injungendo, quod se decentius quo poterit parari faciat et nobiscum in proximo passagio nostro ad partes transmarinas se transferat,' etc., etc.

It is interesting to find that in his prosperity he cared for others, and, after the manner of his day, was ready to help them. The same records relate how, when the Abbey of Coverham, through the wasting inroads of the Scots, lay almost in a state of destitution, Geoffrey le Scrope gave them the advowson of Sedbergh, which was accordingly appropriated to them, that from its revenues they might provide for their needs.[1]

Henry le Scrope, his son and successor, seems to have followed in his father's footsteps, except that he did not hold any judicial office. His name also is one of frequent occurrence in the records. He is an ambassador to treat with the Scots;[2] a commissioner to defend the sea-coast of Yorkshire when invasion is threatened;[3] he is one of those who have charge of David Bruce, and make agreement to surrender him to his fellow-countrymen;[4] he is governor of Calais, of the province of Guienne, and of other possessions across the sea;[5] he, also, can be trusted to negotiate royal marriages;[6] he investigates the exportation of gold and silver;[7] negotiates foreign alliances and terms of truce,[8] and settles strife between nobles at home.[9] It is an equally busy and fully as varied a life, and yet one not prominent in historical pictures.

But there are three members of the family whose names are to be found in Shakespeare, and as we read of them in his writings, we seem to see, to some extent, what manner of men they were. It is Sir Stephen le Scrope, according to Shakespeare, who breaks the tidings of utter ruin to Richard II. The scene is laid on the coast of Wales. The King, with the Bishop of Carlisle and others, hails his own land, and compares his return to the sun chasing away the night. Bolingbroke's treasons shall vanish as the evil things of night at sunrise; the Lord's anointed must reign:

[1] Rymer's Fœdera, ii. 780.   [2] Ibid., iii. 215.   [3] Ibid., iii. 245.
[4] Ibid., iii. 263, 279, 281, etc., etc., 365, 367, 372.
[5] Ibid., iii. 625, 636, 684, 687, etc., 722, 761, 829, 881.
[6] Ibid., iii. 636, 744, 750.   [7] Ibid., iii. 775.
[8] Ibid., iii. 793, 828, 836, 933.   [9] Ibid., iii. 971, 1011.

> 'Not all the water in the rough rude sea
> Can wash the balm from an anointed king:
> The breath of worldly men cannot depose
> The deputy elected by the Lord.'

The Earl of Salisbury enters. He brings tidings of the defection of the Welsh:

> 'O, call back yesterday, bid time return,
> And thou shalt have twelve thousand fighting men!
> To-day, to-day, unhappy day! too late,
> O'erthrows thy joys, friends, fortune, and thy state:'

Richard is dismayed, and becomes pale with fear. He is cheered by others, and for the moment recovers:

> 'Awake, thou coward majesty! thou sleepest.
> Is not the King's name twenty thousand names?
> Arm, arm, my name! a puny subject strikes
> At thy great glory.'

But Scrope enters to tell the worst little by little:

> 'More health and happiness betide my liege,
> Than can my care-tun'd tongue deliver him.'

He tells first of the power of Bolingbroke:

> 'Like an unseasonable stormy day,
> Which makes the silver rivers drown their shores,
> As if the world were all dissolv'd to tears:
> So high above his limits swells the rage
> Of Bolingbroke, covering your fearful land
> With hard bright steel, and hearts harder than steel.'

He then tells how Bushy and Green have fared, how they have made 'peace' with Bolingbroke:

> 'Their peace is made
> With heads, and not with hands: those whom you curse
> Have felt the worst of death's destroying wound,
> And lie full low, grav'd in the hollow ground.'

After a passionate mournful soliloquy from the King, the Bishop consoles him, and, as a last hope, asks where the Duke of York is with his force:

> 'Say, Scroop, where lies our uncle with his pow'r?
> Speak sweetly, man, although thy looks be sour.'

Then Scrope tells the worst:

> 'Men judge by the complexion of the sky
> The state and inclination of the day:
> So may you by my dull and heavy eye,
> My tongue hath but a heavier tale to say.

> I play the torturer, by small and small,
> To lengthen out the worst that must be spoken :
> Your uncle York is join'd with Bolingbroke,
> And all your northern castles yielded up,
> And all your southern gentlemen in arms
> Upon his party.'

The King gives up all hope :

> 'Let them go
> To ear the land that hath some hope to grow,
> For I have none :
> *   *   *   *   *
> Discharge my followers : let them hence away,
> From Richard's night, to Bolingbroke's fair day."[1]

In the second part of 'King Henry IV.' the Archbishop of York, a former Rector of Bowden, is drawn by the same master-hand. He is not a common conspirator bent on personal gain. His soul is full of the wrongs of others, and of the evils of the time. He is persuaded to join with those who are scarcely so disinterested as himself, and he is too honourable to carry conspiracy to a successful issue. So he falls easily into the snare prepared for him, disbands his followers, and is taken to be condemned to death. Perhaps the finest passage ascribed to him is that in which he pours forth his contempt for the fickle multitude :

> 'Let us on ;
> And publish the occasion of our arms.
> The commonwealth is sick of their own choice ;
> Their over-greedy love hath surfeited :
> An habitation giddy and unsure
> Hath he, that buildeth on the vulgar heart.
> O, thou fond many ! with what loud applause
> Didst thou beat heaven with blessing Bolingbroke,
> Before he was what thou wouldst have him be?
> And being now trimm'd in thine own desires,
> Thou, beastly feeder, art so full of him,
> That thou provok'st thyself to cast him up.
> So, so, thou common dog, didst thou disgorge
> Thy glutton bosom of the royal Richard ;
> And now thou wouldst eat thy dead vomit up,
> And howl'st to find it ! What trust is in these times?
> They that, when Richard liv'd, would have him die,
> Are now become enamour'd on his grave :
> Thou, that threw'st dust upon his goodly head,

---

[1] King Richard II., Act III., scene ii.

> When through proud London he came sighing on
> After th' admired heels of Bolingbroke,
> Cry'st now, "O earth, yield us that King again,
> And take thou this!" O thoughts of men accurst!
> Past and to come seem best; things present, worst.'[1]

The third member of the family who is delineated in Shakespeare, is the Henry le Scrope who died a traitor at Southampton. But in this case the delineation is not to be traced in any words of his own. The Second Act of the tragedy of 'King Henry V.' opens with an explanation by the Chorus, how the King is about to sail on an expedition into France, but treachery is at work:

> 'O England!—model to thy inward greatness,
> Like little body with a mighty heart,—
> What mightst thou do, that honour would thee do,
> Were all thy children kind and natural!
> But see thy fault! France hath in thee found out
> A nest of hollow bosoms, which he fills
> With treacherous crowns; and three corrupted men,—
> One, Richard, Earl of Cambridge; and the second,
> Henry, Lord Scroop of Masham; and the third,
> Sir Thomas Grey, knight, of Northumberland,—
> Have, for the gilt of France (O guilt, indeed!)
> Confirmed conspiracy with fearful France.'

The second scene opens at Southampton, in the Council Chamber. The Duke of Exeter, the Duke of Bedford, and the Earl of Westmoreland enter first, and speak with one another of the traitors, their fair-seeming behaviour, and the King's knowledge of their treachery. Then the King and the conspirators enter together. The King commands the Duke of Exeter to set free a prisoner who had 'railed' against the royal person. The traitors dissuade the King from the act of mercy. The King refuses to change his purpose:

> 'We'll yet enlarge the man,
> Though Cambridge, Scroop, and Grey—in their dear care,
> And tender preservation of our person—
> Would have him punish'd. And now to our French causes.'

Then, feigning to hand them their appointments as state commissioners in his absence, he hands, instead, to each,

---

[1] 2 King Henry IV., Act I., scene iii.

the formal indictment for treason. They at once confess and appeal for mercy. But mercy cannot be their due, on their own showing:

> 'The mercy, that was quick in us but late,
> By your own counsel is suppress'd and kill'd;
> You must not dare, for shame, to talk of mercy;
> For your own reasons turn into your bosoms,
> As dogs upon their masters, worrying them.'

Then, turning to his lords, the King speaks to them briefly of the guilt of Cambridge, but at last breaks forth in words of keen and indignant rebuke to Scrope himself:

> 'What shall I say to thee, Lord Scroop? Thou cruel,
> Ingrateful, savage, and inhuman creature!
> Thou that didst bear the key of all my counsels,
> That knew'st the very bottom of my soul,
> That almost mightst have coin'd me into gold,
> Wouldst thou have practised on me for thy use?'[1]
> * * * * *
> O, how hast thou with jealousy infected
> The sweetness of affiance! Show men dutiful?
> Why, so didst thou: seem they grave and learned?
> Why, so didst thou: come they of noble family?
> Why, so didst thou: seem they religious?
> Why, so didst thou: or are they spare in diet;
> Free from gross passion, or of mirth or anger;
> Constant in spirit, not swerving with the blood;
> Garnish'd and deck'd in modest complement;
> Not working with the eye, without the ear,
> And, but in purged judgment, trusting neither?
> Such, and so finely bolted, didst thou seem:
> And thus thy fall hath left a kind of blot,
> To mark the full-fraught man, and best endued,
> With some suspicion. I will weep for thee;
> For this revolt of thine, methinks, is like
> Another fall of man.'

After each has been arrested, Scrope speaks:

> 'Our purposes God justly hath discover'd:
> And I repent my fault more than my death;
> Which I beseech your highness to forgive,
> Although my body pay the price of it.'[2]

The persevering and ultimately successful efforts of his brother, John le Scrope, to recover the forfeited estates

---

[1] 'Quem dictus dominus rex plus aliis diligebat et cui contra quamplures sibi emulos gratitudinis maxime insignia exhibebat.'—Quoted in Drake's Eboracum (Appendix, p. xvi.), from the York City Registers.

[2] King Henry V., Act II., Prologue, and scene ii.

have been already told. None of the later heads of the family come prominently into notice.

Following the same order which has been observed in giving the extracts from the records and registers, an attempt must be made to trace some features in the life and condition of the church. As to the buildings themselves, the churches of Great Bowden, Little Bowden and Harborough bear witness, each in its own way, to that long process which reduced the rough heathenism of England to something like Christianity. Little Bowden has been so altered, and so dealt with in the course of alteration, that only a skilled mind can decipher its evidence. But the western tower and turret are evidently of an early date in English architecture, and the will of its Rector in 1326 proves the existence at that time of the side-chapel of St. Mary, with its own altar, and quaint mediæval wall-painting, recently brought to light. Great Bowden Church has, in its outward features, a history easier to read. With the exception of the tower and dwarf spire, it belongs to the period of architecture usually called Perpendicular, and the work must have been carried out while the Scropes held the manor, even if it were not done at their cost. One early will, and several which belong to the sixteenth century, tell us of its high altar, and we know that there was a chantry, with its chantry-priest, and with property for its maintenance. Harborough Church, externally, tells its own story, as we have seen. It has suffered some changes. The spire of pre-Reformation times was several feet higher, and there were two crockets for every one which is now to be seen. With these exceptions, it stands as it did 450 years since, but cleared, now, of mean lean-to buildings, and perhaps better cared for than ever it was before. The St. Mary's of old time has passed away. Only one doorway, Norman in character, but itself a restoration, remains, and the only thing certain is, that the dead of many centuries lie round and about the poor little building of post-Reformation days.

About the interiors[1] of the churches these records tell us very little. Each of them had its high altar, and at Great Bowden, as at Little Bowden, there was at least one other altar. Probably the one fraternity or guild known to have existed at Harborough had its own altar in Harborough Church. Harborough, it is well known, had a chancel-screen, removed only in the last century, and at Great Bowden there is now to be seen the beginning of the staircase leading to the rood-loft. The nave, in each case, if we may judge from the few specimens of unpaved and unrestored churches in the county, would be fitted with strong oak seats having square ends and panels filled up with a bold carved pattern. The design of the nave roof at Harborough, which dates from the fifteenth century, is dignified in character, with far more of adornment than the rough timbers which, until recently, were to be found in the chancel. At Great and Little Bowden, remains of bold, if not very graceful wall-painting have been brought to light in recent years. At the former the scene depicted is 'The Last Judgment,' at the latter 'Our Lord's Ascension,' the situation being the same in each case, viz., on the north-east wall of the south aisle. In the absence of any pre-Reformation churchwardens' accounts, or inventories of church goods, it can only be inferred that the vestments and ornaments were such as have been frequently described in other churches. At East Haddon, *e.g.*, in the neighbouring county of Northampton, the inventory of a later date includes, a silver chalice, xiiii. ounces in weight, a cope of blue velvet, and one of green; green, red, and white vestments. This was in the reign of Edward VI., and, certainly, at the beginning of the sixteenth century the church goods would include many other things not used afterwards. But a comparison of different inventories proves that there was no absolute uniformity in number, colours, or other points, and the wills given in this volume show that churches were largely indebted to private persons

---

[1] See *Rock's* Church of Our Fathers.

for gifts of church vestments and church plate.[1] In the town records themselves there is no mention of any bells previous to the Reformation, but the wills preserved at Leicester tell us that there were bells in all the churches, St. Mary's included;[2] and this gives some probability to the tradition that some of the bells now in Harborough steeple came from St. Mary's when it fell to ruin.

From the church we pass to the clergy. And first, these records and documents are in themselves sufficient to show that by 'the clergy,' in pre-Reformation times, we must understand not merely those who were either deacons or priests, and who, with few exceptions, served at the altars and in the pulpits of some consecrated church, but all who, in any sense, had a claim to the character of 'clerk,' all who had taken any minor order at episcopal hands, who had received the first tonsure or had been ordained acolytes or sub-deacons, and therefore many who never taught, or said Mass, or did any priestly or ministerial act, though they could hold ecclesiastical benefices, and enjoy by far the greater part of their profits. When we read, therefore, of the 'Rector' or 'Parson' of Great or Little Bowden in 1326, it is not necessarily the man who was himself responsible for the sacred offices in the one church or the other that is brought before us, but the dignified 'clerk,' perhaps a near relative of the lord of the manor for the time being, who had received a certain degree of holy orders, but whose chaplains officiated in that which was, nevertheless, called his church. Thus we have the holders of benefices, who might or might not be priests; some were canons of the cathedral church, some wealthy landowners, some, apparently, useful men of business to their patrons. Many of them held other benefices at the same time, and some were able, frequently, to exchange one benefice for another. We have also

---

[1] See the following wills in this volume: Geoffrey le Scrope, pp. 52, 53; Henry le Scrope (extract), p. 67; Wm. of Wolstanton, p. 74; Agnes Atkinson, p. 218.

[2] See will of John Nubon or Newbon, p. 210; Richard Parych, p. 213; Thos. Alann, p. 220; Edward Fysh, p. 226.

a glimpse of the chaplains or working clergy, chantry-priests and vicars, having their rights well secured against their non-serving or absentee rectors, and of these chaplains we are told there were large numbers in mediæval times.[1] Little is shown by these records of their state, but that little tends to support the conclusions which have been drawn by historical students, that, allowing 'for exaggerated and one-sided statements,' the 'moral influence of the secular clergy was questionable.' 'Idleness and poverty,' 'frivolity,' strife even to bloodshed, and even 'coarse vice,' like that of the laity amongst whom they lived, are proved to have been only too common from the records of the spiritual courts of the Middle Ages.[2] At the same time it is equally clear, even from these scanty records, that the secular clergy were in close relationship with the laity of their day, that every class of society had its members in the clerical order, and that the clergy mingled with others in the administration of charitable gifts, and in the legal forms by which such gifts passed on to succeeding generations. So far we have been speaking of the secular clergy, not of the monastic orders. But the picture is incomplete without some reference to them. Although there was no house for monks or nuns in any of these parishes, there were great abbeys and lesser abbeys near at hand, which must have brought the monastic life in its different phases before the eyes of those who lived here. The great house of Austin Canons at Leicester, called St. Mary de Pratis, had a small property in Harborough itself. The other great abbey of the same order, at Launde, in the remote country district between Harborough and Oakham, enjoyed the patronage of Little Bowden; and near to it was yet another house of Austin Canons, at Owston (Osolveston). In Northamptonshire, about six miles away to the south-east, was the Cistercian Abbey of Pippewell, or St. Mary de Divisis, and between Pippewell and Harborough stood a little hermitage, of

[1] Stubbs' Const. Hy., iii. 395, 396.   [2] *Ibid.*, iii. 402.

which no records exist. The name only is still preserved in a modern farm.[1] About the same distance to the southwest was the Premonstratensian house of Sulby. Of these four, Leicester, Pippewell and Sulby, with others at a greater distance, gave titles for orders to some from these parishes, and, perhaps, drew them from their rough homes and hard life to the comparative comfort and quiet of the monastery, to the orderly work of the carefully cultivated farm, or the patient toil of the scriptorium, and to the only means then open of becoming scholars, or thinkers, or men of devotion. The Knights Hospitallers were so near at their preceptory of Dingley, that another phase of monastic life was not wanting to the men of the Bowdens and Harborough. The rough road between the preceptory at Dingley, and the 'camera' at Swinford, must have lain through the town, and the red military cassock, with its white cross, may have roused the attention of the peasant toiling in the open fields, as naturally as the red coats of the soldiers changing their quarters, or of men riding home after a day's hunting, stir the same common human feeling in those who come from the factory, the cottage, or the shop, in the nineteenth century. In the case of Little Bowden there was a more practical link with the preceptory than that of occasional curiosity. There the Knights Hospitallers were landed proprietors, and had certain manorial rights; probably they were quite as wise and kindly in the exercise of these rights as many who held like rights at the same time, or who afterwards profited by the suppression of the military orders.

A word or two must be said as to the Bishop and the Archdeacons. Even so great a potentate as the Bishop of Lincoln in mediæval times, was not quite outside the little circle of Bowden and Harborough life. From time to time he came to those of his more than thirty manors which were within reasonable distance, to Buckden on the other side of Northamptonshire, in the neighbouring

[1] Bridges' Northamptonshire, ii. 284.

county of Huntingdon, or, nearer still, to Liddington, only about twelve miles down the valley of the Welland, a mile or two distant from it. There he would hold an ordination, or more often commission an assistant Bishop to hold one for him whilst he was engaged in affairs of the State. There he would hold his court for the correction of thieves, and other offenders, for the trial of heretics, for the receiving presentments; and now and again, in one or other of these ways, the Bowdens or Harborough would come before him, and the results in each case would be carefully recorded by his notary or secretary in the registers of his see. The Archdeacons are more in obscurity, so far as these records are concerned, than the Bishops; but every induction then, as now, had to be made by the Archdeacon's authority, if not by himself. From time to time the clergy and wardens would be summoned to his visitation at Leicester, or at Kibworth, at 'Easton by Rockingham,' or at Hallaton, and some of the latest glimpses of pre-Reformation Church life come, as we have seen, from the notes of such visitations in the earlier years of the sixteenth century. Of that gradual upheaval of the level of thought and feeling on religious and social questions which resulted in the events of the next 100 years, there are just a few signs. William of Swinderby, as we have seen, had to read his recantation in Harborough Church. In the sentence against him he is described as a 'Wyclevist,' a sure proof that the great Rector of Lutterworth, only twelve miles distant, was not without sympathizers and followers here.

But the question which is by far the most important remains still to be considered. How far do these facts make known to us the common life of those who lived in the Bowdens and Harborough up to the beginning of the sixteenth century, their daily toil, their dwellings, their food and clothing, their common habits and interests?

Several points have already been noticed, as they were suggested by one or other of the records or documents, taken in the order of their date. On a broad view of them, as a whole, it may be said that we have here set before us two large agricultural communities, whose occupations and interests lay, mainly, in the cultivation of the common fields, according to the system general in most parts of England before the time of the Enclosure Acts. Some trades, indeed, are mentioned from time to time. The 'webster,' or 'wever,' the 'bucher,' the 'mercer,' the 'hosyer,' the 'baker,' the 'draper,' the 'wolman,' the 'roper,' and of course the 'inholder,' in fact, if not in name, are all found. But none of these prove in any way that Harborough was a place of large trade. Most of them would naturally belong to a market-town, and some of them would be found on most manors. Of the two Bowdens might have been said truly, what we know to have been said of one Bowden by the jurors impanelled by the Abbot of St. James's, Northampton, on the collection of the ninth in 1340 : 'there are no traders or dealers there, except those who live by agriculture.' But in trying to picture the agricultural work of the Bowdens and Harborough, as it is indicated in the town documents, we must first banish from our minds nearly all the outward features which are so familiar in the present day. The continuous neat enclosures of grazing ground, stretching in some cases for miles without a ploughed field, and bounded by strong, well-kept hedges, are the work of the last hundred years. In the days of which these records tell, there would be large quantities of waste land, overgrown in all its original wildness, only used as a source of fuel, or of wood for temporary fencing, or for the acorns on which the swine fed. Foxton Moor, Harborough Moor, Bukwell Moor, suggest a feature in the look of things which has so entirely disappeared, that even the very names have long gone out of use. The good, hard, well-made roads, also, which run from village to village, were unknown to the fifteenth century, as entirely as the careful draining, which, in later days, has done so much for large tracts of cultivated land.

What is set before us is a picture of *three* villages, each with its little enclosures, 'tofts' and 'crofts,' close up to the dwellings of those who owned them, and of *two* sets of open fields, one set enjoyed in common by the men of Bowden Parva (St. Nicholas and St. Mary's), the other set enjoyed in common by the men of Bowden Magna and the men of Harborough, its chapelry. It is only to this latter set that the documents now published relate. The enclosure map for Little Bowden is in existence, and gives an accurate representation of the common holdings. The map for Great Bowden and Harborough, unluckily, is missing.

In those of the town documents which give any lengthened description of the holdings in the common fields (Nos. 6, 49, 66, and 96), mention is made of *four* 'fields' in Bowden-Harborough, the North (or Gallow) Field, the South Field, the East Field, and the West Field, but, with one trifling exception, the holdings are only in *three* fields. In No. 6 they are in the South, East and North; in No. 49, in the same; in No. 66, in the South, West and North, and in No. 96, the South, East and North. The system, therefore, which prevailed is that in general use throughout England, viz., what has been called the 'three-field or trinity arrangement.' The North Field, afterwards called the Gallow Field, lay north both of Harborough and Bowden. A place on the road to Leicester is still called Gallow Hill. The allotment land now held under the trustees of the town estate would be part of this field. The South Field would be south of Great Bowden village, stretching down to the Welland below St. Mary's Church; the East Field would be east of Great Bowden village, tending towards Sutton Bassett and Welham, while the West Field was, no doubt, wholly removed from Great Bowden village, immediately west of Harborough town, and as one of the documents describes a holding, in part 'shooting into Lubenham Brook.' But what were these 'fields'?

They have been compared to 'sheets of paper ruled with margins and lines.' Each of the three large 'fields' of arable land (for the great mass of land which was not waste was then under the plough) had several 'furlongs,' as they are frequently called in the foregoing documents, supposed to be about ten acres each in extent, but really very far from uniform in size. These are compared to the separate sheets of paper. They were separated from one another by strips of unploughed land, covered with overgrown turf, called 'balks,' and down one side of them ran other strips called 'headlands,' across the ends of their subdivisions. These subdivisions, represented by the lines of the paper, are the 'acres,' 'half-acres,' 'roods,' 'thirty-falls,' which are particularized in the descriptions of property. The little bits which were left over by this sort of arrangement seem here to have been called 'gores,' and in shape were not unlike those parts of garments which still bear that name. There was a regular succession of cultivation under this system: 'wheat or rye' the first year; 'barley, oats, beans or peas,' the second; 'fallow' the third; and, as a consequence, every occupier or owner had his strips of arable land in each of the three fields, so that he might not be in the predicament of having nothing but fallow land in any one year. From seed-time to harvest each owner or occupier might fence his strips of arable land round. After harvest the fences were removed, and the town neat-herd tended the town cattle on the fields, again become common.[1] Besides these holdings of arable

---

[1] For this description of the open fields, the Editor is indebted to a work already quoted, Pioneers and Progress of English Farming, by R. E. Prothero (Longmans, 1888). An examination of the modern remains of the English open-field system forms the first chapter of Seebohm's English Village Community (Longmans, 1883), and this is illustrated by maps. A reference to these maps suggests one objection to the illustration from sheets of ruled paper, viz., that it gives to the mind the impression of too exact a symmetry and regularity. Imagine the sheets cut into all kinds of odd shapes, and then tacked together with the picturesque irregularity of a patchwork quilt, yet the straight

land, each man, who had common rights at all, had his share of the meadow land, here called 'le Hayeleyis.' These, we are told, were commonly apportioned by lot each year, but they were property which might be legally conveyed with the rest. These also might be fenced off from Candlemas (February 2) to Midsummer Day, while for the other part of the year they were the common pasture.

Such is the broad view of the yearly agricultural life of these parishes. The town documents after the Reformation, up to the date of the enclosure, show how the area of cultivated land was in part enlarged, and the records of certain lawsuits tend to illustrate the yearly customs, and to fill up details; but the main outlines of the picture must have been the same from very early days to the time of George III., and the changes wrought by the Enclosure Acts were nothing less than a quiet, if a necessary revolution.

Many of the names given to the 'furlongs' in the open fields give life and picturesqueness to the scene we have been trying to describe. Goodwyn's Ox, 'the place where Goodwyn's ox died,' seems to tell of one of the oxen then commonly used for the plough, an ox anything but 'strong to labour,' and in whom was 'no decay,' toiling on bravely in the stiff Leicestershire clay, and at last beaten, and lying down there to die. 'Schirdaycotys'—Shire-day-cotes—one of the earliest of all, seems to mark the division between the two counties, the place where the Shire Court may have been held on the confines of two shires. 'Watyrlakis' tells of the swampy, undrained ground near the sleepy, sluggish, but quick-to-flood, Welland. 'Stanhill,' or 'Rockhill,' perhaps proves the truth in detail of the Parable of the Sower in one point, just as the 'balks,' over which the sower walked, or near

---

lines and the borders preserved, and the illustration seems the nearest that can be given of what few, in these days, are able to see with their own eyes.

to which he came as he scattered his seed by hand, may be the key to the meaning of 'the wayside,' in another. 'Brakenbarrowhylt' proves that some sort of ferns were to be found here and there. 'Paddokispyltche' turns our thoughts in another direction. Here, again, was some low-lying ground where the 'paddock,' or toad, was often to be seen, just as 'Craneworth' suggests the idea of a place where such large birds often gathered. 'Le Gallowe' tells of crime and its extreme punishment, often cruelly and coarsely used for offences which do not now demand it. 'Snakesyke' seems to show that snakes were more commonly to be seen than they are in our day, while 'Washford,' 'Marlepyttes' and 'Myllegate' suggest three ordinary parts of village life.

Of the houses which the people occupied, of what they ate, and how they were clothed, there are here but a few glimpses. The obligation to repair a house in 'thacke and modd' supports the descriptions of the common dwellings of our forefathers often given by writers on their social and physical condition. The roughness, the dirt and the inconvenience, even of the better class of houses, the meanness of their appearance without, and their filthy state within, are held to have been one cause of the terrible waves of pestilence which at times almost depopulated whole districts. It is harder to tell from these documents how people fed, or how they were clothed, than how they were housed. The earliest indication is given when Thomas Bernard, handing over his property to his son, reserves to himself a room with a *solar*, showing that his was not a mere labourer's hovel, and at the same time requires that his son shall give him so long as he lives 'competentem et rationabilem victum,' three yards of blanket, and one pair of shoes each year or 12d.[1] The best and fullest information on these subjects is gathered from the wills. They tell us something as to the materials used for garments, the food stored up for

---

[1] See No. 29, p. 171.

consumption, the furniture of some houses, the instruments of some trades, the live-stock attached to the homestead, as well as of the offerings to the Church and the gifts to the community. The inventory accidentally discovered at Lincoln[1] gives a mass of detail as to the possessions of a Harborough tradesman in the early part of the sixteenth century, and suggests a fair amount of wealth and comfort in that class of the community.

It remains only to point out, if possible, how far these documents and records illustrate the history of the town estate, now administered by the trustees elected by the townspeople. Amidst much that is difficult to trace a few points are clear. The old houses formerly used by the poor in Lubenham Lane, and in Dag Lane, or New Street, which were sold in the early part of this century, came down through many generations. The George and Hind Inns can be distinctly traced back more than 400 years, from the date of their being sold in recent times, and the fact that the name 'le Olde George' is found in those days proves that it was no modern compliment to the reigning sovereign, but one amongst many commemorations of 'St. George of Merrie England.' The Hind is quite a modern name. Later records prove that the inn which stood there was called the Peale, no doubt from the bells in the church tower opposite. The enclosure has made such changes that it is no longer possible, like the Harborough antiquary, Mr. Rowland Rouse, just before the Act was carried out, to walk leisurely over the town holdings in the three fields, noting with pencil and paper what strips were missing which had been recorded 120 years before, and what had been added; but, in spite of these changes, it is certain that the George Close, and much of the land to the west of the town, the allotments north of the town, and the land at the west of Great Bowden village, have been charity lands for a very long period. One point as to the objects of the trust seems

[1] See pp. 230-234.

perfectly clear, viz., that the repair of bridges is the oldest object to which its funds may now be devoted. It would be too much to say for certain that the gift to the Guild of the Holy Cross was one for this purpose, though it is known that Guilds of the same title at Birmingham and Stratford-on-Avon were established for this among other objects.[1] But the will of William Neell, in 1439, is a distinct proof that the repair of 'the great bridge' was a charitable object in the reign of Henry VI., and as the property used by the poor passed to the parish officers in more recent times, there is no object within the scope of the existing scheme which can be said, with any certainty, to be of earlier date.

To sum up, the general impression left on the mind by a survey of the records up to the Reformation is one of the continuity and gradual development of country town and village life in this part of England. It is needless to point out at length the enormous differences made by things we use now as a matter of course, by good roads, by the post, by canals, and above all by railways and electricity. But beneath all these, and, perhaps, in spite of them, there are features and institutions which can be traced back so far that we altogether lose sight of their first beginning. The manor, the churches, and perhaps, above all, the Tuesday market, have a long ancestry, and those who use them now are only doing, under different conditions, what others before them did more than 600 years ago. Rockingham is no longer a royal castle in the royal hunting forest, Braybrooke Castle is no longer a baron's stronghold, the Trussells of Marston, the Harcourts and Beauchamps of Kibworth, the Latimers of Burton and Corby, the Bassetts of Sutton and Weston, have passed away, at all events from this district, together

---

[1] Denton's England in the Fifteenth Century, p. 174, and note 3. On roads and bridges generally, see many references in the same; and also English Wayfaring Life in the Middle Ages (Jusserand), Part I., chap. i.

with the great abbeys and the military orders, once so dominant a feature in English life; but life in towns like Harborough, and villages like the Bowdens, is still the life of the English community, and is healthy and prosperous in so far as duty to the community is recognised and discharged faithfully, under the wonderful conditions of modern times.

MARKET HARBOROUGH PARISH RECORDS.

(1) Richard, son of Richard Buckard of 'Mangna Bugedon' gives, grants and confirms to Adam Bernard, for his homage and service, and for twelve shillings in silver then paid, a headland[1] (foreram) in the field of Bugedon, lying between his tillage and the said Adam's enclosure (inter culturam meam et curiam dicti Ade), at 12 peppercorns rent, payable annually at Easter for all services and demands.

No date. (? *Circa* 1180—1200.)

Witnesses: Richard Illing, Robert his brother, Hugo de Meyners, Roger de Meyners, Roger the deacon, David his brother, and many others.

(2) William, son of William Gaugi, of Harbergh, gives, grants and confirms to William de Sowtorp, of Magna Boudon, and Edda, his wife, and their heirs, in return for a sum of money in hand paid, two selions[2] of his land in the fields of Boudon, to hold of him and his heirs for ever at the yearly rent of one farthing, payable at the Annunciation of the Virgin Mary for all secular services and demands.

Witnesses: Tomas Reynold de Magna Boudon, Geoffrey Hunnay, Richard Chapelen, Richard at the Moor, Robert de Dingle of Boudon, Hugo de Foxton of Boudon, William the clerk, and many others.

No date. Probably first half of thirteenth century.

PARTICULARS OF THE PROPERTY.

One selion on Tongsty, between the land of Adam Bernard and the land of Thomas Handrewe de Harbergh.

Another selion, under Scirdaykotys, next the land of Robert Byllyng on the west.

---

[1] Cowel's Interpreter.

[2] *Selion*, ground rising between two furrows. No certain quantity; sometimes more, sometimes less. (Cowel's Interpreter.)

(3) Felicia, widow of John Gerveis, of Stamford, in virtue of her widowhood, grants, remits and quit-claims to Robert of Ocham, burgess of Stamford, and his heirs and assigns, in return for a certain sum of money then in hand paid, all her right and claim which she has, under the name of dowry or otherwise, in certain houses, with their appurtenances, situated in the parish of St. John, Stamford, opposite the parish burial-ground, between a tenement belonging to the Lord Abbot of Crokesdene on the north, and a tenement belonging to the nuns of St. Michael without Stamford on the south.

> Witnesses: John of Eston, Roger of Styandeby, Honorius Pycard, Leonard the furbisher (le furbechur), Peter the tailor (le parmenter), Richard the goldsmith (le orfevure), Peter Ponteis, William the clerk, and others.

Dated 19 Edward I., 'die Veneris proxima post festum Inventionis Sancte Crucis;' *i.e.*, Friday, May 4, 1291 (Old Style).

(4) Roesa, daughter of William Boccard of Magna Boudon, grants and quit-claims to Thomas Chapeleyn of the same town, and his heirs, etc., for the sum of sixpence in silver in hand paid, all her right and claim (together with wards, reliefs and escheats) in an annual rent of one penny, in which the said Thomas Chapeleyn is bound to her for one selion of land on 'le Thwong' and another on 'Maynerdesholm.'

> No date. (? *Circa* 1300.)
>
> Witnesses: Alexander 'le Sweyn,' William at the Church, Richard at the Moor, Richard 'le folur,' Thomas the clerk, and others.

(5) Robert Warin of Haverbergh gives, grants and confirms to John Fot of the same, one rood and a half of his land in the field of Magna Boudon lying on Foxton Moor, next the land of the said John Fot on the north; to hold the same of the chief lord of the fee at the due and accustomed services.

> Witnesses: Thomas Yol of Haverbergh, Thomas Reyner, of the same, John the clerk, and others.

Dated at Haverbergh, 18 Edward II. (regis Edwardi filii regis Edwardi), 'die Mercurii proxima ante festum St. Gregorii;' *i.e.*, Wednesday, March 6, 132⅘.

At the back: 'Le fait Roberti Wareyn.'

(6) Indenture witnessing that Thomas Reyner[1] of Haverbergh gives, grants and confirms to Thomas his son, and Olive, his son's wife, and their lawful heirs, 20 acres of land in the fields of Magna Boudon, at a rent of one rose, payable yearly on the Feast of St. John Baptist (June 24), and on performance in his name of the due and accustomed services to the chief lords of the fees (feodorum illorum); the said property to revert to Thomas Reyner and his heirs in case of failure of lawful heirs.

Witnesses: Richard de Smetheton, Richard de Foxton, Robert de Neuton, Richard Cristien, John Andrewe, Peter Piere, John de Brampton, clerk, and others.

Dated at Haverbergh, 'die Veneris proxima post festum Apostolorum Simonis et Jude,' 17 Edward III.; *i.e.*, Friday, October 31, 1343.

PARTICULARS OF THE ABOVE-NAMED PROPERTY.

In the South Field.

3 roods lying together, extending above the croft of John de Pydele.
1 half-acre, second from the gore[2] on the east.
1 half-acre, second from the gore on the west.
9 roods below the croft of the said Thomas Reyner, extending 'in to Weland.'
2 roods on Stanyhull, second and third from the gore on the west.
7½ roods together against the sun, next the land of Master Geoffrey on the east.
6 roods lying together, extending on Sevenewell, next the land of Adam de Sutton on the north.
1½ roods on Holebergh, next the gore on the west.
2½ roods on Holebergh, next the land of John Bercher on the east.
1 rood on Ouerrademylde, next the headland on the east.
1½ roods 'in to Lobenhambrok,' next the land of Richard de Smetheton on the south.
1 thrittifal against the sun, next the land of Adam Dekne on the west.
1 thrittifal on Nethirrademylde, fourth from the road on the west.
1 half-rood 'in to Lobenhambrok,' next the land of Hugh Luffe on the north.

In the East Field.

1½ roods lying where Godwynes Oxe died (ubi Godwynesoxe morieabatur [*sic*]), next the land of Richard de Smeton on the east.

---

[1] In 1340 Thomas Reyner, of Harebergh, was summoned with about 150 other merchants, etc., to Westminster, on the Monday after Mid-Lent Sunday next ensuing, the King wishing to treat with them on difficult and urgent business. Rymer, Fœdera (edit. 1821), ii. 1114.

[2] *Gares*, called also *gores*, irregular lands. See Best's Farming Book (Surtees Soc.), p. 43; Cf. *ante*, p. 153.

2 roods together on the same furlong, next the land of Thomas Waygnon on the west.

1 rood on the same, seventh from the head (a capite).

1½ roods on Shorthilrene, fourth from the gore on the west.

1½ roods on Helthirne, next the land of Thomas, son of Thomas Yol, on the west.

1 thrittifal 'in to Gasewell,' next the land of Geoffrey Yonge on the west.

1 half-acre on Longehilrene, next the land of John de Pydele on the south.

1½ roods below Kyngestyrne, next the land of Clemency Bate on the south.

3 roods together on the same, next the land of Clemency Bate on the north.

1½ roods on the same, fourth from the gore on the west.

1 rood below Broddole, next the land of William Pachet on the west.

1 rood below Broddole, next the land of William de Godessalve on the west.

1½ roods below Broddole, next the land of John Andreu, chaplain, on the east.

In the North Field.

1½ roods extending 'in to Foxtonegate,' second from the gore on the north.

1½ roods and 1 thrittifal on Shirdaycotis, together, next the land of Thomas Pachet on the east.

2 roods below Portgates, next the gore on the east.

2 roods below Shirdaycotis, next the land of John Andreu, chaplain, on the east.

1 half-acre on Galhou, next the land of the Rector on the north.

1 half-acre at Westwell, next the land of Thomas Averey on the west.

1 thrittifal at Westwell, next the land of Master Geoffrey on the west.

3 roods together on 'le Brest,' next the land of Thomas Piere on the west.

1 rood on 'le Brest,' second from the gore on the west.

1 half-acre in Toucroft, next the land of John Bercher on the east.

3 thrittifals lying together on Nethirportgate, next the land of Adam Dekne on the west.

(7) William Fidel, of Boudon Magna, gives, grants and confirms to Thomas Bernard, of the same place, and Olive his wife, a headland on 'Fidellis-wonge Ourelange-tongate' next the land formerly belonging to Richard Bernard on the south, to hold the same of the chief lord of the fee at the due and accustomed services.

Witnesses: Richard Harper, Richard Boner, Richard Dekene, William Pachet, Robert the clerk, and others.

Dated at Boudon, 17 Edward III., 'die Dominica proxima post festum Purificationis beate Marie ;' *i.e.*, February 8, 134¾.

N.B.—Numbers 1, 4, and 5, were bound together by straw.

(8) Thomas Fleming, of Haverbergh, gives grants and confirms to Hugh Gladman, of the same, one stall in Haverbergh lying next the stall of Matilda de Brampton on the north, to hold of the chief lord of the fee at the due and accustomed services.

<small>Witnesses : Thomas Reyner, of Haverbergh, Thomas de Stanesby, John Andrewe, John the clerk, and others.

Dated at Haverbergh, 18 Edward III., 'die Martis in festo Sancti Thome Apostoli ;' *i.e.*, Tuesday, December 21, 1344.</small>

(9) William, son of Reyner Mannyng, junior, of Haverburgh, gives, grants and confirms to Roger, his brother, and Juliana, the said Roger's wife, and their heirs of the same place, for $4\frac{1}{2}$ marks sterling in hand paid, a certain place with its appurtenances in Haverburgh, which he had by the gift and feoffment of Reyner his father, together with leave to grant, bequeath, sell or assign the same ; the said Roger and Juliana paying yearly to the heirs of Reyner three pence, viz., at the Feast of the Annunciation of the Blessed Mary one penny and a halfpenny, and the same at the Feast of the Nativity of the Blessed Mary, for all accustomed services, suits, courts, and for reliefs and all secular demands : the said rent to be doubled when a relief occurs.[1]

<small>No date. (*Circa* 1350.)

Witnesses : John Seman, of Haverburgh, Thomas Yol, of the same, John Wyldegrys, of the same, Robert Cristien, of the same, Richard the clerk, and others.</small>

(10) Thomas, son of Master Richard 'le leche,' of Haverbergh, gives, grants and confirms to Roger de Clendon, of the same, a tenement with a croft adjoining, formerly belonging to John 'le bailif' in Haverbergh, situated between a tenement formerly belonging to John de Clendon on one side, and a tenement belonging to Hugh

---

[1] *Relief :* 'the money paid by the incoming heir for admission to his inheritance.'—Stubbs, *Select Charters ;* Glossary, 'relevium.'

'le milner' on the other side, to be held of the chief lords of the fee at the due and accustomed services.

> Witnesses: Thomas Reyner, of Haverbergh, Richard de Boresworth, Thomas Cristien, Richard de Leycester, Thomas de Clipston, of the same, and others.

Dated at Haverbergh, 38 Edward III., 'die Lune proxima post festum S. Dunstani ;' *i.e.*, Monday, May 20, 1364.

(11) The same gives, etc., to the same, the property before mentioned, with this further description: ' that is to say, in length, from the king's highway in the town as far as the field of Magna Boudon.' (' Scilicet in longitudine a via regia in villa usque in campum de Magna Boudon.')

> Witnesses: The same, except Thomas de Clipston, instead of whom is Thomas Skynare, chaplain.

Dated at Haverbergh, 39 Edward III., same day; *i.e.*, Monday, May 20, 1365.

(12) Indenture by which John de Beolton, chaplain, gives, grants and confirms to Thomas de Alyngton and Juliana his wife, and their heirs, an annual rent of one rose arising from the lands and tenements which Thomas Reyner, of Haverbergh, holds of him in Haverbergh and Magna Boudon for life, together with the services of the said Thomas Reyner and the reversion of the lands and tenements at his decease, to be held of the chief lord of the fee at the due and accustomed services. The indenture further provides that if Thomas Alyngton and Juliana his wife die without heirs, the aforesaid lands, etc., shall become the property of Thomas Cristian, Thomas, son of Richard de Stonton, and Emma and Letia, daughters of John, son of Thomas Reyner, and their heirs.

> Witnesses: Richard de Foxton, Richard de Boresworth, Thomas Rag, Richard de Leycester, William Andrew de Haverbergh, and others.

Dated at Haverbergh, 41 Edward III., 'die Lune proxima post festum Translacionis Sancti Thome Martiris ;' *i.e.*, Monday, July 12, 1367.

SEAL.

(13) Thomas Marshall, of Haverbergh, gives, grants and confirms to Richard de Byllesdon, chaplain of the Fraternity

of the Holy Cross,[1] of Haverbergh, a yearly rent of one penny, payable by Roger Coo, of Haverbergh, and Margaret his wife, in a house which they hold for life, together with the services of the said Roger and Margaret, and the reversion of the said house, to be held of the chief lord of the fee at the due and accustomed services.

> Witnesses : Richard de Leycester, Thomas Cristien, Thomas Ragg, Thomas Prentys, William Andrew, and others.

> Dated at Haverbergh, 42 Edward III., 'die Lune proxima ante festum Sancti Silvestri Pape et Confessoris ;' *i.e.*, Christmas Day, 1368.

(14) Indenture witnessing that William de Borsworthe, of Haverbergh, grants and demises to Roger Coe, of the same, and Margaret his wife, for life, a messuage in Haverbergh, situated between the tenement of Roger Mayner and the King's highway.

> Rent : 18 silver shillings yearly, payable in equal portions at Easter and Michaelmas.
> Power of re-entry and distraint reserved in case the rent is 15 days in arrear.
> The tenants to maintain and repair at their own expense, and not in any way to alienate.

> Witnesses : Richard de Borsworthe, of Haverbergh, Thomas Cristien, Thomas Rag, Richard de Leycester, Thomas Prentys, of the same, and others.

> Dated at Haverbergh, 47 Edward III., 'die Lune in festo Assumpcionis beate Marie ;' *i.e.*, Monday, August 15, 1373.

(15) Richard Andrew, of Magna Boudon, grants and confirms to William Andrew, of Haverbergh, one selion, containing one rood and a half, of arable land in Magna Boudon Fields, lying on Foxton Moor next the land of William Dekene on the south, to be held of the chief lords of the fee at the due and accustomed services.

> Witnesses : The same as in No. 12.

> Dated at Haverbergh, 48 Edward III., 'in festo S. Georgii ;' *i.e.*, April 23, 1374.

> *Memorandum on the back :* That the above is void if Richard Andrew pays to William Andrew or his attorney 12 silver shillings on the Feast of the Holy Trinity after date ; *i.e.*, May 28, 1374.

---

[1] On Guilds from a religious point of view, see *Rock*, Church of Our Fathers, vol. ii., pp. 395 *et seq.*

(16) Roger Koe, of Haverbergh, and Margaret his wife, remit, release and pardon William de Borsworthe, of the same, in respect of all actions and suits at law, real and personal, which they have against him from the beginning of the world to present date.

> Witnesses : Richard de Leycester, Henry de Leycester, Thomas de Alynton, Roger Mayner, Thomas Rag, Robert Venablis, Hugo Lodore, and others.

Dated at Haverbergh, 1 Richard II., 'die Saturni proxima post festum Sancti Andree Apostoli ;' *i.e.*, Saturday, December 5, 1377.

(17) Thomas Clypston, of Haverbergh, gives, grants and confirms to John de Boresworthe, of the same, one stall in Haverbergh situated in 'le fleyschschamelis'[1] between the stall of Thomas de Alynton on the north and the stall late of Richard de Foxton on the south, to hold of the chief lords of the fee at the due and accustomed services.

> Witnesses : Richard de Boresworth, Richard de Leycester, William de Boresworth, Hugo Lodere, John Whyte, of Haverbergh, clerk, and others.

Dated at Haverbergh, 4 Richard II., 'die Dominica proxima ante festum Annunciationis beate Marie ;' *i.e.*, Sunday, March 24, 138⅞.

(18) Thomas, son of Thomas Clypston, of Haverbergh, remits, releases and quit-claims to John de Boresworth, of the same, and his heirs, etc., all his right and claim in a certain stall in Haverbergh which he had by the gift and feoffment of his father, Thomas Clypston.

> Witnesses : Richard de Boresworth, Richard de Leycester, William de Boresworth, Hugo Lodere, Robert Coley, of Haverbergh, and others.

Dated at Haverbergh, 4 Richard II., 'die Dominica proxima post festum Annunciationis beate Marie' ; *i.e.*, Sunday, March 31, 1381.

(19) Thomas Skynner, of Haverbergh, chaplain, gives, grants and confirms to John, son of John Couper, of the same, a tenement formerly John Baly's in the same, with a croft adjoining, situated between the tenement formerly John de Clendon's and a tenement formerly

---

[1] The English word 'shambles' is derived from *schamel* (Middle English), a bench.—Skeat's Etymological Dictionary.

Hugh Milner's, to hold of the chief lord of the fee at the due and accustomed services.

> Witnesses : Richard de Boresworth, Robert Wenablys, John Walker, of Haverbergh, and others.

Dated, 'apud villam de Sancto Botulpho' (Boston), 6 Richard II., 'die Veneris in septimana Pasche ;' *i.e.*, Friday, March 27, 1383.

(20) William Harper, of Mangna (*sic*) Boudon, gives, grants and confirms to William Andrewe, of the same, 4 roods of land in the fields of Mangna Boudon, to hold of the chief lords of the fee at the due and accustomed services.

> Witnesses : Robert Mychell, of Haverbergh, John Cay, of the same, Richard Bernard, of Mangna Boudon, John Bernard, William Dekene, jun., of the same, and others.

Dated at Mangna Boudon, 7 Richard II., 'die Dominica proxima ante festum S. Petri ad vincula ;' *i.e.*, Sunday, July 26, 1383.

On the back, in two different hands: ' Carta Willelmi Harper de una acra terre.'

PARTICULARS OF THE PROPERTY.

1 rood on Lyzard, next the land of John Mayners on the south.
1 rood on Smethmewe furlong, next the land of Robert Wenham on the west.
1½ roods on [?], next the land of Roger Crysten on the east.
½ rood 'in le Watyrlakes,' next the land of Richard Boresworth on the east.

(21) Richard Leycester and John Couper, both of Haverbergh, attorneys of Sir Thomas Skynner, of Haverbergh, chaplain, acknowledge the receipt of 4 marks, 5 shillings and 4 pence, silver, from William Spycer, of the same, the amount of his written obligation, in consideration of which they release and remit to him all manner of actions, right or claim, in regard to that tenement which Sir Thomas had by the gift and feoffment of Roger de Clendon.

> Witnesses : Richard de Boresworth, Thomas de Alynton, of Haverbergh, John Whyte, of the same, clerk, and others.

Dated at Haverbergh, 7 Richard II., 'die Veneris in festo Sancti Mauri Abbatis ;' *i.e.*, Friday, January 13, 138¾.

(22) Richard Andrewe, of Magna Boudon, gives, grants and confirms to William Andrewe, of Haverbergh, a selion

of arable land containing a rood and a half in the field of Magna Boudon, lying on Foxton Moor, next the land of William Dekene on the south, to hold of the chief lords of that fee, etc., etc.

> Witnesses: Roger Mayner, Richard Bernard, John Bernard, Thomas in le Hirne, John Thurston, of Magna Boudon, and others.

Dated at Magna Boudon, 8 Richard II., 'die Dominica proxima post festum S. Matthie Apostoli;' *i.e.*, Sunday, February 26, 138⅘.

On the back: 'Foxton Mor.'

(23) Thomas Pruston, of Mangna (*sic*) Boudon, gives, grants and confirms to William Spycer, of Haverbergh, one half-acre of arable land, in the field of Mangna Boudon lying on Gasylleseyke next the land of William Walker on the west, which he had by the gift and feoffment of John Pruston, his father, to hold, etc., etc.

> Witnesses: Richard de Leycester, of Haverbergh, Richard de Boresworth, of the same, Richard Barnard, of Mangna Boudon, John Barnard, and Reginald Crystyen, of the same.

Dated at Mangna Boudon, 15 Richard II., 'die Mercurii proxima ante festum S. Marci Evangeliste;' *i.e.*, Wednesday, April 24, 1392.

On the back: 'Thomas Thruston, xxxij.'

(24) Richard Dekene, of Mangna Boudon, gives, grants and confirms to William Andrewe of Haverbergh, 4 pence and 1 halfpenny, yearly rent, called 'cotage rente,' arising from a messuage in 'le west ende' of Mangna Boudon, lying between the tenement of John Ingold and the tenement of John Mayner, to hold, etc., etc.

> Witnesses: Richard Leycester, of Haverbergh, John Cay, of the same, Richard Bernard, of Mangna Boudon, John Dekene, and William Walker, of the same, and others.

Dated at Mangna Boudon, 19 Richard II., 'in vigilia Pasche;' *i.e.*, Easter Eve, April 1, 1396.

(25) Roger Petlyng and Thomas Bate, chaplains, of Haverbergh, give, grant and confirm to William Hely, of the same, one stall in Haverbergh, situated in 'le Fleschamcles,' between the stalls of Thomas Alyngton on the

north, and the stall formerly of Richard de Foxton on the south, to hold, etc., etc.

> Witnesses: Richard de Leycester, steward, Richard Cristian, William Boresworth, John Burton, Robert Dyke, clerk, and many others.

Dated at Haverbergh, 7 Henry IV., 'die Martis proxima post festum Corporis Christi ;' *i.e.*, Tuesday, June 15, 1406.

(26) John Salton, chaplain of the Chantry of Merston Trussel, gives, grants and confirms to William Neell, of Haverbergh, mercer, 10 acres of arable land, with the meadows and 4 pastures, in the fields of Boudon Magna, which he had by the gift and feoffment of Isabella Holme, of Bondon Parva, to hold of the chief lord of the fee, etc., etc.

> Witnesses: John Baxter, draper, of Haverbergh, William Boresworth, of the same, John Hyrne, of Boudon Magna, Richard Hyrn, of the same, and John the parson, of the same, and others.

Dated at Boudon, 5 Henry VI., 'in festo Apostolorum Philippi et Jacobi ;' *i.e.*, Thursday, May 1, 1427.

On the back: 'Le faitt Johannis Salton de Merston clerici.'

(27) Indenture witnessing that whereas Thomas Palmer has bound himself to John Burgh and Reginald Welham, of London, draper, in the sum of £20, the said John Burgh and Reginald Welham release him from his obligation on the following conditions:

(1) That he releases to them and Richard Boresworth, John Baxter and William Neell, of Haverbergh, and their heirs, all his right and claim in 1 messuage, 2 cottages, 7 acres of arable land, and 3 roods of meadow, which they have by the gift and grant of him, the said Thomas, and others his co-feoffees, the release to be accompanied by a warranty clause.

(2) That he causes Everard Dygby, one of his co-feoffees, to execute a similar release without a warranty clause.

(3) That he causes Thomas Warmyngton, of Coventre, 'hosyer,' Richard Warmington, of Haverburgh, and Robert Warmyngton, of the same, to execute a similar release without a warranty clause.

(4) That he delivers, or causes to be delivered to them, all the records and muniments relating to the said properties.

(5) That the foregoing conditions are carried out before the Feast of the Purification of the Blessed Mary next ensuing.

Dated 6 Henry VI., 'die Mercurii proxima post festum Omnium Sanctorum, *i.e.*, Wednesday, November 5, 1427.

On the back : ' Indentura facta per Thomam Palmer.'

(28) Robert Warmyngton, of Haverbergh, gives, grants and confirms to Reginald Cokyn, of Beryhatley,[1] John Burgh, of Withkote, Robert Boresworth, of Haverberg, 'gentilmen,' Thomas Warmyngton, of Coventre, hosier, and William Neel, of Haverbergh, mercer, all his lands and tenements, meadows, etc., etc., in the towns and fields of Haverbergh, Boudon Magna and Lobenham, or elsewhere in Leicestershire, and also all his goods, movable and immovable, of every kind, and in every part of England, to hold, etc., etc.

Witnesses : Thomas Alyngton of Haverbergh, John Warmyngton, of the same, Thomas Shute, of the same, John Page, of the same, John Welham, of the same, and many others.

Dated at Haverbergh, 9 Henry VI., 'die Jovis proxima ante festum Sancte Katerine Virginis ;' *i.e.*, Thursday, November 23, 1430.

(29) Indenture witnessing that Thomas Bernard, of Boudon Magna, hands over and lets to farm to his son Roger, of the same, one messuage situated next the tenement late of Thomas Thurston, on the south, with all the lands, meadows, pastures and pasturages thereto belonging, and a tenement called ' Chapelensthing,' and half a pigeon-house next ' le Gunnesbrok,' in Boudon, for the

[1] Cockayne Hatley, Beds.

term of 6 years after date, at the yearly rent of 20s., to be paid in equal parts on the Feasts of St. Michael the Archangel, the Nativity of Our Lord, Easter, and St. Peter ad Vincula.

The indenture reserves to the said Thomas Bernard, during the said term, 9 acres of arable land, ½ acre of meadow, with 6½ beast pastures, and half the pigeon-house next the Gunnesbrok, 1 room with a solar,[1] with free ingress and egress, and a garden called 'le Kylnzerde,' with the apples. It further covenants that the said Roger shall provide for his father during the said term sufficient food (competentem et rationabilem victum), 3 yards of blanket (tres virgas blanketi), and 1 pair of shoes, or 12d.

Also that, in case of the rent being 15 days in arrear, it shall be lawful to retake possession, and that the said Roger shall execute all repairs at his own expense, leaving everything at the expiration of the term in good order.

Dated 9 Henry VI., 'in festo S. Joannis Baptiste,' *i.e.*, Sunday, June 24, 1431.

(30) John Ingold, of Magna Boudon, senior, gives to William Neell, of Haverbergh, 3 roods of arable land in the fields of Boudon, to hold, etc., etc.

> Witnesses: Thomas Alyngton, John Page, of Haverbergh, Thomas Harper, William Smyth, Thomas Ingold, of Boudon, and many others.

Dated at Haverbergh, 14 Henry VI., 'in die Martis proxima ante festum Pasche;' *i.e.*, Tuesday, April 10, 1435.

PARTICULARS OF THE PROPERTY.

½ acre on Tongstede, between the land of the said William Neell on the east, and the common gore on the west.

1 rood abutting into Haverbergh-more, third from the gore on the east.

(31) William Clerk, of Magna Boudon, senior, gives, grants and confirms to John Shyrewode, of the same,

---

[1] *Solarium*, solar. The upper story of a house.—Liber Albus (Rolls Series), Glossary of Med. Latin.

junior, 5 roods of arable land and meadow in the fields of Boudon, to hold, etc., etc.

> Witnesses : John en le hyrne,[1] Richard en le hyrne, William Harper, Thomas Crystyen, John Clerk, jun., of Boudon, and many others.

Dated at Boudon, 17 Henry VI., 'in die Sabbati proxima post festum Purificationis beate Marie ;' *i.e.*, Saturday, February 7, 1435/9.

PARTICULARS OF THE PROPERTY.

½ acre on Branglondis, next the land of the heirs of John Cort on the west.

3 thirty-falls of herbage (tripartite herbagii) lying together on 'le Hayeleyis,' next the meadow of John Cregis on the west.

1 thirty-fall of herbage, lying on Cranesworth, next the land of John Ingold on the south.

(32) Thomas Grene and Robert Isham hand over, grant and confirm to Henry Leycester, of Haverbergh, one messuage in Haverbergh, situated between the messuage formerly Richard Leycester's, and the messuage of Thomas Cotes, with all the lands, etc., rents, services, etc., which they have in the towns and fields of Haverbergh and Magna Boudon, in the county of Leicester, and in the town and fields of Farndon, or elsewhere, in the county of Northampton, which said messuage, lands, etc., they have by the gift and feoffment of Roger Petlyng, chaplain, to hold, etc., etc. In case Henry Leycester has no legitimate heirs, the property remains to John Leycester, his brother, and his heirs, to hold, etc., etc.

> Witnesses : John Boresworth, of Haverbergh, Thomas Baverey, of the same, William Neell, of the same, John Page, of the same, John Shute, of the same, and many others.

Dated at Haverbergh, 17 Henry VI., 'in die Lune proxima ante festum Translationis S. Thome Martyris ;' *i.e.*, Monday, July 6, 1439.

(33) The will of William Neel, of Haverbergh, dated the 35th (tricesimoquinto [*sic*]) day of November, 1439.

He bequeaths :

> His soul to Almighty God and the Blessed Virgin His Mother, and All Saints.

---

[1] *Herne*, a nook of land projecting into another district, parish, or field.—Forby, p. 157. There is a Herne Lane still in Great Bowden.

His body to be buried in the burial-ground of the Church of the Blessed Virgin.

As mortuary, whatever is right (in nomine mortuarii quod justum est).

To the Church of Saint Mary, vis. viii*d*.

To the chapel of Haverberg, vis. viii*d*.

To Henry Mariothe, clerk, of Welam, xiiis. iiii*d*.

To Thomas Triclowe, of Thorplangton, a servant of his father's, iiis. iiii*d*.

To each of his own servants, iiis. iiii*d*.

For the repair of the great bridge (pontis magni), iiis. iiii*d*.

The residue to be disposed of by his wife Margaret, Robert Averey, chaplain, and Richard Stacy, of Haverberg, who are appointed his executors.

The seal is gone.

(34) Reginald Wellam, citizen of London, and Robert Boresworth, of Harberowe, in the county of Leicester, demise, grant, deliver and confirm to William Neell, of Harberowe, all the lands, tenements, meadows, pasturages, rents and services in Harberowe and Magna Bowden, which they held conjointly with John Burgh, deceased, by the gift and grant of Thomas Palmer, to hold, etc., etc.

Witnesses : John Stonton, John Page, John Stryt, and many others.
Dated at Harberowe, 22 Henry VI., 'undecimo die mensis Marcii ;' *i.e.*, Wednesday March 11, 144¾.
On the back: 'Relaxatio Reginaldi Welham et aliorum.'

(35) [Imperfect.]

Thomas Smyth, of Magna Bowdon, chaplain, and John Smyth, his brother, of the same, give, grant and confirm to Richard Smyth, of the same, and John [   ], all the lands, tenements, meadows, pastures and pasturages inherited on the decease of Robert Hillesley, their late father, and Johan his wife [   ], to hold, etc., etc.

    Witnesses : William Thannyng, of Bowdon, John Smyth, sen., of the same, [   ] Dekon, next the Cross, of the same, and William Brannge, of the same, and many others.

Dated at Bowdon, 24 Henry VI., 'decimo quarto die mensis Maii ;' *i.e.*, Saturday, May 14, 1446.

(36) Thomas Wermington, of Coventre, and Robert Wermington, of Haverbergh, give, grant and confirm to John Heton, Esquire, Laurence Kay, John Grene, Richard Rybell and William Pere, a messuage in Haverbergh, situated between the tenement of Robert Boseworth and that of John Sander, to hold, etc., etc.

    Witnesses : William Neell, John Laughton, John Person, John Page, John Stonton, and others.

Dated at Haverbergh, 26 Henry VI., 'die Veneris proxima post festum Omnium Sanctorum ;' *i.e.*, Friday, November 3, 1447.

(37) John Heton, Esquire, John Grene, Richard Rybell and William Pere, give, grant, and confirm to Thomas Wermyngton, of Coventre, and Robert Wermyngton, of Haverbergh, a messuage in Haverbergh, which they lately held conjointly with Laurence Kay, now deceased, by the gift and feoffment of the aforesaid Thomas Wermington and Robert Wermington, by a deed of fee-simple (per cartam simplicis feodi), to hold, etc., etc.

    Witnesses : William Neell, John Laughton, John Person, John Stonton, Richard Stonton, and others.

Dated at Haverbergh, 27 Henry VI., 'die Veneris proxima post festum Pasche ;' *i.e.*, Friday, April 18, 1449.

(38) The same parties as in No. 36 give, grant and confirm to William Neell, of Keylmersh, and Alice his wife, a messuage in Haverbergh, situated between the tenement lately Robert Boseworth's and that which John Felough holds, to hold, etc., etc.

    Witnesses : Nicholas Joy, John Laughton, John Person, John Stonton, Henry Smyth, and others.

Dated at Haverbergh, 27 Henry VI., 'tertio die mensis Maii ;' *i.e.*, Saturday May 3, 1449.

(39) Robert Wermyngton, of Haverbergh, 'wolman,' gives, grants and confirms to Henry Smyth, of the same, a messuage in Haverbergh, situated between a certain inn, lately Robert Boseworth's, called the Bear on the Hoop (le Bere super le Hope),[1] and the tenement of Robert Wright, with a croft lying between the croft of Henry Leycester and the tenement of Robert Hooke, also all his lands, tenements, etc., in the town and fields of Lobenham, in the county of Leicester.

> Witnesses : Nicholas Joy, Peter Auton, John Person, Walter Coly, William Foxton, and many others.

Dated at Haverbergh, 30 Henry VI., 'die Jovis in festo Sancte Katerine Virginis ;' *i.e.*, Thursday, November 25, 1451.

(40) Indenture witnessing that whereas Robert Wermyngton, of Haverbergh, has by a charter of feoffment given and confirmed to Henry Smyth, of the same, a messuage situated in Haverbergh, as in the said charter is fully contained, the aforesaid Henry, for himself and his heirs, wills and grants that if Robert Wermyngton, or someone on his behalf, shall pay to him, the said Henry, or his attorney, within 15 days after the Feast of S. Dionysius the Martyr, next after date, 6 marks and 9 shillings of lawful English money, or as many pence in cloth (in pannis), *i.e.* 6 marks 9 shillings full value according to the estimate of three or more just and impartial clothiers (secundum quod videbitur per tres aut plures probos pannarios indifferentes), the said charter and seisin delivered by it shall be void.

Dated at Haverbergh, 32 Henry VI., 'quarto decimo die mensis Septembris ;' *i.e.*, Friday, September 14, 1453.

(41) Robert Wermyngton, of Haverbergh, 'wolman,' gives, grants and confirms to John Stukeley, of Merston Trussell, in the county of Northampton, and John his son, of the same, all his lands, tenements, meadows, etc.,

---

[1] *Cf.* Bury Wills, p. 244, 'The Hert of the Hop.' Many an old sign consisted of a carved figure set in a hoop.

in the towns and fields of Magna Boudon and Lobenham. He also gives and grants to the same a croft in Haverbergh, lying between the croft of Henry Leycester and the tenement of Robert Hooke, and the reversion of a messuage situated between an inn called the Bear on the Hoop (le Bere super le Hoope), lately Robert Boseworth's, and the tenement of Robert Wrighte, in the tenure of Henry Smyth, of Haverbergh, by reason of a mortgage, to hold, etc., etc.

> Witnesses : Nicholas Joye, Thomas Gote, Richard Stonton, John Felowes, and William Neell.

Dated at Haverbergh, 32 Henry VI., 'duodecimo die mensis Octobris ;' *i.e.*, Friday, October 12, 1453.

(42) John Stonton, of Haverbergh, gives, grants and confirms to John Schirwode, of Magna Bowdon, and Thomas his son, 6 thirty-falls (tripartetas) of arable land lying in the field of Bowdon, and lying together against the sun, next the land lately Thomas Alyngton's on the west, and one rood and a half of land lying on Stanhill, next the land lately John Simons' on the west, to hold of the chief lord of that fee, etc., etc.

> Witnesses : Richard Stonton, of Haverbergh, John Shute, of the same, Richard West, of the same, and many others.

Dated at Haverbergh, 36 Henry VI., 'decimo octavo die mensis Junii ;' *i.e.*, Friday, June 18, 1458.

(43) William Couper, of Haverbergh, senior, gives, grants and confirms to John Schirwode, of Magna Bowdon, 6 roods of arable land lying in 'le Gallowfeld' of Bowdon, on Schirdecotys, between the land of Nicholas Joy on the west, and 'lez Hadys' on the other part, to hold, etc., etc.

> Witnesses : William Harpar, of Bowdon, William Strannge, of the same, Richard Anneys, of the same, Richard Harper, jun., of the same, and John Basset, of the same, and many others.

Dated at Bowdon, 39 Henry VI., 'tertio die mensis Februarii ;' *i.e.*, Tuesday, February 3, 146^0_1.

(44) John, son of William Coupar, of Haverbergh, remits, releases and quit-claims, for himself and his heirs for ever, to John Schirwode, of Magna Bowdon, all his right and claim in 6 roods of land lying on Schirdecotys, in the field of Bowdon, as described in a deed executed by his father to John Schirwode.

Dated 39 Henry VI., 'decimo die mensis Marcii;' *i.e.*, Tuesday, March 10, 146$^0_1$.

(45) John Neele, of Keylmerssh, in the county of Northampton, gives, grants and confirms to William Dey a messuage in Haverburgh, between the tenement lately John Sanders' on the south, and the tenement of Robert Mallory, Esquire, on the north, to have and to hold of the chief lord of the fee, etc., etc. J. N. also constitutes and appoints William Hay, of Maydewell, his attorney, to deliver possession and seisin of the same.

Witnesses: Henry Leycester, Henry Smyth, Thomas Gylbard, William Wever, and others.

Dated 2 Edward IV., 'septimo decimo die mensis Maii; *i.e.*, Monday, May 17, 1462.

(46) John Wenneham, of Haverburgh, gives, grants and confirms to John Pyfford, of the same, a curtilage[1] situated between the tenement lately Robert Michell's on the south, and a messuage of the said John Pyfford's on the north, and abutting on [   ] of Dag Lane, in Haverburgh, to have and to hold, etc., at the yearly rent of one flower, payable on the Feast of the Nativity of Saint [   ], for all secular services.

Witnesses: Thomas Gylbard, Richard Stonton, Richard Sherman, Richard Brown, John Whatton, and many others.

Dated at Haverbergh, 3 Edward IV., 'die Veneris proxima post [festum] Pasche;' *i.e.*, Friday, April 15, 1463.

(47) Indenture by which Thomas Palmer, John Beyvill and Hugh Beyvill, Esquires, Richard Neell and Thomas

---

[1] A courtyard, or small garden, attached to a house.—Liber Albus (Rolls Series), Glossary.

Gyssing, grant and hand over to Henry Pentynge, kinsman and heir of William Neell, of Haverbergh, lately deceased—*i.e.*, the son of Alice, daughter of the said William Neell—all the lands and tenements, meadows, pastures, etc., etc., in Haverbergh and Bowdon, which lately belonged to William Neell, deceased, to have and to hold to the said Henry Pentynge and his legitimate heirs, of the chief lords of the fee, etc., etc. In case there are no such heirs, the property is to revert to the said Thomas Palmer and the others, and their heirs.

    Witnesses: Henry Leycester, Nicholas Joye, Richard Stonton, Richard Brown, John Whatton, and others.

Dated at Haverbergh, 3 Edward IV., 'die Lune proxima ante festum Sancte Margarete Virginis ;' *i.e.*, Monday, July 18, 1463.

(48) Power of attorney by which Thomas Palmer, John Beyvill and Hugh Beyvill, Esquires, Richard Neell and Thomas Gyssing, appoint Henry Smyth, of Haverbergh, and Robert Smyth, bailiff of Haverbergh, jointly and severally, to deliver seisin to Henry Pentynge of the property above mentioned.

    Dated at Haverbergh. (Same date.)

(49) John Skepper, of Magna Boudon, gives, grants and confirms in frank-marriage[1] to Richard Cristyan, son of Thomas Cristyan, of the same, and Agnes his wife, daughter of the said John Skepper, and their lawful issue, one messuage in Boudon, and 10 acres of arable land in the fields of Boudon, lying separated in different places (in diversis locis separatim jacentes), and 2 pastures.

    Witnesses: John Eston, Richard Harper, Thomas in le hirne, William Graunge, Richard Knyght, and others.

Dated at Boudon, 3 Edward IV., 'die Dominica proxima ante festum S^{ti} Petri quod dicitur ad Vincula ;' *i.e.*, Sunday, July 31, 1463.

DESCRIPTION OF THE PROPERTY.

The messuage lies in the south end (in fine australi), next the lord's messuage on the south and a certain lane on the north. Whence ten acres of land, as follows (et unde decem acre terre) :—

---

[1] *Frank-marriage*: a tenure in tail special, whereby lands or tenements are held to a man and his wife, and the heirs of their bodies, on condition of doing no service to the donor but fealty to the fourth degree.—Bailey's Dictionary (folio 1755).

In the South Field (le Southfeld).

2½ roods lying together on Bukwelmore, next the gore on the west.
1 half-rood on Lyttylhill, next the gore on the east.
1½ roods and 1 thirty-fall towards the Gatemyll, next the land of Thomas Dekyn, senior, on the south.

In the North Field (le Norhtfeld).

1 rood on 'le Estlonge,' next the land of John Basset on the north.
1 rood on the same furlong (quarentena), next the land of John Clement on the south.
3 roods and 3 half-roods lying together on 'le Threnge,' next the gore on the east.
1½ roods on the same, next the Rector's land on the west.
1 selion containing 3 roods on the same, next the land of Richard Petenale on the west.
1 half-acre on 'le Brest,' next the land of the said Richard on the east.
1 rood on the same, next the land of William Harper on the west.
1 rood on Overgrymeswong, next the land of Thomas Cristyan on the west.
3 roods lying together on 'le Gallowe,' next the land of the late William Neell on the east.
1 rood on 'le Gallowe' abutting on Paynesgore.
1½ roods on Warpart, next the land of Thomas Cristyan on the east.

In the East Field (le Estfeld).

1 rood on Lyttylbergh, second from the gore on the north.
1 rood on Snakesyke, next the land of John Russel on the south.
1 half-acre on Sandefurlong, next the land of William Harper on the east.
2 roods together on Musfurlong, next the land of John Basset's heirs.
1 half-rood on Lakefurlong, next the land of the late John Shirwode.
1 rood on the same, next the land of the late John Shirwode.
1 acre together, under Mikelbergh, on the east between the two gores.
1 rood on Mikelbergh, next the land of Richard Swan on the south.
1 thirty-fall on the south part of Mikelbergh, next the land of Thomas Cristyan on the east.
1 thirty-fall on the same, next the land of William Peer on the east.
1 thirty-fall on Mikelbergh, next the land of John Eston on the east.

The property is to revert to the heirs of John Skepper, and Joanna his wife, if Richard Cristyan and his wife die without heirs.

(50) Henry Leycester, of Haverbergh, gives, grants and confirms to Mr. John Fyssher, clerk, and Thomas Fyssher, chaplain, a messuage situated in Haverbergh between his capital messuage[1] on the north and the tenement of

---

[1] *Capital messuage:* that occupied by the owner of a property containing several messuages.—New English Dictionary (Dr. Murray), 'capital,' adj. and sub., A II., 6b.

John Whatton on the south, which messuage was formerly in the tenure of Roger Petelyng, chaplain, to have and to hold of the chief lord of the fee.

> Witnesses : Thomas Gylbard, Robert Smyth, bailiff of Haverbergh, Richard Stonton, Richard Broun, John Whatton, and others.

Dated at Haverbergh, 3 Edward IV., 'die Veneris in festo Sancte Scolastice Virginis ;' *i.e.*, Friday, February 10, 146¾.

(51) [In duplicate.]

The two parts of an indenture by which Agnes, late wife of Nicholas Joy, and Lambert, son and heir of Nicholas Joy, of Haverburgh, hand over, grant and let to farm to Thomas Robert, of Haverburgh, 'bucher,' for the term of his life the following property in Haverburgh :

- A messuage situated between the messuage lately John Parson's, and a tenement of Thomas Crancefelde.
- A bakehouse (pistrinam), situated between the common ropewalk (funarium) and a tenement lately Agnes Warmington's.
- One pasture in the common pasture of Haverburgh.
- Yearly rent to be paid by equal portions at Easter and Michaelmas : 10s. lawful English money.
- Also year by year to the chief lords of that fee 8s. 3d. ; viz., to the heirs of Thomas Walssh, 7s. 6d. ; and to Thomas Trussell, knight, 9d.
- The lessee to repair and maintain at his own expense, and leave everything in sufficient order.

> Witnesses : Richard Curlett, gentleman, Richard Smyth, Robert Smyth, bailiff of Haverburgh, Edmund Pentyng, and others.

Dated at Haverburgh, 4 Edward IV., 'in festo Undecim Mille Virginum ;' *i.e.*, Sunday, October 21, 1464.

(52) Thomas Palmer, of Holt, Esquire, remits, releases and quit-claims for himself and his heirs for ever to Angnes (*sic*) Joye, and Lambert Joye, all his right and claim [in all the lands and tenements] in the town (villa)

and fields of Magna Bowdon, Haverbarugh, Lubbenham, Est Langeton in the county of Leicester, and Farnedon, Parva Oxendon, and Parva Bowdon, in the county of Northampton, which he held with Robert Boseworth, William Weldon, William Nelle, and John Stonton, senior, deceased, by the gift and feoffment of Katherine Leycester, to have and to hold, etc.

> Witnesses : Thomas Langeton, William Iseham, John Langeton, Esquires, Thomas Chapman, of Foxton, Henry Smyth, of Haverbarugh, Henry Balle, of the same, Robert Smyth, of the same, and many others.

Dated 5 Edward IV., 'vicesimo tertio die mensis Octobris ;' *i.e.*, Wednesday, October 23, 1465.

(53) Angnes (*sic*) Joy, of Haverbarugh, gives, grants and confirms to Lambert Joy her son, and Angnes his wife, all her lands and tenements, meadows, pastures, etc., etc., in Haverbarugh, Lubbenham, Est Langeton in the county of Leicester, Farnedon, Parva Oxendon, Parva Bowdon, in the county of Northampton, Follysworth, Stelton and Sawtry in the county of Huntingdon, to have and to hold, etc., etc.

> Witnesses : Robert Smyth, Henry Balle, Edmund Pentyng, John Clyn, Thomas Hawkeworth, and many others.

Dated at Haverbarugh, 5 Edward IV., 'in festo Natalis Domini ;' *i.e.*, Wednesday, Christmas Day, 1465.

(54) Lambert Joy, of Haverborough in the county of Leicester, binds himself to Henry Longe, 'husbondman,' of Parva Bowdon in the county of Northampton, in the the sum of 40s. lawful English money, to be paid on the Feast of St. John Baptist next ensuing.

This bond is of no value if Henry Longe and his assigns hold, possess and enjoy for 13 full years after date the following lands:

In the South Field of Magna Bowdon.

1 acre next the land of Robert Malery.
1 acre in Yngbarowefelde, next the land of Richard Broun.

In the Fields of Faryndon.

1 half-acre lying next the land of the Rector on the east.
1 half-acre towards Brakynbarowhylt,[1] next the land of the Rector on the south.

Dated 6 Edward IV., 'vicesimo primo die mensis Junii;' *i.e.*, June 21, 1466.

(55) [Imperfect.]

Lambert Joy, of Haverbergh, and Agnes his wife, give, grant and confirm to Robert Janyn, of Haverbergh, 'yoman,' one yearly rent of 10s., arising out of certain lands, tenements, etc., in Haverbergh, which Thomas Robert, 'bocher,' of Haverbergh, and Agnes his wife, hold of them by virtue of a pair of indentures, duly executed between them, for the period of Thomas Robert's life.

The rent is payable by equal portions at the Feasts of St. Michael and the Annunciation.

If it is in either case one month in arrear, Robert Janyn has full powers of distraint.

Seisin has been given to Robert Janyn by payment of the sum of 4d., and Thomas Robert has been empowered and caused to become security for the rent by payment of 1d.

Dated 9 Edward IV., 'septimo die mensis Aprilis;' *i.e.*, Friday. April 7, 1469.

(56) Indenture by which Lambert Joy, and Agnes his wife, grant, hand over and let to farm to Robert Janyn, of Haverbergh, 'yoman,' for the term of his life immediately after the decease of Thomas Robart, the lands, tenements, etc., in Haverbergh, which the said Thomas Robart, and Agnes his wife, hold of them for the term of the life of the said Thomas Robart.

One red rose to be paid yearly for the same (if demanded) at the Feast of St. John Baptist.

Also to the chief lords of the fee, yearly, 8s. 3d.; viz.,

---

[1] *Braken*, brakes = ferns (Forby, p. 37). See also New Eng. Dict. (Dr. Murray), 'bracken.'

to the heirs of Thomas Walssh, 7s. 6d., and to Thomas Trussell, knight, 9d.

Robert Janyn and his assigns are to repair at their own cost, and to give up at the end of the term in good order.

Dated 9 Edward IV., 'nono die mensis Aprilis;' *i.e.*, Sunday, April 9, 1469.

(57) Lambert Joy, of Haverbergh, in the county of Leicester, 'gentilman,' binds himself to Robert Janyn, of Haverbergh, 'yoman,' in the sum of £20 sterling, payable on the Feast of St. John Baptist after date.

Dated 9 Edward IV., 'decimo die Aprilis;' *i.e.*, Monday, April 10, 1469.

Condition (*on the back*): This bond is void if the conditions and covenants of the indentures between the same parties, dated April 9, 1469, are duly fulfilled.

(58) Thomas 'in the hyrne,' of Magna Boudon, gives, grants and confirms to John Atwell, of Foxton, 5 acres of arable land and herbage in the north field of Boudon, to hold of the chief lords of the fee, etc.

Witnesses: Robert Dekyn, of Boudon, William Carter, of the same, William Wattys, of the same, John Cristian, of the same, Thomas Skotte, of the same, and many others.

Dated 11 Edward IV., 'in die Sanctorum Philippi et Jacobi; *i.e.*, May 1, 1471.

PARTICULARS OF THE ABOVE-NAMED PROPERTY.

1 half-acre on the plough-land (carucata)[1] abutting 'into Tocroft,' fourth from the gore on the east.

1 half-acre on the same tillage (super eandem culturam),[2] sixth from the gore on the west.

1½ roods on the same, seventeenth from the gore on the west.

3½ roods together, on 'le Breche,' next Boudon Church land on the west.

---

[1] A measure of land, varying with the nature of the soil, etc., being as much as could be tilled with one plough (with its team of eight oxen) in a year; a plough-land.—New Eng. Dict. (Dr. Murray) 'carucate.'

[2] Cultura sæpe sumitur pro modo agri qui colitur et aratur.—Du Cange.

1 rood with a headland of herbage abutting 'into Fargatys,' sixth from the gore on the north.

1 rood lying on the plough-land abutting 'into Tocrofte,' on the upper part of the said plough-land, the fifth rood from Fargatys.

1 half-acre on the said plough-land, thirteenth from Fargatys.

1½ roods on Midillfurlonge Weste.

2 roods together, on 'le Weste breste,' abutting on the domain (territorium) of Banlonds.

1 thirty-fall (triparticum) lying next the domain of the Rector on Comynmarlepyttes.

(59) Lambert Joy, son of Nicholas Joy, of Haverbarough, and Agnes his wife, give, grant and confirm to Robert Jennyn, of the same, and Margaret his wife, two tenements and one pasture in Haverbarough, to hold, etc., and appoint John Elyner, their attorney, to deliver seisin.

DESCRIPTION OF THE PROPERTY.

One tenement, situated between the tenement of John Kelyng, clerk, late the tenement of John Wenham, on the north, and the tenement of Robert Mallory, late the tenement of Robert Crancefelde, on the south, extending (et extendit se) from the highway (via regia) on the east, as far as the Field of Magna Bowdon, on the west.

Another tenement, called a shop (unam shopam), otherwise called the common bakehouse (communam [sic] pistrinam), situated between the tenement of John Pyfford on the south, and the common ropewalk (funarium) on the north.

Dated 11 Edward IV., 'quarto decimo die Julii ;' *i.e.*, Sunday, July 14, 1471.

(60) Lambert Joy gives, grants and confirms to Robert Gennyn, the same property described as above, and appoints the same attorney to deliver seisin.

Dated 11 Edward IV., 'die Dominica proxima post festum Sancte Margerete Virginis ;' *i.e.*, July 14, 1471.

(61) Thomas Holande, of Snaithe in the county of York, 'yoman,' binds himself and his heirs, etc., in the sum of £20, lawful English money, to be paid on Easter Day after date.

Dated 13 Edward IV., 'die Martis proxima ante festum Sanctorum Symonis et Jude ;' *i.e.*, Tuesday, October 26, 1473.

No condition attached.

(62) John Tythewell, 'gentilman,' Robert Coldham, 'fyshemonger,' and John Freman, grocer, citizens of London, hand over, demise, enfeoff, deliver and confirm to Henry Pentyng, citizen and fishmonger of London, all the lands and tenements, rents, reversions, etc., etc., in the towns, parishes, and fields of Harborowe, Bowdon, and Throp Langton, which they hold by his grant and confirmation, to hold, etc.

> Witnesses : Robert Geny, bailiff of Harborowe and Bowdon (tunc ballivo), Richard Broun, John Waton, and many others.

Dated 15 Edward IV., 'ultimo die mensis Septembris ;' *i.e.*, Saturday, September 30, 1475.

(63) The same persons appoint Thomas Gilbert, of Harborowe, William Cok, of the same, and William Harper, of Bowdon, their attorneys to deliver seisin.

(64) William Palmer and Richard Langeton, Esquires, Thomas Chapman, John Freseby, of Carleton, Richard Sherman, senior, of Haverbergh, and John Eleyne, of the same, hand over, deliver and confirm to Lambert Joye, of Haverbergh, all those lands and tenements, meadows, pastures, with tofts, crofts, rents, reversions, and services, etc., in the towns and fields of Magna Boudon, Haverbergh and Lubbenham in the county of Leicester, and Farendon in the county of Northampton, which they hold by his grant and feoffment, to hold, etc.

> Witnesses : Robert Burdon, of Haverbergh, Richard Sherman, Richard Broun, Richard Fraunces, William Marshall, of the same, and many others.

Dated 16 Edward IV., 'vicesimo sexto die mensis Maii ;' *i.e.*, Monday, May 16, 1476.

(65) Lambert Joy, of Haverbergh, 'gentilman,' binds himself to Robert Longe of the same, 'webster,' in the sum of £10, lawful English money, to be paid on the Feast of St. Michael the Archangel next after date.

Dated 16 Edward IV., 'sexto decimo die mensis Decembris ;' *i.e.*, Monday, December 16, 1476.

Condition (*on the back*) : This bond is void if Robert Longe and Alice, his wife, hold peaceably, etc., a messuage and two pastures for the term of twenty years, after the death of Henry Longe, according to the terms of indentures executed between the parties to the bond at the same date.

(66) Walter Marchant, of Boudon Magna, and Johanna his wife, give, grant and confirm to John Peche, of Haverbergh, 10 roods of arable land and meadow, and one ox-pasture (pasturam unius grossi animalis), lying scattered (divisim) in the fields of Boudon, to hold, etc., etc.

Witnesses : Richard Harper, jun., of Boudon, Thomas Harper, Thomas Annes, Robert Cartar, Thomas Scotte, of the same, and many others.

Dated at Boudon, 17 Edward IV., 'in die Sancti Marci Evangeliste; *i.e.*, April 25, 1477.

PARTICULARS OF THE PROPERTY.

In the South Field.

1 half-acre and 1 half-rood of arable land below Efilde, next the lord's gore there on the east.

2 roods lying on Stockefurlong, one east of the land of John Griggs, clerk, the other west of the same.

In the West Field.

1 thirty-fall (triparticum) on Waterlakes, next the land late Robert Boresworth's on the east.

1 rood on Stretefurlong, abutting on the highway, next the land late William Nele's on the east.

In the North Field.

1 half-rood on Shorte Rockehill, next the land late John Griggs' on the north.

$1\frac{1}{2}$ roods on Nether Wylardisgate, next the land of Thomas in the Hyrne on the east.

1 half-acre lying in the East field, on Hayleys, next the meadow of Thomas Harper on the west.

The aforesaid pasture lies among the common pastures of the town of Boudon.

Tied to the preceding: A power of attorney, appointing Robert Janyne, of Haverbergh, and Thomas Scotte, of Boudon, to deliver seisin. Same date.

(67) Lambert Joye, of Haverbergh, gives, grants and confirms to John Peche, of the same, $11\frac{1}{2}$ roods of arable

land and 1 pasture in the south fields of Boudon Magna, to hold, etc., etc.

> Witnesses : Robert Burdon, of Haverbergh, Richard Sherman, of the same, John Eleyne, of the same, Thomas Scotte, of Boudon, Richard Harper, jun., of the same, and many others.

Dated at Haverbergh, 17 Edward IV., 'in die Sabbati proxima post festum Ascensionis Domini ;' *i.e.*, Saturday, May 17, 1477.

PARTICULARS OF THE PROPERTY.

1½ roods on Smalthornes, next the land late Thomas Walshe's on the west.

1 rood abutting into Lubbenham broke, next the land late Hugh Beyvile's on the south.

1 rood on the same, next the land of the said Hugh on the north.

1 rood on the same, next the land of Thomas Deken on the north.

1 rood on the same, next the land of the said Hugh Beyvile on the south.

2 roods on the same, next the gore there on the south.

1 rood abutting into Penytherne, fifteenth from the gore on the north.

1 rood on the same, seventeenth from the gore on the north.

1 rood on the same, nineteenth from the gore on the north.

1 rood on the same, twenty-first from the gore on the north.

The aforesaid beast-pasture lying among the common pastures of the town of Haverbergh.

(68) Lambert Joye remits, releases and quit-claims to John Peche all his right, title, estate, claim, interest and demand in the before-mentioned property.

> Dated 17 Edward IV., 'in die Lune proximo post festum Ascensionis Domini ;' *i.e.*, Monday, May 19, 1477.

(69) Lambert Joy appoints Richard Fraunces, of Haverbergh, his attorney to deliver seisin of the same property.

(70) Indenture by which Richard Barone, of Haverbergh, hands over, grants and lets to farm to Richard Fraunces, of the same, a messuage situated in Haverbergh in Lubbenham Lane, next the messuage of Thomas Pope on the east, and a toft, late Robert Mallory's, on the west, for the term of 12 years, on payment of a peppercorn rent yearly, on the day and feast of the Nativity of

the Lord, if demanded, and of the due and accustomed services to the chief lords of the fee.

> Witnesses: John Eleyne, of Haverbergh, Lambert Joye, John Umfray, Robert Barkar, John Lowte, of the same, and many others.

Dated at Haverbergh, 18 Edward IV., 'in die Translacionis Sancti Thome Martiris;' *i.e.*, Tuesday, July 7, 1478.

(71) Richard Barone, of Haverbergh, gives, grants and confirms to Richard Fraunces, of the same, a messuage in a street there called Lubbenham Lane (in venella ibidem vocata Lubbenham Lane), next the messuage, late Thomas Pope's, on the east, and next the toft, late Robert Mallory's, on the west.

> Witnesses: John Eleyne, of Haverbergh, William Whatton, John Piffeford, Hugh Avercy, William Lowte, of the same, and many others.

Dated at Haverbergh, 18 Edward IV., 'quinto die mensis Januarii;' *i.e.*, Tuesday, January 5, 147$\frac{8}{9}$.

(72) Henry Pentyng, citizen and fishmonger of the city of London, gives, grants and confirms to Lawrence Fyncham, Robert Creket, Robert Coldcham, citizens and fishmongers, London, and Robert Janyn, 'yoman,' all his lands, tenements, etc., in the towns and fields of Harborowe and Bowdon Magna, in the county of Leicester, to hold, etc.

> Witnesses: William Cok, of Harborowe, Robert Carter, of Bowdon, Thomas Scot, of the same, and others.

Dated at Harborowe, 19 Edward IV., 'sexto die mensis Maii;' *i.e.*, Thursday, May 6, 1479.

(73) Power of attorney, by which Henry Pentyng empowers Richard Browne, and William Serle, to deliver seisin of the property above-mentioned.

Dated 19 Edward IV., 'septimo die mensis Maii;' *i.e.*, Friday, May 7, 1479.

(74) Power of attorney, by which John Peche, of Haverbergh, empowers Sir John Belyngham, chaplain, and Robert Welyngore, of Haverbergh, to enter and take possession of all his lands and tenements, etc., in the

town and fields of Boudon Magna, and to deliver seisin of the same to William Blake, chaplain, of Haverbergh, Thomas Gylbert, junior, of the same, Richard Burdon, Lambert Joye, John Gleyne, John Umfraye, John Brewode, of the same.

Dated 19 Edward IV., 'quinto decimo die mensis Novembris;' *i.e.*, Monday, November 15, 1479.

(75) Power of attorney, by which Richard Fraunces, of Haverbergh, empowers Richard Browne, and Robert Wellyngore, of the same, to enter and take possession of a messuage in Lubbenham Lane, situated between a messuage, late Thomas Pope's, on the east, and a toft, late Robert Mallory's, on the west, and to deliver seisin of the same to William Blake, chaplain, of Haverbergh, Thomas Gylbert, junior, of the same, Richard Burdon, Lambert Joye, John Gleyne, John Umfraye, and John Brewode.

Dated 19 Edward IV., 'sexto decimo die mensis Januarii;' *i.e.*, Sunday, January 16, 1479/80.

(76) Lawrence Fyncham, Robert Creket, Robert Coldeham, citizens and fishmongers of London, and Robert Janyn, 'yoman,' remit, release and quit-claim to Henry Pentyng, citizen and fishmonger of London, all their right, title, etc., etc., in all the lands and tenements which they lately held by his gift and feoffment.

Dated 20 Edward IV., 'undecimo die Aprilis;' *i.e.*, Tuesday, April 11, 1480.

(77) [Imperfect.]
Henry Pentyng, citizen and fishmonger of London, gives, grants and confirms to Robert Janyn, all his lands, tenements, rents, etc., etc., in the fields of Magna Bowedone, Harborowe and Lubbenham, in the county of Leicester.

(Power of attorney is added, but the names are obliterated.)

Witnesses : William Cok, of Harborowe, Robert Carter, of Magna Bowedon, Thomas Scotte, and many others.

Dated at Harborowe, 21 Edward IV., 'primo die Maii;' *i.e.*, Tues-

(78) Richard Eston, son of Robert Eston, of Boudon Magna, and John Harcorte, of Dyngeley, remit, release and quit-claim to Robert Janyne, of Haverbergh, all their right, claim, etc., in 2½ acres of land in the fields of Boudon, which the said Robert Janyne held by the grant and confirmation of Robert Eston, of Boudon, aforesaid, according to terms of a deed dated at Boudon, July 2, in the 21st year of Edward IV.

> Witnesses : Richard Petenale, of Boudon, Richard Harper, jun., William Graunge, of the same, and many others.

Dated at Boudon, 21 Edward IV., 'vicesimo sexto die mensis Julii ;' *i.e.*, Thursday, July 26, 1481.

(79) Richard Reynold and Thomas Bytteswell remit, release and quit-claim to Robert Janyn, bailiff of Sybertoft, all actions, suits, etc., etc., with reference to the collection of rents, or other exercise of his office as bailiff.

Dated 22 Edward IV., 'ultimo die Octobris ;' *i.e.*, Thursday, October 31, 1482.

(80) Thomas Myryell, of Bytteswell, in the county of Leicester, 'gentilman,' binds himself to Thomas Entwysull, Esquire, sheriff of the said county, in the sum of £20, to be paid on the Feast of St. Michael the Archangel next ensuing.

Dated 1 Richard III., 'nono die Augusti ;' *i.e.*, Saturday, August 9, 1483.

(81) Richard Swan, of Boudon Magna, binds himself to Robert Longe, of Haverbergh, in the sum of forty shillings, to be paid on the Feast of the Annunciation.

Dated 1 Richard III., 'quinto die mensis Decembris ;' *i.e.*, Friday, December 5, 1483.

On the back is written the condition in English as follows : 'The condicon of this obligat' is this y^t if w^{t}in wretyne Robart longe his heyres & assignez haue and holde and pesably receyve an acr^e & a rode of arabyll lande lyenge w^{t}in ye Weste Felde of Mekell Boudon w^{t}oute any vexacon or t^{o}ble of Ric^d Swan w^{t}in bonden his heyres or assignes the wiche ye said Robart hath p'chased of ye said Richard y^t then ye obligacon for no thynge be had or ellys to stande True & Stronge.'

(82) John Kynge, of Magna Boudon, in the county of Leycester, gives, grants and confirms to Robert Janen, of Haverbergh, one croft, and the third part of one headland, in the town and fields of Boudon, to hold, etc.

> Witnesses : William Walkeleyn, of Boudon, Robert Carter, Thomas Annes, Nicholas Jakes, Robert Harper, of the same, and many others.

Dated at Boudon, 1 Richard III., 'vicesimo septimo die mensis Januarii ;' *i.e.*, Wednesday, January 27, 148¾.

DESCRIPTION OF THE PROPERTY.

The messuage is situated in the town of Boudon, between the messuage of William Harper on the north, and the messuage of William Collys on the south, and extends from the King's highway on the east to the field of the town on the west. The third part of a headland abuts on the said croft.

(83) William Clerk, of Haverbergh, gives, grants and confirms to Robert Janyn, of Haverbergh, a thirty-fall (unam triparticatam) of land lying in the fields of Magna Boudon, in the west field of the town of Boudon on Waterlakes, next the land called 'Tudges' land on the north.

> Witnesses : Lambert Joye, of Haverbergh, Richard Fraunces, of the same, Robert Carter, of Boudon, Nicholas Jakes, Richard Crystian, of the same, and many others.

Dated at Boudon, 1 Richard III., 'vicesimo primo die Marcii ;' *i.e.*, Sunday, March 21, 148¾.

(84) Thomas Harper and William Harper, of Magna Boudon, give, grant and confirm to Robert Janyn, of Haverbergh, a messuage and three-parts of a selion, lying in the town and fields of Boudon, to hold, etc.

> Witnesses : Richard Harper, of Boudon, Thomas Annes, Richard Carter, William Harper, son of Richard Harper, John Sawnders, of the same, and many others.

Dated at Boudon, 2 Richard III., 'vicesimo die mensis Julii ;' *i.e.*, Tuesday, July 20, 1484.

DESCRIPTION OF THE PROPERTY.

The messuage is situated next the tenement of Thomas Smyth, son of Richard Smyth, on the south, and the tenement late John Kynge's on the north, and extends from the King's highway on the west to the boundary of the third part of a selion on the east.

(85) Richard Harper and John Walkeleyn remit, release and quit-claim to Thomas Harper, of Magna Boudon, all their right, claim, etc., in a messuage and three-parts of a selion lying in the town and fields of Boudon (the same described in the preceding), to hold, etc.

> Witnesses: William Wakeleyn, of Boudon, Nicholas Jakes, Robert Carter, Richard Valentyn, Robert Harper, of the same, 'et multis.'

Dated at Boudon, 3 Richard III., 'sexto decimo die Julii;' *i.e.*, Saturday, July 16, 1485.

(86) Lambert Joie, of Haverbergh, in the county of Leicester, gent., gives, grants and confirms to Robert Janen, of the same, 3 acres and 1 rood of meadow lying in the fields of Magna Boudon, and 1 pasture lying in the common pasture of Haverbergh, to hold, etc.

> Witnesses: Richard Browne, of Haverbergh, Richard Fraunces, of the same, Thomas Annes, of Boudon, Thomas Harper, John Sawnders, of the same, and many others.

Dated at Boudon, 3 Richard III., 'vicesimo quarto Julii;' *i.e.*, Sunday, July 24, 1485.

On the back: 'Carta Lambti Joye de xiij rod prᵃti et una pastur'.

DESCRIPTION OF THE PROPERTY.

1 acre on 'le Hayleys,' next the land of Robert Janen on the west.
1 thirty-fall on the same, next the land of John Crystian on the east.
1 half-rood on Fulforth, next the land of Leonard Acton on the east.
1 half-rood on Paddokispyltche, at the Whiteston, next the land of the Chantry there on the east.
1 rood on the same, next the land of John Crystyan on the east.
1½ roods on the same, next the land of Richard Harper on the west.
1 rood on Overgyfhoke, next the land of the Rector there on the west.
1 thirty-fall on Craneworth, next the land of the Rector there on the north.
1 half-acre on the same, next the land of John Dekyn on the south.
1 rood on 'le Halough,' next the land of Richard Peche on the east.

(87) John Clerk remits, releases and quit-claims to William Clerk, all his right, title, etc., in a messuage in the town of Haverbergh, situated next the bridge of

Haverbergh on the east, and the land of William Isham on the west.

> Witnesses: Lambert Joee, of Haverbergh, Richard Brown, John Glen, Richard Fraunces, William Wotton, and many others.

Dated at Haverbergh, 1 Henry VII., 'sexto die Maii;' *i.e.*, Saturday, May 6, 1486.

(88) William Dey, of Haverbargh, gives, grants and confirms to Robert Astell, and Alice his wife, a messuage, and a rood and a half of land lying in the town of Haverbargh and the fields of Magna Boudon, and appoints John Mayne his attorney to deliver seisin of the same.

> Witnesses: Robert Janen, of Haverbargh, Lambert Joee, Richard Browne, Richard Fraunceys, and Nicholas Barett, of the same.

Dated at Haverbargh, 3 Henry VII., 'quinto decimo die Januarii;' *i.e.*, Tuesday, January 15, 148¾.

The messuage is situated next the messuage of John Haddon on the south, and the messuage of the heirs of Robert Bosseworth on the north, the rood and a half lie on Holbarogh, next the land of Thomas Kyng on the west.

(89) Robert Swan, of Boudon Magna, remits, releases and quit-claims to Richard Oxton all his right, title, etc., in a messuage situated in Boudon between the tenement, late John Ingold's on the east, and a lane called Hyrn Lane[1] on the west, which he held together with Simon Kynnesman, Esquire, John Burgh, John Palmer, of Carleton, and John More, of Boudon, now deceased.

> Witnesses: William Walkeleyn, of Boudon, Nicholas Jakes, Roger Crafte, Richard Carter, and Thomas Kenett, of the same, and many others.

Dated at Boudon, 3 Henry VII., 'quarto decimo die Maii;' *i.e.*, Tuesday, May 14, 1488.

(90) Lambert Joee, of Haverbargh, gives, grants and confirms to John Marsh, and Margaret his wife, a messuage called 'le mylne house,' with a horse-mill built in the said messuage (cum uno molendino equino in dicto

---

[1] See p. 172, note.

messuagio edificato), situated in Haverbargh between the messuage of Richard Burdon on the north, and the messuage of Robert Burdon on the south, to hold, etc.—annual rent to the heirs of William Trussel, chief lords, ninepence silver—William Wafer, of Haverbargh, appointed attorney to deliver seisin.

>Witnesses : Thomas Sherewode, of Haverbargh, William Wetton, John Brewode, John Archer, and William Serle, of the same, and many others.

Dated at Haverbargh, 5 Henry VII., 'tertio die Novembris ;' *i.e.*, Tuesday, November 3, 1489.

(91) Robert Swanne, of Boudon Magna, gives, grants and confirms to Robert Janen, of Haverbargh, two acres of his land lying in the fields of Boudon, and appoints Roger Crafte, Thomas Harper, and William Harborowe, of Boudon, his attorneys, to deliver seisin of the same.

>Witnesses : Richard Marston, of Boudon, William Harper, son of Richard, Nicholas Jakes, William Carter, and Robert Bassett, of the same, and many others.

Dated at Boudon, 6 Henry VII., 'decimo die mensis Marcii ;' *i.e.*, Wednesday, March 10, 1490.

DESCRIPTION OF THE PROPERTY.

1 rood of herbage in 'le Hayleyes,' next the land of Robert Janen on the east.

1½ roods on Shirdycotes, next the land of Robert Roper on the west.

5 selions, containing 1 acre and 1 half-rood, on Rokhill, next the lord's on the east.

1 headland, containing 1 rood, on long Rokhyll, next the land late John Sherewode's on the north.

(92) Thomas Harper, of Boudon Magna, senior, remits, releases and quit-claims to Robert Janen, of Haverbargh, all his right, title, etc., in the property specified in the preceding, which he lately held, together with John Walkeleyn, deceased, along with other lands and tenements, by the gift and feoffment of Robert Swanne, of Boudon.

>Witnesses : William Walkeleyn, of Boudon, Richard Marston, Nicholas Jakes, Robert Bassett, and John Fyssher, of the same.

Dated at Boudon, 6 Henry VII., 'duodecimo die mensis Marcii ;' *i.e.*, Friday, March 12, 1490.

(93) Thomas Smyth, son of Richard Smyth, late of Boudon Magna, gives, grants and confirms to Robert Janen, of Haverbargh, all his tenements, tofts, crofts, rents, reversions and dues in the town of Boudon, together with half a headland in the fields of Boudon, next the land of John Clerk, and 40 feet in length of one selion abutting on the gates of Robert Janen's messuage (quadraginta pedes unius selion' . . . abbutt' usque portas messuagii prefati Roberti), formerly Thomas Smyth's.

> Witnesses: Thomas Harper, of Boudon, Nicholas Jakes, William Brewster, Richard Carter, and John Fyssher, of the same, and many others.

Dated at Boudon, 6 Henry VII., 'octavo die Junii;' *i.e.*, Wednesday, June 8, 1491.

William Walkleyne and Roger Crafte are appointed attorneys to deliver seisin.

(94) Margaret Staunton, widow, gives, grants and confirms to Robert Janyn a close in Haverbergh, lying next the land of Leonard Acton on the south, and all her arable lands, lying in the fields of Boudon Magna, for the term of her life, at a rent of 4s. yearly, payable in equal portions at the Feasts of Easter and St. Michael the Archangel. Richard Fraunnceys is appointed attorney to deliver seisin of the same.

> Witnesses: Ralph Shirley, knight, Thomas Kewell, serjeant-at-law, Thomas Entwysull, Esquire, and many others.

Dated 7 Henry VII., 'duodecimo die Octobris;' *i.e.*, Wednesday, October 12, 1491.

(95) Robert Clyff, otherwise called Robert Roper, of Boudon, 'housebondman,' appoints Everard Dygby, Esq., of Stoke Dry, in the county of Rutland, and Robert Jenyn, of Harborough, 'yoman,' his attorneys, to enter upon 2 acres of land lying in the fields of the town of Bowdon Magna, and to deliver seisin of the same to Sir Robert Duston, of Bowdon, clerk.

Dated 7 Henry VII., 'vicesimo tertio die mensis Januarii;' *i.e.*, Monday, January 23, 149½.

Name at the foot: J. Barkby.

(96) Richard Cristyan gives, grants and confirms to Robert Janen 6 acres of arable land, lying in the fields of Boudon Magna, to hold, etc., and appoints Nicholas Barrett, of Haverbargh, and Richard Carter, of Boudon, attorneys to deliver seisin of the same.

> Witnesses: William Walkeleyn, of Boudon, Roger Crafte, William Brewster, Robert Bassett, and Thomas Harper, of the same, and many others.

Dated at Boudon, 9 Henry VII., 'penultimo die Julii;' i.e., Wednesday, July 30, 1494.

Particulars of the Property.

In the East Field (in campo orientali).

1 half-acre lying together on Shulfebrode, next the land of Edward Derby on the east.

1 half-acre on Moreforelong [sic], next the land of Robert Bassett on the east.

1 half-acre under Mykelbarogh northe, next the land of William Walkeleyn on the west.

1 half-acre, extending into Wasshford, next the land of William Judde on the east.

1 rood on Mekylbarogh, next the land of the late Richard Dekanne on the south.

In the south Field (in campo australi).

1 half-acre, extending into Myllegate, next the land of Nicholas Deken on the south.

3 roods together, lying on Efell, next the lands of Boughton Chantry on the east.

1 rood under Efell, next the land of William Walkeleyn on the west.

1 rood on Overtoftys, next the land of the late William Grawnge on the east.

1½ roods next the common balk,[1] in Russhygore, on the west.

1½ roods in Wyllerspyttes, next the land of John Norewyche on the east.

In the North Field (in campo boriali).

1 thirty-fall on Rokhyll, next the land of Thomas Horsham on the north.

1 rood on 'le Galowe,' extending up to Paynesgore and the King's highway, next the land of Thomas Horsham on the north.

1 half-acre on Overgrymeswonge, next the land of William Goodman on the east.

1½ roods on Shortebanham, next the land of the Chantry of Boudon on the west.

---

[1] *Balk*: 'a ridge of land left unploughed to serve as a boundary, either between two contiguous occupations or two divisions of the same farm, in an unenclosed cornfield.'—Forby, p. 13; New Eng. Dict. (Dr. Murray), 'Balk,' II. 3; Halliwell's Archaic. Dict., 'Balk,' 1.

(97) John Browne gives, grants and confirms to Robert Janen a messuage of his, and two ox pastures (duas pasturas grossorum animalium), lying in the town and fields of Haverbargh and Boudon Magna, to hold, etc., and appoints George Alleyn his attorney to deliver seisin.

> Witnesses: John Archer, of Haverbargh, Nicholas Barrett, John Brewode, of Haverbargh, Thomas Harper, of Boudon, Thomas le Herne, of the same, and many others.

Dated at Haverbargh, 10 Henry VII., 'vicesimo secundo die Novembris;' *i.e.*, Saturday, November 22, 1494.

PARTICULARS OF THE PROPERTY.

The messuage is situated in Haverbargh, next the tenement of Leonard Acton on the south, and the tenement formerly Thomas Neell's on the north.

The two pastures lie in the common pastures of Boudon.

(98) Thomas Smyth, of Boudon Magna, senior, gives, grants and confirms to Robert Janen $6\frac{1}{2}$ roods of arable land, lying in the West field of Boudon, to hold, etc., and appoints John Rudde, of Boudon, his attorney to deliver seisin of the same.

> Witnesses: Nicholas Jakes, of Boudon, Thomas Benett, Robert Bassett, John Fyssher, and John Cristyan, of the same, and many others.

Dated at Boudon, 10 Henry VII., 'primo die mensis Februarii;' *i.e.*, Sunday, February 1, $149\frac{4}{5}$.

PARTICULARS OF THE PROPERTY.

1 half-acre on 'le Breeste,' next the land of Richard Browne on the west.

2 roods lying together, on the same tillage (culturam), third and fourth from 'le Foxtongate' on the west.

$1\frac{1}{2}$ roods on Pylwelfurlong, next 'le Tudges' land on the east.

1 on the same tillage (una super eandem culturam), next the land late 'le Grygges' on the east.

(99) [Attached to 98.]

Thomas Smyth, son of William Smyth, heir of Thomas Smyth, his grandfather, releases and quit-claims to Miles Roos, Thomas Watton, Thomas Foxton, John Newsham, John Hardyng, Richard Wele, Richard Cade, and John Tybbis, enfeoffed of $6\frac{1}{2}$ roods of arable land by the gift and feoffment of John Janyen, son and heir of Robert Janyen, all his right, title, etc., to the same.

> Witnesses: Roger Crafft, of Boudon Magna, Richard Deken, Richard Herper, Robert Warde, Robert Deken, and Nicholas Deken, of the same.

Dated at Boudon, 3 Henry VIII., 'vicesimo die mensis Aprilis;' *i.e.*, Tuesday, April 20, 1512.

(100) Receipt from Nicholas Vaws, knight, High Sheriff of Northamptonshire, acknowledging the payment by John Stanley, Esquire, lord of Sybertoft, by the hands of John Janyen, his bailiff, of 53s. 1d. for serjeanty,[1] due the Michaelmas preceding.

> Signed by William Lane, Under-Sheriff.

Dated 12 Henry VII., 'quinto die Novembris;' *i.e.*, Saturday, November 5, 1496.

(101) Lambert Joee gives, grants and confirms to John Janen a messuage, in the town of Haverbargh, one tillage[2] (cultura) of arable land, and one piece of meadow, lying in the fields of Boudon Magna, to hold, etc.

> Witnesses: Thomas Sherewode, of Haverbargh, Richard Marchall, senior, of the same, Thomas Harper, of Boudon, William Harper, son of Richard, of the same, and Richard Carter, of the same, and many others.

Dated at Haverbargh, 12 Henry VII., 'vicesimo primo die mensis Septembris;' *i.e.*, Friday, September 21, 1497.

PARTICULARS OF THE PROPERTY.

The messuage is situated between the tenement of Henry Manne on the north and the tenement of Robert Burdon on the south, and extends from the King's highway on the east, up to the field on the west.

The tillage (cultura) lies in the fields of Boudon on Crowethornhyll.

The piece of meadow lies in the field, and is called Potersholme Este, and extends from the lord's meadow on the west, to the bridge on the east.

(102) Lambert Joee appoints John Archer and Henry Manne, of Haverbargh, his attorneys to enter upon the

---

[1] *Serjeanty*, a tenure of land by peculiar service of special duty to the person of the lord.—Stubbs, *Select Charters;* Glossary, 'sergantia.'

[2] See p. 183, note 2.

above property and deliver seisin to John Janen, of Haverbargh.
Witnesses and date as above.

(103) John Marssh, of Haverbargh, and Margaret his wife, give, grant and confirm to John Janen, the property described in the preceding.

N.B. The description is the same as in the preceding, except that Henry Manne's messuage is to the north.

Witnesses: John Archer, of Haverbargh, Henry Manne, Thomas Sherewode, William Byron, and Thomas Foxton, of the same.

Dated at Haverbargh, 12 Henry VII., 'quintodecimo mensis Agusti (*sic*), *i.e.*, Tuesday, August 15, 1497.

(104) Nicholas Barrett, of Haverbargh, appointed attorney to deliver seisin of the same.
Witnesses and date the same.

(105) Richard Janen, of Haverbergh, gives, grants and confirms to Nicholas Barrett, and Anne his wife, a piece of land lying in the town and fields of Haverbargh and Boudon Magna, to hold, etc. The said piece of land is called 'Smeton leyes,' and abutts on 'Crowethorne hyll' on the south, and the land of Leonard Acton on the north.

John Browne and Thomas Foxton, of Haverbargh, are appointed attorneys to deliver seisin of the same.

Witnesses: Richard Fraunces, of Haverbargh, John Brewode, of the same, Thomas Sherewode, of the same, Nicholas Jakes, of Boudon, and William Brewster, of the same.

Dated at Haverbargh, 13 Henry VII., 'decimo die mensis Junii;' *i.e.*, Sunday, June 10, 1498.

On the back: 'M^d of Smeton leyzes.'
'for ye leis w^{t}in ye willows in ye horse faire at hau'browge.'

(106) Stephen Alyngton, otherwise Adyngton, of Little Canfeld, in the county of Essex, son and heir of William Alyngton, late of Haverborgh, gives, grants and confirms to John Fayrehed, senior, and John Clerk, senior, of Takeley, in the county of Essex, all the lands, tenements,

meadows, etc., in the towns and fields of Haverbergh, Bowdon Magna and Bowdon Parva, which formerly belonged to William Alyngton his father, and which have descended to him by right, to hold, etc.

John Jenen, of Haverbergh, appointed attorney to deliver seisin.

Dated at Haverborgh 14 Henry VII., 'quarto die mensis Septembris ;' *i.e.*, Tuesday, September 4, 1498.

On the back : 'Testes deliberacionis seisine et sigillacionis hujus carte sunt Johannes Scott, Johannes Stonhard, Nicholaus Clerk et alii multi de Takeley infrascripta.'

(107) John Fayrehed, senior, and John Clerk, senior, of Takeley, give, grant and confirm to John Jenen, of Haverborgh, 'gentilman,' the property described above, which they held conjointly by the gift and feoffment of Stephen Alyngton, to hold, etc.

Witnesses : Thomas Sherwode, Nicholas Barrett, Richard Fraunces, and John Brown, of Haverborgh, and many others.

Dated at Haverborgh, 14 Henry VII., 'decimo die Septembris ;' *i.e.*, Monday, September 10, 1498.

(108) Stephen Alyngton (as above) gives, etc., etc., to John Janen, of Haverborgh, the property described in the preceding, to hold, etc., and appoints John Archer, mercer, and Henry Man, of Haverborgh, his attorneys to deliver seisin.

Dated at Haverborgh, 14 Henry VII., 'decimo die mensis Octobris ;' *i.e.*, Wednesday, October 10, 1498.

(109) Thomas Kongullton, of Coventry, hosier, binds himself and his heirs, etc., to Thomas Swafeld, in the county of Rutland [no place given], gentleman, in the sum of £14 sterling to be paid on the Feast of St. Peter ad Vincula next ensuing.

Dated 16 Henry VII., 'decimo die mensis Octobris ;' *i.e.*, Saturday, October 10, 1500.

On the back : ' Kongullton de [   ] Th. hunyng, (?) tayllour.'

(110) This indentur', made be twene John Janen, of Haverbargh, in the County of Leyc', on theoon pty, and Elizabeth Harp, late the wyff of John Harper, wydowe, of Meche Boudon, in the said County, on the other pty, witnessith that the said Elizabeth hath frely Bargayned and solde unto the said John Janen hur dowery, the wiche she hath in a mease, late the fore said John Harper', in Boudon fore said, and the said mease is sett nexte the mease of Thomas Harper, the sone of Richard, on the weste syde, and the lane callyd Ferrōs lane on the Este Syde, for the wiche dowery the fore said John Janen, he his heyres, executōs, or assiges, gauntteth to pay to the said Elizabeth, or her assiges yerely durenge all lyff, ijs. viijd. of lawefull mony of Yngland, that is to say at Ester and Mychelmas, be yevene porcōns, and if the said Rentte of ijs. viijd. be behyende on paid at any of the fests be fore said, if hit be asked and nat paid, thanne hit shall be lawefull to the said Elizabeth and hur Assignes to distres in ye said mease, and the distresse so takyn to kepe holde and dryve a way unto ye seid Rentte be fully contente. To ye wiche Covenūttes well and truly to be performed, holdyn, and kepte, the partyes be fore said to theis indentures ent'chaungeably have sett thair Seilles, wretyn at Boudon, fore the xxvjth day of the moneth of Juin, the yere of the reigne of Kyng Henry the vijth aft' the Conqueste the xvjth.

(111) Richard Harper, son and heir of John Harper, late of Boudon Magna, gives, grants and confirms to John Janyn, of Haverberghe, his tenement in Boudon, situated next the tenement of Thomas Harper, son of Richard Harper, on the west, and the lane called Ferrors lane on the east, to hold, etc.

  Witnesses : Thomas Schirwode, of Haverberghe, William Merschall, of the same, John Archer, of the same, Henry Mann, of the same, Richard Janyn, of the same, and many others.

Dated at Haverberghe, 17 Henry VII., 'xviij° die mensis Novembris ;' *i.e.*, Thursday, November 18, 1501.

(112) John Janen gives, grants and confirms to John Browne, John Archer, Thomas Sherewode, William Marsschall, Thomas Grey, Robert Astell, William Browne, baker, George Whylan, Richard Archer, William Browne, 'wefer,' William Repyngton, Robert Browne, baker, Nicholas Barre, John Dutton, William Archer, Henry Leycester, Thomas Fraunces, John Archer, junior, Richard Barrett, Thomas Marschall, all his lands, tenements, meadows, etc., etc., with all and singular, etc., etc., etc., in the towns and fields of Haverbargh and Boudon Magna, to hold, etc., and appoints Sir William Benett, chaplain, and Thomas Foxton, of Haverbargh, his attorneys to deliver seisin of the same.

> Witnesses : Henry Manne, John Hardy, John Barford, Thomas Repyngton, of Haverbargh, Roger Crafte, Richard Carter, Nicholas Jakes, Richard Harper, and John Cristyan, of Boudon, and many others.

Dated 19 Henry VII., 'tertio die Maii ;' *i.e.*, Tuesday, May 3, 1503.

On the back: 'Jhon Jennins dede.'

(113) John Vycars and Agnes his wife give, grant and confirm to Thomas Sherewode, John Browne, Richard Archer, George Wyllan, and William Marschall, their messuage, in the town of Haverbargh, which formerly belonged to Lambert Joee, deceased, and is situated next the messuage of Thomas Clerk on the south, and the messuage of Robert Burdon on the north, to hold, etc.

> Witnesses : John Archer, of Haverbargh, Thomas Grey, William Browne, Robert Browne, and Thomas Clerk, of the same, and many others.

Dated at Haverbargh, 20 Henry VII., 'quato (*sic*) die Octobris ;' *i.e.*, Friday, October 4, 1504.

(114) John A-vicars and Agnes his wife give, grant and confirm to Thomas Scherewoode, John Brown, Richard Archer, William Marchall, and George Welan, a messuage in Haverborough, late John Janen's, situated between the tenement of Thomas Clerke on the south, and the tenement of Robert Burdon on the north, and extending from

the King's highway on the east as far as the field on the west, to hold, etc.

> Witnesses: John Archer, of Haverborough, Robert Astell, Henry Manne, Thomas Foxton, William Sander, of the same, and many others.

Dated at Haverborough, 20 Henry VII., 'die Luna (*sic*) proxima ante festum Sancti Dionisii;' *i.e.*, Monday, October 7, 1504.

(115) John Archer, William Marsschall, Thomas Grey, Robert Astell, William Brown, baker, William Brown, 'wefer,' Robert Brown, baker, William Archer, Thomas Fraunces, Thomas Marschall, demise, hand over, deliver and confirm to Miles Roos, bailiff of Bowdon Magna and Haverburgh, Thomas Whatton, Thomas Foxton, mercer, John Newsham, Thomas Smyth, John Hardyng, Richard Cade, Richard Weyle, and John Tybbys, all those lands, tenements, etc., etc., which they lately held conjointly with John Brown, Thomas Sherewode, George Welan, Richard Archer, William Repyngton, Nicholas Baret, John Dutton, Henry Leycester, John Archer, junior, and Richard Baret, deceased, by the gift, grant and confirmation of John Janen, to hold, etc., etc., and appoint William Wyllyngore their attorney to deliver seisin of the same.

> Dated 24 Henry VII., 'vicesimo quarto die mensis Septembris;' *i.e.*, Sunday, September 24, 1508.
>
> *On the back:* 'The dede frō yᵉ friste feffies. In truste too oother feffies.'

(116) William Marchall remits, releases and quit-claims to Miles Roos, bailiff of Magna Bowdon and Haverburgh, Thomas Whatton, Thomas Foxton, mercer, John Newsham, Thomas Smyth, John Hardyng, Richard Cade, Richard Weyle, John Tybbys, all his right, title, etc., in a messuage in Haverburgh, which he lately held conjointly with Thomas Sherewode, John Brown, Richard Archer, George Weland, deceased, by the gift, grant and confirmation of John A-vycars and Agnes his wife.

> Dated 24 Henry VII., 'vicesimo quinto die Septembris;' *i.e.*, Monday, September 25, 1508.

DESCRIPTION.

The messuage is situated between the tenement of Edward Fyshe on the south, and that of Robert Hasylryg on the north, and one head (caput) extends from the King's highway on the east, and another head (caput) extends as far as the field on the west.

(117) [In English.]
Indenture dated 'the xxvj. day of September, the xxiiij. yeer of ye reign of Kyng Henry the vijth,' witnessing that Myles Roos, 'baylly of Myche Bowdon and Haverburgh,' Thomas Whatton, Thomas Foxton, mercer, John Newsham, Thomas Smyth, John Hardyng, Richard Cade, Richard Weyle, and John Tybbys, have 'dymysed, taken, and to ferme leten to William Marschall, a messuage and L. acres of arrable and medowe, and a holme called Pyllokesholme, with v. nett pastures with thapptences in ye Townes and Felds of Myche Bowdon and Haverburgh, from ye Fest of Seynt Michell tharchungell next after date . . . un to the end and terme of ix. yeers then next folowyng,' at a yearly rent of iiij. marks iijs. and iiijd., payable 'at the Fest of the Annunciation of our lady and Seynt Michell tharchungell.'

Description of the messuage as in the preceding.

Covenants.
  against arrears of rent
    to 'paye, acquyte and discharge Myles Roos, etc., against the cheyff lords of the fee.'
    to 'kepe, susteyne and maynteyne, and suffyciently repeyr as in Thacke and Modd.'
    if W. M. will take the premises, etc., again at the end of the term, 'he shall be a fore ony oder persone under ye pric of vis. viijd. of ony persone.'

(118) John Archer demises, hands over, delivers, and confirms to Miles Roos, Bailif of Bowdon Magna and Haverburgh, and others (as in the preceding), five acres of arable land and herbage in the North field of Bowdon

Magna, which he held conjointly with John Clen, Nicholas Baret, Robert Janen, Lambert Joy, William Serle, John Brewode, Richard Fraunces and William Wotton, late of Haverburgh, deceased, by the gift, grant and confirmation of John Atwell and Thomas Atwell, of Foxton, to hold, etc.

Dated 24 Henry VII., 'vicesimo sexto die Septembris;' *i.e.*, Tuesday, September 26, 1508.

The description of the land corresponds with that in No. 58, except that for 'carucata,' 'cultura' is given, and Langbarowe is said to 'abutt in to Tocrofte.'

(119) Thomas Williams, of Rolson (Rolleston), gives, grants and confirms to William Johnson all his lands, meadows, etc., in the fields of Bowdon Magna, to hold, etc.

Witnesses: Richard Deken, of Boudon, Richard Carter, Robert Deken, William Serll, and Thomas Richard, of the same, and many others.

Dated at Boudon, 5 Henry VIII., 'tertio die mensis Decembris;' *i.e.*, Saturday, December 3, 1513.

(120) This indenture made the vth day off Maye, in 6th yere of the reigne of Kynge Henry the viiith, wyttenesseth that Thomas Waterhouse, of the Scoles, in the parishe of Rotherham, Nayler [hath], payed in to the hands of John Adames, of Harborowe, yrynmownger, xxs. of lafull money in the [   ] underwritten. That is to say, the saide John graunteth by these presents that, by the grace of God, durynge the space of a hole yere next ensuynge in everi vi. weks of the yere, shall by and [   ] xxxs. worth nayles of said Thomas, of souche sorts and price as they be agreid opon. And at thend off the saide yere the said John Adames to recontent and pay to the saide Thomas or his assignes the said xxs. And for the performacon of the same byndeth hym, his heires or assygnes, by thies presents to the said Thomas or his assignes in the some of xls. In wyttenes whereof to theis presente indentures, parties beforesayd ayther to

other hath putt their seyles Giffen the day and yere before wrytten.

(121) Thomas Parmynter, clerk, Edmund Haselwode and William Pope, remit, release and quit-claim to Agnes Pope, widow, all their right, title, etc., in two tenements with gardens and closes in Haverburgh, of which one tenement with a garden lies in 'le High strete' between a tenement or inn called 'le Belle' on the north, and a tenement late Leonard Acton's on the south, and the other lies in Lubenham Lane between the land of Leonard Ackton on the east, and the land of Robert Haselrygge on the west, and the King's highway on the north, which messuages, etc., they lately held with others, together with Agnes Pope and Thomas Hobbys, clerk, deceased, by the gift and feoffment of John Pope, late of Bowdon Parva, in the county of Northampton, daughter of the said Agnes, to hold, etc.

Dated 6 Henry VIII., 'vicesimo quarto die Januarii;' *i.e.*, Wednesday, January 24, 151¼.

(122) Agnes Pope, widow, gives, grants and confirms to Robert Astell, of Harverburgh, 'chapman,' two tenements with gardens, etc., etc. (as in the preceding), to hold, etc.

Robert Kynge 'weyver' and Robert Collys, baker, appointed attorneys to deliver seisin.

    Witnesses: Antony Roos, gentleman, Nicholas Hardying, John Hardyng, John Dooles, Miles Rychardson, Miles Fysche, Thomas Richards, and many others.

Dated at Harverburgh, 6 Henry VIII., 'quinto die Februarii;' *i.e.*, Monday, February 5, 151¼.

(123) Agnes Pope, of Northampton, in the county of Northampton, widow, remits, releases and quit-claims to Robert Astell, of Harverburgh, 'chapman,' all her right, title, etc., in the property described in the preceding.

Dated 6 Henry VIII., 'decimo die Februarii;' *i.e.*, Friday, February 10, 151¼.

(124) Indenture by which Richard,[1] Abbot of the Monastery of St. Mary of the Meadows, Leycester and the Convent of the same hand over, grant and let to farm to Robert Astell, of Haverburgh, a toft in Haverburgh, in a certain street called 'lubnamlayn,' situated between the land of Robert Hasylrigg, merchant (marcatoris [sic]), on the east, and the land of Richard Osburn on the west, and abutting on the land of Thomas Richardson on the south, and on the King's highway on the north, for forty years from the next Easter after date, at a yearly rent of 12d. payable on the Feast of the Annunciation.

A yearly payment of 4d. is also to be made to the Lord of Harborough and his heirs as chief rent.

Dated at the Monastery in the Chapter House, 6 Henry VIII., 'septimo die mensis Marcii ;' *i.e.*, Wednesday, March 7, 151$\frac{4}{5}$.

(125) Thomas Pulteney, of Mysterton, Esquire, by special desire of Edward Boresworth, son and heir of Thomas Boresworth, deceased, remits, releases and quit-claims to Rowland Walker, of Haverborugh, all his right, title, etc., in a tenement in Haverborough called 'le Olde George,' situated between the tenement of George Langton on the north, and a tenement formerly Leonard Acton's on the south.

Dated 9 Henry VIII., 'decimo die mensis Augustii ;' *i.e.*, Monday, August 10, 1517.

(126) Robert Astell, of Northampton, mercer, gives, grants and confirms to John Parvyn, of Northampton, 'marchaunt,' Richard Bowers, Edward Aylmer, Thomas Wondeley, Robert Longe, and John Hardyng, of Harburgh, all his lands, tenements, etc., etc., in the towns and fields of Harburgh, Bowdon Magna and Lubenham, to hold, etc., for the performance of his last will and testament (ad usum et intencionem ad performandam ultimam voluntatem mei predicti Roberti Astell).

[1] Richard Pexall, 1509-1533. — Nichols' Leicestershire, i. 275 ; Dugdale, vi. 462.

William Bowghton and John Forster are appointed attorneys to deliver seisin.

Dated 12 Henry VIII., 'vicesimo die Octobris;' *i.e.*, Saturday October 20, 1520.

(127) [Attached to the preceding.]

M^d that I, Robert Astell, of Northampton, mercer, the xxth day of Octobr', in ye yeer of our Lord God a M^{l}DXX., and in the yeer of the reign of Kyng Herry the viiith xiith, make and ordeyn this my last wyll concernyng my londs, teñts in Harburgh, Moch Bowdon and Lubenham, in the Countie of Leyc', that is to wytte that all my Feoffees stand and be scasid of and in all my londs and teñts in Harburgh, Moch Bowdon and Lubenham aforeseid, to the use and behof of me, the seid Robert Astell, for terme of my lyf. And after my decesse, then I will that all my londs and teñts aforeseid shall remayne un to William Heyr, my pryntyse, for his diligent and good servyce, to have and to hold to hym and to his heyeres for ever, upon the condicon that then the wyf of me, the said Robert Astell, to have a annuell rent of xxs. by yeer for hir Jointo^r and dower going owt of the foreseid londs and teñts for terme of hir lyf annexed un to this my Feoffement. In witnesse wherof to theys presents, I have putte my Seale the day and yeer aboveseid.

EXTRACTS FROM WILLS, ETC.,

PRESERVED AT THE DISTRICT REGISTRY OF THE PROBATE COURT AND REGISTRY FOR THE ARCHDEACONRY OF LEICESTER.

COPIES IN THE REGISTER BOOKS.

Book I.

Fol. 8. May 12, 1516. William Burditt, of Bowdon.

my soull to All myghty Gode to our lady Saint Marie and to all the holy company of hevyn:

my body to be buried in the Church yard off Mych Bowdon:

for myrtuary[1] aftur the custam and maner off the cuntre:

to the church off Lincoln vjd:

to the hy alter off Bowdon vjd:

to the reparacon of the causey befor my dour xij^d:

to William my sone a blake bulloke:

to Janet my daughter a rede bulloke:

The residue .... to Alys my wyffe whome I orden my executrix w^t William my sone to be my executor.

Supervisors: Richard Harper, Richard Carter, William Jo [   ].
Present: Richd Morden, Roger [   ], Martyn Holcott.

---

[1] *Myrtuary*, mortuary: a gift left by a man at his death to his parish church. See Cowel's *Interpreter*, and the references there given. Skeat (Etymological Dictionary) says: 'a fee paid to the parson of the parish.'

Fol. 173 (*in dorso*). *September* 17, 1522. *Thomas Dennett, of Mych Bowdon.*

my soull to God Almyghty Our Lady Sent Mary and all Sents :

my body . . . in the Church yard of Peter and Polle of Bowdon :

for my mortuary my best goods after the custome of the towne :

to hy auter for thyth, etc., forgot viij^d :

to the Church of Lincoln vij^d :

to the repellacon off the hye auter and welfare of the sayde churche of Myche Bowdon one penny :

my executors to pay of my goods :—

to John Smyth son of Thomas x marks at Michaelmas 1524 :

to Thomas Smyth son of Thomas v li (£5) at Michaelmas 1527 in which he is indetted to me by reason of his executorship to their father :

The residue . . . . to Angnes Denet my wyffe and John Denet . . . my executors.

> Overseers : Richard Dekyn, Wm Bowgton, Robert Johnson, each to have xij$d$.
> Witnesses : Sir Wm Gasken, prest, Wm Sowther, chantre prest, John Corte, John Dekyn, Tho Smyth.

Fol. 184 (*in dorso*). *March* 12, 1523. *John Nubon or Newbon, of Bowdon Magna.*

my body . . . in the churche yard in Gret Bowdon :

for my mortuary (as in the last will) :

to the hye alter viij^d : to o^r lady off Lincoln ij^d :

to the reparacon of the bellys xl^d : to my gostly father iii^s iiij^d :

to Robt my sonne iiij^d : to my buryall xx^s for me and for my good frends :

> Executors : Alys, my wyfe, & Thomas Castey, my sonne. John Deykyn & Richd Hogs, overseers.
> Wytnes : Robt Marson, Thos. Strang.

Fol. 195. *July* 8, 1522. *Thomas Foxton, of Haverborowe, husbandman.*

my solle to God Allmyghty my plasmator,[1] to the Intemat[2] Virgyn and mother of God oure lady Sent Mary w⁽ᵗ⁾ all the sentts off hevyn :

my body to be buryed Jn the churchyard off oure lady In Atharne, my best beyst, At the Electyon off the farmer, to my mortuary: to the mother church of Lincoln iiij⁽ᵈ⁾: to the hye auter of Sent Denys Chapell for thything forgott vj⁽ᵈ⁾: to the parrych Church off oure lady in Atharne xx⁽ᵈ⁾: to the Chappell of Sent Denys in Harborow xx⁽ᵈ⁾: Also I wyll y⁽ᵗ⁾ Wyltm Foxton my eldyst sonn have my cotage w⁽ᵗ⁾therto pertaynynge y⁽ᵗ⁾ Abutts of the grene byneth the Bell[3] In Harborow for terme of hys lyve, and after hys decesse I wyll y⁽ᵗ⁾ John Foxton my son have the seyd cotage w⁽ᵗ⁾ apurtenans to the same to hym and to hys herys of hys body laufully begotn, so that he gyve to the chyld⁽ʳ⁾en of Rychard Foxton one tym xiij⁽ˢ⁾ iiij⁽ᵈ⁾ to pray for the sowle of there gransir: Also I wyll y⁽ᵗ⁾ John Foxton my sone have my best cart w⁽ᵗ⁾ the teyme to yt belongyng, y⁽ᵗ⁾ ys to say horse and horse geyr w⁽ᵗ⁾ all therto perteng, a plow ij harows ij neyt and a calfe: Also I gyve to Wyltm Foxton my sone a shod[4] carte ij harrows a cowe w⁽ᵗ⁾ a bulloke ij ewys and ij lambys: Also I gyve to Rychard Foxton my sone A cow and a calfe and A bald colte A nowe And A lambe: And to Cecely hys daughter A lambe: Also I gyve to Jōn Gray a lond[5] of barly next the whet

---

[1] Creator. 'Thy hands have . . . fashioned me' (plasmaverunt, Vulg.) Job x. 8.

[2] *Intemerate*, undefiled.

[3] The Bell Inn here spoken of was in the Sheep Market, at the Lubenham Lane corner. On a pane of glass in one of the houses there the outline of a face is roughly scratched, and the following words are added: 'A. W. Bryan breakfasted here August 10, 1764; and, admiring the Harborough Loaves, eat 16 of them with great Pleasure. A. W. B. had a pretty good stomach.—M. A. Sale.'

[4] *Shod, shud*, subs.: a shed.—Forby's Vocabulary of East Anglia, p. 297. *Shod*, covered.—Halliwell's Archaic Dictionary, 2.

[5] *Lond:* a subdivision of an unenclosed field; fields into furlongs; furlongs into 'londs.'—Forby, p. 200.

lond and ij butts of peyse: Also I gyve to John Gray A cowe A nowe A lambe vj^s viij^d in money, and to Alys hys wyffe A payre of harden[1] shets, And to Thomas hys sone A shepe: Also to the parrych churche Lubnam xx^d: Also I wyll y^t Wyll'm my son have hys lyvinge w^t my wyfe or w^t John my sone wych of them he can best Agre w^t: The resydew of my goods not beqwethyd I wyll remayn in the hands of Marget my wyffe and John Foxton my sone, whom I make myne executtors, they to pay my dets and perform my wyll, the Resydew as they thynke best in dyscharyg of ther conscyens.

Testibus Syr Michall Marten, Thomas Wels, Thomas Hudson w^t other mo: I wyll y^t Robt Ranold of Lubnam be supervyser of thys my wyll and he to have for hys labor A payr off howysse.

Fol. 225. *February* 2, 1521. *John Peryns, of Harborow.*

I, Jhon Peyrins of Herdeborow husbandman in my good and hole mynde beyinge laud and prasinge to Gode Almyghty:

my body . . . in the church yerd off Herdeborow:
my best beyst for my principall:[2]
to oure moder church off Lincoln iiij^d:
oon acre off wheyt to the payntynge off the rodlofte:
another acre a peisse to the reparacon off the church:
The Residew . . (my funerall expenses excepte) . . holly to Yssabell my wyffe and to my chyldern.

    Sole executrix: Yssabell, my wyffe.
    Wytnes: John Kirkby.

Fol. 236. *No date. Year of proof,* 1521. *Agnes Harper, of Bowdon.*

to the church of Bowdon ij^d:
to Robert my brother a shepe:
to Rich. Russell and Margrett Russell ether off yem a shepe:

---

[1] Made of coarse flax.—Bury Wills (Camden Soc.), p. 261.

[2] *Principall:* 'sometimes used for a mortuary or corse-present.'—Cowel's Interpreter, (edit. 1727, with Appendix).

to Wyllm Harper a new and a lame :

to Marget Russell my best kyrtyll :[1]

to Alice Harper the wyff of Ric Harper my best russet kertyll and my best cape :

to Agnes Stevens a russett kyrtell and a lambe :

to Elsabell Merston a lambe :

my mother to deliver this stuff and dispose the Resydew as she thynk best, Thes berynge wittnes :—

   Willm Harper, Mrg. Brest, Alice Harper.

Fol. 252 (in dorso). November 14, 1520. Richard Parych, of Mych Bowdon. Proved in St. Mary's by the Castle, Leicester, November 5, 1521.

my body to be beried in the Church yerd off Seynt Petre and Paulle of Mych Bowdon : My best beest to be my mortuary : To the hey alter for tything *oblit* and negligente forgoten ij^d : to the repellynge of the alter and church vj^s viij^d :

to the bellis off ye same church iiij^d : to the church of Lincoln, ij^d :

to Elizth Welles xx^s : to John Lyghton xiij^s iiij^d and my best wosted dublet :[2]

to Sir Wyllm my gostely father xij^d to pray for me :

I wyll that my two garnars[3] situate in my measse [[4]] as hers for evermore : I wyll that John Dekyn ye elder and John Lyghton off Mych Bowdon my feoffers have and hold all my landds and tenements mewdowys pasturs and lesurs w^t all theyre app^{r}ten^{a}ces in the towne and Feldes off Bowdon . . to the usse of John Deken myn executor oon twlmoneth and a day nixt enseuyinge my decesse, to pay my detts and avoyed the chargs concernynge my testa-

---

[1] *Kirtle :* a sort of gown, or petticoat, used rather vaguely.—Skeat. Forby (p. 184) says that it was an outer petticoat to protect the other garments from dust in riding, and that in his day it was scarcely ever heard of, 'since pillions are so gone out of use.'

[2] 'An old-fashioned garment for men, much the same as a waistcoat.'—Bailey's Dictionary.

[3] *Garnars :* granary, storehouse for corn. 'That our garners may be full and plenteous with all manner of store.'

[4] Some words are clearly omitted in the Register Book.

ment, and after the seid yer ffully exspyred I wyll that my seid feoffers have and hold all my seid landes with all the premisses to the usse of John' Burgesse my mother, durynge all the terme of her lyff, off the cheif lordes off the fee by dew service and custome, and after the decesse off the seid Jone my mother I wyll that my seid feoffers and other to be made by them have and hold for ever all my seid landes and tenants with all the premisses . . . to the usse of Wiłłm Johnson my brother, and to his eldest hayer malle, hole w'out partyon, and Frome the seid eldest her' male to his hares male, and in faute of here male to the usse off his eldest heer feymale, w'out particon, and to her eldest heer male in forme aforesaid, and in faute off yssu lynyally descendynge to Returne to the next heer male, the eldest off hyme or heer y^t have hade the usse off my seid landds, evermore w'out particon, and to descend after the Forme aforeseid for ever, and in faute off yssu descendynge off the seid stoke off Wiłłm Johnson as ys aforeseid I wyll that my seid feoffers and others to be made by them have and hold all my seid landes etc. . . . to the usse off the seid towne off Boudon and Church Reeffes[1] off the same for ever, remembering alway that I wyll the said Rich Pech wyll (sic) y^t ye seid Wiłłm Johnson and his heeres, both male and Feymall, towshynge, and the Church Reeffees havynge the usse and profitts off all my seid landds, yther off them durynge ye tyme, kepe yerly in the seid church off Bowdon ye xviijth day off Novembr oon *obbite*[2] with *placebo*[3] and *dirige*[4] and messe off *requiem*[5] all w^t nott off *commendacon*[6] w'out not (*sic*), to the valour of xiij^s iiij^d, for the soule of Ryc' Pech and the soule

---

[1] Churchwardens.—Bury Wills, p. 254.

[2] Office for the Dead, performed at the funeral and after.—See above, pp. 52, 61, will of Geoffrey le Scrope. Also the Anniversary Office for the Dead.

[3] The first word of the antiphon in Vespers for the Dead.

[4] The first word of the antiphon in Matins for the Dead.

[5] Mass for the Dead.—See Proctor on the Common Prayer, p. 416, notes ; Bury Wills, p. 250.

[6] Commendation of Souls, in the Sarum rite—certain psalms sung over the corpse just before the Mass.

off John Pech and John' Burgesse, my father and my mother, and all crysten soules, and causaynge our seid soules in the seid church off Bowdon to be prayd for every Sonday in the beed Roolle[1] perpetually dispossynge, and to the [ ] off the seid town beynge present and syngynge in all the seid service, to the executor off the offic v^d, to y^e deken v^d, to the parych clerke beynge subdeken iij^d, to ych other prest $iiij^d$, to v off the ablest quermen ych off them ij^d, to every off the quermen i^d a peysse, to every chyle syngynge in the seid service ob.($\frac{1}{2}$d.). The Residew of the seid sume to wax and offerynge paid for to be exspent on bred al and chesse and gyffyn[2] to the pepull present at the seid service and prayinge for the seid soulles: and yff ytt happen the foreseid Willm Johnson or eny off the seid heeres or townschype or Church Reeffs, havynge the usse and profytt off my seid landes, to fayll and kepe not ye seid *obit* and bed Roolle in forme aforeseid, then it shalbe leyfull to the baley off the seid towne, officer to the Lord Scrope, to enter into all the seid landes and into every parcell off them and distreyn to the valure off oon yeres rent, and to prysse ye seid dystresse by theyre Sutters, and the seid officer w^t the money so levied to kepe the seid *Obitte* and bed Roolle y^t oon yer in forme aforeseid, And the Residew off the seid Rent take to his owne usse for his labo^r, and so to do as often as the seid parties make Fautt in the seid *obite* and bed rooll kepynge, the Residew off my goodds her befor not bequeythed, my detts payd, the costs off my sepulture and other chargs content and performed, I gyff and bequeyth to the seid John Deken, whom I make my executor and John' Burgesse my mother oversear, that my seid executor trewly perform my will and dispose for the elth off my soule as it seemeth hym me best to sped and best to

---

[1] List of deceased benefactors to be remembered in the offices, read on All Saints' Day.—Bury Wills, p. 252. The Book of Life, or Bead Roll.—*Rock*, vol. ii., p. 342. On the Funeral Services according to the Old English Ritual, see *Rock*, vol. ii., p. 469 *et seq*.

[2] On Doles to the Poor at Funerals, see *Rock*, vol. ii., p. 493; vol. iii., p. 36 *et seq*.

please Almyghty Gode. In wittenesse wheroff I the seid Ric' Pech to this my present testament have sett my sealle, thes witnesse Sir Wiłłm Gaskyn, parysh prest, John Lyghton, skryvener, and Thomas Burgesse of the same, w^t many other moo.

Fol. 258. *September* 28, 1521. *Proved September* 30, 1521.
William Bacar in the towne of Harborow.

'beyinge hole in mynde with stabull reson and parfytt remembrance all thoffe I be with Almyghty Gode sore visit, Ferynge the departynge off my soule and body comynge nygh' . . .

' my soule to my Plasmator and redemer God Almyghty and to the Intemeraytt vyrgyne his glorius mother o^r lady Saynt Mary, to the gydynge off the holy Archangell Mychell, the provest off paradyse, and to the intercession off all the celestiall company, off the name off my mortuary after the custome off the cuntre or as the churche law shall require.'

' my body . . . in the church yerd off o^r lady's parysh in Arthorne and to the seid churche I bequethe ij^d : to the chapell off Seynt Denesse in Harborow and to the reparacon of the same ij^d : to the fabricacon off o^r lady Cathedrall Church in Lincoln xij^d : to the hy alter off o^r lady Church in Arthorne xij^d : to Wiłłm Hyll my heldest sone xx^s : to Thos. Hyll my son xx^s : to Margaret Hyll my dowghter, xx^s : to Anne Hyll, my youngest dowghter, xx^s : to Annys Marshall, my servande, xij^d : yff y^t chaunch any off my chyldern to decesse, that ther parts be devided amonge my chyldern y^t be over lyft : yff y^t chaunch theym all to depart from this world, I wyll y^t ther parts be gydyth at the dyscrecon off my wyff . . . my wyff to have my horsmylne durynge her lyff, and after the decesse off my wyff, I wyll wych off my sonnys plesyth my [sic.] wyff the best to have hyt, that goith to the bacar-craft to have the mylne, yff not wich off my sonnys that goth to the bacar-craft to have the said mylne, yff y^t they go to the bacar-craft, to ther proper use, yff ij of [my] sonnys or all them go to the forseid occupacon, I wyll the forseid mylne be devided to them y^t goth to ye seid occupacon, yff yt forten my sonnys departe or non off them go to the forseid craft, I wyll y^t the said mylne chane remayn to my wyff to do w^{t}all what she thinks best: the Resydew off my goods not bequered I wyll y^t be at dispocisson off Elyzabeth my wyff, whome I make and orden my lawfull executrix . . . by the oversyght off Rouland Walker my neybour, and he to have for his labo^r iij^s iiij^d

    Witteness : Sir Mychall Martyn, Rouland Walker, Wyllm Marchall, Jhon Hardynge, w^t others moo.

Fol. 270. 1521. Thomas Mariott, of Bowdon Magna.

my body . . . in the Church yerd off Peter and Paulle in Gret Bowdon: for my mortuary after the usse and custome off the towne: to the hey alter, vj^d: to o^r lady of Lincoln, ij^d: to my gosteley fader xij^d, and I wyll ytt be done for ye soules [erasure] : to my ij chyldern vj sheype : also them ij viij marks, the lynger lyver to have the hole yff they depart : I make my wyff my executrix and my gostele fader : [supervisor?] Thomas Harper : Item I bequeyth to the curatt off Bowdon Magna for his labour my best cott and my best hoysse, and to my syster Dykynson iiij yerds off cloth to make her a petticott.

    Wittenes : dominus curat Thomas Watton.

Fol. 273. August 12, 1521, proved September 21, 1521.
    Richard Syddyll, of Harborow.

my body . . . in the church yard off our Lady off Bowdon :

for my mortuary my best qwyke best aftur the custome and maner off the cuntre : to the church off Lincoln iiij^d : to the hy alter off Saint Mare church in Mych Bowdon iiij^d : to Saint Mare Church off our lady off Bowdon xx^d : to the reparacon of Harborow chapell xij^d : to the reparacon off Dyngley church xx^d : The resydew . . . to my wyff . . . sole executrix.

    Witnesses : William Browne, John Tybbys, John Foster, w^t oder moo.

Fol. 278 (in dorso). No date. William Harper, of Bowdon.

to the church off Bowdon iij^s: Willm Harper, a sheype: to Robt my brother, a sheype: to Richard Russell and Margaret Russell, ether off them, a shepe: to blynd Ryc' Harper, a shepe: to Rychard Lokyn, a dublett a pare off hose and my best cape: to Alice Harper a pare off hose, and Agnes my mother to deliver this and to dispose the Residew.

> Witnesses: Willm Harper, Agnes Hawnes, Anne Jarvis, Alice Harper.

Fol. 296. February 20, 1526. Agnes Atkinson, widow, of Harborow.

my body ... in the church yard off our Lady in Ardrone:

my best goods for my mortuary as custome and maner is:

to the mother church off Lincoln iiij^d: to the hy alter off Saint Mare xx^d:

to the Chapell off Saint Dennys one goblett off sylver and a peysse:

my best pane to Willm Chester: to John Smyth my secund pane:

to Margaret Hudeson on pott off a galone and a halffe:

to Johan Chester my second gyrdyll: to Elizabeth Cooke on father bede ande a matres: to John Smyth on matres: to John Chester my best gowne: to Elizabeth Purser my best kyrtyll: to Dorathe Smyth my secund kyrtyll: to Joh'ne Clerke my secund gowne: to Elizabeth Cooke my warst kyrtyll: to the neytherds wyffe my petycott:

The residew of all, etc. etc., to Robt Browne and to John Purser ... executoures.

> Wytnes: Willm Marshall, John Manne, Willm Chester, Sir Curat ther, & John Smyth, w^t other moo.

This is the trewe Intent off my last wyll and deyde off Feofament, Fyrst I wyll ande declare that my feoffers William Marshall, Rowland Walker, Thomas Richard-sone and Thomas Pawlmer stande Feoffed and seasyd in one Mese wᵗ the appurtynauncs as yt is sett in Harborough in the which I do dwell, Into the use and profett off the towneshippe off the same, unto sych tyme the some off ten pounds off Lawfull money off England be clearly paid off the rent off the foreseid Messe to the seid towneshype, to the intent to by to the seid chapell off Saint Dennys a suyt off vestments, and aftur the contacion (*sic*) and full paymentt of the seid tene pounds I wyll my foreseid Feoffars staund seasyd to the use and profett off John Alann ande to his ayres off his body Lawfully be gottyn for ever more, to have and to hold the foreseid messe wᵗ the appurtynauncs after the custom and maner off the lordshype, and for lake off Lawfull yssue off the seid John I wyll the seid meysse wᵗ the appurtynauncs returne to the towneshype off Harborough, ytt to have ande to hold aftur the custome and maner off the lordeshype wᵗ servys thertoo dett or accustomed for evermore.

Fol. 318 (*in dorso*).   *November* 27, 1517.   *Richard Cade, of Harborow.*

my soulle to Allmyghty God and to his moder our lady Saint Mary and to all Sancts: my body to be beryed in the Church yarde of Saint Marys: my best beast to be my mortuary: to yᵉ moder church of Lincoln viijᵈ: to Saint Mary Church xxᵈ: to yᵉ chapell of Harborow xijᵈ: to yᵉ highe alter iiijᵈ: to yᵉ parish churche of Asheley xijᵈ: to yᵉ parish churche of Weston xijᵈ: to yᵉ chapell of Sutton xijd: to Saint Nicholas Church of Litill Bowdon xijᵈ: Also A trentall[1] of massys to be sayd for me xˢ: to Martyn of Rowell ijˢ: to Robart Knytt A merray cott:[2] to Annes Hakett xxᵈ: to Agnes Wainwright xxᵈ: to Robt Knytte my best dublett: to Harry Wanwright my secunde dublett: to John Cade ijˢ: to yᵉ bellys iijˢ iiijᵈ: to John,

[1] Thirty masses said on as many different days.—Proctor on the Common Prayer, p. 417, note.
[2] 'A cote of murre color.'—Bury Wills, p. 133. Dark-brown, or dun.—Kersey's Dictionary (1715). Dark-red, the sense being properly 'mulberry-coloured.'—Skeat.

parish prest of Saint Maryes xviij^d: to Sir Hugh xij^d: to Margr: Golde xx^d: to Helenor Sumtyng my servant iij^s iiij^d: I wyll y^t Richard Page of Carrylton shall have a lede, a mawnger, a rake and thelys,[1] beynge at ye sygne of Swanne in Harborow, if y^t he woll pay for them ye money aforseyd [*erased*] vj^s viij^d: also I wyll y^t master Wiłłm Pope shall resave of my wyff v sponneys of Silver w^t a par of beds[c] ye price xxvj^s viij^d, and they to be solde for ye helthe of my soull don, except ye man y^t leyd yem to plege woll come and pay for theme.

    The residew . . . to Agnes my wyffe . . . my executrix.

        Witnesses : Wiłłm Brown, Robert Gryme, & oder moo.

Fol. 321.   Thomas Alann.   No date.

    my body . . . in the Church yard of Saincte Maries of Bowdon : my best beast to be my mortuary : to ye mother Church of Lincoln vj^d: to the Reparaccons of the bellys in Saincte Marys Church viij^d, and to the bellys of Haverborough viij^d, and to the highe alter of Haverboroughe iiij^d: to my v children v shep prec' x^s: the Resideue . . . to Johan my wif to pay my detts and to dispose for the wele of my soule . . . my wif . . . my executrix . . . Robt Grene supervisor.

        Witness : Wiłłm Brown, John Smyth, w^t many moo.

Fol. 333.   December 20, 1515.   Richard Harper, of Grete Bowdon.

    my body . . . in the Church yard of Peter and Poule of Grete Bowdon : to be my principall my best beaste : to the Church of Lincoln iiij^d: to the high auter of Bowdon xij^d: to the welfar of the Church of Bowdon a quarter of malt : to Wiłłm my sonne my house as it apperith by a dede : to the said Wiłłm xv sheep and my best shode cart : to the said Wiłłm v marks : to the said Wiłłm my colt :

---

    [1] *Theal:* a board, a plank, a joist (*Leicestershire*).—Halliwell's Archaic Dictionary.
    [2] A pair of beads.

to Robt my sonne my Lond that was sometyme Robt Harpers as it aperith by a dede : to the said Robt xv sheip : to the said Robt v marks : to Annes my daughter v li (£) : to the said Annes xx sheyp : to Willm Harper the sonne of Thomas Harper a foll : The residue . . . to Agnes my wif . . . my executrix, wt Thos Harper my brother and Robt Russell . . . oversears, Christopher Campynett, John Crestian, and Richd Carter.

Witnesses : Sir Richd Moden, Mgr Wm Sotherey, chauntrey preste, Richd Annys, & Martyn Hoolkot, wt many other moo.

Fol. 349 (in dorso). January 3, 1518. Peter Hyll, of Bowdon Magna.

'I Peers Hyll of Grett Boundon' . . .
my soule to Almyghty God to his moder Saynt Mary and to all the holy company of hevon : my body . . . in the Church yerde of Peter and Paule : to my prynsipall my best mare : to the high Awter iiijd : to the works of oure lady of Lyncoln iiijd : to every oon of my chylder ij shepe : The residew . . . to my wyff . . . myne executrix wt Thomas Harper, Thes wytnessynge :—Richard Mordon, John Hyll, Robt Merston wt other moo.

On fol. 361 there is another copy of this will. The only differences are (1) 'Mych Bowdon' instead of 'Grett Boundon.' (2) Ric. Mordon, Curat ther.

Fol. 361 (in dorso). September 18, 1518. Proved September 21, 1518. Rich. Sharpe, of Gret Bowdon.

my body . . . in the church yard of Grett Bowdon : for my principall my best goods after the maner and custome off the towne : to the hy alter of Mych Bowdon iiijd : to the church off Lincoln iiijd : to Richard my sone ij sheype : to Elizabeth my syster on sheype : the residue to Alys my wyffe . . . my executrix.

Wittness : William Sotherey and Thomas Richard wt oder moo.

Fol. 440 (*in dorso*), 441, 442.

Testamentum Willmi Sotherey capellani perpetui Cantariæ in ecclesiâ parochiali de Bowdon Magna fundatæ.

Dated October 1, 1523.   Proved November 26, 1523.

I, Sir William Sotherey Chauntre prest,[1] off Mych Bowdon w^tin the dioc. off Lincoln . . .

my body to be buried in the Chapell off our Lady in the Church off Peter and Pole off the said towne off Mych Bowdon before the South corner off the alter: my best beyst for my princypall: for my tythes offerings and other dewtyes unpaid:—to the hy alter of Mych Bowdon ij^s: to the church off Lincoln iiij^d: to the box off pardon[2] at the Freer Austyns[3] in Leicester for me and for my moder and for my fader iij^d, And lykewysse to the pardon off the Holy Gost iij^d: to the reparating off the hy alter and church off Mych Bowdon xx^s: to mending off briggs and causes off the same towne off Bowdon vj^s viij^d: to the reparacon off Frysby church apon Wreyke iij^s iiij^d: to the reparacon off the Almshousse in Mych Bowdon iij^s iiij^d: to William Wygington and Johane hys wyffe xxiij^s iiij^d: also I forgyffe to the said W. W. his rent dew to me at the making heroff: to Will̄m Sotherey the sone off John Sotheyrey all my cart beysts and cart and cart gayres a cowe and two sheype: also I doo forgyffe Rauffe Pole his rent and dett that he owes me: to Alys Pole ij yards and a halffe off hardyne and a yard off flaxen and iij yards off woollen: to Anne Pole a Cot Cloth and a smoke and iiij^d in money; to Rob̄t Pole a shart and iiij^d: to Will̄m Pole a shart and iiij^d; to Johane Facone ij yards off carsey[4]: to Agnes Fawne a smoke and iiij^d: to Alyce Sotherey a yerlying

---

[1] On Chantries and the duties of Chantry Priests, see *Rock*, vol. iii, pp. 104 *et seq.*

[2] On Pardoners (sellers of Indulgences), see English Wayfaring Life in the Middle Ages, pp. 312 *et seq.*

[3] Austin Friars, see Nichols' Leicestershire, i., 300, 301.

[4] *Kersey:* coarse, woollen cloth.   Skeat's Etymological Dictionary.

bulloke and a smoke and a aprone: to Johane Facone a yerling bulloke and xij^d: to Sir Thomas Frysby x^s: to Richard Sotherey x^s: to Sir Richard Andrew, prest, to say daily *placebo* and *dirige* and also *comendacons*, and daly to remembre me in his masse, and to say dayly this collec *Deus cui proprium est misereri*[1] w^t the *secreta*[1] and *post communio*[1] unto my xxxth day vi^s in money: to Agnes Shawe my servand iij^s iiij^d for hyr reward, and yff shoo doo forth hyr hole yer servys w^t my syster, then I wyll that shew have hyr hole yer wagys: to every oon of all thes churches her aftur folowing xij^d, that is to wytt, to Gaddesby, Bowdon Parva, Harborow, to our Lady Church in the fylds, to Lubbenham Church, Foxton, Kyrke Langton, Thorp Langton, Welham, Weston, Sutton, and Dyngley: to every oon off the pour folks dwelling in the Almeshousse in Mych Bowdon aforeseid the day of my buriall iiij^d: . . . that at my vij day ych oon of them to have a penny, And soo in lyke maner at my xxxth day every oon off the seid pour folks w^{t}in the seid Almeshousse to have a penny: to every prest being at my buriall vj^d: to every clerke synging in his mannes brest 1^d: to every chyld 1^d: to every prest off the same towne off Mych Bowdon beying present at masse and *dyrige* apon my vij^t day iiij^d: and to vij off the queremen off the same towne, yff they be present at my masse and *dirige*, ych oon off them ij^d: and too two synging chylderyn adyr off them 1^d: and at my xxx^t day in lyke maner: . . . to the Priores and Convents off the three howses off Freers in Leicester and too the Whit Freers in Stamford, to pray for my soule, ych off the seid howses v^s viij^d, so as ych off the seid Priors and Convents do syng halffe a trentall off masses for my sole, and also to syng a mase off *requiem* with *placebo* and *dirige* and *comendacon* tyll every masse: to every oon off my gode chylderyn iiij^d: Also I wyll that my Feoffers and other to be made in tyme to tyme have and hold all my Lands tenements medowes pastoures and leasoures in the towne and fylds

---

[1] Three collects in Mass for the Dead. See *Missale Romanum*. 'Missæ pro defunctis.' 'In die obitus seu depositionis defuncti.'

off Mych Bowdon, to the ousse off Wiłłm Sotherey sone off John Sotherey and his eldest heyre male, hole w*t*out particion, for evermore, to the intent and kepyng off a *obbott* yerly in the church off Mych Bowdon to the valour of x^s by yer, for my soule and for all crystyne soulles, in maner ande forme specified in a Indenture annexed to my feoffament, declaring more opynly the intent theroffe : And for faut off yssue off heyre mayle dissendyng off the seid Wiłłm I wyll that all the seid Lands w^t all the premisses holly remayne to William Fawne my godesone and to the next ayre male off his body begotyne, and to dissend to the next ayre male for ever, hole w*t*out particion, to the intent and use off performyng and kepyng off my yerly *obett* w*t*in the parysh church off Mych Bowdon aforeseid : And in defaut off yssue off heer mayle dissending off the seid William Fawne, to remayne to the Church reves off the seid Mych Bowdon, And they to se my *obett* yerly to be kepped w*t*in the seid church off Mych Bowdon, for my soule my fader's soule my moder's soule and for all crystyn soulles to the some and valour of x^s as is befor rehersed : The residew off all my goods unbequeathed I gyffe and bequeath, aftyr this my wyll be performed my detts pade and my funerall honestly performed and done, to Wiłłm Sotherey the sone of John Sotherey and to Johane Fawne the daughter off John Sotherey, whome I orden and make my sole executoures, they to dysposse for the helthe off my soule and all crystyne soulles as they shall thynke most expedient.

  Supervisoures : John Sotherey, Sir Richard Andrew, prest, John Crystyan, Rauffe Pole, and ych off them to have for ther laboures vj*s*. viij*d*.

  Wytnes : Sir Wiłłm Gaskyne, parysh prest off Mych Bowdon, Robt Ward, John Harper, and Wiłłm Serle, w^t many other moo.

Fol. 329. *December* 24, 1517 (*in Latin*). *Robert Wellingtore.*

Corpus meum in Cimiterio Sancte Virginis de Hardron sepeliendum : optimum bonum meum more mortuarii condonandum : matrici ecclesiæ de Lincoln viij*d*.: altari summo de Haverborough pro ejus supportacione xij*d*.: Ecclesiæ beatæ Virginis Mariæ de Hardon iijs. iiij*d*.: Johanni Hankynson unum Lintheum telarium anglice 'a Linen horne' cum sex falleris textoriis anglice 'wth sex weving geyres.'

Et meam togam meliorem preter optimam do et lego dicto Johanni Hankynson quam quidem optimam togam do et lego Katerinæ Fuller famulæ meæ: Thomæ Hudson unum lintheum telarium cum sex phaleris textoriis : volo insuper ipsum Thomam pro precio convenienti pre aliis emere et habere de rebus meis textrinis quicquid sibi videtur utile : . . . domino Thomæ Wellingtore pro termino vitæ suæ naturalis : Et post ejus mortem volo Robertum Wellingtore nepotem meum ipsud habere messuagium in quo permaneo cum suis commoditatibus et pertinentibus : Et Aliciam Grene alteram possidere messuagium cum suis pertinentibus : Cui etiam Aliciæ do et lego omnia mea utensilia quæ ad familiam pertinent ad artificium textoris pertinencia : Et si contingat quod alter eorum puerorum et uterque puer sine successore legitime nato et sine successoribus legitime natis moriatur : Tunc volo ipsud messuagium sic vacans aut ipsa messuagia sic vacancia in usus pios et necessarios villæ et capellæ de Haverborough

Translation.

... my body to be buried in the Cemetery of the Holy Virgin of 'Hardron' (Arden). My best goods to be given by way of mortuary : to the mother church of Lincoln, 8*d*.: to the high altar of Harborough for its maintenance, 12*d*.: to the Church of the Blessed Virgin Mary of ' Hardon,' 3*s*. 4*d*.: to John Hankinson, 'a Linen horne,' ' with sex weving geyres '[1]

And I give and bequeath to the said John H. my second-best coat, my best coat I give and bequeath to Katharine Fuller, my servant : to Thomas Hudson a ' linen horne with six weaving gears :' Moreover, I will that the said Thomas have first right to buy, at a fitting price, whatever seems useful to himself from my weaving goods : ... to Sir Thomas Wellingtore for his life (and after his death I will that Robert Wellingtore, my nephew, shall have it) the messuage in which I dwell, with its conveniences and appurtenances. And that Alice Green have my other messuage with its appurtenances. To whom the said Alice I also give and bequeath all my articles which belong to the household and pertain to the weaving trade. And if it chance that either of these boys and each boy die without successor or successors lawfully born, then I will that the said messuage so void, or the said messuages so void, pass and be given for pious and necessary uses to the town and chapel of Harborough, at the disposition of the

---

[1] *Gear*, s. : stuff ; tackle of any sort.—Forby, p. 130.

per disposicionem duorum villicorum anglice 'Townysmen' de Haverborough comutanda danda et pro anima mea disponenda: Residuum vero bonorum meorum non legatorum do et lego prefato domino Thomæ Wellingtore ad disponendum pro salute animæ meæ, prout sibi videtur maxime meritorium, quem quidem Thomam Wellingtore ordino et constituo meum verum executorem: In cujus tamen absenciâ Magistrum Willelmum Sherp clericum et Willelmum Marshal exoneravi funeralia de bonis meis ministrare ac verum de rebus meis omnibus Inventarium per visum Johannis Jankynson et Thomæ Hudson conscribere et rotulare: quos etiam Willelmum Sherp et Willelmum Marshall hujus meæ voluntatis ultimæ supervisores preordinavi, quorum utrique, viz., Willelmo Sherp et Willelmo Marshall pro eorum labore et diligenciâ do et lego iij*s.* iiij*d.* hiis testibus Johanne Hardyng, Willelmo Bowton, Johanne Foster de Haverborough cum multis aliis.

two 'Townsmen' of Harborough, and be disposed for the good of my soul. The residue of my goods not bequeathed I give and bequeath to Sir Thomas Wellingtore, to be disposed of for the health of my soul as shall seem most worthy to himself, whom, the said T. W.. I ordain and constitute my true executor. In whose absence I have permitted Master William Sharp, clerk, and William Marshall to provide the funeral rites from my goods, and, under the oversight of John Jankinson and Thomas Hudson to write and enroll a true inventory of all my property, whom, the said William Sharp and William Marshall, I have ordained as supervisors of this my last will; and to each of them ... for their labour and care, I give and bequeath 3*s.* 4*d.* These bearing witness: John Harding, William Bowton, John Foster, of Harborough, with many others.

Book II.

Fol. 43. November 6, 1518. Proved January 9, 15$\frac{18}{19}$. Edward Fysh, of Harborow.

my body ... in the church yard off Saint Mares off Mych Bowdon: to the Church off Lincoln viij^d: to the hy alter off Harborow church viij^d: to the maynteyng off the belles off Sanct Mares vj^s viij^d: to the supportyng off the belles off Harborow chapell x^s: ... that a trentall off masses be done in the Blake Freers in the horsse market in Northampton x^s: to Robt Matoke a folding tabyll and a cappe: to my chyldern xx marks to be devyded evenly among theme by even porcions, and yff any off them depart, the part off them that soo dous dy w^t eshew, or at they cum to Lawfull age, ther parts to remayne to the longer lyver off the sade chylderon, And yff they all departh then I wyll that Agnes my wyffe have all ther partyes and dyspoose the same at hyr plesoure : . . . to Ric' Fysh my sone v marks vj^s viij^d, And yff he depart w^{t}out yshow then hys chyld part to retorne to his other brother and systerres :—to Ric' Matoke my best purl : Also I wyll that my executoures do cause a trentall off masses to be sunge for my soul where so ever they plase, and for the same I bequeth x^s : to my gostly fader Sir Thruston xx^d: The resydew . . . to Anne my wyffe . . . my sole executrix : being present, Rob͡t Matoke . . . oversere.

    Wytnes : Freer Ricardus Metley, Robertus Matoke, Margeria Jopper, w^t oder moo.

to every gode chyld that I have . iiij^s:

Fol. 49. Thomas Goodrych, of Bowdon Magna, the xxvj^t daye off December, the yere of owre Lord God, A thosande v hundreth and xxx^{to}.

my body to be beryed in the churche of the holy Appostuls Peter and Paule in Mych Bowden : for my mortuare as the law wyll : to the churche of Bowdon vj^s viij^d : to the hy awter of the same churche xij^d : to the moder churche of Lincoln vj^d : to the bying of one boke to the seyd churche of Bowdon xls : to the Chantre one brase pott having long Fete : to my too god childerne iij^s iiij^d : to ye iij awturs of Freres at Leycestr x^s : to oure Lady Frerys at Stamford iij^s iiij^d : to the mendyng of the hey ways in Boudon ix (?) quarter of malt : for one trentall of messes x^s : the resydue . . . to Alys my wyffe. Sir Thomas Olever, preyst, Richard Annys and Thomas Kesten . . . my lawfull executurs, Sir Robert Westone to be oversear

    Wyttnes : Sir George, Curude, paryche preist, Robt Warde, John Harper, Roger Kyrby w^t other moe.

Wills in Bundles.

Bundle 2. November 3, 1526. Wyllyam Grene.

my body ... yn ye churchyerd of Sent Mary yn Alderne: my best good for my mortuary: to ye hye auter for tyths forgottyn iiij^d: to our lady yn Lyncolne iiij^d: to my goostly fader iiij^d: to iij churchs xij^d: to Robt my sun one Ambrey[1] a cofer[2] A tabulle my best bras potte A payre of flaxen sheets a mattres a coverlett ij bedstydds ij short forms ij smalle tresulls A puter dysshe A platter A candelstycke ij tubbs and al my hoole schappe: to Annys my daughter one mattres a payre of harden shets ij candelstycks A cofer ye tabull in ye halle a shorte forme ij bedstydds A tubbe A platter and A puter dysshe: thes be my detts, Inprimis for woode to mayster Ratclyffe vij^s, Item for Osmunds vij^s, Item to Thomas Brydgman iij^s iiij^d, Item to Annys Symon xvj^d: Item for my rent xvj^s, Item I bequeth to Jone my wyfe al my goods moveable and unmoveable unbequeythed, to dyspose for my soule As she thynckes best, she being my full executyor and Thomas Brydgman, Ryc' Spryggs supervysors.

Wytnesse: Sir Wyllyam Clarke, my goostly fader, Ryc' Man', Johan' Francys, George Balantyne, wyth many moo.

November 28, 1528 (in 1529 bundle). Margaret Sexton, of Parva Bowdon.

my body ... in the church yard off o^r Lady in Arthern: to the mother church of Lincoln ij^d: for my tythes forgotyn iiij^d; to Saint Denys chapell xvj^d: to Saint Mare church off Gret Bowdon [   ] to Lubnam church viij^d:

---

[1] *Armarium*, a cupboard. 'A cupboard, either in the recess of a wall, or as a separate article of furniture.'—New English Dictionary (Dr. Murray), 'ambry,' I., gen.

[2] A chest, trunk, or box.—Bury Wills, p. 243.

to Lytyll Bowdon church viij^d: to John Gray's chylder iij sheype: to Cecely Sexten a sheype: to Agnes Sexten a sheype: John Foxton my sone... my executor, and John Gray my supervisor:

Wytnes: Thomas Foxton, William Smyth, John Dybbys, Richard Foxton, Robt Butler, w^t other moo.

(In the '1529' bundle) very imperfect and indistinct.
Auguste 6. William Clerke, of Harborow.

to hy alter off Harborow vj^d: to the chapell off Saint Dennys off Haverborow, all my boks: to my father [   ] gownes and thre dubletts ij off them off woursted and the other off bukeskyne: to Sir Ryc' my best bonnet[1]: to [   ] Wysaw my jerkyn[2] off chamelete[3] and colars therat: to William Chester my hate and best hosse: to Ric' Mane my fustyan jaket and a payr off shets: to [   ] Addames my warst gowne my wynter jaket a dublet and a payr off hosse ande a sharte: to Helen Barker my bede y^t I ly in, y^t is to say a matres a bolster a payr off shets and a coverlet: to John Wayn a payr off hosse, a payr off shone: to Robt Cully iij^s iiij^d: Robt Crowne and Robt [   ] my executoures, Willm Chester, Supervisor

Wytnes: T Foxson, Rich [   ], and John Smythe.

In bundle 2. Year 1539, but dated May 13, 1520.
Thomas Harper, of Gret Bowdon.

my sole to Gode and to o^r lady Sent Mary and to all the holy cumpeny of heven... my body... in the Church yard of Bowdon: to my pryncipall j gre colte: to the hy auter

---

[1] *Bonett:* a head-dress for men and boys.... In England, superseded in common use (app. before 1700) by *cap*, but retained in Scotland; hence sometimes treated as='Scotch cap.'—New English Dictionary (Dr. Murray), 'bonnet,' I., a.

[2] *Jerkyn:* a short upper coat, or jacket.—Kersey, Bailey, Skeat.

[3] *Camlet:* a name originally applied to some beautiful and costly Eastern fabric, afterwards to imitations and substitutes, the nature of which has changed many times over.—New English Dictionary (Dr. Murray), 'camlet,' *sb*.

iiij^d: to Lincolłe iiij^d: Item I bequethe yerly to be downe for me and my wyfe at our yerdaye[1] iiij^s, wych schall be taken and downe by my executors of ye grownd and close callyd Adamys yard: to the church a quarter of malte: I will y^t on of my executors have the close on yer and the tother a nother yer so thatt these my wyll be performyd:

The Residew . . . I gyfe to Rychard Harper and John Harper my sonnys . . . my executors, and Richard Decon to be supervisor.

Wytnes: Sir Richard Morden, Thomas Goodrych, Robert Marson, w^t other.

FOUND IN ONE OF THE VISITATION RECORDS IN THE BISHOP'S REGISTRY, LINCOLN.

Inventarium omnium bonorum et debitorum Agnetis Smyth de Haverborough viduæ nuper defunctæ appreciatum secundum discrecionem virorum Fide dignorum videlicet Johannis Archer Thomæ Whatton Thomæ Foxton Ricardi Deken et Willelmi Marchall factum apud Haverborough predictum quinto decimo die mensis Decembris Anno Domini Milesimo quingentesimo nono hiis testibus Milone Roos generoso Willelmo Sotherey clerico et domino Ricardo Parkyn capellano Sic incipit in primis:

Translation.

Inventory of all the goods and debts of Agnes Smyth, of Harborough, widow, lately deceased, valued at the discretion of men worthy of credit, viz., John Archer, Thomas Whatton, Thomas Foxton, Richard Deacon, and William Marshall, made at Harborough aforesaid the 15th day of December, A.D. 1509, these being witnesses: Miles Roos, gentleman, William Sotherey, clerk, and Sir Richard Parkyn, chaplain. Thus it beginneth, in the first place:

LVI sheppe prec'	lvjs.
Item a Boere Fedde v shots[2] and A Sowe ...	xijs. viij$d$.
Item A Cok and iiij hennys	vj$d$.
Item in Gold and Silver...	vli. vjs. viij$d$.

[1] See before, p. 52, note 1.
[2] *Shot, shoat:* a half-grown pig.—Forby. p. 297. A young pig that has done sucking.—Bailey's Dictionary.

Item iij Ryngs off Silver and a Peer off bedys	xxij*d*.
Item In wax ij^c and half and half a quartern[1]...	vij*li*. iiij*s*. iiij*d*. *ob*.
Item In Talow LV ston	xxxvj*s*. viij*d*.
Item i Fedir bedde and iiij bolsters	viij*s*.
Item vj peer off flaxen shets ... ... }	xx*s*.
Item vj peer off harden sheets ... ... }	
Item iij Kovers off Bedds	ix*s*.
Item v Kover leddys	vij*s*.
Item In salt Fyshe xcvij warpe[2] and half ...	xxxiij*s*. iiij*d*.
Item v mattrasses & vj blancketts	xvi*s*.
Item ij woll weyllys[3] A hekkett[4] A stryke[5] and ij sekkys	ij*s*.
Sum^a ... ... xxij*li*. xiij*s*. vj*d*. *ob*.	
Item viij pelows & ix peloberys[6]	vj*s*.
Item vj silver sponys	xiij*s*. iiij*d*.
Item A silver spone A pleage For	viij*d*.
Item iij laton[7] Basons and A laver and a Basyn off Peuter	v*s*.
Item vij laton Candell stykks	ij*s*. viij*d*.
Item a Chayffyng dyshe[8]	viij*d*.
Item ij peuter Salts and oon of ston	iij*d*.
Item vj brasse pottis	xx*s*.
Item ij Caudernys[9] and A lityll pane and a Skelett[10]...	ij*s*.
Item iij gret panys	v*s*.
Item ij leddys and iij wort ledds[11]	xvj*s*.

---

[1] £7 4*s*. 4½*d*. for 2 cwt. 2 qr. 14 lb. is at the rate of 55*s*. per cwt.

[2] *Warp*: 'four of fish.' Halliwell's Archaic Dictionary (1). *East*. Still used at Harwich for four, and in the Isle of Man for three.

[3] Wool-wheels.

[4] ?=*Hackle*: an instrument for separating the coarse part of flax or hemp from the fine.—Collins' Library Dictionary. *Hekel*, v. : to comb hemp. Hartshorne. *Salopia Antiqua*, p. 462.

[5] The name of a measure; originally an instrument with a straight-edge for levelling off (striking off) a measure of grain.—Skeat.

[6] Cloths for laying over the pillows.—Bury Wills, p. 256.

[7] A hard mixed metal resembling brass.—*Ibid.*, p. 246.

[8] A vessel to hold burning charcoal or other fuel for heating anything placed upon it; a portable grate.—New English Dictionary (Dr. Murray), 'chafing dish.'

[9] *Cauldron*: a large kettle, or boiler.—*Ibid*.

[10] *Skillet*: a small pot, usually made of bell-metal, with a long handle. —Bury Wills, p. 260, from Forby and others. A small boiler in an iron frame, with an iron handle; of brass, not of copper or iron.— Forby, Supplement, p. 45.

[11] Vats for the wort. *Lead* (Halliwell's Archaic Dictionary): a vat for dyeing. *North*. A kitchen copper is sometimes so called. For *wort* see Halliwell, sub. voc. 'grout' (1), quotation from Kennett.

Item xviij peuter plates vj peuter dysshes vij saucers v potagers of peuter and ij peuter potts	ixs. ijd.
Item A turned Chayer & A Cownter	vjs. viijd.
Item ij Almres[1]	vs.
Item Ric' Beelle flaxman for hony	iijli. & od mony.
Item ij hony baggs a buckett wt a chene & ij hors lokks	ijs.
Item ij serpless' a cheys rakke[2]	ijs. vjd.
Sum[a]	vijli. xixs. viijd.
Item iiij Spitts A peer off coberdes & the toon is broken a gredierne	iiijs.
Item a hony brake[3]	ijs.
Item A chyst A Koffer & An olde Arke[4] ...	iijs. iiijd.
Item A mantell	iis.
Item ij Silver harnest gyrdells	xxs.
Item ij Whomens gownys & ij Kyrtells ...	xijs.
Item v thredon kerchyffs	iiijs. iiijd.
Item a blake bonett nekkyde & i off Redde & A nother bonett of violett	ijs. iiijd.
Item ix bedsteds ij Furmes[5] ij stolys xiij trestulls viij bords	viijs.
Item vj yards off white carsey	iiijs. vjd.
Item vj yards off Rocett[6]	ijs. vjd.
Item iiij bord clothes	iiijs.
Item ij towells flaxon	xxd.
Item ij towells hardon	iiijd.
Item viij napkyns playn	xijd.
Item iiij Apurnes & iij Smokkys	ijs.
Sum[a]	iijli. xiijs.
Item v coshons A Bankker iij pentyd clothes in the hall	iiijs.
Item vij Selers[7] over Bedds and A Curten ...	iiijs.
Item In tymbir	xxs.
Item In Fyer wode	xxs.
Item vj lomys	ijs.

---

[1] Small cupboards, in the wall or moveable.—Bury Wills, p. 244. See before, p. 228.

[2] *Cheese-rack:* a rack to dry cheese on.—Halliwell's Archaic Dictionary, 'cheese-fatt.'

[3] *Brake*, sb.[3]. 3. New English Dictionary (Dr. Murray): In brewing and similar processes, a wooden mill to crush green fruits, hops, etc. Halliwell's Archaic Dictionary (16), a mortar. *North.*

[4] A large chest.—Bailey. A chest or box.—Skeat.

[5] Still in use in Leicestershire for 'forms.'

[6] *Russet*, reddish brown; hence applied to a coarse brown rustic dress.—Skeat.

[7] *Selers.* See above, p. 57, note 6.

Item iiij payllys and iij Kymnells[1]	xviij$d$.
Item a growt lome[2] and a lome For grenys	vj$d$.
Item a peer off pott henggells and A brandert[3] & A peer off chenys in the parler	vj$d$.
Item In woll iij ston and half	xs.
Item In lath iiij^c	xij$d$.
Item ij bemes and i peer Stollys & Wheyghts & peysses	vs.
Item In Sope	ix$s$.
Item A bare Franke[4]	xij$d$.
Item A peer off tonggs & a peer off belows	viij$d$.
Item A half barell & tiere theron	xij$d$.
Item A bunshe of Whier	xvj$d$.
Item A Barell & A Stryke off Salt and more therein	viij$d$.
Item iiij baken flyxes a sadyll A bowe A pilliun & A bridull	vj$s$.
Sum^a	iiij$li.$ viij$s.$ ij$d$.
Item A hachet & A Fryyngpanne	viij$d$.
Item A masshyng Fatt & bultyng lome[5] yiling Fatt[6]	iiij$s$.
Item ij barells A candell stokke & A choppyng Knyffe & A trowgh	ij$s$.
Item in peysse and hey	xs.
Item A Fyrkyn & hony therin	ij$s$.
Item A redde cloth	jd.
Item ix Ryffes[7] off onyons A mele Syff & a clensyng Syff	viij$d$.
Item A stryke off Whete & certayn malt hemmyd in w^t bords	ij$s.$ viij$d$.
Item A Bare off ierne in y^e Chimney in y^e hall	xij$d$.
Item John Hornbe of Lubnam for dette	xiiij$s.$ viij$d$.
Item Sir Rayff Glascott of Stoke	vj$s.$ viij$d$.

---

[1] Said to mean the same as kemling ... a brewer's vessel or powdering tub.—Nares' Glossary.—See Hartshorne, *Salopia Antiqua*, p. 480.

[2] Probably a tub to put ground malt in.—See Halliwell's Archaic Dictionary, 'grout' (1). 'Loome,' a tool, implement. Best's Farming Book (Surtees Soc.), p. 49.

[3] *Brander*, v.: to boil or grill; the instrument on which the meat is *brandered* or grilled—a gridiron. *Brandreth* or *brandrith*, an iron tripod fixed over the fire, on which a pot or kettle is fixed. Brockett's *Glossary of North Country Words*. See New English Dictionary, 'brander,' 'brandreth.'

[4] *Frank*: a place to fatten a boar in; a sty.

[5] A sifting instrument.—See New English Dictionary, 'bolting.'

[6] A brewing-vat, 'yele-house.'—Halliwell's Archaic Dictionary, 'a brewing-house.' 'Yelfate.' *Archæologia*, vol. xxi., p. 277, note 5, 'gylevat or guilevat.'—See Howson's Craven Guide, p. 115.

[7] ? Rifts. *Rift* (4): a pole or staff.—*Ibid.*

Item Colmans wyff off Foxton	x*d*.
Item Willm Thedyngworth off Mycul Oxton¹	iij*li*.
& A ston of blak wolle	iij*s*. iiij*d*.
Ric' Smyth off Laughton for candell	ij*s*.
Item Willm Marchall	xviij*d*.
Item John Croft off Stoke	xx*d*.
Item John Bayly of Sutton for malt	ij*s*. viij*d*.
Item Spenser off Welingborogh for candell ...	ix*s*.
Sir Edmunde off Stoke	x*d*.
It Pope of Litull Boudon	ij*s*. iiij*d*.
John Walker off Braybroke for lent mony ...	xij*d*.
Edmunde Porter of Keteryng	iij*s*.
Herry Ocham of Cotyngham	viij*s*.
Sir Christopher	xxvj*s*. viij*d*.
John Tybbys	lis. ij*d*.
Sum͞a ... ... vj*li*. xj*d*. (erased), x*li*. xviij*s*. ix*d*.	
Sum͞a tot¹ ... ... xlix*li*. v*s*. iiij*d*. ob.	

N.B.—The totals, including the sum total, seem to be inaccurate, with one exception.

---

¹ Great Oxendon.

APPENDIX I.

EXTRACT FROM THE ISHAM MSS.

(*T. T., fol.* 2, 3.)

[The hamlet of Little Oxendon was situated at some distance from Little Bowden Church, in the direction of Great Oxendon and East Farndon, the boundary stretching up to a point on or just beyond the road between those two parishes. Bridges, writing at the end of the last century, states that in his time there was only one house standing, but that there were remains of others, and that the site and position of the chapel could be clearly traced.[1] There is still one house which bears the name, and this is at the limit of the hamlet furthest from Little Bowden. The acreage is given in recent directories as 740 acres. It would seem that at the beginning of the fifteenth century the place was one of some importance, having a number of householders.

The extract now given refers to the chapel mentioned on page 125 of this volume. It was known to Bridges, and is briefly mentioned by him.[2] Its interest is varied, and more than local. It gives some idea of the duties of a parish chaplain in these parishes, and records some features of parish life. A summary of its purport is given below in English.]

CAPELLA DE PARVA OXENDON.

Universis sanctæ matris ecclesiæ filiis presentem processum nostrum inspecturis vel audituris, Johannes

---

[1] Bridges' Northamptonshire, ii. 8.
[2] *Ibid.*, ii. 9.

Hauberk, decretorum doctor, Officialis Lincoln., salutem in amplexibus Salvatoris. Ad universitatis vestræ indubitatam noticiam deducimus per presentes Nos, auctoritate nostrâ ordinariâ, inter partes infrascriptas, sententiam diffinitivam tulisse et provulgasse, sub eo qui sequitur tenore verborum :—In Dei nomine, Amen. Auditis et intellectis meritis causæ subtractionis invencionis unius Capellani, certis temporibus missas et alia divina officia in Capellâ de Oxendon celebraturi et inhabitantibus dictam villulam de Oxendon sacramenta et sacramentalia ministraturi, necnon subtractionis aliorum officiorum sive serviciorum divinorum, quæ coram nobis Johanne Hauberk, decretorum doctore, Officiali Lincoln., aliquamdiu vertebatur, inter Ricardum Esthorn, Johannem filium ejusdem, Johannem Wryth, Johannem Taylour, Ricardum Margary, Nicholaum Grene, Johannem Whytyng, Rogerum Clerk, communitatem sive majorem partem villulæ de Oxendon parochiæ de Bowdon Parva facientes, partem actricem, ex parte unâ, et dominum Johannem Exenford, Rectorem ecclesiæ parochiæ de Bowdon Parva predicta, partem ream, ex alterâ, oblato libello per dictam partem actricem coram nobis vicesimo quarto die mensis Marcii anno Domini millesimo cccc^{mo} quinto in ecclesiâ parochiali de Farndon Lincoln. dioc. pro tribunali sedentibus, et per dictam partem ream recepto, cujus tenor talis est :—In Dei nomine, Amen. Coram vobis honorabili viro Magistro Johanne Hauberk, decretorum doctore, Officiali Lincoln. Ricardus Esthorn, Johannes filius ejusdem, Johannes Wryth, Johannes Taylor, Ricardus Margery, Nicholaus Grene, Johannes Whytyng, Rogerus Clerk de Oxendon de parochiâ de Bowdon Parva, Lincoln. dioc. communitatem seu majorem partem dictæ villulæ de Oxendon facientes, contra dominum Johannem Exenford, Rectorem ecclesiæ parochialis de Bowdon Parva predictâ, et contra quemcunque in judicio legitime introvenientem pro eodem, dicunt, allegant, et in jure proponunt quod, de laudabili antiquâ approbatâ et legitime prescriptâ consuetudine, onus inveniendi et sustentandi perpetuis temporibus sumptibus et expensis ipsius domini Johannis Rectoris unum capellanum sufficientem et idoneum missas celebraturum et dicturum duobus diebus in singulis septimanis in Cappellâ de Oxendon predictâ, videlicet, diebus Martis, Jovis, ac omnibus et singulis annis futuris imperpetuum unam missam in festo Sancti Nicholai, tresque missas in festo Natalis Domini, cum vesperis primis et secundis dicti festi et Natalis Domini, necnon in festo Epiphaniæ Domini missam cum pleno servicio, ac in festo Purificacionis Beatæ Mariæ unam missam, in die Dominicâ Ramis palmarum unam missam cum pleno servicio, ac diebus Mercurii, Jovis, et Veneris, sive noctibus proximis, ante festum Paschæ, plenum servicium nocturnum, necnon in vigiliâ Paschæ missam cum pleno servicio, ac in festo Paschæ missam cum pleno servicio, ac vigiliâ Ascencionis Domini unam missam et campum dictæ villulæ processionaliter circumiturum et deambulaturum, in festo Ascencionis Domini unam missam cum pleno servicio, ac vigiliâ Pentecostes unam missam cum pleno servicio, necnon die Pentecostes missam cum pleno servicio, quodque die Cinerum missam et cineres daturum, ac die dedicacionis dictæ ecclesiæ de Bowdon missam cum pleno servicio, ac in festo Mariæ Magdalenæ missam cum pleno servicio, ac in festo Omnium Sanctorum missam cum pleno servicio, ac die sepulturæ quorumcunque inhabitancium vel inhabitandorum in dictâ villulâ ab hâc luce migrancium unam missam, necnon singulis diebus Dominicis per singulos annos panem benedictum et aquam benedictam in dictâ capellâ confecturum et singulis diebus Dominicis memoriam tantum de Dominicâ cum precibus more dominicali dicturum, et infirmos in dicta villulâ visitaturum, ac omnia et singula sacramenta et sacramentalia, sepulturâ dumtaxat exceptâ, inhabitantibus dictam villulam ministraturum, necnon missam pro quocunque inhabitante in dictâ villulâ de Oxendon ab hâc luce migrante, et pro sepulturâ canonicâ obtinendâ ad ecclesiam de Bowdon predictâ deportato, per se vel capellanum suum, in dictâ ecclesiâ de Bowdon, ante ipsius deportati sepulturam, celebraturum, ad dictum dominum Johannem Rectorem, quamdiu Rector ejusdem ecclesiæ de Bowdon extiterit et erit, pertinuit, pertinet, et pertinere debet etiam in futuro, prefatus tamen dominus Johannes, Rector predictus, hujus onus agnoscere et subire, secundum formam superius specificatam, non curavit nec curat, sed invencionem et sustentacionem hujus capellani per nonnulla tempora subtraxit nequiter et injuste, et subtrahit in presenti, in animæ suæ grave periculum et cultûs divini diminuscionem ac omnium et singulorum dictam villulam de Oxendon inhabitancium perendinum (?) dampnum non modicum et gravamen, Quæ omnia et singula sunt vera, notaria, manifesta et famosa, et per partem dicti domini Johannes Rectoris, in presenciâ dictorum inhabitancium et aliorum fide dignorum, sepius et ex certâ scienciâ recognita et confessata, et super eisdem in villâ de Bowdon et Oxendon et locis circumvicinis laborat publica vox et fama, et laborabat ante quamcunque litem in hâc parte motam, Quare, probatis in hâc parte de jure probandis, petunt predicti Ricardus, Johannes, Johannes, Johannes, Ricardus, Nicholaus, Johannes et Rogerus, pro consuetudine supradictâ ac ipsius consuetudinis vigore, onus inveniendi et sustentandi hujus capellani, secundum modum formam et effectum superius expressatum, ad dictum dominum Johannem Rectorem et suos successores, Rectores qui pro tempore erunt in dictâ ecclesiâ de Bowdon Parva, pertinuisse, pertinere et pertinere debere imperpetuum, per vos dominum Officialem Lincoln. finaliter et diffinitive pronunciari et declarari, ulteriusque fieri, statui, et decerni in premissis et ea concernentibus quæ dictaverunt canonicæ sanctiones, premissa proponunt et petunt predicti Ricardus, Johannes, Johannes, Johannes, Ricardus, Nicholaus, Johannes, et Rogerus, conjunctim et divisim, jure et beneficio in omnibus semper salvo : Factâque litis contestacione affirmative, ad eundem per dictam partem ream sic dicendæ—narrata prout narrantur vera esse et idem petita prout petuntur fieri debere : juratis hinc inde de calumpniâ et de veritate dicendâ, productisque tunc ibidem nonnullis testibus per dictam partem actricem, quibus in formâ juris admissis, juratis, et diligenter examinatis, eorumque testimoniis dictis et sepoibʒ (?) de consensu partium publicatis, et quia dicta pars rea, ut dixit, nichil contra dictos testes seu eorum dicta dicere seu allegare voluerit, nec aliqua in jure seu in facto consistencia proponere, de consensu utriusque partis supradictæ per nos in dicto negocio fuerat conclusum, et subsequenter partibus predictis coram nobis pro tribunali judicialiter sedentibus, videlicet, quarto die Decembris anno Domini millesimo ccccmo sexto in ecclesiâ parochiali Sancti Martini, Leycestr. legitime comparentibus et sententiam diffinitivam in predictâ causâ fieri petentibus, ad prolacionem sententiæ, Christi nomine primitus invocato, et de consilio juris peritorum nobis in hâc parte assidencium, procedimus in hunc modum : quod nos Officialis antedictus per acta et inactitata, producta, et exhibita, et confessata in dictâ causâ, et legitima documenta in eâ parte nobis ministrata, invenimus dictam partem actricem intencionem suam in libello suo deductam sufficienter et legitime fundasse et probasse pro consuetudine supradictâ, et ipsius consuetudinis vigore onus inveniendi et sustentandi perpetuis temporibus, sumptibus et expensis ipsius domini Johannis Rectoris, unum Capellanum sufficientem et idoneum, missas celebraturum et dicturum duobus diebus in singulis septimanis in Capellâ de Oxendon predictâ, viz., diebus Martis et Jovis, ac omnibus et singulis annis futuris imperpetuum unam missam quolibet festo Sancti Nicholai, tresque missas in festo Natali Domini, cum vesperis primis et secundis dicti festi Natali Domini, necnon in festo Epiphaniæ Domini missam cum pleno servicio, ac in festo Purificacionis Beatæ Mariæ unam missam, in die Dominicâ Ramis palmarum unam missam cum pleno servicio, ac diebus Marcurii (sic), Jovis et Veneris, sive noctibus proximis, ante festum Paschæ, plenum servicium nocturnum, ac vigiliâ Paschæ missam cum pleno servitio, ac in festo Paschæ missam cum pleno servitio, ac vigiliâ Ascensionis Domini unam missam et campum dictæ villulæ processionaliter circumiturum et deambulaturum, ac in festo Ascencionis Domini unam missam cum pleno servicio, ac vigiliâ Pentecostes unam missam cum pleno servicio, necnon die Pentecostes missam cum pleno servicio, quodque die Cinerum missam et cineres daturum, ac die dedicacionis dictæ ecclesiæ de Bowdon missam cum pleno servicio, ac in festo Mariæ Magdalenæ missam cum pleno servicio, in festo Omnium Sanctorum missam cum pleno servicio, ac die sepulturæ quorumcunque inhabitancium vel inhabitandorum in dictâ villulâ de Oxendon ab hâc luce migrancium unam missam, necnon singulis diebus Dominicis per singulos annos panem benedictum et aquam benedictam in dictâ capellâ confecturum et eis parochiæ ibidem existentibus daturum et ministraturum, ac singulis diebus Dominicis memoriam tantum de Dominicâ cum precibus more dominicali daturum, et infirmos in dictâ villulâ visitaturum, ac omnia et singula sacramenta et sacramentalia, sepulturâ duntaxat exceptâ, inhabitantibus in dictâ villulâ ministraturum, necnon missam pro quocunque inhabitante in dictâ villulâ de Oxendon ab hâc luce migrante et pro sepulturâ canonicâ obtinendâ ad ecclesiam de Bowdon predictâ deportato, per se vel capellanum suum in dictâ ecclesiâ de Bowdon, ante ipsius deportati sepulturam, celebraturum, ad dictum dominum Johannem Exenford Rectorem et suos successores in dictâ parochiâ de Bowdon Parva, pertinuisse, pertinere et pertinere debere imperpetuum, ac ipsum Dominum Johannem invencionem hujusmodi capellani certis temporibus injuste subtraxisse, finaliter et diffinitive pronunciamus et declaramus in hiis scriptis. Constat nobis Officiali supradicto de rasurâ istarum dictionum—*missam cum*—in decimâ octavâ lineâ ac de interlinear' istius dictionis — *missam* — supra quadragesimam secundam lineam, et de interlinear' istarum dictionum—*de Oxendon* —supra quadragesimam septimam lineam, a capite computando, quæ approbo eggo (*sic*) Officialis antedictus. In quorum omnium et singulorum premissorum testimonium sigillum officii nostri presentibus apposuimus. Datum apud Lydyngton vicesimo secundo die mensis Septembris anno Domini millesimo cccc^{mo} septimo.

[On March 24, 1405, before John Hauberk, Doctor of Canon Law, Official of the diocese of Lincoln, in the parish church of Farndon, Richard Esthorn, John his son, John Wryth, John Taylor, Richard Margery, Nicholas Green, John Whytyng, and Roger Clerk, being the community or the major part of the community of the hamlet of Little Oxendon, in the parish of Little Bowden, lay a complaint against John Exenford (? Oxenford), Rector of Little Bowden, to the following effect:

Whereas by ancient and prescribed custom the *onus* of finding and maintaining a chaplain to perform certain duties in the hamlet of Little Oxendon, has always rested upon the Rector of Little Bowden for the time being, the said John Exenford (or Oxenford) has wrongfully neglected to provide and maintain such a chaplain and is neglecting to do so at the time of the complaint, in peril of his own soul, to the lowering of Divine worship and to the serious loss of the inhabitants.

That this neglect is a matter of common knowledge, and has been confessed by the said Rector; that common talk and rumour in Bowden, Oxendon, and the neighbouring parishes, are at work on the matter, and have been at work long before this complaint. Wherefore the complainants pray that the *onus* of providing and maintaining a chaplain to perform these duties may be judicially declared to rest upon the Rector and his successors, and that all else may be done to give canonical sanction to the obligation.

The defendant having had the opportunity of hearing and replying to the complaint, witnesses having been examined in support of it, and no adequate answer having been offered in contradiction, either in law or in fact, the parties appear before the Official, in St. Martin's,

Leicester, on December 4, 1406. The Official there pronounces sentence to the effect that the contention of the complainants is established, and that the *onus* of maintaining and providing a chaplain to discharge the duties enumerated does rest upon the Rector of Little Bowden and his successors.

The declaration of sentence is signed and sealed at Lydington, September 2, 1407.

Duties of the Chaplain of Little Oxendon, twice enumerated.

On the Tuesday and Thursday in each week, one mass: on the Feast of S. Nicholas, one mass, and on Christmas Day, three masses, with the first and second vespers on each of those festivals: on the Epiphany, one mass with full service: on the Purification of the Blessed Virgin, one mass: on Palm Sunday, one mass with full service: on the Wednesday, Thursday, and Friday before Easter or the next nights, full night service: on Easter Eve, mass with full service: on Easter Day, the same: on the Vigil of the Ascension, one mass and the going round and perambulating in procession the 'field' of the hamlet: on Ascension Day, one mass with full service: on the Vigil of Pentecost (Whitsun Eve), one mass with full service: on the day of Pentecost (Whitsun Day), the same: on Ash Wednesday, mass and the giving of ashes: on the dedication day of Little Bowden church, mass with full service: on All Saints' Day, the same: at the burial of any inhabitant, one mass: on each Sunday in year, making Holy Bread and Holy Water in the chapel and giving them to those present, saying the memorial of the Sunday and prayers after the use of Sunday. The Rector is also bound, either himself or by his chaplain, to say mass in Little Bowden church before the interment of any inhabitant of Little Oxendon whose body has been brought to Little Bowden church to be interred.]

APPENDIX II.

(ISHAM MSS. *U. U.*, *fol.* 105.)

SCIANT presentes et futuri quod ego Rogerus Clerk dedi concessi et hac presenti cartâ meâ confirmavi Nicholas Gryffon armigero Advocacionem ecclesiæ de parva Bowdon in comitatu Northampton, cum omnibus, etc., etc. Salvâ quâdam pensione tresdecim solidorum et quatuor denariorum de dictâ ecclesiâ exeunte Habendum, etc., etc.

Datum die Martis proxima post festum Omnium Sanctorum anno regni regis Henrici sexti post conquestum tricesimoquinto.

[Roger Clerk gives, grants and confirms to Nicholas Gryffon, Esquire, the advowson of the church of Little Bowden, save and except a pension of 13*s.* 4*d.* yearly, due therefrom, to have and to hold, etc.

Dated Tuesday next after All Saints' Day, 35 Henry VI., A.D. 1456.]

The pension of 13*s.* 4*d.* was the property of Launde Abbey. In some memoranda belonging to Bishop Bokingham's time, though not included in the large volume bearing that title, a royal writ is recorded which requires the Bishop to cause Thomas, rector of Little Bowden (Thomas Tyberay, see p. 124), to answer before the King's Court for being 4 marks in arrear in payment of this charge of 13*s.* 4*d.* to Walter Baldok, Prior of Launde. Date of the writ, November 8, 17 Richard II., A.D. 1393.

INDEX.

ABKETTLEBY (Leic.), 103
Abonetoun, Roger, 119
Acton (Ackton), Leonard, 192, 195, 197, 199, 206, 207
Adames, John, 'yrynmownger,' 205
Addames (   ), 229
Ad Ecclesiam, Ricardus, 44
Adelingfleet (Yorks), 19
Adyngton. See 'Alyngton'
Aids, 11
Ainderby with the Steeple (Yorks), 36, 67, 81, 86
Airmyn (Yorks), 31
Alb, 54, 55
Alburgh, John, 85
Allann, Johan, 220
  ,,   John, 219
  ,,   Thomas, Will of, 220
Alleyn, George, 197
Allington (Ailyngton), William of, Rector of Fifehead, 39, 40
'Almres' ('Ambrey'), 228, 232
Almshouse (Great Bowden), Bequests to, 222, 223
Altars, Bequests to, 51, 53, 209-211, 213, 216-222, 225-227, 229
Alton, John of, chaplain, 74
Alyngton (Aylyngton), Juliana de, 164
  ,,   ,,   Thomas de, 164, 166-168, 170, 171, 176
Alyngton (alias Adyngton), Stephen, of Little Canfield, Essex, 199, 200
Alyngton (alias Adyngton), William, 199, 200
Amice ('Amita'[*sic*]), 53-55
Anchorites, Bequests to [Doncaster, Hampole, Kirkby Wiske, Lincoln (Holy Trinity), Stamford (St. Paul's)], 58
'Ancoradensis, Johannes Episcopus,' 133
Andrew, 'Hesteln,' 44
  ,,   Johannes (chaplain), 44-46, 161-163
Andrew, Richard, 165, 167

Andrew, 'Sir R. prest,' 223, 224
  ,,   Rogerus, 44
  ,,   William, 167, 168
Annadown (Enachdunensis), Thomas, Bishop of, 132
Annes (Annys), John, Churchwarden of Great Bowden, 97, 101, 134
  ,,   ,,   Richard, 176, 221, 227
  ,,   ,,   Robert, 134
  ,,   ,,   Thomas, 186, 191, 192
Apesthorpe, Prebend, 43
Apparels (paruræ), 55
Apulthorp, John of, 56
  ,,   William of, 56
  ,,   (Apesthorpe, Notts), Bequest to the church, 54, 55
Archer, John, 194, 197, 199-204, 230
  ,,   Richard, 202, 203
  ,,   William, 202, 203
Arcubus, S. Mary de, Dean of, 118
Arden, St. Mary's in ('our Lady in Ardrone,' 218; 'our Lady in Arthern,' 228; 'our Lady's parysh in Arthorne,' 216; 'the parych church off our Lady in Atharne,' 211; 'the Holy Virgyn off Hardron,' 225; 'our Lady off Bowdon,' 217; 'St. Mare Church off our Lady off Bowdon,' 217; 'Sent Mary yn Alderne,' 228; 'Saincte Maries of Bowdon,' 220; 'Saint Mares off Mych Bowdon,' 226; 'the Blessed Mary in Little Bowden in the fields,' 53; 'our Lady church in the fylds,' 223; 'Sent Mare Church off Gret Bowdon,' 228; 'Saint Mary's,' 219; 'Saint Mare Church in Mych Bowdon,' 217; 'the blessed Mary in the fields in Great Bowdon,' 91, 92); position of church and parish, 1, 2, 5-8; chapelry of Great Bowden, 13-15; bequests to the church, 53, 173, 211, 216-219, 225, 228; burial-ground for Harborough, 91,

Index
245

92, 173, 211, 216-219, 225, 226, 228; chancel reported out of repair (1510), 110; bequests to the bells, 220, 226; present church, 145; St. Mary's land, 3
Ardern, John of, Rector of Wakely, 28, 45
'Arke,' 232
Armilausa, 58
Arnhale, Ralph, Rector of Little Bowden, deprived, 116-118
Arthur, Prince of Wales, 113
Arundel (Thomas), Archbishop of Canterbury, 62
Arundel, Master A. of, 115
   ,, Richard, Earl of, 32
   ,, Thomas, Earl of, 66, 69
Asgarby, Prebend, 60
Ashes, giving of, 240, 242
Ashley (Northants), Bequest to the church, 219
Askeby, William de, notary, 123
Askerby, Thomas de, 115
Asplande, John, Churchwarden of Harborough, 110
Astell, Alice, 193
   ,, Robert, 'of Haverburgh, chapman,' 'of Northampton, mercer,' 193, 202, 203, 206-208
Astley, Thomas of, 137
Aston, 116
At Gate (ad portam), Henry, 17
Atkinson, Agnes, Will of, 218
Atte Mor, Richard, 159, 160
   ,, Thomas, 44
Atte Thorn, Robert, son of William, 132
At the Church, William, 160
Atwell, John, of Foxton, 183, 205
   ,, Thomas, of Foxton, 205
Auton, Peter, 175
Averey, Hugh, 188
   ,, Robert, chaplain, 173
   ,, Thomas, 44, 46, 162
'Avez,' 57
A-vicars. See 'Vicars'
Aylmer, Edward, 207

'Bacar,' William (Hyll), Will of, 216
'Bacar-craft,' 216
Bacheler, William, Canon of Lincoln, 37, 45
Baddeby, Thomas, 121
'Bailif,' John le (John Baly), 47, 65, 163, 166
Bailiff, The ('baylly'), 17, 102, 198, 203, 204, 215
Bakehouse (pistrina), The common, 180, 184

Baker, 202, 203
Balantyne, George, 228
'Bald Colte,' 211
Baldok, Walter, Prior of Launde, 243
Bale, John, Vicar of Tokby, 124, 127
Balle, Henry, 181
Balme, Robert, of the bakehouse, 58
Banbury, 130, 134
Banquers (or bankers), 57, 232
Barber, William, son of Thomas, 59
Barett (or Barrett), Anne, 199
   ,, ,, Nicholas, 193, 196, 197, 199, 200, 203, 205
Barett (or Barrett), Richard, 202, 203
Barford, John, 202
Barkby, J., 195
Barker (or Barkar), Godfrey, 12
   ,, ,, Helen, 229
   ,, ,, Robert, 188
Barnet, 137
Barone, Richard, 187, 188
Barre, Nicholas, 202
Basin (pelvis), 74
Basing, Nicholas, of Bassingbourn, 12
Basset, John, 176, 179
   ,, Robert, 194, 196, 197
Bassingbourn (Camb.), 12
Bate, Clemency, 162
   ,, Thomas, chaplain, 44, 80, 168
   ,, Walterus, 44
Bath (lavacrum), 74
Baverey, Thomas, 92, 172
Bawtry, John of, 56
Baxster, John, son of Richard, 133
Baxter, John, draper, 169
Bayly, John, of Sutton, 234
Bead-roll, 215
Beads, Pair of, 220, 231
Bear on the Hoop (le bere super le hope), 175, 176
Beaufort, Cardinal, 48, 81
Beaumont family, 113
Beauvale, Bequest to, 54
Bedford (S. Paul's), 135
   ,, Archdeaconry of, 124
   ,, Duke of (John, brother of Henry V.), 143
Beelle, Richard, flaxman, 232
Belers, Hamon, Subdean of Lincoln, 38, 60
Bell, John, 133
Bellerby (Yorks), 86
Bells, Bequests for :—
   Great Bowden, 210, 213
   Harborough, 220, 226
   S. Mary in Arden, 220, 226
Belvoir, John of, Subdean of Lincoln, 60

Belyngham, John, chaplain, 103, 108
'Bemes' (of weighing instruments), 233
Benefend, 12
Benett, Thomas, 197
  ,, William, chaplain, 202
Benniworth (Beningworth), William de, 115
Bercher, John, 161, 162
Beringarius ('Beringarium meum'), 55
Berkhamsted, Honour of, 7, 113
Bernard (or Barnard), Adam, 16, 18, 19, 159
  ,,   ,, John, 167, 168
  ,,   ,, Richard, 74, 162, 167, 168
  ,,   ,, Roger, 170, 171
  ,,   ,, Thomas, 155, 162, 170, 171
Berth, Johannes, 44
Bertlot, Master L., 130
Beryhatley (Cockayne Hatley, Beds), 170
Beuon (?), R., 115
Beverley, Richard of, Subdean of Lincoln, 60
Beyvill, Hugh, esquire, 177, 178, 187
  ,, John,   ,, 177, 178
Biddenden (Bydingdon) (Kent), 90
Biggleswade (Bikyllswade), 135
Billesdon, Richard de, Chaplain of the Guild of the Holy Cross, 164, 169
Birmingham, 157
Bishopthorpe (Yorks), 124
Bitteswell (Leic.), 190
Blake, William, chaplain, 103, 189
Blanket, blankets, 57, 155, 171
Blaston (Leic.), 5
Bobton, Laurence of, 17
Boccard, Roesa, 160
  ,, William, 160
'Bocher' or 'Bucher,' 103, 180
Bolton (Yorks), 34
Bolton, John of, chaplain, Rector of Great Bowden, 39, 47, 164
Boner, Ricardus, 44, 45, 162
'Bonett' (man's), 229
Books, Bequests of, 53-57, 227, 229
Booth, Robert, LL.D., Rector of Great Bowden, 101, 104, 105
Boresworth (Husband's Bosworth, Leic.), 110 [207
Boresworth (or Bosworth), Edward,
  ,,   ,, Robert, 170, 173-176, 181, 186, 193
  ,,   ,, Thomas, 207

Boresworth (or Bosworth), John de, 166, 172
  ,,   ,, Richard de, 164-168, 169
  ,,   ,, William de, 165-167, 169
Boston (Villa de Sancto Botulpho), 167
Botreaux, The Lord de, 69
Bottesford (Leic.), 45
Boucer, Hugh, Lord de, 69
Boughton, Chantry of, Land belonging to, 196
Bould, Alexander, 119
Boungarth. See 'Lincoln'
Bourne, The Abbot of, 118
Bow, S. Mary le (S. Mary de Arcubus), 118
Bowde, Thomas, Rector of Great Bowden, 105, 106
Bowden Magna (Great Bowden) [Bugedon, 4; Buchedon, 10; Bukedon, 11; Budon, 13; Boudon, 14; Bowedon, 90; Bowdon, 33; Mekell Boudon, 190; Mych, or Myche, Bowdon, 204, 209; Moch Bowdon, 208; Magna Bowedone, 189; Gret, Grett, or Grete Bowdon, 210, 220], Parish described, 1-3; manor of Bowden-Harborough, 4, 5, 8, 9, 11-13, 18, 19, 27, 28, 31-38, 66, 69-73, 81-89, 94, 103-105, 109, 135-137; benefice, value of, 14, 24, 43, 112; suit as to right of presentation, 79, 80; rectors, 13, 19-21, 24, 28, 29, 36, 37, 39, 40-43, 47, 61, 63, 73-77, 90, 91, 94, 101, 105, 106, 109-112; vicars and chaplains, 14, 24, 25, 47, 54, 109-111, 210, 219, 221, 224, 227, 230; churchwardens, 101, 109-111, 214; assistant to the rector, 28, 29; church, 15, 73, 109, 145; bequests to the church, 52, 53, 67, 74, 210, 220, 227; church land, 183; chantry, foundation of, 95-100, tradition as to, 101; chantry-priest, 210, 221, 222; chantry, land of the, 192, 196; bequests to, 227; churchyard, reconciliation of, 26; clerical disorder at, 25, 26; clergy, A.D. 1292, 24, 25; poor, bequests to, 54, 223; almshouse, 222, 223; rectory, or parsonage, 111, 112; commonfields, 3, 152-155; inhabitants (lay subsidy roll, 1 E. III.), 44; choir, bequests to, 215, 223; 'Adamy's yard,' 230; 'Bukwel Moor,' 151; 'chapelensthing,' 93, 170; 'Ferrors Lane,' 108, 201; 'Gallow Hill,' 152; 'le Gunnesbrok,' 93, 170, 171;

Index. 247

'Hyrn Lane,' 107, 172, 193; 'le Kylnzerde,' 93, 171; 'parsonage gate,' 111, 112; the south end, 178; 'ie weste ende,' 66, 168; 'next the Cross,' 174; wall-painting in the church, 146

Bowden Parva (Little Bowden, Northants)[Bugedun, 112; Bugedon, 114; Buggedon, 115; parva Buwedon, 115; Budon, 116; parva Boudon, 116; Bowdon parva, 124; parva Bodon, 126], parish described, 1-3; ecclesiastical divisions of, 1, 2; in Domesday, 5, 6; early manorial history, 6-8; summary of later manorial history, 113, 114; gift of the benefice to Launde Abbey, 114; grant of the benefice to N. Griffyn, 243; value of the benefice, 119; rectors, 114-119, 121-132; chaplains, 114-116; assessment for a ninth (1342), 119, 120; church, 121, 145; bequests to the church, 121, 219, 228; wall-paintings in the church, 146; advowson attached to portion of the manor, 128; day of dedication, 237, 240; Burton's Fee, 113; Latimer's Fee, 113; pension to Launde Abbey, 234

Bowden, A. of, Canon of Lincoln, 58
,, Master Richard of, 25, 26
,, Master Roger of, 25, 26
,, William of, chaplain, Vicar of Great Bowden, 14
,, Sir William, parish chaplain of, 54

Bowers, Richard, 207
Bowghton (or Bowton), William, 208, 210, 226
Brake (or Brackele), Stephen, Rector of Little Bowden, 125, 128
Brampton (Brampton Ash, Northants), 74
Brampton, John de, clerk, 161
,, Matilda de, 163
'Brandert,' 233
Brannge, William, 174
'Brase pott having longe fete,' 227
Brass, 57
Braybrooke (Northants), 234
'Bred, al, and chesse,' to be given at a funeral, 215
Brest, Margaret, 213
Breviary (portiforium) of the York use, 56, 74
Breviary, noted, of the Sarum use, 56
Brewode, John, 189, 194, 197, 199, 205

Brewster, William, 195, 196, 199
Bridgeman (or Brydgeman), John, 134
,, ,, Thomas, 228
Bridges, Bequests and grants for repair of, 157, 173 (' pontis magni '), 222
Brokesby, Bartholomew, 86, 87
Browne, John, 132, 197, 199, 200, 202, 203
Browne, little John, 58
Browne, Richard, churchwarden of Great Bowden, 111, 177, 178, 180, 181, 185, 188, 189, 192, 193, 197
Browne, Robert, baker, 202, 203
Browne, Robert, churchwarden of Great Bowden, 111, 218
Browne, William, churchwarden of Harborough, 110, 112, 217, 220
Browne, William, 'wefer,' 202, 203
,, William, baker, 202, 203
Bruce, David, 140
Bryan, A. W., 211
Buci, Robert de, 5, 6, 112, 114
Buckard, Richard, 159
Buckden (Hunts), 20, 130, 132, 134, 135, 139
Buckingham, Gilbert of, Bishop's Chancellor, 118
Budon, Magister Johannes de, 44, 45
'Bukeskyne,' 229
'Bulting lome,' 234
Bunney, Nicholas, priest, 25
Burbache, Master J., Canon of Lincoln and vicar-general, 133
Burditt, Alys, 209
,, Janet, 209
,, William, will of, 209
Burdon, Richard, 185, 189, 194
,, Robert, 187, 194, 198, 202
Burgess, Jone (or Johanna), 214-216
,, Thomas, 216
Burgh, John, chaplain, 56
,, John, of Withcote, 169, 170, 173, 193
Burghersh Chantry. See 'Lincoln'
Burton, Herbert of, Rector of Little Bowden, 115, 116
Burton, John, 169
Burton, Master William, of (Lincoln), 52
Burton, William de, 113
,, William, 133
Burton Constable (Yorks), 85, 86
Burton Latimer (Northants), 157
Bussy Hugh, chaplain, 52
Butler, Robert, 229

'Butts off peysse,' 212
Bylling, Robert, 159
Byron, William, 199
Bytteswell, Thomas, 190

Cade, Agnes, 220
  ,, John, 219
  ,, Richard, 197, 203, 204, 219 (will)
'Calaber,' 58
Calais, 140
Caldwell (Leic.), 9
Cales (or Caleys), William, of Ainderby, confessor to John, Lord le Scrope, 81, 82
Cambridge, Chancellor of the University, 62
Cambridge, Earl of (Richard), 66-69, 143
Campden, John of, 17
Campynett, Christopher, 221
Canfield, Little (Essex), 199
Canterbury, Archbishops of : Stratford, 32, 34, 120 ; Arundel, 62 ; Chichele, 82, 90
Cantilupe, William de (1), 9, 11, 13, 15
  ,, ,, (2), 12
Canvas, 57
Capital messuage, 179
Carlisle, Bishop of (Thomas Merkes), 140, 141
Carlton (Carlton Curlieu, Leic.), 5, 111, 185
  ,, in Kesteven (Linc.), 77
  ,, John of, Canon of Lincoln, 60
  ,, Kyme, Prebend, 52, 60
  ,, cum Thurlby, Prebend, 60
'Carsey' (Kersey), 222, 232
Carter, Richard, 193, 195, 196, 198, 202, 205, 209, 221
Carter, Robert, 186, 188, 189, 191, 192, 205
Carter, William, 183, 194
Carthusians, 54
Carucata. See 'Field-names and descriptions'
Castey, Thomas, son of John Nubon, 210
Catesby, Hugh of, 121
  ,, John, son of Hugh, 121
  ,, Simon, ,, ,, 121
'Caudernys,' 231 [92
Caumbrygge, Katharine, Will of, 91,
'Causeys,' Bequests to repair, 209, 222
Cave, Geoffrey of, Rector of Little Bowden, 116

Cay, John, 167, 168
'Cercum' (?), 55
Chace, William, 119
Chalcombe, Waryn of, justiciar, 17
Chalice, 53, 54
Chambre, John, M.D., Rector of Great Bowden, 106, 109, 112
'Chamlette,' 229
Chantry and Chantry-priest. See 'Bowden Magna'
Chapelen, Richard, 159
'Chapelensthing,' 170
Chapeleyn, Thomas, 160
Chaplain, Nicholas, of Benefend, 12
Chaplain of Little Oxendon, Duties of the, 235-242
'Chapman,' 206
Chapman, Thomas, of Foxton, 181, 185
Charterhouse, Bequest to, 54
Chasuble (casula), 52, 55
'Chayffing dyshe,' 231
Chessmen ('tabellæ annelit''), 55
Chester (St. John's), Dean of, 125, 126
  ,, Johan, 218
  ,, John, 218
  ,, William, 218, 229
Chesterfield, Richard, Canon of Lincoln, 64
'Cheysrakke,' 232
Chichester, 62, 63
Chief rent, 194
Choir, Bequests to, see 'Bowden Magna'
Chonde, John, 68
Christian (Cristian, Cristien, Cristyan, Crystyen), John, 134, 135, 183, 192, 197, 202, 221, 224
Christian, Reginald, 168
  ,, Richard, 12, 161, 169, 178, 179, 191, 196
Christian, Robert, 163
  ,, Roger, 44, 97, 167
  ,, Thomas, 164, 165, 172, 178, 179
Christian, William, 133, 134
Churches (Bowden and Harborough), probable dates, ornaments, fittings, etc., 15, 145-147
Churches, Bequests to :—
  ,, Great Bowden, 52, 53, 67, 74, 210, 220, 227
  ,, Little Bowden, 121, 219, 229
  ,, Harborough, 53, 173, 211, 212, 216, 217, 219, 228, 229
  ,, S. Mary in Arden, 53, 173, 211, 216, 217, 219, 223, 225, 228

Index. 249

Churchyard, Reconciliation of. See 'Bowden Magna'
'Churchyard of Herdeborow,' 212
'Ciphum,' 55
Cistercians, 54 [87
Clarence, Thomas, Duke of, 67, 69,
Clarke, 'Sir Wyllyam, my goostly fader,' 228
Claypole (Notts), 56
Clement VI., Pope, 122
Clement, John, 179
Clementines, The, 57
Clen, John, 205
Clendon, John de, 163, 166
  ,, Roger de, 163, 167
Clergy, The, 131, 132, 147, 148
Clerical disorder, Instance of, 25, 26
Clerk, John, 192, 195
  ,, John, sen., of Takely, Essex, 199, 200
Clerk, John, jun., 172
  ,, Nicholaus, de Takely, 200
  ,, Thomas, 202
  ,, Thomas the, 160
  ,, William the, 159, 160
  ,, William, churchwarden of Great Bowden, 97, 101, 171, 191, 192
Clerke, Johane, 218
  ,, Roger, 127, 128, 236, 241, 243
  ,, Roger, of Haloughton (Staff.), 129
Clerke, William, of Harborough, Will of, 229
Clifford, John, Lord de, 69
Clifton (Yorks), 86
Clinton, William, Lord de, 69
Clynton, William de, 32
Clippeton, Robert de, 10
Clipston, Thomas de, 164, 166
Clone (or Clune), John of, Rector of Great Bowden, 63-65
Cloth and clothiers, 175
Clyff, Robert (alias Robert Roper), 195
Clyn, John, 181
'Cofer' ('Koffer'), 228, 232
Coft, Richard, 133
Cok, William, 185, 188, 189
Cokayn, John, 86, 87
Cokyn, Reginald, of Beryhatley, 170
Coldeham, Robert, citizen and fishmonger, 185, 188, 189
Coley, Robert, 166
'Collman's wyff off Foxton,' 233
Collys, Robert, baker, 206
  ,, William, 191
Cologne, Orphrey of, 53

Colston, Thomas, notary public, 129
Colwick (Notts), 123, 124
Coly, Walter, 175
Colyn, John, 68
'Commendacon, not(e) of,' 214, 223
Commendatory letter (G. le Scrope), 39, 40
Commissions as to the manors of the Scropes, 85, 89
Confessor, Licence to choose, 38
Conyers, Christopher, Escheator of Yorkshire, 84
Coo (or Koo), Margaret, 165, 166
  ,, Roger, 165
Cooke, Elizabeth, 218
Co-opertorium, 55
Cope (capa), 53, 67
Corby, Willelmus de, 44
Corby Latimer (Northants), 113, 157
Corder, Adam the, 17
'Corio bulliet', 55
Cornwall, Earl of (Edmund), 7
  ,, ,, (John of Eltham), 30-32, 35, 139
Corporal (corporale), 53
Corpus Christi, Guild of, Bequest to, 55
Cort (or Corte), John, 172, 210
'Cotage rente,' 168
Cotes, Thomas, 172
Cottingham (Northants), 234
Couper, John, 133, 167
  ,, John, son of John, 166
  ,, John, son of William, 177
  ,, William, 176
Coventry, 170, 174, 200
  ,, Carthusian priory near, 134
Coventry and Lichfield, Bishop of, 62
Coverham (Yorks), 35, 36, 53, 85, 87, 140
Coverham, Abbot of, 53
'Craft,' 216
Crafte, Roger, 193-196, 198, 202
Crancefelde, Robert, 184, 189
  ,, Thomas, 180
Cranoe (Leic.), 5
Crecy, 137
Cregis, John, 172
Creket, Robert, citizen and fishmonger, 188, 189
Croft, John, of Stoke, 234
Crofte, 'William in ye,' 121
Crokesdene, Abbot of, 160
Cromwell, Lord (Ralph), 81
Cross, Silver, Bequest of, 54
Crouthorp, Osbert of, 17
Crowne, Robert, 77, 229
Cruets (fiolis), 53, 54

Crusade, Rector of Great Bowden joins in, 21-24
Cryspe, John, chaplain, Rector of Little Bowden, 124, 125, 127, 128
Cully, Robert, 229
Cultura. See 'Field Names,' etc.
Culworth, Robert of, clerk, 29
'Curatt,' 217, 221
'Curia,' 159
Curlett, Richard, 'gentleman,' 180
Curtains (curtinis), 57, 70
Curtilage, 177
Cusancia, William de, 35
Cushions ('cussynez'), 57

David, King of Scotland, 7
Davyson, 97
Debts forgiven by will, 210, 222
Decem librarum, Prebend, 60
Decretals, The, 57
Deken (Dekene, Dekan, Dekon, Dekne, Dekyn), Adam, 161, 162
 ,, ,, ,, John, 168, 192, 210, 213, 215
 ,, ,, ,, Nicholas, 196, 198
 ,, ,, ,, Richard, 44, 45, 109, 110, 112, 168, 196, 198, 205, 210, 230
 ,, ,, ,, Robert, 111, 183, 198, 205
 ,, ,, ,, Thomas, 179, 187
 ,, ,, ,, William, 165, 167, 168
Demesne, Ancient, 48, 49
Dennett, 'Angnes,' 210
 ,, John, 210
 ,, Thomas, Will of, 210
Denys, St. (St. Dionysius), 15, 93, 175, 211, 216, 218, 219, 228, 229
Derby, Edward, 196
 ,, William, 98, 100
Derby, County of, 137
'Deus cui proprium est misereri,' 223
Dey, William, 177, 193
Digby, Everard (1), 93, 169
 ,, ,, (2), 108, 195
Dingle, Robert de, 159
Dingley (Northants), 190
 ,, Bequests to the church, 217, 223
 ,, Preceptory, 149
'Dirige,' 214, 223
Dishes, Silver, Bequest of, 55
Domesday Book, Extracts from, 4-6
Doncaster, 58
Donnington, Robert of, 56
Dooles, John, 206
Dorchester (Oxf.), 119
Dorset, Thomas, Earl of, 69
Draper (citizen of London), 169, 173
Drayton, 126
Drayton, Henry, 125
'Dublet,' 213, 218, 219, 229
Durham, Bishop of (Thomas Langley), 82, 83
Duston, Robert, clerk, 169
Dutton, John, 202, 203
Dybbys, John, 229
Dyke, Robert, clerk, 169
'Dykynson, my syster,' 217

East Field, the (campus orientalis). See 'Fields'
Easton by Rockingham (Great Easton, Leic.), 45, 150
Eddlesborough (Bucks), 22, 24
Edenstowe, Henry of, Canon of Lincoln, 52
Edmondthorpe (Leic.), 45
Edward the Confessor, 4
Edward I., 16, 18, 20, 21, 23-25
Edward II., 27, 28
Edward III., 30-34
Edward IV., 95-100
Edward V., Grant by, 103, 104
Eleanor of Provence, Queen, 13, 18
Eleyne, John, 185, 187, 188
Elizabeth, wife of Edward IV., 95, 98
Ellyngstryng (Yorks), 86
Ellyngton (Yorks), 86
Elyner, John, 184
Encampment, Supposed Roman, 3, 4
English, Earliest bit of (1483), 190
Entwysall (or Entwysull), Thomas, esquire, 108, 190, 195
Escheator, 70, 96, 97
Escheats, 160, 190
'Esquire, My,' 59
Essendon (Herts.), 21
Esthorn, John, 236, 241
 ,, Richard, 236, 241
Estlyngton, Beatrice of, 58
Eston, John of, 160, 178, 179
 ,, Richard, son of Robert, 190
 ,, Robert, 190
Eventale (ventaille), 56
Evington (Leic.), 45
Exchanges of benefices:
 Great Bowden and Biddenden (Kent), 90
 Little Bowden and Oadby, 118, 119
 ,, Colwick, 123, 124
 ,, St. John's Hospital, Lutterworth, 125

Exchanges of benefices (*continued*):
    Little Bowden and Drayton, 126
        ,,   St. Mary Magdalene's (V.), Oxford, 127
    Little Bowden and Lapworth, 129
    Lapworth and Gumley, 130
Exchange of manors:
    Whitgift, etc. (Yorks), and Nayland, etc. (Suff.), 31-33
Exenford (? Oxenford), John of, Rector of Little Bowden, 236, 240, 241
Exeter, Duke of (Thomas Beaufort), 82, 83, 143

Facone, Johane, 222, 223
'Falleris (or phaleris) textoriis anglice weyving geyris,' 225
Fallisle, John, 121
    ,,   Thomas, 121
Fandon, Master John of, 53
'Fanon' (maniple), 55
Farendon, John of, notary, 117
Farndon (East Farndon, Northants), 2, 4, 172, 181, 182, 185, 236
Farndon Fields, 182
Fawdon, John, Rector of Sturneton, 36
Fawne, Agnes, 222
    ,,   Johane, 224
    ,,   William, 224
Fayrehed, John, of Takeley, Essex, 199, 200
Feliskirk (Yorks), Sir John of, 56, 57
Felough (Felowes), John, 174, 176
Felton, Robert, Rector of Great Bowden, 78-80, 90
Feoffees, the first, Deed from, 106, 107, 203
Ferrars, Sir William de, of Groby, 86, 87
Fidel, William, 47, 162
'Field, William in ye,' 121
Fields, The Common, of Great Bowden, 152-154, 179
    ,, the East Field, 152, 161, 179, 186, 196
    ,, the North or Gallow Field, 30, 93, 152, 162, 176, 179, 186, 196, 204
    ,, the South Field, 152, 161, 179, 181, 196
    ,, the West Field, 152, 186, 190, 191, 197
Field-names (1343 and 1655), 46
Field-names and descriptions:
    'Against the sun,' 93, 161, 176
    Balk, The common, 153, 154, 196

Field-names and descriptions (*contd.*):
    Brakynbarowhylt, 155, 182
    Branglondis or Banlonds, 93, 102, 172, 184
    'Le Brest or Breeste, le Weste Breste, le Breche,' 46, 162, 179, 183, 184, 197
    Broddole, 46, 162
    Bukwelmore, 102, 151, 179
    'Carucata,' 183, 205
    Comyn marlepyttes, 102, 155, 184
    Cranesworth, or Craneworth, 93, 155, 172, 192
    Crowthornehyll, 197, 198, 199
    'Cultura' (tillage), 159, 183, 197, 198, 205
    Efell or Efilde, 102, 186, 196
    'Le Estlonge,' 102, 179
    Fargatys, 102, 184
    Fidelliswonge oure langetongate, 162
    'Into Foxtongate,' 162
    'Le Foxtongate,' 197
    Foxton Moor, 30, 151, 160, 165, 168
    Fulforth, 105, 192
    Galhou, 'le Gallowe,' 46, 155, 162, 179, 196
    'Into Gasewell,' 'Gasylleseyke,' 46, 162, 168
    Gatemyll, 179
    Godwyne's ox, 'ubi Godwyne's oxe moricabatur,' 46, 154, 161
    Gore, Gores, 153, 161, 162, 183, 184, 187
    'Le Grygges,' 197
    'Lez Hadys,' 176
    'Le Halough,' 105, 192
    'Haverbergh more,' 151, 171
    'Le Hayeleyis (Hayleys), 93, 154, 172, 186, 192, 194
    'Headland' (forera), 153, 159, 162, 194, 195
    Helthirne, 162
    Holebergh, 46, 161, 193
    Kyngestirne, 46, 162
    Laconwell, 46
    Lakefurlong, 102, 179
    Langbarowe, 205
    'Into Lobenham brok,' 161, 187
    Longehilrene, 46, 162
    Long Rokhill, 194
    Lyttylbergh, 102, 179
    Lyttylhill, 102, 179
    Lyzard, 167
    Maynerdesholm, 16, 27, 160
    Mekylbarogh, Mykelbarogh, Mikelbergh, 179, 196

Field-names and descriptions (contd.):
  Midillfurlonge, 102, 184
  Moreforelong (sic), 107, 196
  Musfurlong, 102, 179
  Myllegate, 155, 196
  Nethirportgate, 46, 162
  Nethirrademylde, 46, 161
    ,, Wylardisgate, 102, 186
  Ouerrademylde, 46, 161
  Overgrymeswong, 179, 196
  Overgyfhoke, 105, 192
  Overtoftys, 107, 196
  Paddokispyltche, 105, 154, 192
  Paynesgore, 179
  Penytherne, 102, 187
  Portgates, 46, 162
  Potersholme, Este, 198
  Pyllokesholme, 107, 204
  Pylwellfurlong, 107, 197
  'Quarentena,' 179
  Rokhill or Rokhyll, 194, 196
  Russhygore, 107, 196
  Sandefurlong, 102, 179
  Scirdaykotys, Schirdecotys, Shirdaycotis, Shirdycotes, 16, 46, 154, 159, 162, 176, 177, 194
  'Selion,' 159, 160, 164, 165, 167, 191, 192, 194, 195
  Sevenewell, 46, 161
  Shortebanham, 107, 196
  Shortehilrene, 46, 162
  Shorte Rockhill, 102, 186
  Shulfebrode, 107, 196
  Smalthornes, 187
  Smethmewe, 66, 167
  'Smeton leyis,' 107, 199
  Snakesyke, 102, 155, 179
  Stanyhull, 46, 154, 161, 176
  Stockefurlong, 102, 186
  Stretefurlong, 102, 186
  'Territorium,' 184
  'Le Threnge,' 102, 179
  'Thrittifal,' thirtyfall, 161, 162, 172, 176, 184, 186, 191
  'Le Thwong,' 160
  Tocroft or Toucroft, 46, 162, 183, 184, 205
  Tongstede or Tongsty, 16, 159, 171
  'Triparteta,' 176
  'Triparticata,' 191
  'Triparticum,' 184, 186
  'Tripartita,' 172
  'Tudges land,' 191, 197
  Warpart, 102, 179
  Wasshford, 107, 155, 196
  Waterlakes, 66, 154, 167, 186, 191

Field-names and descriptions (contd.):
  Westwell, 46, 162
  Wyllerspyttes, 196
  Yngbarowefelde, 102, 181
Fifehead (Wilts), 39
Fishmonger (citizen of London), 103, 185, 188, 189
Fiskerton, John of, Vicar-Choral of Lincoln Cathedral, 59
Fisshwyk, William, clerk, 62
FitzHugh, Henry, Lord, 82, 83, 85
FitzHugh, Robert, 7
'Flaxen shets,' 228, 231, 232
Flaxflete (Yorks), 89
Flaxman, 232
Fleming, Thomas, 163
Fletcham, John de, 36
'Fleyschschamelis,' 'fleschameles,' le, 166, 168
Flint, 50
Folesworth ('Follysworth') (Hunts), 181
'Folur le,' 27
'Folur, Thomas le,' 160
Food and clothing, 155, 156
Forster, John, Rector of Great Bowden, 78-80
Forster or Foster, John (1520), 208, 217, 226
Fosse (Linc.), Bequest to, 54
Fosse Way, The, 4
Fot, John, 160
Four Stalls, The. See 'Harborough'
Foxton (Leic.), 5, 181, 183, 233
  ,, Bequest to the church, 223
  ,, Moor. See 'Field-names'
Foxton (or Foxson), Cecely, 211
  ,, John, 211, 212, 219, 229
  ,, Margaret, 212
  ,, Richard, 211, 229
  ,, ,, of, 119, 161, 164, 169
  ,, Thomas, 'mercer,' 197, 199, 202, 203, 204, 211 (will), 229, 230
Foxton, William, 175, 211, 212
Framland Wapentake or Hundred, 5, 45
Frampton (Linc.), 54, 60
Francis (Francys, Fraunces, Fraunceys), Joan, 228
  ,, ,, ,, Richard, 185, 187-189, 191-193, 195, 199, 200, 205
  ,, ,, ,, Thomas, 111, 202, 203
  ,, ,, ,, William, 17
'Franke,' 233
Frank-marriage, 178

Index. 253

Freeman, William, Rector of Colwick, Rector of Little Bowden, 123
Freman, John, citizen and grocer, 185
Freseby, John, of Carleton, 185
Freyby (Fraby, Frayby), John, chaplain, 109-111
Friars, Austin, Leicester, Bequest to, 222
Friars, Black, Northampton, Bequest to, 226
Friars, 'three howses of,' Leicester, Bequest to, 223
Friars, White, Stamford, Bequest to, 223
Frisby upon Wreake (Leic.), Bequest to the church, 222
Frysby, Thomas ('Sir'), 223
Fuller, Katherine, 225
Funeral, Entertainment at, 51
  ,, Money to be spent at, 210, 215
Furbisher (furbechur), Leonard the, 27, 160
'Furmes,' 232
Fus, John le, 17
'Fustyan,' 222
Fyncham, Laurence, citizen and fishmonger, 188, 189
Fynche, John, chaplain, 74
Fysh (Fyshe, Fysche), Agnes, 227
  ,, ,, ,, Edward, 204, 226 (will)
  ,, ,, ,, John Welere, 68
  ,, ,, ,, Miles, 206
  ,, ,, ,, Richard, 227
Fyssher, Mr. John, clerk, 179, 194, 195, 197
Fyssher, Thomas, chaplain, 103, 179

Gaddesby (Leic.), Bequest to the church, 223
Galby (Leic.), 5
'Garnars,' 213
Garston (Yorks), 86
Gartree Deanery, 14
  ,, Dean of, 14, 123
  ,, Wapentake or Hundred, 5, 18, 19, 44, 45
Gascoigne, Sir William, Chief Justice, 62
Gasken, or Gaskyne, William, 'prest,' 'parysh prest off Mych Bowdon,' 210, 216, 224
Gategang, Master Henry, Rector of Welton beyond Humber, 56, 59
'Gaudez,' 57
Gaugi, William, 159

Gaukewell (Gowkeswell), Bequest to, 54
'Gentilman,' 103, 170, 200
Geny or Geuyn. See 'Janen'
Geoffrey, Vicar of the north portion of Graffham (?), 39
Geoffrey, son of Bernard, 10
'George, Le olde,' 156, 207
Gerard, Thomas, 44
Gerveis, Felicia, widow of John, 160
'Geyr,' 'geyres,' cart, 222
  ,, ,, horse, 211
  ,, ,, weaving, 225
Ghent, 35
Gilbert, Gylbert, Gylbard, Thomas, 97, 177, 180, 185
Gilbert, Gylbert, Gylbard, Thomas, jun., 189
Gladman, Hugh, 163
  ,, Johannes, 44
Glascott, 'Sir Rafe,' of Stoke, 233
Glen or Gleyne, John, 189, 193
Gloucester, Duke of (Humfrey), 81
Godchildren, Bequests to, 121, 223, 227
'Goddetis,' 55, 56
Godesalve, Willelmus de, 44, 46, 162
Godwin, 6
Golde, Margaret, 220
Goldesborough, Anthony of, Canon of Lincoln, 38
Goldsmith (Orfevure), Peter the, 160
Goodman, William, 196
Goodrych, Alice, 227
  ,, Thomas, Will of, 227, 230
Gores. See 'Field-names'
'Gostely father,' 210, 213, 217, 227, 228
Gote, Thomas, 176
Graffham (?), 39
Grange (Grainge, Graunge or Grawnge), William, churchwarden of Great Bowden, 97, 101, 178, 190, 196
'Gransir,' 211
Grantchester, 129
Gray, Alys, 212
  ,, John, 211, 212, 229
  ,, Marget, 212
  ,, Thomas, 212
  ,, William, 212
Graystock, John, Lord, 85
Grene (or Green), Alexander le, chaplain, 121
Grene (or Green), Alice, 227
  ,, ,, Annes, 228
  ,, ,, John, 174
  ,, ,, Jone, 228
  ,, ,, Nicholas, 236, 241
  ,, ,, Robert, 220, 228
  ,, ,, Thomas, 172
  ,, ,, William, 228

Greenwich, Walter of, 123
Grey, Thomas, 202, 203, 212
    ,,   Sir Thomas, 67-69, 143
Griffyn (Gryffyn) family, 7
    ,,   ,,   John, 113
    ,,   ,,   Nicholas, 129, 130, 243
    ,,   ,,   Richard, 132
    ,,   ,,   Thomas, 131
Griggs, John, 186
'Gris,' 58
Groby (Leic.), 87
Grocer (citizen of London), 103, 185
'Growtlome,' 233
Gryme, Robert, 220
Guienne, 67, 140
Guilds :
    Holy Cross, Harborough, 48, 157, 164
    Corpus Christi (York), 55
Gumley (Leic.), 110, 130
Gunwardeby, John of, 35, 36, 82, 86, 87
'Gyrdyll,' 218
Gyssing, Thomas, 178

Haddon, East (Northants), 146
    ,,   John, 193
'Hadys, lez.' See 'Field-names and descriptions'
Hakett, 'Annes,' 219
Hallaton (Halughton) (Leic.), 45, 65, 150
Halle, Joan de, 74
    ,,   John, 68
Haloughton (Staff.), 129
Halton, Peter of, Rector of Claypole, 56
Hamelyn, Lawrence, 68
Hand-napkin (manutergium), 74
Handrewe, Thomas, 159
Hankinson, John, 225
Harborough, Market [Haverbergh, 161; Haverberghe, 201; Haverborgh, 199; Haverburgh, 163; Haverbargh, 94; Haverbarugh, 181; Haverboroughe, 220; Haverbarough, 184; Haverborough, 181; Haverborugh, 207; Haverborow, 229; Haverborowe, 211; Haverbrowge, 199; Harberghe, 132; Herbergh, 53; Hareberghe, 33; Harburgh 79; Herburgh, 101; Harverburgh, 206; Herdeborow, 212; Harberowe, 173; Harborowe, 189; Hareburgh, 65], chapelry of Great Bowden, 2; extent and boundaries, *ib.*; no separate common fields, 3; supposed Roman remains at, 4; erroneous supposition as to manor of, 6; not named in Domesday, 8 ; Manor of Bowden-Harborough, 8, 9, 11-13, 18, 19, 27, 28, 30, 31, 35, 36, 48, 49, 66, 70-73, 81-89, 94, 103, 105, 109; mill in the Pipe Roll, *temp.* Ric. I., 9 ; market on Monday, A.D. 1219, 10; altered to Tuesday, 1221, 10 ; tolls at, 12, 17, 18 ; first mention of church at, 14, 15 ; probable dates of church, 15, 25, 145 ; dedication, 15 ; bequests to, 53, 173, 211, 212, 216, 217, 219, 228, 229 ; bequests for the bells, 220, 226 ; clergy, A.D. 1292, 25 ; inhabitants (Lay Subsidy Roll, 1 Ed. III.), 44-46; William of Swinderby reads recantation at, 65 ; fair, 93; churchwardens, 109-111; trades, 151 ; ' town and chapel,' bequest to, 225 ; townsmen (Villici), 3, 226 ; 'le Belle,' 206, 211 ; 'the Swanne,' 220 ; 'Dag Lane,' 102, 156, 177 ; 'le fleysschamelis,' 66, 80, 165, 168 ; 'le olde George,' 47, 156, 207 ; 'the Hind,' 156 ; 'the Peale,' 156 ; 'the Grene,' 211 ; 'le High Strete,' 206 ; 'Harborough Moor,' 93, 151, 171 ; 'Four Stalls,' 47, 66 ; Market Cross, 94, 174 ; 'Horsefair Close,' 107 ; 'the Horsefair,' 199 ; 'George Close,' 156, 'the bridge of Haverbergh' (Chain Bridge), 107, 192 ; Lubenham Lane (Coventry Road), 102, 156, 187, 188, 206, 207, 208, 211 ; 'Lobenham brok,' 152, 161 ; 'le Mylne house,' 193 ; 'the Great Bridge,' 92, 173 ; 'Sheep Market,' 102
Harborough (Warw.), 9
Harborowe, William, 194
Harcorte, John, of Dingley, 190
'Harden,' 212, 222, 228, 231, 232
Hardy, John, 202
Hardyng, John, 197, 203, 204, 206, 207, 217, 226
Hardyng, Nicholas, 206
Harington, John, Canon of Lincoln, 118
Harlande, John, churchwarden of Harborough, 109
Harper, Agnes, 212 (will), 218, 221
    ,,   Alice, 213, 218
    ,,   Elizabeth, 201
    ,,   John, 201, 224, 227, 230
    ,,   Ricardus, 44, 45
    ,,   Richard, 162, 176, 178, 186, 187, 190-192, 198, 200 (will), 202, 209, 213, 220, 230

Index.

Harper, 'blynd Richard,' 218
" Robert, 191, 192, 202, 212, 221
Harper, Thomas, 97, 171, 186, 191, 192, 194-198, 201, 217, 221, 229
Harper, William, 97, 167, 172, 176, 179, 185, 191, 194, 198, 213, 218, 220, 221
Harper, William, Will of, 218
Harpham, John, 57
Haryndon, John, Lord de, 69.
Haselwode, Edmund, 206
Hastynges, Sir Richard, 86, 87
Hastyngs, Richard, 113
Hasylrygg (Hasylrigg, Haselrygge), Edmund, 206
" " "
Robert, 'merchant,' 204, 206, 207
Hathern, —, sister of G. le Scrope, 56
Hauberk, John, Doctor of Canon Law, Official of the Diocese of Lincoln, 235, 236, 241
Hawkesworth, Thos., 181
Hawnes, Agnes, 218
Hay, William, of Maydewell, 177
Haydor (Linc.), Bequest to the church, 54
Haydor (Linc.), Inscription in the church, 56 [60
Haydour cum Walton, Prebend, 43,
Haynton (Henton, Somerset), Carthusian priory, Bequest to, 54
'Head' (caput), in the Common Fields, 162
Headland (forera). See 'Field-names'
Hebden, Brother William of, 54
'Hekkett,' 231
Helagh (Yorks), 86
Helmet, 56
Heltwelle (Holwell, Leic.), 103
Hely, William, 168
'Hengells, pott,' 233
Hengham Castle, 134
Henry, chaplain, Vicar of Little Bowden, 114-116
Henry V., 82, 83, 87, 88; extract from inventory of the effects of, 70
Herbage, 87, 137, 172, 183, 184, 204
Herberd, Agnes, 44
Heresy, Heretics, 65
Hermitage, The, 148, 149
Hertford, Dean of, 28
Heton, John, 174
Heynenges (Hevenynge) (Linc.), Cistercian nunnery, Bequest to, 54
Heyr, William, 'pryntysse,' 208
'Heyways,' Bequest for mending, 227
Hill, J., Rector of Gumley, 130

Hillesley, Joan, 174
" Robert, 173
Hilling, Richard. See 'Illing'
Hillingdon, 129
Hilton, Sir Robert, Sheriff of Yorkshire, 85
Hirne (or Hyrne, 'en le Hirne;' 'in le Hyrne')
" " " John, 169, 172
" " " Richard, 169, 172
" " " Thomas, 168, 178, 183, 186, 197
Hirne or Hyrn Lane. See 'Bowden Magna'
Hobbys, Thomas, clerk, 206
Hogs, Richard, 210
Holande, Thomas, of Snaith, Yorkshire, 184
Holbech (Linc.), 133
Holcott, Martyn, 209, 221
Holme, Isabella, 169
'Holme,' 107, 204
Holt (Leic.), 93, 180
Holt, Sir John, of Brampton, 74
Holy Bread and Holy Water, 240, 242
Holy Trinity, Figure of the, 51
'Hony brake,' 232
Hook (Yorks), 31
Hooke, Robert, 175, 176
Hore, Walter, 68
Horkesley, Great and Little (Essex), 31
Hornbe, John, of Lubenham, 233
'Horse-faire at Haverbrowge,' 199
'Horse-mill,' 107, 193, 216
Horsham, Thomas, 196
'Hors lokks,' 232
Hospitallers, Knights, 113, 149
'Hosyer,' 170, 200
'House-bondman' ('husbondman'), 103, 181, 195
Houses, 155
Howdenby, Thomas, 'literate,' 101
Hudson (or Hudesone), Margaret, 218
" " Thomas, 212, 225, 226
Hugate, William, Canon of Lincoln, 60
Hugh the justiciar, 12
Hull, Carthusian house at, Bequest to, 54
Human, Thomas, 119
Hunfrid, 5, 6,
Hunnay, Geoffrey, 159
Huntingdon, John, Earl of, 69
" Simon, Earl of, 7, 114

Huntingdon, Honour of, 7, 113, 114
Huntingfield, Lord, 55
Hunton (Yorks), 86
Hunyng (?), Th., 'tayllour,' 200
Huse (Hosy, or Husy), William of, Rector of Carlton in Kesteven, Rector of Great Bowden, 50, 77-79
Hyll, Anne, 216
  ,, Elizabeth, 216
  ,, John, 221
  ,, Margaret, 216
  ,, Peter (or 'Peers'), Will of, 221
  ,, Thomas, 216
  ,, William, son of William, 'Bacar,' 216

Illing, Richard, priest, 10, 25, 159
  ,, Robert, 159
Ilston (Leic.), 5
Ingham, John, Fellow of the Burghersh Chantry, 59
Ingmanthorp (Yorks), 35
Ingold, Adam, 44
  ,, John, 168, 171, 172, 193
  ,, Thomas, 171
'Intemerate' Virgin, 211, 216
Irford (Linc.) (Premonstratensian nunnery), Bequest to, 54, 59
Irnham, Lambert of, Chaplain, 40, 52, 53
Iron, 57
Ironmonger ('yrynmownger'), 205
Isabella, Queen, 27, 28, 30, 36
Ischam (or Isham), Robert, 172
  ,,   ,, William, 181, 193
Iue, Johannes, 44
Ivo, Brother of Bernard, 10
  ,, son of Roger, 10

Jakes, Nicholas, 191-195, 197, 199, 202
Janen (Janyen, Janyn, Jeny or Geny, Jenen, Jenyn, Jennin), John, Bailiff of Sibbertoft, 106, 107, 112, 198-203; 'Jhon Jennins dede,' 202
  ,,   ,,   ,, Richard, 199, 201
  ,,   ,,   ,, Robert, 'yoman,' 'bailiff of Harborough and Sibbertoft,' 'bailiff of Magna Bowden and Harborough,' 97, 102, 182-186, 188-198, 205
Jankinson, John, 226
Jarvis, Anne, 218
Jerkyn, 229
John, 'parysh prest off S. Maryes,' 220

John, sacrist of Lincoln Cathedral, 59
John, son of a Harborough chaplain, 17
John the clerk, 163
  ,, the kitchen-boy, 58
  ,, the parson, 169
Johnson, Robert, 210
  ,, William, 103, 104, 205, 214, 215
Jopper, Margeria, 227
Jordan the Knight, 17
Joy (Joie or Joce), Agnes, 180-182, 184
  ,,   ,, Lambert, 'gentilman,' 180-189, 191-193, 198, 202, 205
Joy (Joie or Joce), Nicholas, 174-176, 178, 180
Judde, William, 196
Judith, Countess, 5-7, 112, 114

Karlyll, Richard, 132
Kay, Lawrence, 174
Keilesey, Master John of, 56
Kelmarsh, Robert of, 17
  ,, Roger of, 119
  ,, (Keylmarsh) (Northants), 92, 174, 177
Kelsey, North, Prebend, 60
Kelyng, John, Rector of Great Bowden, founder of the chantry, 94-103, 184
Kenett, Thomas, 193
Kenilworth Castle, 9
Kent (Cancia), Walter of, Rector of Great Bowden, 20
'Kertyll,' 213, 218, 232
Kesten, Thomas, chaplain, 109, 111, 227
Kettering (Northants), 234
Kewell, Thomas, serjeant-at-law, 108
Kibworth (Leic.), 2, 150, 157
Kilsby, William of, 119
Kilvyngton (Yorks) ('S. Wilfrid'), Bequests to the church, 67, 74
Kirby, Roger, 227
Kirkby Wiske (Yorks), 58
Kirkby, John, 212
Kirkeby (Kirby Belers, Leic.), Augustinian priory, Bequest to, 56
Kirklyngton (Yorks), 38
Knight, Richard, 97, 178
Knytt, Robert, 219
Koe. See 'Coo'
Kongulton, Thomas, of Coventry, 200
'Kylnzerde, le.' See 'Bowden Magna'
'Kymnells,' 233

Kynge (or Kyng), John, 191
",, ",, Oliva, 44
",, ",, Robert, 'weyver,' 206
Kynge (or Kyng), Thomas, 44, 193
Kynnesman, Simon, Esq., 193
Kynwolmersh, William, clerk, 83

Lafford (Sleaford), 38
Lambeth, 90
Lancaster, Henry, Earl of, 137
",, Thomas of, son of Henry IV., 50
Lane, William, Under-Sheriff of Northants, 198
Langton Church ('Kyrke'), Bequest to the church, 223
Langton, East, 181
",, Thorpe, 173; Bequest to the church, 223
Langton (or Langeton), George, 207
",, ",, Johanna, 101
",, ",, John, 181
",, ",, Richard, Esq., 185
",, ",, Thomas, 181
Lapworth (Warw.), 129, 130
Latimer, Alianore de, 113
",, Elizabeth le, 113
",, William de, 7, 113
'Laton,' 231
Laughton (Leic.), 234
Laughton, John, 174
Launde, Prior of, 26, 40, 41, 114, 243
",, Abbey (Leic.), 114-117, 123, 124, 243
Laver (aquarium), Bequest of, 55
Lawrence, Alice, 121
",, Simon, of Preston Capes, Rector of Oadby, Rector of Little Bowden, 118, 119, 132; his death and will, 121, 122
Leavenheath (Suff.), 31
'Leche, Magister Ricardus le,' 47, 163
Leicester, 18, 137; abbey (S. Mary de pratis), 40, 133, 148, 207, 213; Abbot of, 40, 41, 74-76; St. Margaret's, 65; S. Martin's, 65, 239, 241, 242; St. Mary's, 65; St. Mary's-by-the-Castle, 213; Austin Friars, bequest to the 'box of pardon,' 222; 'three howses of Freers,' 223; 'iij awturs of Freres,' 227; Archdeacon of, 20, 26, 36, 41, 46, 75, 76, 80, 91, 102, 106, 150; Bailiff of, 137
Leicestershire, Sheriff of, 48, 86
Lexington, W., Obit of, 61

Leycester, Henry de, 166, 172, 175-179, 202, 203
Leycester, John, 172
",, Katharine, 181
",, Richard of, steward of the manor, 80, 164-169, 172
Leyot (or Layed), John, Dean of St. John's, Chester, 125, 127, 128
'Librum qui incipit cum rubro,' 'cum cubas dicas,' 56
Lilford (Lilleford), John, LL.D., Rector of Great Bowden, 91, 94
Lillyng, Thomas, 58
Lincoln, 44, 50, 51, 54, 59, 60, 90, 101, 121, 122; Boungarth, 54; mendicant friars, bequest to 54; St. Margaret-below-the Close, bequest to, 54, 55, 61; anchorite at Trinity Church, bequest to, 58; Burghersh Chantry, 59; poor, bequest to, 51; Bishops of, 30, 32, 38, 48, 65, 76, 81, 105, 108-111, 114-135, 149, 150; Archdeacon of, 60
Lincoln Cathedral: Canons in residence, 51; 'facientes magnam residenciam,' 60; canon's income for one year, 61; custodians of altars, 51; chaplains wearing the habit, 51; vicars, 51, 52; ditto of the second grade, 52; vicar-choral, 59; poor clerks, 51, 57; choristers, 38, 39, 51, 57; vergers, 51; ringers and their attendants, 51; dean, 52; sub-dean, 38, 60; vice-chancellor, 52; succentor, 52; fellow of the Burghersh Chantry, 59; sacrist, 59; 'Clericus Communæ,' the, extracts from the accounts of, 60, 61; high altar, 51; belfrey, 50; bequests to, 51, 121, 209, 210-213, 216-222, 225-228, 230
Lincolnshire, Defence of the coast, 137
'Lintheum telarium,' anglice, a linen-horne, 225
'Literatus.' See 'Howdenby, Thomas'
Llandaff, 52
Lodore, Hugh, 166
Lok, John, 68
Lokyn, Richard, 218
'Lome,' 232, 233
'Lond' ('londs'), 211, 221
London, 169, 173, 185, 188, 189; Charterhouse, bequest to, 54; Old Temple, 37, 79, 90
Longchamp, Daniel de, Rector of Great Bowden, 13, 14, 20

17

Longe, Alice, 185
,, Henry, 'husbondman,' 181, 185
,, Robert, 185, 186, 190, 207
Loughborough (Loucheborough), 65, 137
Louth Park, 40, 64, 125
Lowte, John, 188
,, William, 188
Lubenham (Leic.), 2, 170, 175, 176, 181, 185, 189, 208; bequests to the church, 212, 223, 228, 233
Ludlow, William of, Vicar of Riccall, 63
Luff, Hugo, 44, 46, 161
Luton, 134
Lutterell, or Le Outrell, Beatrice de, sister of Geoffrey le Scrope, 56
Lutterworth, 111, 125, 137; Bailiff of, 137
Luvetoft (Lovetoft), Nicholas of, Rector of Great Bowden, 19-21
Lydda, Augustine, Bishop of, 134
Lyddington (Rutl.), 39, 40, 63, 77, 92, 106, 117, 118, 123, 133, 134, 150, 242
,, Prebend, 60
Lyghton, John, 'skryvener,' 213, 216
Lyons, Council of, 21

Maidstone, Walter of, bishop's crucifer, 117
Maidwell (Northants), 177
Mallory, John, Sheriff of Leicestershire, 87
,, Robert, esquire, 177, 181, 184, 187-189
Malory, George, Rector of Little Bowden, 131
Maniple (fanon), 55
Mann (or Manne), Henry, 198-203
,, ,, John, 218
,, ,, Richard, 228, 229
'Mannes brest, clerk syngyng in his,' 223
Mannyng, Juliana, wife of Roger, 163
,, Roger, son of Reyner, 163
,, William, 98, 100
,, William, son of Reyner, 163
Manor, The, 135-137
Manor of Bowden-Harborough, Grants of, 8, 9, 12, 13, 18, 27, 28, 30, 31, 70-73, 103, 104; value of, 12, 18, 32, 55; reserved rent from, 35; settlement of in the Scrope family, 35, 36; succession to, 49, 66, 90, 94, 105, 109; forfeiture of, 69-71; restoration of, 81-89
Manor of Bowden Parva, 1-4, 112-114
Manors, The, in Domesday, 4-8

March, Edmund, Earl of, 66-69
Marchant, Joanna, 186
,, Walter, 186
Margaret of France, Queen, 18, 27, 28, 30
Margary, Richard, 236, 241
Mariothe, Henry, clerk, of Welham, 173
Mariott, Thomas, Will of, 217
Market, The, at Harborough, 10, 11
Marlow, Nuns' (Merlawe Monialium), 20
Marsh, John, 193, 199
,, Margaret, 193, 199
Marshal, John, Earl, 69
Marshall (Marschal, Merschall), Annys, 216
,, ,, ,, John, 134, 135
,, ,, ,, Richard, 198, 217, 218, 226, 230
,, ,, ,, Thomas, 164, 202, 203
,, ,, ,, William, 185, 201-204, 218, 226, 234
Marston (Marson or Merston), Elsabell, 213
,, ,, ,, John, 132, 133
,, ,, ,, Richard, churchwarden of Great Bowden, 97, 101, 194
,, ,, ,, Robert, 210, 221
Marston Trussell (Northants), 157, 169, 175
Marten or Martyn, 'Syr Michall,' 212, 217, 219
'Martyn off Rowell,' 219
Masham (Yorks), 35, 85, 86
Mashvat (massefactum), 74, 233
Mason, William, vicar-general, 110
Mass of the Blessed Virgin Mary 'in honorem Corporis Christi,' 51
Mathew, Walter, 58
Mathon, Thomas, 92
Matilda, daughter of Waltheof and Judith, 7
Matoke, Richard, 227
,, Robert, 226, 227
Mauduit, Robert de, 8
,, William de, 8
Maurice of the kitchen, 58
Mautravers, John, Lord de, 69
Mawdit, Willelmus, 44
Mayne, John, 193
Mayner, John, 168
Mayner, Thomas, 119

Index.   259

Mayners, Adam, 44
  ,,   Isabell, 44
  ,,   Rogerus, 44, 165, 166, 168
Mayo, John, Bishop of, 135
'Mazer' (murreus), 56
Medbourne (Leic.), 4, 5, 45, 93
Melbourne, John of, Rector of Great Bowden, 35-37, 39
Melton Mowbray, 45, 65, 137; Bailiff of, 137
Mendicant friars, 54
Mercer, 170, 200, 203, 204
Mereton, 11
'Merray cott, A,' 219
Merton College, Oxford, Warden and Scholars of, 129
Metley, 'Freer Ricardus,' 227
Meyner (or Meyners), Hugo de, 159
  ,,   ,,   Roger de, priest, 24, 25, 159
Michell, Robert, of Harborough, 124, 127, 167, 177
Milner, Hugh le (Hugh Milner), 47, 163, 167
Misterton (Leic.), 207
Monaldus (? Monardus), 57
Monasteries near Harborough, 148, 149
Mondeyn (or Mundeyn), William, 125, 126, 128
Morden (or Moden), Richard, 'curat,' 209, 221, 230
More, John, 193
Moris, G. de, 115
Mortain, Count of, 5-7, 112
Mortimer, Roger, 30, 31
Mortuary, 173, 209-211, 213, 216-220, 227
Mounte, Joan de la, 74
Mustarder, Richard le, 17
'Mylne-chane,' The, 217
'Mylne-house, le,' 107, 193
Myryell, Thomas, of Bitteswell, 190

Nayland (Suff.), 31, 32; value of the manor of, with its members, 31, 32
'Nayles,' Agreement as to, 205
Neele (or Neell), Alice, 174
  ,,   ,,   John, of Kelmarsh, 177
  ,,   ,,   Margaret, 173
  ,,   ,,   Richard, 177, 178
  ,,   ,,   Thomas, 197
  ,,   ,,   William, mercer, 91, 92, 103, 157, 169-171, 172 & 173 (will), 174, 176, 178, 179, 181, 186
Neuton, Robert de, 161

Nevill, William, of Rolleston and Holt, 93
Nevyll, Sir Richard, 85
Newcastle-on-Tyne, 50, 69
Newsham, John, 197, 203, 204
'Neyt,' 211
'Neytherd,' 218
Nicholas IV. (Pope), 21-24
'Ninth,' Assessment for a, 119, 120
Non-residence, Licences of, 37, 64, 78
Norewyche, John, 196
North Field, the, (campus borialis). See 'Fields'
Northampton, 17, 18, 48, 49, 137; All Saints', 132-134, 206-208; Black Friars in the Horse Market, 226; Abbot of St. James's Without, 119, 120, 151; Archdeacon of, 114-119, 125-128, 130, 131
Northampton, County of, 137
Northamptonshire, Sheriff of, 10
Northumberland, Earl of, 62
  ,,   Henry Percy, Earl of, 85
Norton, 5
Norwich, 36
Nottingham, 31, 32
  ,,   County of, 137
Novel disseisin, 10
'Nowe' (or 'newe'), A, 212, 213
Nowres, Henry de, 10
  ,,   Juliana de, 10
Nubon (or Neubon), Alys, 210
  ,,   ,,   John, Will of, 210
  ,,   ,,   Robert, 210

Oadby (Leic.), 118
Oakham, 148
Obit, 52, 214, 215, 224
Ocham, Robert of, 160
  ,,   'Henry, of Cotyngham,' 234
Ocle, William of, 74
Olever, 'Sir Thomas, preyst,' 227
Ordinations, Extracts from lists of, 132-134
'Orfevure le,' 27, 160
Orget, Roger, 11
Orlton, Adam de, Bishop of Winchester, 32
Orphreys, 52, 53
Osburn, Richard, 207
'Ostiensem in lectura,' 55
Ostiensis (Segusio, Cardinal de), 56
Ousefleet (Yorks), 31
Overston, Geoffrey of, 17
Owston (Osolveston) Abbey, 148; Abbot of, 26, 40, 41

17—2

Ox (or beast) pasture ('unius grossi animalis'), 171, 186, 187, 197
Oxendon Magna (Northants) ('Mycul Oxton'), 132, 233, 235
  ,,   Parva, 125, 181, 235-242
Oxendon, Ricardus de, 44
Oxendon Parva, William de, 7, 113
Oxenford (?). See 'Exenford'
Oxford, 106, 124; St. Mary's, 38, bequest to, 53; Balliol Hall, bequest to, 53; Christ Church, 112; St. Mary Magdalene's, 127; Merton College, 129
Oxford, Richard of, 115
  ,,   Richard, Earl of, 69
Oxton, Richard, 193

Pachet, Thomas, 162
  ,,   Willelmus, 44-46, 162
Page, John, 121, 170-174
  ,,   Richard, of 'Carrylton,' 220
Palmer, John, of Carleton, 193
  ,,   Katharine, of Holt, 93
  ,,   Thomas, esquire, of Holt, 93, 169, 170, 173, 177, 178, 180
  ,,   William, esquire, 185
Pardon, box of, Bequest to, 222
  ,,   of the Holy Ghost, Bequest to, 222
Parkyn, 'Sir Richard,' chaplain, 230
Parliament, payment of members, exemption from contributing to, 48, 49
Parliaments, 44, 65, 120
'Parmenter, Le,' 27, 160
Parmynter, Thomas, clerk, 206
Parochial divisions of the Local Board district, 1, 2
Parson (or Person), John, 174, 175, 180
Parson (or Person), Thomas, 134
Paruræ (apparels, 'paroures'), 55
Parvyn, John, of Northampton, 'marchaunt,' 207
Parych (or Pech), Richard, Will of, 213, 214, 216
'Parych clerke being subdeken,' 215
'Parysh prest off Mych Bowdon,' 224
  ,,   ,,   off St. Maryes,' 220
Pawlmer, Thomas, 219
Payments to lords of the fee, 180
Peche, John, 186-188, 215
  ,,   Richard, 192
'Peloberys,' 231
Pentyng, Edmund, 180, 181
  ,,   Henry, citizen and fishmonger, 103, 178, 185, 188, 189
Penyton, John, 68
Pere (or Peer or Piere), Peter, 161

Pere (or Peer or Piere), Thomas, 44, 46, 162
  ,,   ,,   ,,   William, 174, 179
'Peridod,' 55
Person. See 'Parson'
'Personatum,' 115
Perte, Johanna, 55
Peryns, John, Will of, 212
  ,,   Yssabell, 212
Peterborough, 17, 132
  ,,   Abbot of, 17
Petlyng, Roger, chaplain, 80, 103, 168, 172, 180
Petnale, Richard, 97, 179, 190
Pexall, Richard, Abbot of St. Mary's Abbey, Leicester, 207
Philippa, Queen, 31, 32
Pickwell, Theobald of, Dean of Gartree, 14
Piffeford, John, 188
'Pigeon-house,' 170
Pigiun, Clement, 115
'Pilliun,' 233
Pipewell, 17, 132-134, 148
Pipewell, Thomas of, 17
Piskre (Lithuania), 49
Pittance (pictancia), Bequest for a, 54
'Placebo,' 214, 223
'Plasmator,' 211, 216
Plate, Bequest of, to Harborough Church, 218
Pledge, Things 'laid to,' 220
Plumpton, Lady Isabella, 55
  ,,   Sir Robert of, 55
Pole, Alys, 222
  ,,   Anne, 222
  ,,   Rauffe, 222, 224
  ,,   Robert, 222
  ,,   William, 222
'Polydore, Master' (Polydore Vergil), Rector of Church Langton, 110
Ponteis, Peter, 160
Pontieu, 139
Poor, the, Bequests to, 51, 54; doles to, at funerals, 215
Pope, Agnes, of Northampton, 206
  ,,   John, of Little Bowden, 206, 234
Pope, Thomas, 187-189
  ,,   William, 206, 220
Popham, Sir John, Constable of Southampton, 68
Porter, Edmund, of Kettering, 234
  ,,   Sir William, 70-73, 78, 79, 81, 88, 90
Portsmouth, 137
'Post-Communio,' 223

Pownall, Venerable A., Archdeacon of Leicester, 46
'Prank,' Horse called, 74
Prentys, Thomas, 133, 165
Prestbury, Ralph, Doctor of Canon Law, Rector of Little Bowden, 127, 128
Preston, John, 85
,, Robert, 57
,, Roger of, 121
Preston Capes, 118
'Principall,' 212, 220-222, 229 [133
'Prissinensis, Willelmus, Episcopus,'
Property, Dispersion of, in the open fields, 178
'Provest off paradyse' (St. Michael), 216 [123
Provision under papal letters, 122,
Provisors, Statutes of, 122, 123
Pruston, John, 168
Pruston, Thomas, 168
'Pryntyse,' 208 [207
Pulteney, Thomas, Esq., of Misterton,
Purser, Elizabeth, 218
,, John, 218
'Puter,' 228, 231, 232
Pycard, Honorius, 160
Pydele, John de, 161, 162
Pyfford, Geoffrey, 110, 111
,, John, 177, 184, 188

Quadring (Linc.), 52
Quarentena. See 'Field-names and descriptions'
'Quermen,' Bequests to, 215, 223
'Quia emptores,' Statute of, 30
Quit-rents: a farthing, 159; a rose, 161, 164; one penny, 165; a flower, 177; a peppercorn, 187; twelve peppercorns, 152; one red rose, 182
'Qwyke best,' 217

Rag, Thomas, 164-166
Ranesby, Thomas de, 44
Ranold, Robert, of Lubenham, 212
'Ratclyffe, Mayster,' 228
'Rathlurensis, Thomas, Episcopus,' 133, 134
Reedness (Yorks), 31
'Reeffes,' Church, 214, 215
Reliefs, 160, 163
Repyngton, Thomas, 202
,, William, 202, 203
'Requiem, Mass of, 214, 223
Retford, Richard of, D.D., 123
Reyner (Rayner, Reigner), Emma, 164
,, ,, ,, Letia, 164
,, ,, ,, Olive, 161

Reyner (Rayner, Reigner), Thomas, 44, 45, 160, 161, 163, 164
Reyner (Rayner, Reigner), Thomas, son of Thomas, 161
Reynold, Richard, 190
,, Thomas, 159
Riccall (Yorks), 29
Richard II., 67, 68, 140-142
Richard the clerk, 163
Richard, Thomas, 205, 221
Richards, Thomas, 206, 221
Richardson, Myles, 206
,, Thomas, 207, 218
Richmond (Yorks), 36; Archdeacon of, 60
Ripon, 138
Robert, son of Hugh, donor of Little Bowden benefice to Launde Abbey, 114
Robert the clerk, 162
Robert the coachman, 58
,, ,, John, son of, 58
Robert the mercer, 119
Robert, Agnes, 182
,, Thomas, 'bucher,' 180, 182
Robyn, Rogerus, 44
Rockingham, 137, 157
Roger the deacon, 159
'Rogerus filius Reginaldi,' 44
Rolleston (Leic.), 93, 205
Roman roads near Harborough, 4
Rome (S. Maria Major), 23
Roodloft (Harborough), Bequest for painting the, 212
Roos, Anthony, gentleman, 206
,, Myles, gentleman, 'baylly of Myche Bowdon and Haverbergh,' 109, 110, 112, 197, 203, 204, 230
Roper, Robert, 194
Ropewalk (funarium), The common, 180, 184
Rotherham, 205
Rothley (Leic.), 5, 9
Rothwell (Rowell) (Northants), 10, 11, 119, 219
Rouceby, John of, Canon of Lincoln, 60
Rouse, Rowland, 156
Rowell, John of, Rector of Little Bowden, 114
Rowth (?), William de, 36
Rudde, John, 197
Rudyng, Master John, 95
Russel (Russell), John, 179
,, ,, Margrett, 212, 218
,, ,, Richard, 212, 218
,, ,, Robert, 212, 221
Russet, 58, 213, 232

Rutland, 120, 137, 195, 200
Rybell, Richard, 174
Rychevyll, Richard, Rector of Little Bowden, 126-128
'Ryffes off onyons,' 233
Rykeman, Peter, Rector of Little Bowden, 129, 130

Saddington (Leic.), 12
Sadyler, John, son of John, 133
St. Albans, Robert of, Rector of Essendon, Rector of Great Bowden, 20, 21, 24, 28, 29, 36, 112
St. Botolph's, Prebend, 60
St. Martin, Roger of, 17
St. Mary in Arden. See 'Arden'
St. Omer, William of, justiciar, 17
Salisbury, Thomas, Earl of, 69
    ,,   Earl of, 141
Salt meat, 57
Salton, John, chaplain of the chantry, Marston Trussell, 169
Sander (Sanders, Saunders), John, 174, 177, 191, 192
    ,,   ,,   ,,   William, 203
Sandon, Ralph, Rector of Little Bowden, 128, 129
Sandwich, 137
Sawtry (Hunts), 181
Scoles, Rotherham, 205
Scott (Skotte), John, of Takeley, 200
    ,,   ,,   Thomas, 183, 186-189
Scraptoft (Leic.), 109
Scrivener, 216
Scrope, Geoffrey le, chief justice, 31-35, 43, 60, 61, 87, 92, 138-140
Scrope, Henry le, first Lord Scrope of Masham, 35, 39, 48, 49, 55, 61, 63, 64, 87, 137, 140
Scrope, Master Geoffrey le, Rector of Great Bowden, Canon of Lincoln, etc., 35, 38, 39, 40-43, 47; his will, 50-60, 161, 162
Scrope, Ivetta le, wife of Geoffrey le, 35
Scrope, Richard le, knight, 36
    ,,   William le, knight, 36
    ,,   Richard le, Lord, of Bolton, 36
Scrope, John le, fourth lord, of Masham and Upsall, 36, 74, 81-91, 94, 144
Scrope, Geoffrey le, eldest son of Henry, first Lord, 49
Scrope, Stephen le, second Lord, of Masham, 49, 50, 55, 61, 65, 77, 81, 87, 140-142

Scrope, Lady Johanna le, wife of Henry, first Lord, 55
Scrope, Lady Matilda (or Marjory) le, wife of Stephen, second Lord, 55, 78, 79
Scrope, Master Richard le, Rector of Great Bowden, Archbishop of York, 55, 56, 61-63, 65, 142, 143
Scrope, Henry le, third Lord, of Masham, 66-72, 81, 83, 87, 143, 144
Scrope, Elizabeth le, wife of John, fourth Lord, 81, 94
Scrope, Geoffrey le, brother of Henry, third Lord, 82, 87
Scrope, Stephen le, brother of Henry, third Lord, 82, 87
Scrope, Thomas le, fifth Lord, of Masham and Upsall, 94, 97, 98, 100, 101, 103
Scrope, Thomas le, sixth Lord, of Masham and Upsall, 94, 105, 106
Scrope, Henry le, seventh Lord, son of Thomas, sixth Lord, 105, 109
Scrope, Ralph le, eighth Lord, son of Thomas, sixth Lord, 105, 109
Scrope, Geoffrey le, ninth Lord, son of Thomas, sixth Lord, 105, 109
Scrope, Alice le, 105
Scrope, Elizabeth le, wife of Thomas, sixth Lord, 105, 106
Scrope, Henry le, Lord, of Bolton, 105
Scrope family, line of entail, 87, 88
Secreta, 223
Sedbergh (Yorks), gift of the advowson to Coverham Abbey, 140
Seisin by payment, 182
'Selers,' 57, 70, 232
Selion. See 'Field-names and descriptions'
Seman, John, 163
Serjeant-at-Law, 84, 195
Serjeanty, 198
Serle (or Serll), William, 188, 194, 205, 224
'Serpless,' 232
Servants and attendants, Bequests to, 58
Sewale, William, of Southwell, Rector of Little Bowden, 123
Sexaginta Solidorum, Prebend, 60
Sexton (or Sexten), Agnes, 229
    ,,   ,,   Cecely, 229
    ,,   ,,   Margaret, Will of, 228
'Sextum et Clementinum cum glosis,' 56
Shangton (Leic.), 5
Sharpe, Alys, 221

Index.   263

Sharpe, Elizabeth, 221
  „   Richard, 221 (will)
  „   Master William, clerk, 226
Shawe, Agnes, 223
Sheep, Price of, 220, 230
Sheets, 57
Shepper, John, 97
Sherman, Richard, 177, 185, 187
  „   William, Rector of Little Bowden, 130
Shirley, Ralph, knight, 108, 195
'Shod carte,' 211, 220
'Shone, payr off,' 229
'Shopa,' 184
'Shots,' 230
Shute, John, 172, 176
  „   Thomas, 170
Shyrewode (Schirwode, Sherewode), John, 171, 176, 177, 179, 194
Shyrewode (Schirwode, Sherewode), Thomas, 176, 194, 198-203
Sibbertoft (Northants), 102, 190, 198
Silton (Yorks), 86 [7
Simon of Senlis, Earl of Huntingdon.
Simons, John, 176
'Sir Christopher,' 234
'Sir Curat ther,' 218
'Sir Edmunde off Stoke,' 234
'Sir George, curude, paryche preist,' 227
'Sir Hugh,' 220
'Sir Thruston, my gostly fader,' 227
'Sir Wyllm, my gostely father,' 213
'Skelett,' 231
Skepper, Agnes, 178
  „   Joanna, 179
  „   John, 178, 179
Skynare, Thomas, chaplain, 47, 164, 166, 167
Slake, John, Rector of Little Bowden, 130, 131
Sleaford, 38, 64, 78, 133
Smeeton (Smeeton Westerby, Leic.), 5
Smetheton, Richard de, 161
'Smoke,' A, 222, 223, 232
Smyth, Agnes, Inventory, 230-234
  „   Henry, 92, 174-178, 181
  „   Hugh, 119
  „   John, 173, 174, 210, 218, 220, 229
  „   Richard, 173, 180, 191
  „   Richard, of Laughton, 233
  „   Robert, bailiff, 102, 178, 180, 181
  „   Thomas, 133, 173, 191, 195, 197, 203, 204, 210
  „   Thomas, churchwarden of Harborough, 109

Smyth, Thomas, chaplain, 173
  „   William, 171, 197, 229
Snaith (Yorks), 184
'Solar,' 155, 171
Soltania, John, Bishop of, 133
Sotherey (Sowther), William, 'chantre prest,' 101, 210, 221; his will, 222-224, 230
  „   „   Alys, 222
  „   „   John, 223, 224
  „   „   Richard, 223
  „   „   William, son of John, 222, 224
Southampton, 68-71, 87, 143
Southampton plot, 67-70, 143, 144
South Field, The (campus australis). See 'Fields'
Southwell, 52, 123
Sowtorp, Edda de, 159
  „   William de, 159
Spaldwick (Hunts), 25, 26
Sparewe, Robertus, 44
'Spenser off Welingborough,' 234
Spoons, Silver, 220
Spridlington, Alice of, 57
  „   Thomas of, 57
Spryggs, Richard, 228
Spycer, William, 167, 168
Spyer, Ralph, Rector of Little Bowden, 129
Stacy, Richard, 173
Stamford, 17, 18, 27, 116, 160; St. Paul's, 58; Austin Friars, 133; St. Mary's-at-the-Bridge, 134; White Friars, 223; 'oure Lady Frerys,' 227; St. John, 160; Nuns of St. Michael Without, 160
Stanesby, Thomas de, 163
Stanley, John, esquire, Lord of Sibbertoft, 198
Staunton, Margaret, widow, 108, 195
Stauren, William of, 117
Steer, John, 68
Stepney (Stevenhythe), 94, 130
Stevens, Agnes, 213
Steward (senescallus), 80, 169
Stilton (Stelton, Hunts), 181
'Stirlay' (Strelley), Magistra, 111
Stockton, Augustine of, 123
Stoke (Stoke Albany, Northants), 233, 234
Stoke Dry (Rutl.), 93, 108, 195
Stoke-by-Nayland (Suff.), 31
Stoke Hundred (Northants), 5
'Stole,' 55
Stonhard, John, of Takeley, 200
Stonton, John, 173, 174, 176, 181
  „   Ricardus de, 44

Stonton, Richard, 174, 176-178, 180, 191
Storer, John, 126
Stow Park, 26, 28, 65
Strange (or Straunge), Thomas, 210
,, ,, William, 176
Strangeways, James, 86, 87
Stratford-on-Avon, 157
Stratford, J., Archbishop of Canterbury, 32, 120
Streatley, Master John, Dean of Lincoln, 52
Stretton (Leic.), 5
'Strike,' A, 231, 233
Stryt, John, 173
Stukeley, John, of Marston Trussell, 175
Sturneton, 36
Styandeby, Roger of, 160
Subsidy, Lay, 1 E. III., Bowden and Harborough names, 44-46
Suffolk, Michael, Earl of, 69
Sulby Abbey (Northants), 133-135
Sumpter, William, of Somerby, Rector of Little Bowden, 122, 123
Sumtyng, Helenor, 220
Surgeon, William the, 17
Sutton, Adam de, 44, 46, 161
,, Thomas of, Canon of Lincoln, 60
Sutton Bassett (Northants), 152, 234; bequests to the church, 219, 223
Sutton Freerby (Yorks), 86
Swafelld, Thomas, 200
Swan (or Swanne), Richard, 179, 190
,, ,, Robert, 193, 194
'Swanne, The sygne of the,' 220
Sweyn, Alexander le, 160
'Sweyn le,' 27
Swinderby, William of, 65, 150
Swinford (Leic.), 149
Syddyll, Richard, Will of, 217
Symon, Annys, 228
'Syngyng chylderyn,' Bequest to, 223
Synyngthwait, Thomas de, clerk, 36
,, William de, Rector of Ainderby-with-the-Steeple, 36

'Tabellarum annelit',' 55
Table-cloth (mappa), 74
Tailor (parmenter), Peter the, 160
Takeley (Essex), 199, 200
Talbot, Gilbert, Lord de, 69
Tapestry, 57, 70
Taylor, John, 236, 241
Territorium. See 'Field-names and descriptions'
'Thacke and modd,' Tenant to repair in, 108, 204

Thannyng, William, 174
Thedyngworth, Rogerus de, 44
,, William, of 'Mycul Oxton,' 233
'Thelys,' 220
Thomas filius Hugonis, 44
,, Thomæ, 44
,, chamberlain to Geoffrey le Scrope, 57
'Thomas at Parson's,' 119
Thomas of the stable, 58
'Thomas, Bishop in the Catholic Church,' 134
Thoresby, John, Archbishop of York, 124
Thorpe, Ralph of, 17
'Thrittifal' (thirty-fall). See 'Field-names and descriptions'
Thurston, John, 168
,, Thomas, 170
'Tillage' (cultura), 159, 183, 197, 198
Tilton (Leic.), 93, 108
Tirwhit, Robert, 85
Titchmarsh (Northants), 128
Tithe-forgotten, Bequests to pay, 210, 211, 213, 222, 228
Toft, William, chaplain, 92
Tolls, 12, 17
Tombstone, 74
Torches at funerals, 51, 73
Torkesey (Linc.), 54
Tours, Money of, 18
Towton (Yorks), 93, 137
Trades, 151
Trentall of masses, 219, 223, 226, 227
,, ,, half a, 223
'Tricesimoquinto die,' 172
Triclowe, Thomas, of Thorpe Langton, 173
Trigot, Thomas, 103, 104
Triparteta.
Triparticata. } See 'Field-names and
Triparticum. } descriptions'
Tripartita.
Tru-sel (or Trussell), Thomas, knight, 180, 183
Trussel (or Trussell), William, 137, 194
Tunicles, 52
'Twentieth,' a, 44
Tybbis, John, 197, 203, 204, 217, 234
Tyberay, Thomas, Rector of Little Bowden, 124, 243
Typler, John, 101
Tythewell, John, 'gentilman,' of London, 185

Ufford, Robert de, steward of the household, 32

Ulsi, 6
Umfray, John, 188, 189
Upham, John, 68
Upsall (Yorks), 86, 91, 94, 97, 106

Valentyn, Richard, 192
Vaux, John, of Quadring, chaplain, 52, 57
Vaws, Nicholas, knight, High Sheriff of Northants, 198
Veel, John, 68
Venablis (Wenablys), Robert, 166, 167
Ventaille (eventale, ventaculum), 56
Vestments, 52, 53, 55, 219
'Villicorum anglice Townysmen,' 226
Vincent, William, 81, 82
Visitations (Bishops' and Archdeacons'), 24, 25, 101, 109-111
Vycars (A-vicars), Agnes, 202, 203
,, ,, John, 202, 203

Wainwright, Agnes, 219
,, Harry, 219
Wakefield, 137
Wakely (Herts), 28
Wakelyn (or Walkelyn), John, 133, 134, 192, 194
Wakelyn (or Walkelyn), William, 191, 192, 193-196
Walkere (Walker), John, 167
,, ,, ,, of Braybrooke, 234
,, ,, Rowland, 207, 217, 218
Walkere (Walker), William, 44, 168
Walmesford, Hugh of, Canon of Lincoln, 37, 45
Walsssh, Thomas, 180, 183, 187
Waltham Holy Cross, 37
Waltheof, Earl of Northampton, 7
War, Supply of men for, 137
Waravill, R. de, Canon of Lincoln, 115
Ward, Thomas, Escheator of Leicestershire, 96, 97
Warde, Henry, sister of, Nun of Irford, 59
,, Robert, 198, 224, 227
Wards, 160
Warmington (Warmyngton or Wermington), Agnes, 180
,, ,, John, 170
,, ,, Richard, 170
,, ,, Robert, 'wolman,' 170, 174, 175
Warmyngton, Thomas, of Coventry, 'hosier,' 170, 174

Warner, Walter, 56
'Warp' (of fish). 231
Warrenne, Earl of, 17
,, John de, Earl of Surrey, 32
Warsopp, John of, Canon of Lincoln, 60
Warwickshire and Leicestershire, Sheriff of, 9, 12
Waryn, Robert, 44, 45, 160
,, Roger, son of Robert, 132
Waterhouse, Thomas, of Scoles, Rotherham, 'nayler,' 205
Watkin, John, chaplain, 111
,, Richard, chaplain, 110
Watling Street, 4
Watton (Whatton or Wotton), John, 177, 178, 180, 185
,, ,, ,, Thomas ('dominus curat'), 197, 203, 204, 217, 230
,, ,, ,, William, 188, 193, 205
Wattys, William, 183
Wax, Price of, 231
Wax-tapers at funerals, 51
Waygnon, Thomas, 162
Wayn, John, 229
Wayver (Weyver, Wefer, or Wafer), William, churchwarden of Great Bowden, 111, 177, 194
'Webster,' 103, 185
'Wefer,' 202
Welborn, John of, Canon of Lincoln, 60
Welburne, William, Canon of Lincoln, 60
Welden (or Weldon), William, 92, 181
Wele (or Weyle), Richard, 197, 203, 204
Welham (Leic.), 152, 173; bequest to the church, 223
Welham, John, 170
,, Reginald, citizen and draper, of London, 169, 173
Welland, river, 2, 27, 107, 150, 161
Welles (or Wels), Elizabeth, 213
,, ,, Thomas, 212
Wellingborough, 234
Wellingore (or Wyllyngore), Robert, 188, 189
,, • ,, Thomas, 134
,, ,, William, 203
Wellingtore, Robert, Will of, 225
,, 'Sir Thomas,' 225, 226

Welton, Prebend, 60
„ Robert of, 37, 45
Welton-beyond-Humber, 59
Welton Rivall, Prebend, 60
Wenham, John, 177, 184
„ Robert, 167
West, Richard, 176
West Field, The. See 'Fields'
Westby, Thomas, 135
Westminster, 71, 83, 96
Westminster II., Statute of, 36
Westmoreland, Ralph Nevill, Earl of, 85, 143
Weston-by-Welland (Northants), 157; bequests to the church, 219, 223
Weston, Gilbert, Canon of Lincoln, 122
Westone, 'Sir Robert,' 227
Wetton, William, 194
Whatlows, Cecilia, 57
'Whiteston,' The, 192
Whitgift (Yorks), 31, 32; value of the manor of, with its members, 31, 32
Whitwell, Richard of, Rector of Little Bowden and Canon of Lincoln, 37, 38, 117-119
Whyland (Wyllan, Welan, Weland), George, 202, 203
Whyte, John, 166, 167
Whytyng, John, 236, 241
'William, priest,' 25
'William, son of Thomas Barbour,' 57
William the baker, 58
William the cook, 58
William, little, of the kitchen, 58
Williams, Thomas, of Rolleston, 205
Wills :
    Alann, Thomas, 220
    Atkinson, Agnes, 218
    Bacar, William, 216
    Burditt, William, 209
    Cade, Richard, 219
    Caumbrygge, Katharine, 91, 92
    Clerke, William, 229
    Dennett, Thomas, 210
    Foxton, Thomas, 211
    Fysh, Edward, 226
    Goodrych, Thomas, 227
    Green, William, 228
    Harper, Agnes, 212
    „ Richard, 220
    „ Thomas, 229
    „ William, 218
    Hyll, Peter, 221
    Lawrence, Simon, Rector of Little Bowden, 121

Wills (continued) :
    Mariott, Thomas, 217
    Neell, William, 173
    Nubon (or Newbon), John, 210
    Parych, Richard, 213-216
    Peryns, John, 212
    Scrope, Geoffrey le, Rector of Great Bowden and Canon of Lincoln, 50-60
    Sexton, Margaret, 228
    Sharpe, Richard, 221
    Smyth, Agnes (inventory), 230-234
    Sotherey, William, chantry priest, 222-224
    Syddyll, Richard, 217
    Wellingtore, Robert, 225, 226
    Wolstanton, William of, Rector of Great Bowden, 73-75
Winchcombe, W., Canon of Lincoln, 115
Winchester, Bishops of, 32, 84
Windmill, 95, 98
Winwick, Richard of, Canon of Lincoln, 60
Wiston (Wissington, Suff.), 31
Witham (Linc.), Bequest to, 54
Withcote (Leic.), 170
Witton, West (Yorks.), 43
'Wolman,' 175
Wolstanton, William of, Rector of Great Bowden, 64; will and memorial brass, 73-77, 132
Wondeley, Thomas, 207
Worcester, Bishop of (Carpenter), 129
'Wort ledds,' 231
Woulhouse, Master John, 91
'Woursted,' 229
Wraby, John, Rector of Biddenden, Kent, Rector of Great Bowden, 90, 91
Wrawby, 123
Wright (or Wryght), John, 236, 241
„ „ Robert, 175, 176
Wroxton, 78
Wybern, Alexander, 119
'Wycclevista,' 65
Wycliffe, John, Rector of Lutterworth, 150
Wyginton, Johane, 222
„ William, 222
Wyldegrys, John, 163
Wylughby, Robert, Lord de, 69
Wymondham, 45
Wysaw (   ), 229

Yardley, 123

Index.

'Yerday,' 230
'Yiling fatt,' 234
Yol, Thomas, 160, 162, 163
  ,,   ,,   son of Thomas, 162
'Yoman,' 102, 103, 195
Yonge, Geoffrey, 37, 44, 45, 47, 162
  ,,   Roger le, 119
York, 60, 62, 69 ('Mickellyth'), 138, 139

York, Archbishops of, Neville, 64;
  Thoresby, 124
  ,,   Richard, Duke of, 95, 98
Yorkshire, Defence of the coast, 140
  ,,   Escheator of, 84
  ,,   Sheriff of, 85

Zona, 57
Zousche, William, Lord de, 69

Elliot Stock, Paternoster Row, London.

www.ingramcontent.com/pod-product-compliance
Lightning Source LLC
Chambersburg PA
CBHW032117230426
43672CB00009B/1763